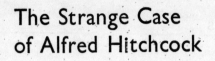

The Strange Case
of Alfred Hitchcock

The Strange Case of ALFRED HITCHCOCK

or
The Plain Man's Hitchcock

RAYMOND DURGNAT

FABER AND FABER   3 Queen Square   London

First published in 1974
by Faber and Faber Limited
3 Queen Square London WC1
Printed in Great Britain by
Butler & Tanner Ltd, Frome and London
All rights reserved

ISBN 0 571 09966 1

720532
60.0092424
(c

Acknowledgements

The text which follows is extensively rewritten and expanded from a series of articles which bore the same title and appeared in *Films and Filming* between February and November, 1970. The chapter on *Strangers on a Train* appeared in the March 1969 issue, as part of the sections devoted to script-writing within a series entitled *Images of the Mind*. The chapter on *Psycho* appeared in *Films and Feelings*, and was reprinted in Albert J. LaValley's *Focus on Hitchcock* (Prentice-Hall, 1972), together with the April 1970 section of the *Films and Filming* series. The comments on *Rich and Strange* derive from *A Mirror For England*. For general encouragement, corrections and comment I should like to express my indebtedness to Robin Bean, editor of *Films and Filming*, John Kobal, for providing many stills, Frank Pike at Faber and Faber, Julian Fox, Barrie Patterson for comments and corrections, Colin MacArthur and David Meeker at the British Film Institute for enabling me to see *Vertigo* for a second time, and to Hunter Films Ltd. for very kindly loaning me a print of *Lifeboat*.

Contents

Illustrations

Isn't it a fascinating design? One could study it for ever.
Alfred Hitchcock, on *Strangers On A Train*

The Record

CHAPTER 1

The Thirteen Lives
of Alfred Hitchcock

Alfred Joseph Hitchcock was born in London on the 13th August, 1899. The son of a poultrymonger, his early life was spent in North London, and he was educated at Saint Ignatius' College, a Jesuit school, until his declared interest in engineering induced his parents to send him to the School of Engineering and Navigation. Eventually he went to work for the Henley Telegraph Company, taking evening classes in art and moving to the advertising department.

From the age of 16 he had been sufficiently fascinated by the cinema to read, 'not just film and fan papers, but the professional and trade journals'. He remembers the impact made on him by American pictures rather than British, and recalls in particular Griffith, Murnau and Fritz Lang's *Der Mude Tod* (*Destiny*).

In 1920 he heard that Paramount-Famous Players-Lasky were opening an Islington Branch and submitted sub-title cartoons for a novel on which they were working. Thus he embarked on the first phase of his career, comprising initially graphic and then also editorial work (including rewriting of sub-titles) on the silent films listed in the filmography.

He designed, or rewrote, the titles for such silent films as *Call of Youth* and *The Great Day* (Hugh Ford, 1921), *The Princess of New York* and *Tell Your Children* (Donald Crisp, 1921) and *Three Live Ghosts* (George Fitzmaurice, 1922).

His first producing-directing initiative occurred when, in 1921, he embarked, in association with the actress Clare Greet, on a film whose subject was the ordinary people of London. It lived up to its title, *Number Thirteen*, being, according to Hitchcock, 'no good', even as far as it went, but it ran into money troubles and was never completed. In 1922 Hitchcock stepped in to complete *Always Tell Your Wife*, in collaboration with its producer-star, Sir Seymour Hicks, when its director fell ill.

After Balcon-Saville-Freedman Productions took over the studio, Hitchcock found a variety of employments, from assistant director, art director, scenarist and editor, on a quintet of films directed by Graham Cutts.

The third phase of Hitchcock's life may be described as his 'scenarist' period (1922–25). Five films were produced by Michael Balcon and directed by Graham Cutts (*Woman to Woman*, 1922, *The White Shadow*, 1923, *The Passionate Adventure*, 1924, *The Blackguard* and *The Prude's Fall*, both 1925).

(4). 1925–27. For Michael Balcon at Gainsborough, Hitchcock directed *The Pleasure Garden* (1925), *The Mountain Eagle* and *The Lodger* (both 1926), *Downhill* and *Easy Virtue* (both 1927).

(5). 1927–33. For John Maxwell at British International Pictures, Hitchcock directed *The Ring* (1927), *The Farmer's Wife* and *Champagne* (both 1928), *The Manx Man* and *Blackmail* (both 1929, the latter marking the transition to sound). Then followed an episode in *Elstree Calling*, *Juno and the Paycock* and *Murder* (all 1930), *The Skin Game* (1931), and *Rich and Strange* and *Number Seventeen* (both 1932). Hitchcock then produced *Lord Camber's Ladies* (directed by Benn Levy) and directed *Waltzes from Vienna* (1933).

(6). 1934–36. At Gaumont British, with Ivor Montagu or Michael Balcon producing, Hitchcock directed *The Man Who Knew Too Much* (1934), *The Thirty-Nine Steps* (1935), *Secret Agent* and *Sabotage* (both 1936).

(7). 1937–38. For Edward Black at Gainsborough, Hitchcock directed *Young and Innocent* (1937) and *The Lady Vanishes* (1938).

(8). In 1938 Hitchcock was approached by David O. Selznick, and the years from 1938 to 1947 may loosely be described as the Selznick Period, although diversified by one-shot associations with other producers. Before his departure for Hollywood, he directed, for Ponner-Laughton-Mayflower, *Jamaica Inn* (1939). In Hollywood, he directed *Rebecca* (Selznick, 1940), *Foreign Correspondent* (Walter Wanger, 1940), *Mr. & Mrs. Smith* and *Suspicion* (both produced by Hitchcock at R.K.O.-Radio, 1941), *Saboteur* (Frank Lloyd–Jack Skirball, 1942), *Shadow Of A Doubt* (Jack Skirball, 1943), *Lifeboat* (Kenneth MacGowan at 20th-Century-Fox, 1944), *Bon Voyage* and *Aventure Malgache* (Ministry of Information, GB, 1944), *Spellbound* (Selznick, 1945), *Notorious* (Hitchcock at R.K.O., 1946) and *The Paradine Case* (Selznick, 1947).

(9). 1948–49. For Transatlantic Pictures, which he had formed with Sidney Bernstein of Granada, Hitchcock directed *Rope* (1948) and *Under Capricorn* (1949).

(10). 1950–54. For Warner Brothers: *Stage Fright* (1950), *Strangers on a Train* (1951), *I Confess* (1953), and *Dial M for Murder* (1954).

(11). 1954–56. At Paramount: *Rear Window* (1954), *To Catch A Thief* (1955), *The Trouble With Harry* and *The Man Who Knew Too Much* (both 1956). *The Wrong Man* (1957) was a last film at Warners, followed by *Vertigo* (Paramount, 1958), *North-by-North-West* (at M.G.M., 1959) and *Psycho* (Paramount, 1960).

(12). From 1955 Hitchcock embarked on a parallel career as producer, presenter and occasionally writer-director of television films. Jack Edmund Nolan gives the total number of hour or half-hour films appearing under the Hitchcock banner between 1955 and 1963 as 353, and details twenty directed by Hitchcock himself.

(13). 1963–72. At Universal: *The Birds* (1963), *Marnie* (1964), *Torn Curtain* (1966), *Topaz* (1969), *Frenzy* (1972).

Hitchcock's creative shifts and turns bear some relationship to these producer periods. Although *The Lodger*, *Blackmail*, *Murder* and *Number Seventeen* had drawn attention to Hitchcock as a director of thrillers, it was his Gaumont British and subsequent Gainsborough periods which established him as 'the Master of Suspense'. It is to these films, together with the four thriller forerunners (the last two rarely revived) to which critics refer when they speak of the 'English Hitchcock' as opposed to the American Hitchcock. But, in fact, there are three, clearly distinct, English Hitchcocks. His first Gainsborough period stresses romantic subjects. His British International period abounds in adaptations of dramatic and literary subjects. His Gaumont British and second Gainsborough periods group the picaresque comedy thrillers. Of this characteristic genre, two further clear examples appear during the first three Hollywood years, but a series of visually somewhat 'enclosed' drama-thrillers, with 'women's film' production styles become the predominant style of the Selznick era, and culminate in the two Transatlantic films. Hitchcock remains aloof from the underworld *film noir*, a genre in which his work might have been sharper and harder. Quite possibly the influence of Selznick had sensitized him to themes and settings which enabled him to combine suspense with a middle-class 'women's angle'. The Warner Brothers period shows no clear direction, but one can see the first of Hitchcock's Paramount group as marking a gradual increase in the general dramatic, visual and poetic complexity which can be accommodated around or within the suspense. In this respect his evolution is in line with Hollywood's gradually more adventurous spirit. After *The Birds*, however, Hitchcock appears as a Hollywood 'conservative', making a magisterial use of its traditional elements, without using new stylistic and thematic freedoms.

But any distinction into periods must remain schematic. Thus the devotee of chronological periods must wish that *The Wrong Man* had been made in 1954 instead of in 1957, when it would fit neatly into the Warner's era and pair with *I Confess*. But it doesn't, and there are so many possibilities, some purely to do with contract-making, that to attempt too detailed a spiritual evolution would be fruitless and unreal. Clearly one must also stream Hitchcock's work, vertically as it were, into genres and themes.

A. Romantic novels, e.g., *The Pleasure Garden*, dominate his first two Balcon periods. Much later, the three Selznick films represent a return to this kind of material, albeit at a suaver and swisher level, with an intensification of the sustained suspense and the moralising, more slickly deadpan rather than more profound. *Marnie* is obviously related to the same genre.

B. The B.I.P. films enabled Hitchcock to cast a wry and inquisitive eye over various facets of the British scene. The presiding spirit could be described as dramatic realism, and it is our contention that its infiltration of subsequent thrillers, as *against* their novelettish plushness, often accounts for much of their richness: as in *Shadow Of A Doubt, Rear Window, The Trouble With Harry*. The opening of *Blackmail* (which precedes virtually all the Grierson documentaries) and the first half of *The Wrong Man* qualify for the designation 'semi-documentary', as it was later applied to British films like *North Sea* and *San Demetrio London*.

C. The Hitchcock thriller had appeared before the Gaumont-British period (e.g., *The Lodger* for Balcon, *Blackmail* for Maxwell), but this period—in which Ivor Montagu's participation is perhaps important—introduces the classic thriller sextet. The last two suggest slackening creative tensions, and it might be argued that Hitchcock's best form reappears only when the general Hollywood climate becomes more sophisticated.

D. In contrast to the dramatic realism looming so large in the English film, the American Hitchcocks tend, for the usual Hollywood reasons, to centre on wish-fulfilment high life. But the picaresque odysseys (*Foreign Correspondent, Saboteur*), occasionally involve ordinary people. Other films endow their glossy milieux with a certain poetic queasiness.

E. Many Hitchcock films take the form of a picaresque pursuit, which may at first seem the polar opposite of such claustrophobic, single setting films as *Lifeboat*, *Rope* and *Under Capricorn*. But often Hitchcock counterpoints the sealed situation (e.g., a hostile couple handcuffed to each other) against the chase. *Rear Window* plays the sealed against the kaleidoscopic (the various windows opposite) in another way. So the picaresque background provides a special form of that same isolation which inspires the enclosed films.

F. Hitchcock's films undoubtedly show a concern with moral values, although exactly which values are involved, and how simple, or single-minded, they are, has yet to be sufficiently debated. Of fifty-two major films two hinge on a specifically Catholic theme, while three hinge on and are moralised in specifically Freudian terms.

G. Hitchcock's work shares with the fiction feature genre a dramatic and thematic structure derived from the traditions of 19th-century narrative plays and novels. It is characteristic of these forms that interest in the fortunes of one or more individuals involves the inter-action of dramatic, moral, social, philosophical, poetic, and any other matters arising, although the autonomy and interaction of each separate area is strictly subordinated to, sometimes even occluded by, the individualism emphasised by the dramatic perspective.

H. Aesthetic interests are not secondary in Hitchcock's work, and internal evidence supplies no reason to doubt his remarks to the effect that what interests him is the way of telling a story. Nonetheless, he must have a story to tell, i.e., sequences of human experiences to evoke. It is obvious that an interest in aesthetic form, whether primary or subordinate, may go parallel with a repetitive thematic, retained partly for reasons of personal preference and partly as popular with audiences.

All these Hitchcocks have produced sharp critical controversies. Through the '40s and '50s, English and American critics, and the older generation of French critics (like Jean-George Auriol of *La Revue du Cinéma*, 'father' of *Cahiers du Cinéma*) vastly preferred the English thrillers, for their visual speed, comic realism and varied social canvases, and their preferred American films were closest to that style (*Foreign Correspondent*, *Saboteur*, *Shadow Of A Doubt*, *Strangers On A Train*). Hitchcock's other American films struck them as clever, but sleek, slick and empty. A minor English artist, a major English enter-tainer, seemed to have become just a velvet glove on the leaden fingers of David O. Selznick. *Notorious* suggested that, as his own producer, he had turned into another Selznick himself. André Bazin, the 'senior wrangler' of *Cahiers*, could not see Hitchcock as an artistic master, and nor did the French Left (*Positif, Premier Plan*).

So far as the Anglo-Saxon critics were concerned, their preference was fortified by aesthetic theories favouring fast and varied visual movement (as more cinematic), a realistic social atmosphere (as opposed to highlife glamour), and location settings. Hitchcock's strong points were seen as his pure cinematic style, which lifted his compound of melodrama and realism to a level of felt excitement roughly comparable with the chase across the salt flats at the end of *Stagecoach*. And for these critics that sort of thing was quite enough, since they felt that the cinema had its own lyrical way of redeeming material which might otherwise be considered banal. This can be described as the Manvell-Lindgren line. They inherited earlier comments about the 'Hitchcock touch', praising manipulations of the medium which some younger critics found rather gimmicky—like the distortions of a woman's voice saying 'Knife!' as the word rasps on the nerves of the guilty heroine (*Blackmail*), or the cut from a woman screaming to a whistling locomotive emerging from a tunnel (*The Thirty-Nine Steps*). These examples were part of the older generation's honouring of 'pure cinema', i.e., cinematic style, as against the literary approach, and Hitchcock in certain ways shared their aesthetic appreciation. For, given the rather different cinematic idioms obtaining during the '30s, they were far less extraneous than they may now seem. Far from being mere gimmicks, they were genuine climactic extensions of form. John Grierson's was a lone voice raised against this emphasis, when he argued that the critics' emphasis on the 'touch' was turning Hitchcock into a mere aesthete, that *Murder* and *The Skin Game* were thematic poppycock, and that Hitchcock's strong point was his feeling for everyday realism. This line was maintained by Lindsay Anderson whose *Sequence* articles implicitly reproached Hitchcock with staying at the Savoy. In other ways, however, Grierson's and Anderson's approaches come very near to the present writer's.

Quietly different from the Manvell-Lindgren and Grierson-Anderson lines alike was the *Sight and Sound* approach, identifiable from the early '50s. Being, as Tony Richardson remarked, 'anti-cinema', it satisfied itself with the most obvious and traditional literary qualities on the level of script, and a liberal humanism of a traditional middle-class kind. By these standards contemporary Hitchcock, of the '50s, was not only boring but often vaguely nasty. However, nostalgia, critical

politics and the inertia of habit prevented the—logically necessary—
dismissal of English Hitchcock as nasty also. In contrast Hitchcock's
French detractors were always ready to accept troubled views of
human nature, and criticised Hitchcock for uninteresting accounts of
human experiences.

The first radical revaluation of Hitchcock came through the columns
of *Cahiers du Cinéma* and in particular the work of Eric Rohmer and
Claude Chabrol. To Hitchcock's moral preoccupations they were,
perhaps, sensitised by sharing with him a Roman Catholic background
or sympathies. In Hitchcock's films they felt that they discerned a
consistent theme of a transference of guilt, such that the apparently
innocent are also partly guilty, that curious affinities between heroes
and villains appear, and that the villains incarnate temptations to
which, on some secret or unconscious level, the heroes have yielded,
and for which they must be memorably punished, or from which
they must be purified, by some sort of trial, concluding in a chastening
awareness.

This approach gave a much-needed new awareness of Hitchcock.
Reservations about it form much of the substance of this study, and
will be unfolded as it goes.

An analogous approach was made by Jean Douchet, for whom
Hitchcock's real inspiration was an esoteric occultism, based on 'the
duel between Light and Shadow, therefore of Unity and Duality'.
Thus the opening long shot of *Psycho*, showing an entire town in
daylight, is contradicted by the second shot, of one particular room, in
semi-darkness. 'In two shots, Hitchcock expresses his subject . . . the
eternal and the finite, existence and nothingness, life and dreams.' It is
in line with Douchet's mixture of neo-Platonism and Manicheanism
that his sentence structure equates the shot of the embracing couple
with the finite, nothingness and death. But one might well object
the meanings attributed to the two shots can be reversed. The two
lovers are, successfully or otherwise, attempting to reach spiritual
eternity, existence and life, while the opening shot suggests the *false*
unity of a complacent, smothering society. Douchet's method is as fascinating as any delirium of interpretation can be, but overlooks too
much to explain Hitchcock adequately. Thus he considers mealtimes
as occasions of the absorption of substances (i.e., matter into mind),
without so much as thinking of the importance of mealtimes in family
and social life, of their *social* spirituality. And sometimes his schema-
tisation is inaccurate, as when, on *Vertigo*, he writes that in Hitchcock
'every representative of the established order (policeman, judge,

statesman, etc.) is a representative of God'. What then of the detective who fakes the evidence and frames an innocent man in *Blackmail*? Or of the lecherous judge in *The Paradine Case*? Or of Castro in *Topaz*, whom all Hitchcock's heroes are supposed to be thoroughly justified in subverting? Is God a liar, a lecher, a Communist? Thus Douchet impoverishes Hitchcock, misreading his dramatic dialectic as simplistic allegory. One's suspicions are aroused also by Douchet's remark that 'All great artists say more or less the same thing.'

None the less, such interpretations possess their own creative fascination and influence such writers as Noel Simsolo and the contributors to *Études Cinématographiques*.

The rising generation of English critics saw things another way altogether, and contrary to a widespread English impression, the approaches of Ian Cameron and Victor Perkins in *Movie* bore no resemblance either to Chabrol and Rohmer's or to Douchet's. Refusing to equate cinematic style with the obvious aesthetic 'touch', or to remain content with script, they stressed instead the manipulation of audience attentions, sympathies and reactions. They emphasised, not a hidden symbolism, but an overt level of dramatic and moral experience. And this approach has subsequently been vindicated by its close relationship to the actual questions and answers which Hitchcock sets himself in working out a film.

The present writer would likewise insist that the real Hitchcock touch is a more diffuse affair than a moral schema, or points of style. It comprises a certain conjunction of elements, the absence of even one of which gives us a feeling of atypicality. The story ingredients include (1) violent death, (2) a physical or mental chase in which we identify with a pursued pursuer, so that (3) virtue appears menacing and indulgence deceptive, while (4) amorous badinage (or tormenting) proceeds and (5) hero and heroine are offered some dramatically plausible choices between good and evil and (6) 'greys are everywhere' (the remark is Hitchcock's, although Chabrol and Rohmer substituted for it a transference of guilt, which is quite a different thing). There is a sense of having penetrated from an apparently tolerant, even permissive, world, to a grimmer one, whose cruelties seem, confusingly, both amoral and morally unremitting. In the British thrillers, everyday worlds of familiar foibles and eccentricities momentarily part to reveal grimmer patterns. There is usually, however, an affirmative return to a normally comfortable world.

In *Movie* and in his book, Robin Wood worked out another interpretation of Hitchcock the moralist. Its basic co-ordinates were a mixture of evangelical fundamentalism secularised, and an aesthetic whose theory, at least, if not its application, owed something to F. R. Leavis. Despite parallelisms with Chabrol and Rohmer, the moral tone was substantially different, the emphasis lying on individual responsibility and the consequences of its absence. It might have been so developed as to emphasise its basic contradictions with the French critics' Catholicism, as well as their idea of Jansenism. However, one's objections to Robin Wood's moral interpretations are parallel. He doesn't consider the possibility that any moral system other than one might be involved, and this assumption seems to me to risk depriving Hitchcock's films of much of their interest, as well as evading the problem, and possibilities, of comparing moral codes. None the less, Wood's attention to moral and dramatic detail, without benefit of metaphysic, aligns itself with the other *Movie* pieces in clarifying the level, form and nature of the films' contents. As in the case of the Chabrol and Rohmer approach, the present writer's divergencies and alternatives will become apparent as the analysis proceeds.

In general, those for whom Hitchcock was the master of the 'touch' preferred his English films to his American period. Conversely, those for whom Hitchcock was a moralist preferred his Hollywood period to his English period. Two critics for whom Hitchcock was finally an entertainer have adopted more consistent attitudes to his whole work. For François Truffaut, Hitchcock is above all the showman-manipulator; he refers to Hitchcock's moral vision as a kind of artistic credential, but he clearly has no interest whatsoever in finding out anything new about it. Truffaut, we know, loves (*a*) intimate movies and (*b*) movies as circus; Hitch's cat-and-mouse games with suspense fit both requirements perfectly. One might well be tempted by the theory that Truffaut's feeling for Hitchcock is a kind of nostalgia. The younger man, specialist in emotions of vulnerable passivity, desperately longs for, and hero worships, the slick, subtle mastery with which Hitchcock torments his audience. So far, too, Truffaut has depended on a childlike hero for his best inspiration (*Les Quatre Cents Coups*, *Tirez Sur Le Pianiste*, *Jules et Jim*), while his later films evidence a certain dryness. How professionally enviable, therefore, the wily aplomb with which the older man has varied his utterly reliable thematic! In Truffaut's search for Hitchcock's triumphs of manipulation, one can see the younger artist forgetting the silver and gold of his true inspiration, in the style of Renoir, for the sawdust and tinsel daydream of meticulous control over one's audience and one's professional destiny.

Chabrol's own films closely transpose the Hitchcock thematic into the settings, style and terms that interest Chabrol. And critical paradox continues in an infinite regression, for Gavin Millar, who efficiently ferrets out all Hitchcock's artistic weaknesses, notably his reliance on certain popular stereotypes, is also English high priest of the Chabrol cult. Unfortunately, his dismissal of Hitchcock relies heavily on a selection of his least interesting moments which, abundant as they are, isn't the whole story. For the question remains of distinguishing what is valid in each director's work from what is less so or not so, and one might easily reverse Millar's preferences, by hazarding that if Chabrol is the more consciously schematic moralist it is because his characters have so little internal existence as to remain derisory caricatures of bourgeois habits, or merely symbols for metaphysical and theological diabolisms, all of which would contrast with Hitchcock's calculated and commonsensical view of human nature. Chabrol, then, would be a young and callow Hitchcock, unstably veering between the intellectual and the clownesque.[1]

Given the variety of possible positions, it's curious, or perhaps it's only too typical, that one fairly obvious possibility was hardly argued. This is that Hitchcock has always been an entertainer whose work can, on occasion, and for one reason or another, reach a degree of sophistication and intensity such that his material takes on sufficient truth, urgency and challenge to qualify as a significant artist (and whether he's a minor or a major one is another matter again; but to be a minor artist is no mean achievement). It then becomes as impossible to try to discredit *Psycho* by ridiculing, however justifiably, a scene in *Foreign Correspondent*, as to suppose that all Hitchcock's films fall into one of only two possible categories: the major and the minor masterpiece. Just because of the thematic similarities, the distinction is, precisely, whether the screw is relaxed into banality or twisted towards the crunch, and how far the drama is false or felt.

[1] *Les Cousins* (as suggested in *Films and Feelings*) would be the one Chabrol film whose Hitchcockian schema is authentically felt through.

CHAPTER 2

Moral Codes:
Mainstreams and Challenges

Before turning to individual films, it might be interesting to glance
at the relationship between Hitchcock's moral implications and
common assumptions.

The initial English reaction to Chabrol and Rohmer's establishment of moral patterns was to dismiss them as a delirium of interpretation. In doing so it ignored the equally important point, of whether
moral interpretations of some sort or another were appropriate. This
dismissal was worse than cavalier, as Robin Wood had no difficulty
in showing. For every drama involves moral pros and cons, and none
more naturally than detective stories, to which Hitchcock's films either
belong or are closely related. If the earlier critics hadn't discussed
Hitchcock's moral patterns it was because they took them for granted,
as part and parcel of any drama; whereas critics of the '50s didn't
bother with them, because, having decided that Hitchcock's films
were boring, stuffy and nasty, it seemed to them to follow that the
moral patterns underlying them hadn't been translated into experience-
able artistic terms.

To become interesting the moral patterns would have to be (1)
translated into or related to dramatic experience and (2) differ significantly, when so translated, from those which are run-of-the-mill in
entertainment anyway. Here it seems relevant to comment on the
extent to which the transference of guilt operates in run-of-the-mill
detective stories. For a certain morality, of guilt, apparent innocence,
and retribution, is built into the detective story. The ultra-traditional
Agatha Christie-type tale, in which any one of x close relatives had
the means, the motive, and, in one way or another, the temptation or
the inclination, to murder irascible but pitiable Uncle Ebenezer,
fulfils most of the moral points of the so-called Hitchcock thematic,

especially in some variant in which the nastiest person proves, to our chagrin, that the nicest person did it, and so might we. Hitchcock himself points out that if you remove the old-fashioned will-library-butler-detective syndrome, and do the same story in a chase format, centring not on the classic detective but on a pursued pursuer, you have his characteristic Hitchcock formula. And doubtless it was evolved in response to cinematic facilities (movement) as well as to a shift in public mood (from the stern affirmations of 19th-century morality to the uneasier guilts and fears of our own). At any rate the furtive hero, rather than the supremely assured detective, dominates the modern thriller. Another factor in the shift from detective story to thriller is the evolution from the prim stiffness of older middle-class life to the less furtive brutalities of the wider public.

Hence all the points which Chabrol and Rohmer can discover in Hitchcock are to be found also in such films as (in ascending order of artistic merit) Michael Anderson's *Chase a Crooked Shadow* and *The Naked Edge*, J. Lee-Thompson's *Cape Fear*, and Robert Siodmak's *Phantom Lady* which, despite a disappointing dénouement, rivals, in expressionist atmosphere and structure, Orson Welles's *The Lady From Shanghai*, which is the ultra-Hitchcock. If the analysis of *Johnny Guitar* in *Films and Feelings* has any validity, then the same moral thematic is altogether at home in the West. Indeed, Nicholas Ray's film, translated into modern settings and murder instead of the Wild West and gunplay, would be bolder than all but a handful of Hitchcocks, luring us as it does into an identification with chastened guilts. Incidentally, even *Chase a Crooked Shadow* shows more daring than any Hitchcock film until *Psycho*, in so far as our principal identification is with the apparent innocence of the actually guilty party. One can add to the films mentioned above what is not so much a mixed bag as a random sample of one-offs by other directors: not only Anthony Asquith's *A Cottage On Dartmoor* (what Asquith might have done, in the way of Hitchcockery and more, had Balcon not neglected him for Hitchcock during those critical years!), Otto Preminger's *Laura* and *Angel Face*, Billy Wilder's *Double Indemnity*, Arthur Woods's *They Live By Night*, Clouzot's *Le Corbeau* and *Quai des Orfèvres*, and Thorold Dickinson's *Secret People*, maybe Roman Polanski's *Repulsion* and *Rosemary's Baby*, and certainly Bunuel's *El* (a counterpart, as a study in domestic paranoia, of *Suspicion*). Thus, in terms of dramatically experienced transference of guilt the most searchingly Hitchcockian films are by a wide variety of other directors. And by such criteria, Hitchcock only occasionally makes the first team, albeit plying a wily bat in the 2nd or 3rd XI.

It also becomes apparent that the moralists' preference for later over earlier Hitchcock is eminently reversible. Since the British thrillers combine Hitchcock's perennial thematic with a wider variety of realistic social vignettes than Hitchcock's '40s films, they combine two layers of interest instead of one, revealing the later films as slow and over-emphatic, repeating without deepening their dramatic material. The earlier films are quick, sharp, lean and economical, while the '40s films are slow and flabby—more bulk, less brain, hippopotami trying to be ferrets. But the question of dramatic richness is, as I shall try to suggest, closely bound up with the strength or weakness, not so much of Hitchcock's different streams or periods, as of different films within each category.

There is also the question of one's attitude towards these backgrounds and details. The earlier critics disliked in the Hollywood films the glamour and daydream formulae which Hitchcock usually follows slavishly and applies lavishly, whereas the English films abounded in those little vignettes opening on to real, English, life. For the earlier critics these were, primarily, an admirable way of authenticating the melodrama and suspense: but this sense of authentication involved a covert appeal to neo-documentary notions of realism. Conversely, the younger English critics were less appreciative of authentication by this kind of realism, which neo-realism, T.V. documentary and cinéma-vérité had all rendered unexceptional. Moreover, both the French and the English generation of anger and satire were a little ill at ease with anything English and retrospective, and far more at home with that familiar Hollywood stylisation of affluence to whose idioms they had come to accept as an artistic convention, rather than merely rejecting them as a lie. The authenticating details left them unmoved, or seemed merely to interrupt the action, to impede meditation. They might, with some plausibility, although they didn't bother, have argued that Hitchcock's asides didn't go deeper than *Coronation Street* anyway.

Here perhaps this critic should confess a bias. Much of his childhood occurred during the later '30s, and was lived in Hitchcock's London, at that social level. For him the effect of a nostalgia altogether, but altogether, different from nostalgia in the camp sense is strong indeed, and not only in Hitchcock's films, but in others of the era which have any authenticity about them. And it must also be remembered that realism in the '30s was a rarer and more difficult achievement, that the director couldn't just point a T.V. camera in the street. He had first to notice certain details, love them enough to remember and to recreate them, and lastly to slide them deftly into a thriller context. And these difficulties affect, not simply our knowledge of those details, but those details in themselves, as they appeared on the screen. They are in no sense as throwaway as pebbles; they are cherished like jewels.

That sense of the typical which later can lead Hitchcock into tourist-trap stereotypes (as Millar remarks) doesn't, on his home ground, play him false. I can vouch, from vivid memories and a child's sharp eye, that Hitchcock's English era is in another class altogether from Ealing's England. And I would suggest that that touch returns in some of the sparer, glossier details in his later Hollywood films.

There is a sense in which the nearest recent film to the pre-war English Hitchcocks is Norman Cohen's *Till Death Do Us Part*, because its period flavour is so right. That the one is contemporary and the other retrospective is a secondary distinction. For in both cases it's a matter of realism invested, by reconstruction, with all the preciousness of memory.

An analogous (not an identical) quality redeems even the patently cheap artificiality of the model shots in *No. 17*, which have a kind of irreal halo, like the cameo within the 'Rosebud' globe of *Citizen Kane*. These effects—a piercing realism, and a vibrant irrealism—aren't accidental. They relate to Hitchcock's curious blend of insight and insulation, understanding and solitude, sympathy and manipulation. The effect is enhanced not by the fact of melodrama, but by the poetic quality which melodrama at its best may possess. Thus it might be said that Hitchcock is unique *neither* as a moralist, *nor* as a realist, *nor* as a dramatist, *nor* as a melodramatic poet, but that he sometimes attains a certain balance between the four, in which each enriches the other, allowing him perfection within a limited but significant sector of experience. His best films, and his best scenes, are those where the melodrama becomes poetic and the realism a sceptical reverence for our ordinary lives; those which trace the infiltrations of dream, nightmare and reality. It's precisely this mixture which distinguishes *Rear Window*, *Vertigo*, *Psycho* and a few others from those which blend agreeably suspenseful entertainment with the merely aesthetic pleasure of their originality and mastery of style.

Hitchcock's emptiest films move, merely, from a never-never land of plush simplicities to melodramatic banalities. But even in the most thoughtful films the experience lies not so much in the vision to which one penetrates, nor indeed in the vision from which one penetrates, as in the sense of a process of penetration. Hitchcock's films can't be justified by reference to any one layer; their artistic impact is in the intermeshing of layers. In the less interesting films he persuades us, if we are willing, or undemanding, that the superficial world with which he begins does seem to us an adequate account of the world. In other words, he first cretinizes us a little before leading us into dramatic complexities something like those with which more sincere, less cunning artists begin. But if we are to promote Hitchcock to major artistic status, then he has to begin with a vision as sophisticated as ours is already, and lead us to a newer vision which at first we can grasp only partially and turbulently but which, as it steadily colours our outlook on the real world, vindicates itself by its clarification of reality. In other words, the fact that Hitchcock's sinister universe resembles Kafka in melodrama, or that bizarre affinities of mood and form link *North-by-North-West* and *L'Avventurà*, doesn't mean that Hitchcock has the artistic calibre of Antonioni. It is to say only that Antonioni and Hitchcock are like two rivers arising from the same range of mountains. One, surfacing on one slope, runs in one direction, towards the sea of spiritual understanding. The other, surfacing on another slope, runs in the other direction, towards escapist nonsense. Antonioni clarifies and explains, if only by directing us to the enigmas of experience and silencing the chatter of false explanation. Hitchcock usually conjures up our nightmares only to shunt our minds into complacencies of conformism and unreality. In his dramas, Hitchcock moves from a novelettish complacency to an uncertainty worthy of, but hardly deeper than, that of an ordinary middlebrow novel. Sometimes, on the contrary, one may prefer the superficial level to the revealed pattern—find Hitchcock's films interesting as they record everyday notations and uncertainties, and lose interest as the plot thickens and the observation thins.

None the less, there remains an area in which *North-by-North-West* has its affinities with *L'Avventurà*. The thrillers (more often than the dramas) have their convulsions of poetic strangeness—the slumped corpse in the Alpine Chapel producing the *sostenuto* organ-note which soars from the Alpine church out over the holiday snows, the old lady menacingly accepting revolvers on her collection-plate, the burly, frightened, Protestant criminal-detective falling from the Catholic cathedral tower. Many have spoken of Surrealism, although it's also an anti-Surrealism in that these incongruities assert a universe not of libido, but of the ascendancy of inhibition and fear. 'The fact is, I practise absurdity quite religiously'—rather than religion quite absurdly.

One critical trick with Hitchcock's minor movies is to suggest that the suspense is created principally out of our moral criticisms of the hero (and of ourselves), and only secondarily out of our anxiety that the hero and his conformist morality should enjoy their happy and reassuring triumph over the villain and his villainy. This view is undermined not only by Hitchcock's comments about his preoccupations, but by simple commonsense accuracy about our experience, as spectators. It may be that the highly sophisticated spectator of *Strangers On A Train* may derive pleasure from seeing the ways in which Bruno does what Guy would do if he were as wicked as Bruno, but it is also true that most of our suspense comes from the fact that Guy is the good guy and Bruno is the bad guy, and that although Guy is to blame for not going to the police the moment he smelt a rat this is a crime of which thousands of Hollywood good guys are equally guilty. It's true that Hitchcock often gives his good guys a grey streak and makes his bad guys briefly but really sympathetic or pitiable, but so do many other melodramatists. In such terms, Hitchcock has still to attain the sophistication of, say, Clouzot's *Le Corbeau* or *Le Salaire de la Peur*. It's not until *Psycho* that Hitchcock takes so much as one step beyond the conventional moral polarities (I don't say the *absolute* moral polarities, of soot and whitewash, which went out with Theda Bara). After seeing a Hitchcock movie, it may be interesting to wonder whether that dear old lady pouring tea in the Dainty Tudor Café isn't really carrying secret messages on behalf of the man in the green felt hat, but it's doubtful whether Hitchcock's movies provoke reflections on the duplicity or opacity of human nature any more effectively than, say, Michael Anderson's *The Naked Edge*, an effective, perfectly unimportant thriller, in which Deborah Kerr, worried about her husband Gary Cooper, speculates, 'Can you sleep with a man for seven years without realising he's a murderer?' The answer, very obviously, is Yes, though the answer matters less than the sense of alienation which it introduces.

Indeed all murder mysteries depend on the spectator's readiness to believe in a demoniac undertow to everyday relationships. *The Shame* has the edge over most detective stories in this respect, and *Strangers On A Train* is just so much footie-footie with guilt compared with, say, Billy Wilder's *Double Indemnity*, which, without contrivance, without symbolism, teaches you through Fred MacMurray what it's like to discover that the woman you love wants you to murder her husband and be sure she gets the extra insurance, what it might feel like to murder a man who takes you as a friend and genuinely likes you, only then to find that your beloved wants the designated successor to her embraces to do the same job on you, and what it's like to then be in that very Hitchcockian position of being condemned by an elder colleague (Edward G. Robinson), who's also been a lifelong friend, with pitiless severity, in the name not just of decency, but also of suspicious avarice. Only one Hitchcock film so much as tiptoes deep into that territory; and *Psycho* keeps us, right through to the end, identified with the conventional and the unsuspecting.

In a timid way Hitchcock allows us to believe, or half-believe, for a few moments, that maybe Guy intends to murder Bruno's dad. And Chabrol and Rohmer argue that this exemplifies Hitchcock's desire to enlighten us as to, or upset us by showing, how thin the dividing line between innocence and murder. Yet there's no real reason why Hitchcock shouldn't, quite without equivocation, have shown us Guy confronting Bruno's dad in order to weigh him up. We can all understand how exasperation or infatuation or panic can bring a hero towards the intention of murdering, whether in Murnau's *Sunrise* (where the man loves his victim), or in *Double Indemnity*, or in Tay Garnett's *The Postman Always Rings Twice*, or in George Stevens's *A Place in the Sun*, or so on and so forth. Hitchcock's revelations about the human capacity for depravity wouldn't surprise any reader of the London *News of the World*; for they represent a very traditional and popular view.

Hitchcock's limitations may be exemplified by his way with the bad guys in *North-by-North-West*. He tells Truffaut that he split the villain up into three separate characters because there seemed no way of making one man seem 'smooth and distinguished' and 'threatening' at the same time. Given Hitchcock's success in doing just that with the Joseph Cotten character in *Shadow Of A Doubt*, one wonders if the real reason wasn't, after all, something to do with the sheer mechanics of having one man turn up in an improbable number of places, and the need to give him a confidante who can become his apparent opposite and part-antagonist, so as to exteriorise his internal contradictions. The combination is a cliché, and at other times Hitchcock says it's always best to make your villain a suave and charming fellow. None the less the remark indicates a recoiling from just the sort of psychomoral paradox which a less cunning and more conscientious artist might relish. And Gavin Miller accurately indicates the limitations of *Shadow Of A Doubt*: 'Smalltown family life is not really

SCAH—B

represented at all, but only a sort of cleaned-up *Saturday Evening Post* version of it. Here the worst sins are pop and his crony discussing murder on the verandah, and the greatest household curse smart kids. There's nothing here of the strains of real living, as W. C. Fields might represent them in just such a household. And when Uncle Charlie comes to do his murders, well he doesn't really impinge either. He's a figure from Nightmare, not the American Dream, from back East, from the past. Nor is his aberration a criticism of society. He fell off a bike when he was a kid and bumped his head.' The presentation of the ordinary is deceptive and the menace is unreal.

It's ironic that critics who disdained Richard Brooks's quite deliberate subversion of *The Brothers Karamazov* should accept as a Dostoievskian moralist a director who first offers us, as a view of life, a cover from the *Saturday Evening Post*, and then lifts us to the level of Agatha Christie. All too often no attempt is made to revivify a plot by acting, the characters remaining half-*Vogue* mannequin (a wish fulfilment blank to accommodate our participation) and half-social being. One can illustrate this briefly in terms of *Psycho* and *Repulsion*. Polanski's film, basically, is *Psycho*, with three twists. (*a*) The psycho is a girl. (*b*) Whereas Hitchcock works us cautiously from the normal world to 'inside Norman Bates', Polanski starts off inside and keeps us there. (*c*) Hitchcock explains Norman Bates in terms of childhood complexes (without excusing him), whereas the childhood photograph on which Polanski concludes tells us no more than her present 'photograph'. Polanski, operating in the 'zone' between Hitchcock and Bunuel, helps us to see just how broad that zone is. At his best, Hitchcock, remaining nearer moral fundamentalism, and devoid of Polanski's bizarre mixture of frivolity and nihilism, has his own power. Usually, he is happy to frisk about within the purlieus of all the consensus platitudes.

The argument may be shifted from the level of basic moral pattern to that of overt experience, i.e., the shot-by-shot orchestration of our responses. In *Marnie*, says Robin Wood, 'We are caught up in her rhythm of moving, so that we share for a moment her trance-like state' (and certainly Hitchcock's sense of rhythms of movement is one of the finesses which he shares with Murnau), while, in *Psycho*, 'the overhead shot with its complicated camera-movement communicates to us precisely that sense of metaphysical vertigo . . . a sense of sinking into a quicksand of uncertainties, or into a bottomless pit'. (Hitchcock gives another account of the reason for that overhead shot, i.e., disguising the fact that he is deceiving the audience, but

Robin Wood's point remains true (for any given stylistic configuration, e.g., a shot can fulfil a variety of functions at once, and indeed, normally does so).

A danger in such shot-by-shot exegesis in philosophical terms is of making any series of reverse-angles between murderer and victim, or policeman and blackmailer, look like a clash of philosophies, whereas what an audience is in fact seeing is a battle of wits, or simply alternating enthusiastic approval and hatred. In any case shot-by-shot exegesis may seriously underestimate the extent to which the 'mosaic' is seen as a whole (as it must be, if Eisenstein's concept of montage is to make sense, or, indeed, for a sequence of shots to be read as a continuous scene). But one's diffidence about certain of Robin Wood's claims for Hitchcock spring from another source. Demonstrating the richness of the overt dramatic experience in Hitchcock, he opposes 'Strutt, complacent, self-righteous, a man devoid of human warmth and generosity', and Marnie, 'haggard, drawn, face drained of all colour, clinging to a gun without realising she is holding it, moving forward like a sleepwalker . . . "victimised" indeed by a whole complex past'. Here, the critic is beginning to write like a novelette; how far, one wonders, is this a reflection on his material? The answer is, perhaps, that it's a reflection on the critical process. Reduced as the critic so often is to indications which are a peculiar mixture of synopsis, comment and description, it can be hard to avoid stereotyped phrases (a study of bad prose in good criticism might be interesting). Second, difficulties arise in translating movie images into words. But the third answer is, perhaps, that one reason why novelettes are so popular is because they're so interesting. There's a curious severity in film criticism as opposed to its literary counterpart. No one holds it against Winston Graham that his novel *Marnie* isn't a masterpiece; it's enough that it's an interesting, intelligent middlebrow novel, and no one feels obliged to claim that it is much more than that. One may well suspect that what highbrow film critics are discovering, when they vaunt Hitchcock's *œuvre* as a whole, is that lower-middle-brow art may be not only not contemptible but even more interesting than their lowbrow cult objects, like the glib Pop art exploitation of the *persona* of Marilyn Monroe.

At this point it becomes possible to see why Hitchcock, rather than another director, should have become a cult moralist. He combines those lowbrow elements (guns, glamour, melodrama) which link in with highbrows' fondness for the lowest common denominators of the popular arts. The very prudence with which Hitchcock draws back from any moral challenge to the consensus enables the critics to *discover* how close he comes to a moral challenge—and nothing pleases a critic more than being able to discover hidden connections. The older critics' dispraise of the Hollywood Hitchcock as compared to English Hitchcock made this transatlantic figure strategic in the campaign to rehabilitate Hollywood. His very repetitions made the case for his being an *auteur* all the more conclusive. His apolitical Catholicism fitted in with the idealistic reaction of the Chabrol–Truffaut *Cahiers* generation against the leftish social realism which had dominated film criticism a few years before. His dry, terse, texture suited cosmopolitan intellectuals who weren't looking for emotional involvement so much as traits of style to notice and symbols to think about. Lastly, and most important, Hitchcock's series of twists and turns are sufficiently intricate to arouse our alertest interest. In *Chase A Crooked Shadow* our identification figure, the 'persecuted victim' (Anne Baxter), turns out to be the guilty party, the 'blackmailers' are detectives, she fooled us and perhaps herself. The turnaround is more drastic than anything in *Strangers On A Train*. But the whole film has only this one twist, which doesn't need interpreting, the rest being straightforward suspense, which is 'blocked' in in a fairly obvious way, quite without Hitchcock's finesse and speed of fluctuation and shift.

Schematically, we may say that Hitchcock's virtuosity enables him to provoke an easy yet powerful dramatic response while introducing a variety of eddies which, without weakening the emotional current, complicate our involvement—not profoundly, but rapidly, back and forth. He catches us in that semi-serious, semi-infantile area where we accept innocent and wicked as real moral states, and then insists that we grow up, a little. Since moral absolutes are both ineradicable and infantile, he can do what he likes with us for a little while, twisting us from earnestness to doubt, to fear, and back and forth through many nuances and combinations at each twist. Certainly it's all on the level of cat's cradle rather than of knotty moral points. But Hitchcock's bold style and sensitive cunning enables him to introduce more twists more deftly and faster than any other thriller director. He puts us in that delicious entertainment state, of semi-childlike (and not merely childish) tizzy which is usually worth our time and his, but is more like fairground fun for the mind than the highest artistic experience. Hitchcock uses the analogy of a baby swinging in order to enjoy a safe fear. It is the need for safety which clips Hitchcock's artistic wings.

Sometimes, though, these earnestnesses doubts and fears, do take us across the boundaries of our more adult assumptions and experiences. They involve us with more complex characters, or in new configurations of religious absurdity. A special urgency does result from the death, in *Psycho*, of our two successive identification figures, two brutal slaps in the face of our conditioning by Hollywood into a kind of romantic egoism whereby the hero's best pal may die but the hero, never. In delicate counterpoint is the 'fishtail' of contradictory identifications and condemnations as we discover the several layers of Norman Bates, layers more devious than the three faces of Eve. Maybe *Psycho* is only just on the right side of the line of artistic maturity—indeed, it's of its nature that it must be, or our simplicity, our natural fundamentalism, couldn't be so massively involved. The structure of *Psycho* endows it with a violence quite lacking from Polanski's intriguing yet curiously affect-lacking counterpart. Hitchcock is surely one of the cinema's great melodists—if one considers the successsion of expectations and surprises as the narrative equivalent of melody.

In more dramatic movies like *Phantom Lady* and *Quai des Orfèvres*, our fuller involvement with more diffuse feelings and problems distracts us from, slows and blurs, the crisp sharp Hitchcock schemas, which depend on a certain lightness and superficiality. His is a realm of crystal rather than weights, of prisms rather than burdens. For obvious reasons (notably the lack of cultural prestige from which film criticism has so long suffered) film critics regularly feel obliged to rationalise their interest in a director by claiming him as a neglected master; a man who offers all the fun of the fair has to become a serious and stern moralist; and so on. It's of the essence of art that these descriptions aren't mutually exclusive. But the dangers are obvious enough. A celebration of moral banality as extremely profound not only fortifies spiritual complacency but becomes a confusionist pretext for what shouldn't need a pretext, namely, joy derived from agreeable entertainment and from a masterly manipulation of the medium. For if Hitchcock has emerged as an *auteur*, it is not simply on the strength, or weakness, of his thematic. But it was to their aesthetic delight as well as to a sharpness of experience that the older critics referred when they wrote appreciatively of the 'Hitchcock touch', praising its fast movement, quick cutting, brisk close-ups and all the other characteristics of the English version of the Eisenstein aesthetic. The younger French critics were more interested by Hitchcock's camera-movements, which loomed larger in his '40s period than before, and in connection with which they rightly evoked the names of Murnau and Ophuls. The *Movie* critics, as we have seen, developed a third approach, studying the structure and integration of the visual and the narrative-literary mechanisms, the links in the chain of content.

Certainly the older critics, having fetishised their notions of montage, did scant justice to Hitchcock's astonishing virtuosity. Eisenstein's theories, which they hardly understood, seemed to have driven completely from their minds even the dimmest memory of the Murnau style, whereby a sequence, or even a film, might be based on a steady rhythm of movements, including camera-movements; and Hitchcock had the cinematic sense to go even further than Ophuls in Europe, before Ophuls. As Bazin pointed out, the ten-minute take was really a modified form of classical montage, in that the camera slid from one conventional set-up to another, rather than finding new configurations. Certainly Hitchcock made no secret of the practical, rather than aesthetic, reasons behind the procedure: the hope of completing a film in nine takes. None the less the creepy-crawly effect was new, and appropriate to the moral slitheriness of the principal characters, and it easily antedates Renoir's equally practical reasons for another continuous take technique in *Le Testament du Dr. Cordelier*. When Hitchcock adapted T.V. techniques (in *Psycho*), it was far more calculatedly and successfully, in a manner disciplined by the most sensitive aspects of classical narrative editing. The secret of Hitchcock's versatility is his constant references to what he calls 'pure cinema'—sharp angling, bold close-ups, taut cutting, the narrative crispness and emphasis on personal involvement characteristic of Hollywood classicism (the published storyboard sequence for *The Birds* illustrates that virtual alternation of event shots and reaction shots so typical of the American style). In the '40s this emphasis led to a concentration on head-and-shoulders close-ups which wasn't without a certain monotony. Since then new lens and colour have given his films more air to breathe, and even the big close-ups sustain a sense of continuing space. In every film the integration of dramatic and visual content has a singlemindedness which is a kind of immaculacy, of perfection, and cannot but be a source of purely aesthetic pleasure.

This is far from consigning Hitchcock's films to some limbo of *merely* aesthetic connoisseurship. For if Symbolism at its least interesting tended to abstraction in the sense of a merely exquisite formalism, the example of music, and subsequent developments in abstract painting and concrete poetry (abstract meaning concrete!), have made it quite clear that forms abstracted from representational

significance may possess significance of many kinds. In their acceptance of Hollywood asininity as a move towards abstraction, the *Cahiers*
critics were indicating a theoretical aesthetic possibility, even if their
choice of cases reached a pitch of imbecility whose reasons must have
included a culturally pathological disdain of the humane and a lazy
dilettantism which loved observing the differences between, say,
Hitchcockian and Republic travelling mates but avoided having to
think about anything culturally more important. A pale echo of
Symbolism was never far away from *Cahiers* of the period, and it must
be said that Hitchcock's work (transference of guilts apart) represents a rare admixture of, on one hand, melodramatic excitement,
with its free play of robust anxieties, and, on the other, an aesthetic
sensibility which few, if any, melodramatists have possessed. The
mixture is as intriguing as it is rare.

The present study seeks to indicate a middle road between those for
whom Hitchcock is a Master, but a Master of nothing, and those for
whom Hitchcock is regularly rather than occasionally a profound and
salutary moralist working, not through homily, but through a therapeutic process of involvement (which, it might be added, constitutes a
valuable widening of the Aristotelian notion of *catharsis*). In the
course of constrasting Hitchcock's movies with the James Bond epics,
Robin Wood implies that either a film is a work of art or it is a
nothing; but, quite apart from any contentions about the nuances of
travelling mattes, our contention will be that Hitchcock's less interesting films are quite as careful, structured and coherent as his best ones,
the difference lying not in the structure but in the content which is
structured. Thus, a proper structural analysis concludes, not in tables
of opposites, but in an adequate description of the diverse elements
which create the emotional atmospheres of a sequence of scenes. In
this way structural analysis can begin to do something like justice to a
sense of the authenticity and richness of lyrical textures, and the disputes between the two schools, which would have occurred had they
so much as possessed a common language in which to dispute, can
be replaced by a synthesis. Ideas are not a structure 'beneath' the
surface, nor the dry bones, nor even the musculature of the flesh; the
two shade into one another imperceptibly and necessarily. Conversely,
any structure is a structure of atmospheres as much as it is a structure
of ideas. The terms of our analyses will be traditional enough: theme
and variation, continuity and rupture, expectation and surprise, the
interweaving (separation and superimposition) of themes, contrast and
similarity, harmony and dissonance. These patterns are compatible

with a certain degree of latitude in response, which helps to explain why a work of art can affect so many people in roughly similar emotional ways even though their responses differ as widely as they do, although excessive divergence will produce anomalous reactions.

Before turning to individual films, however, it is as well to indicate an attitude to the common assumption that Hitchcock's films must between them figure forth some coherent (even if evolving) moral or philosophical attitude to life. Extreme *auteur* theory, may it rest in peace, has taught us a great deal, and among the things it should have taught us is the extent to which a man's art may be inspired by the irresoluble, insurmountable and inescapable contradictions and incoherences between contradictory instinctual drives, social aims and value-systems. The cultural links between *auteur* theory, romantic individualism and Aristotelian logic encourage us to assume the equation: 'One artist, one philosophy'. But Saul may become Paul, and a man may hesitate throughout his life between mutually exclusive life-styles, while a variety of notions, ranging from that of unconscious conflict to that of bad faith, acknowledge what we all know from our experience of interactions between internal conflict and external circumstances, that the mind incorporates diverse configurations of emotion and aim which can innocently and harmoniously co-exist until a particular dilemma inaugurates a chain reaction of conflicts. In other words, a film is as likely to be about a discovered incoherence as to be an affirmation; and this incoherence is no more reducible to one underlying issue than human nature is.

Of a situation in *I Confess*, Bogdanovich asked Hitchcock if the priest and his beloved slept together during the storm, and Hitchcock replied, 'I hope so. Far be it from me as a Jesuit to encourage that kind of behaviour.' That bland contradiction, far from being the result of moral unpreparedness, is typical enough of people's attitudes, and Hitchcock certainly counts on his interlocuter's understanding it as a settled and wordly attitude. Equally, any account of the film's experience and moral ought to bear this sort of ambivalence in mind. Clearly Hitchcock relishes his remark's provocative mixture of anxiety and liberation, a mixture which is as characteristic of intellectual paradox as of the best Hitchcockian situations.[1]

[1] And although to make connections between interviews is rather more dubious even than taking any interview remark as gospel (for reasons discussed in *Jean Renoir*), it looks as if Hitchcock introduces his 'Jesuitry' so as to sharpen the contradiction. For when Bazin told him what a Jansenist was, and described them as the enemies of the Jesuits, Hitchcock remarked that he had to free himself from his Jesuit education to make *I Confess*, i.e. that that was a de-Jesuitised film. Cer-

In the same way, no modern society has a single-system ideology. Quite apart from our plurality of cultures, the ideology of any culture is an agglomeration of beliefs whose relationship, far from being structurally logical, is a matter of historical evolution and the whole cultural-economic situation. Thus in Anglo-Saxon cultures we find a mixture of the Protestant ethic, psychoanalysis, unreflective hedonism, enlightenment optimism, patriotism, and so on and so forth. It is obvious that a director as concerned with his films' acceptability as entertainment must have a sharp sense of the balance of factors within the consensus. Hitchcock has commented that, in England, he could work in a more or less spontaneous way, reckoning that his personal responses were closely related to his audience's (even so, he has commented on some serious mistakes, notably in *Sabotage*). But in America he found such a variety of ethnic and regional subcultures that he had to work a great deal more reflectively, and this, I would suggest, resulted in the slower, simpler, more emphatic and methodical style of the '40s Hitchcocks. It also helps one understand certain characteristics of the general Hollywood style, notably its fixation on strong simple conflicts whose elements are so stacked as to work across a variety of value-systems while avoiding controversies which might confuse or exasperate important audience groups. Thus a hero who is a Catholic priest will also be personable—played by Montgomery Clift—and pitched against characters who won't confuse the sympathies which we feel for him on one count if not on the other. Not that this catch-all structure need rule out complications—of a sort. Thus a Catholic priest who is a minor character may have a mean face—and it is up to audiences to decide whether his meanness is a comment on Catholicism, or on Christianity, or simply an acknowledgement that priests vary as much as other men. Any result of his actions would have an equal variety of possible meanings. The influence of the Catholic lobby was usually sufficient to ensure that any mean-faced priest would be accompanied or opposed by a pleasant-faced one.

---

tainly he wouldn't appear to have freed himself in a Jansenist direction; quite the reverse, given the libertarian drift of his remark. One possibility among many is that what, specifically, he freed himself from was a certain reverential fear which hindered his understanding of the priest as a man of very fleshly passion and a slightly suspect vocation; and if that possibility can't be confirmed neither can it be dismissed. Otherwise Hitchcock has consistently said that his moral thinking isn't specifically Jesuit or even Christian, although he has also said that he remains a (negligent) Roman Catholic. The contradiction is familiar enough in many an *homme moyen morale*.

In *Torn Curtain*, the Communist scientist relaxes his vigilance over a good meal and wine and in the presence of a beautiful American girl. And the moral might be that self-indulgence is always weakness and dangerous; or that Communism is so unnatural that it can't allow natural human pleasurable responses; or both; and several other possibilities besides. It is of course possible for an artist to so organise his whole action as to rule out ambiguities; but it is also possible for him to so organise it as to maintain them. And restricting ourselves for the moment to this simple situation, it is evidently likely that the scene will provoke different moral responses in people of different moral dispositions. Uncomplicated anti-Communists will uncomplicatedly rejoice at any chink in the Communist armour, as will those people who are relatively unconcerned about the Red Peril and think that American spies are just as naughty as anyone else's spies but vastly prefer handsome and audacious Paul Newman and beautiful and loyal Julie Andrews to anyone else in sight, and as a result react negatively to the East Germans. Not that the film ever becomes a soot-and-whitewash affair, for Paul Newman behaves badly to Julie Andrews, and the Russians are intermittently humanised. But provided a general polarity of hope-and-fear exists, these confusions will extend and enhance our excitement, not only by making everyone concerned more plausible, but as a certain mixture of bewilderment and conviction may do.

Another example of sliding-scale morality may be useful. In a piece for *Take One*, Hitchcock says, of James Stewart's interest in the people over the way, 'If you want to be really mean towards the character in the film you could call him a Peeping Tom. I don't think it's necessarily a statement of morality because it's a matter of "fact".[1] When

---

[1] Although it depends just what you mean by 'Peeping Tom'. A similar word, 'voyeurism' has all but lost its original meaning. Once referring to people who had definite erotic excitement by watching sexual activity, it has now been extended, under the influence of that spiritual valetudinarianism, not to say hypochondria, which is the modern intellectual's equivalent of Victorian ailments, to mean anyone who shows any curiosity about anyone else, as opposed to such three-layer sublimations as reading a book about Hitchcock's film about a photographer who looks at people without a professional pretext. No-one has ever suggested that Stewart's peeping is much more than the very weakly sexualised curiosity of an invalid who doesn't much like reading, is quite rightly bored with glossy magazines and television, and, being an intelligent person, begins weaving his observations into speculations which he plays at making as realistic as possible. The invalid lady opposite my window as I write this does it all the time, elbows on the sill; and unlike some critics, I really don't feel she deserves 'punishment' for it; on the contrary, I hope she has a very sharp mind and eye and spots all sorts of interesting things.

Grace Kelly says that they're a couple of fiendish ghouls because they're disappointed that a murder hasn't been committed she's speaking the truth. They were a couple of ghouls.' Which might seem severe enough—although even so Hitchcock had been equivocal. On one hand: 'If you want to be really mean . . .', and on the other, they're not just peepers, they're fiendish ghouls. But it would be idle to erect on this theories about Hitchcock condemning his hero, or secretly condemning him while allowing his audience to be more indulgent about him. 'Fiendish ghoul' no more means 'fiendish ghoul' when Hitchcock says it than it does when Grace Kelly says it—for after all she goes on to marry Jeff. Hitchcock's mixture of indulgence (Jeff isn't a Peeping Tom *morally*) and stricture is all of a piece with everyone's understanding that a normal person can be both naughtily curious and crave morbid excitement without being guilty of anything in particular. It should be no more difficult to understand than the proposition that although both Hitchcock and his spectators are guilty of enjoyably thinking about murders neither he nor we have connived at murder.[1] One doesn't have to choose between angelism on the one hand or a Jansenist view of total depravity on the other; one can accept, as I think Hitchcock does, that a great many human attitudes are the result of morally mixed motives, so that there's nothing particularly illogical in simultaneously expressing disapproval and indulgence of an action, or even approval and disapproval, or oscillating between degrees of censure or approval depending on which particular aspect or context of an action is being considered. One very traditional form of this is the view that certain murders are altogether understandable and sympathetic but that none the less they have to be punished, and this kind of double-entry moral book-keeping is comprehensible to all (except partisans of one-dimensional logical equations). As Hitchcock remarked to Bogdanovich, 'The critic on *The Observer* called this a horrible film because a man was looking out of the window at other people. I thought that was a crappy remark. Everyone does it, it's a known fact, and provided it is not made too

---

[1] Most of us quite rightly want some sort of awareness of the experiences involved in states of affairs of which we heartily disapprove. To refuse to acquaint oneself with anything of which one disapproves is not only to refuse to read a novel with wickedness in it that isn't heavily moralised over but just another form of 'We don't wish to know that,' i.e. a form of smugly complacent spiritual suicide. This isn't to pretend that morbid delectation is necessarily absent from an interest in morally anomalous experience. It's obvious that a policeman is only too pleased to detect a crime and may be disappointed to find that what promised to be a 'nice juicy murder' (and that's a significantly common phrase) has some perfectly innocent explanation. James Stewart here is functioning as a detective.

vulgar, it is just curiosity. People don't care who you are, they just can't resist looking.' Why else, one might ask, is the paper for which that fastidious critic wrote called *The Observer*? Does it refrain from printing distasteful news as religiously as *The Christian Science Monitor*? Of course not. Does it review crime fiction regularly? Of course it does. It's part of our cultural pathology that critics easily apply to movie characters a morality quite as inapplicable to anything else as that imposed by the Hollywood system itself, and for diverging from which, Hitchcock was, as we shall see, bitterly attacked by so-called 'intellectual' critics. But to see Hitchock's attitude to the audience's tolerance of moral imperfection as sternly therapeutic corrective treatment is only another aspect of a perfectionism for which there is, in fact, no clear warrant in Hitchcock's work. What morally balances James Stewart's systematic peeping and ghoulishness in his attitude to his quarry; and far from being a horrible one it's a morally mediocre one: quite complacent, rather patronising, not particularly kind or unkind, neither altogether unconcerned nor indefensibly interfering. It's equally true that there's no aspect of his attitudes which one shouldn't also have qualms about. The pathology, and the complacency, lies in the Hollywood system's, and in the critic's, attempts to replace the ambiguity of qualms by the certainty of either impeccability or condemnation.

Hitchcock's expertise includes a rare sense of how far dramatic conflicts can be complicated, and in which ways, so as to enhance rather than weaken the polarity of hope and fear which itself remains emphatic and simple enough to galvanise everybody. A primary concern of this study is to observe a mechanism which is primarily a dramatic one, although some of these dramatic factors also happen to be moral ones. In drama even more rapidly than in philosophy, axiological issues (questions of moral value) soon open into questions of where happiness lies (felicitology), of human perfection for its own sake (characterology), and of successful styles of conduct (praxiology),[1] not to mention all the relationships between man, subgroups and society, as well as between individuals and God. If one takes all these issues into account, it rapidly becomes apparent that the so-called 'transference of guilt' only makes sense given a specifically Roman Catholic philosophy of life. And this no critic has so much as attempted to find in Hitchcock's films. Failing which there seems no reason not to prefer an interpretation to which both the films'

---

[1] These categories are borrowed from Maria Ossowska, *Social Determinents Moral Ideas*, University of Pennsylvania, 1970, and Routledge & Kegan Paul, 1971.

underlying good-bad polarities and the Anglo-Saxon moral consensus would tend: the good aren't immune from the temptations which have corrupted the bad, but resist them, yielding to only a minor degree, the difference between heroes and villains remaining significant, since in matters of human behaviour quantitative differences become qualitative ones.

Although our view of Hitchcock's moral positions (in the plural) is developed throughout the text, a few preliminary remarks about Hitchcock's general orientation may be in order. Chabrol and Rohmer assume that Hitchcock's vision is impregnated by a Roman Catholicism which, for whatever reason, has become as severe as Jansenism. This is reasonable enough, but can easily obscure a pervasive cultural influence. Jansenism, in its pure form a heresy, is the result of Calvinist influence on the Roman Catholic Church, although, like Calvinism itself, it can be traced back to the Augustinianism which is securely lodged within Catholic thought. Hitchcock's sense of an implacable, severe, but somehow just moral order may well have come to him via the influence, on the British middle and lower-middle classes, of Puritanism, which is the English expression of Calvinism. It's true that pure doctrinal Calvinism had begun to wane before it was overlaid by the anti-Calvinism which Methodism, and the evangelical revival, brought from the Church of England (whose influence otherwise on the lower urban classes is notoriously conspicuous by its absence and which in any case was doctrinally too flexible to exert a hard-edge line). Thus English nonconformism uses an optimistic, evangelical, even latitudinarian language, as opposed to Scottish nonconformism, where pure Calvinism persisted more forcefully. But the Jansenism theory meets an even more effective objection in the fact that Hitchcock was educated by Jesuits who, in several crucial theological aspects, are not only anti-Jansenist but nearer Anglican latitudinarianism than the Augustinian facet of Roman Catholicism. So if we are to assume a predominant theological influence then Hitchcock's morality turns out to be, not Jansenist at all, but characteristic of Anglo-Saxon lower-class Protestantism, in its capacity for rapid oscillation between a post-Wesleyan evangelical optimism and a grimmer, more punitive view of human depravity, which, as Calvinism waned, was none the less assimilated into the Protestant ethic. And the Protestant ethic, with its emphasis on individualism as to salvation in this world, as in the next, would agree with the overt and conventional good-bad polarity, but accord ill with any transference of guilt, an idea which is closer to the world of Bernanos and Mauriac (although it appears, unconvincingly, like an importation, in Graham Greene). All of which suggests that the idea of a transference of guilt is a French Catholic importation into Hitchcock's films. The latter rejoin the Calvinist streak in Anglo-Saxon culture which assumes that every human being is naturally capable of every depravity anyway—a streak which inspires the traditional detective story and helped Anglo-Saxon culture to accept the idea of an unconscious libido as the French did not. Thus Hitchcock's recourse to overt Freudian ideas can hardly be dismissed as merely a mask for Jansenism.

When Bogdanovich asked Hitchcock if he had been influenced by his Jesuit mentors, Hitchcock's reply was quite explicit. 'The Jesuits taught me organization, control and to some degree analysis. . . . As far as any religious influence goes, at the time I think it was fear. But I've grown out of religious fear now. I think I have. . . . I don't think the religious side of the Jesuit education impressed itself so much upon me as the strict discipline one endured at the time.' Ironically, therefore, the *relative* leniency of Jesuit theology was outweighted by the *relative* severity of Jesuit discipline—although anybody educated in many schools, including C of E, Methodist, and non-denominational ones, in London early in the century, or even much later, was likely to find his daily life dominated, as Hitchcock's seems to have been, by fear of something analogous to the Jesuit fathers' 'cane made of very hard rubber . . . you spent the whole day waiting for the sentence to be carried out'. Pedagogical severity and doctrines of the relative facility of salvation are, after all, independent variables.

A man's philosophy, and his artistic inspiration, is more likely to derive from the texture of everyday life, and a whole socio-ideological conglomerate, rather than from any one -ism. Hitchcock's films accommodate a variety of moral interpretations. But Hitchcock, with his vivid memories of an altogether unpleasurable suspense, comes, as artist-entertainer, to devote himself to inflicting a vicarious, fictitious and altogether delightful suspense, on a grateful victim. In this alteration of situation and role the Freudian notion of 'repetition-compulsion' as a basis of play finds a classical example; the tortured turned torturer, but amiably. Hitchcock might, of course, have learned such fear in almost any English school, including a public one—although not, perhaps, that conjunction of fear and 'organization and analysis', a conjunction which may help to explain his characteristic control of construction. Freudian theory would immediately remind us, as would common-sense, that that conjunction itself would require the response of a particular temperament.

What is interesting, though, is the possibility that Hitchcock's particular temperament inspired him to re-invent the severity of Jansenism for himself. It's even more likely that his sense of the English atmosphere attuned him to all that Calvinism, secularised, bequeathed to its less liberal aspects. Non-Calvinist orthodoxy allows for predestination; 'God foreknew and sorrowed, that you would, alas, abuse his gift of freewill, and sin, and damn yourself into the eternal fire.' The Calvinist speciality is double predestination: 'God created you such that you would damn yourself, yet you, having damned yourself, deserve to be punished.' And with it goes a change in the attitude ascribed to God: 'God, having created you as he did, cannot sorrow over your damnation.' A keynote of the Hitchcock world is its sense of a manipulated order, with Hitchcock, like the Calvinist God, arranging his narrative machines, and adjusting his characters' weaknesses exactly to their allotted role. Calvinism, too, answered, heroically, drastically, and cruelly, a problem which Christian orthodoxy has never contrived to solve: if God created everything, how did evil enter the world? Calvin accepted God's responsibility for evil, adding that good and bad are defined purely by God's arbitrary decision, and not by their inherent characteristics (since this would mean that God's decision was dependent on the nature of good, that his choice was not free, and that, in effect, good was God's God, thus dethroning God, which explains why Calvinism easily adapts to secularisation). In its dependence on the arbitrary preference of an inscrutable God, Calvinism leads directly to religious absurdity, and to a paranoiad fear and terror analogous to that of a Calvinist adrift in a meticulously programmed but pitiless world. If the English never developed a literature of extreme situations, a minor reason may be that the Calvinists had already given a special intensity to moral self-scrutiny through the diary—a moral self-scrutiny, attended with extreme fear, in which every thought, being an index of damnation or salvation, was in itself an extreme situation. And Calvinism normally ensured that absurdity led to fear, not complacency. Many who seem saved are damned, for secret or unconscious sins, but all who, because they sin, seem damned, *are*. Things can only be worse than they seem.

The implacable, indifferent face of a Calvinist God is evoked in those impassive faces: the Egyptian God past which the detectives hound their prey in *Blackmail*, or the Statue of Liberty, that American deity, from which the Nazi hangs in *Saboteur*, or the American Presidents carved into Mount Rushmore. Indeed, Hitchcock's films are

Calvinistic machines, since, as Raymond Chandler ruefully remarked, Hitchcock requires characters to fit predetermined action and settings. Not that the characters may be merely passive; they are required to show initiative, resilience, courage and all sorts of moral qualities. And many Hitchcock films feature that curious sense of a manipulation by an external master leaving no more than little chinks of chance or pluck through which the characters may slip to salvation; the eyes of needles, as it were.

Calvinism, like other extreme, heroic and paradoxical positions, is an unstable one, and slips easily into its own antitheses (just as the Puritans began as would-be theocrats and rapidly became champions of capitalist liberties). And Hitchcock's work involves a streak, even, of rebellion against God, although it takes a peculiar form. Hitchcock *becomes* God. His characters clamber, perilously, about *his* portly, enigmatic face, for his, and our, amusement. Hitchcock, like Bunuel's Robinson Crusoe, looks down at the scurrying ants, and disposes of them. The audience is in a middle position; part immune, part God, part victim. Douchet sees *Rear Window* and *Vertigo* alike as meditations on the punishment awaiting the men whose spectatorial and creative activities make them rivals of God. One may accept this level of meaning, but reverse its sense: Hitchcock strolls by—God, incognito, unrecognised, unseeing. Hitchcock is like God playing as many practical jokes on human beings as he can—jokes in rather poor taste. His bland countenance begins to look less like that of the conventional Christian God than that of the Calvinist God whose cruelty is immune from all pleas. But it also reveals a dreamy, mischievous human pleasure. It begins to look like that of Sade, although a doleful victim's air may replace the explosive energy usually associated with Sade's. It's as that *cold* face is allowed to emerge that Hitchcock becomes most challenging. His two Christian films are suspiciously solemn, as if the intention were there, but the experience is paraphrased by an ill-at-ease respect, or an ambiguous contrivance.

For once, it may be, publicity images are truer than the critical consensus. Slogans like 'Stories they wouldn't let me do on T.V.' imply a saturnine, more than whimsical wryness, which can't quite be got on to the screen but which he thus, surreptitiously, shares with us. 'I am the Master of Suspense. I know more than you will be allowed to know.' If only, the image hints, the visual screen were as free from squeamish censorship as the 'nice juicy murders' which folklore soaks up from newspapers as earlier it soaked them up from penny dreadfuls and public hanging broadsheets. Hitchcock gives Truffaut detailed synopses of three of those English crimes which are so regularly less decorous than Orwell allows in his *Decline of the English Murder*. 'In the Mahon case the man killed a girl in a bungalow in a seafront in southern England. He cut up the body, and threw it piece by piece, out of a train window. . . . But he didn't know what to do with the head, and that's where I got the idea of having to look for the victim's head in *Rear Window*. What Patrick MacMahon did was to put the head in the fireplace and light the fire . . . the heat of the fire made the eyes open wide, as if they were staring at Mahon. He ran out to the beach screaming, with the storm pouring down on him . . . one of the four chief inspectors of Scotland Yard came to see me . . . and he told me . . . he needed to have some indication of the time at which it was put in the fire and how long it had taken to burn. So he went down to the butcher's shop, bought a sheep's head and burned it in the same fireplace.'

Fastidiousness, one may suppose, explains why such details feature in Hitchcock so rarely. But it is also a curious fact that gruesome crimes of a type which fascinate the readers of the Sunday press rarely find their way on to the screen, or only in heavily bowdlerised guise. That the screen is a visual medium is nothing to do with it; the screen is not a visual medium when it chooses not to be; throughout *Rope* we became very concerned for a corpse of which we are vouchsafed scarcely a glimpse. The real reason, I suggest, is that the cinema has traditionally depended on audiences vaster even than those of the Sunday newspapers, a goodly proportion of which would be offended, rather than fascinated, by the misanthropic implications of such material, deeply embedded as it is in a certain stratum of folk culture. And Hitchcock recounts those tales, meticulously, from memory. Their spirit reaches the screen very occasionally. Those aspects of *Psycho* are deftly transposed into Grand Guignol, and their moral meaning is unleashed only in the murder of Gromek in *Torn Curtain*, in extenuating circumstances.[1] What is more freely and frequently allowed though is a sense of moral mischief. Whether through fearfulness or prudence. Hitchcock has refrained from expressing this side of his mind other than coyly, or in the fates of subsidiary and unsympathetic characters, or in the 'religious absurdity' of Hitchcock the poet. He

[1] The few sentences cited above afford one opportunity after another for a Hitchcockian orchestration, even to the sensuous contrasts of water (the seafront, the storm) and fire; spaces limitless and constricted; immobility (the homely fireside) and movement (the train); and the repetition by the detective of the acts of the murderer, in the very same fireplace (which qualifies, by Chabrol's and Rohmer's logic, for a transference of guilt).

described to Truffaut his vision of a film about food and what happens to it—as waste, it's poured by the ton into the sea. The vision hardly needs psychoanalysis, particularly if one thinks of all the things that happen to food. 'Your theme,' says Truffaut, 'might almost be the rottenness of humanity,' and Hitchcock does not demur. Of a certain kind of pessimism, about which film critics, especially if they are young and Anglo-Saxon, incline to be hypochondriac, but which unfortunately perhaps can't be dismissed as subhuman or unintelligent, Aldous Huxley, I think, coined the phrase, 'the excremental vision', and its reflection is evident enough in the work of Sade, of Swift, of Huxley himself, of Céline, of the swamp-and-bathroom syndrome in *Psycho*. Its full integration with preoccupations not unlike Hitchcock's appears in the novels of Gerald Kersh, some of which are so savage as to be, by traditional Anglo-Saxon standards, unfilmable. Clouzot's three masterpieces catch something of that pessimism: the Clouzot in Hitchcock is kept waiting in the wings, as it were. Thus the interrupted kissing in *Notorious* was inspired, says Hitchcock, by the sight of a young French couple holding hands even while the youth was urinating against a factory wall. The Clouzot of *Quai des Orfèvres* would have liked that. A comparison with Simenon is virtually mandatory; and Simenon's best seems to me to be caught by Autant-Lara's *En Cas De Malheur*. The comparison is partly a matter of American and French film-making frameworks, with the latter creatively more flexible, and general audiences more sympathetic to irony and pessimism. Hitchcock has steered consistently clear of the *film noir*, although his ventures towards its mood resulted in *Sabotage* and *Psycho*. About the box-office failure of the first he is thoroughly repentant; and he shot *Psycho*, rapidly, in T.V. style, as if in precaution against the risks he felt he was taking. 'People will say, It was a terrible film to make. The subject was horrible, the people were small, there were no characters in it.' Perhaps the sadness of Hitchcock's career is the disparity between the film-making worlds in which he lived and a vision lying so close under the surface as to appear briefly and more disruptively sometimes than if the *film noir* framework had existed around it. Even his English thrillers conclude in two relatively light and facetious efforts, while in Hollywood Hitchcock's patron was David O. Selznick, a fascinating, but hardly a hard-edged, film-maker, and Hitchcock's picaresque thrillers were so alien to Hollywood theories of undistracted identification that not until 1959 can he combine their pace with a star whom he felt to be adequate. Hitchcock's mixture of complacent surroundings and eruptions from the moral underworld can have its own impact—the killing of the boy in *Sabotage* being an example; regularly, however, the shock is deprived of connections, encapsulated, reduced to an anomaly signifying no more than that the world preserves a certain capacity for anomalies. What is more freely and frequently allowed expansion is a sense of moral mischief which may evoke Polanski—albeit Polanski is a little too sophisticated, a little too playful. The real meaning of *Rosemary's Baby* is 'Two thousand years of Christianity led only to us, so why shouldn't the Devil equally become Son of Man. Things will go on much as before, or possibly be a bit more startling, a bit more fun.' Polanski is New Morality, Hitchcock is Old Morality. *Rope* might have been intended for people who, like Polanski, irresponsibly play with moral ideas. Graham Greene, another believer in the improbability of happiness, hopes that somebody up there will manage a few minor and furtive miracles somehow and give us the strength to go on joylessly suffering; and Hitchcock paraphrases that idea in *The Wrong Man*. Otherwise, though, he seems to believe in a healthy fear: don't tempt providence (or the box-office), lie low, maintain an insulation of mental order, be humorous and afraid, prudent and safe. Sade counselled bravado, Hitchcock mediocrity and a little bit of luck. His creative vision is in uneasy suspension between a Calvinist fear of God and an identification with a Calvinistic God, who, many people will remark, comes close to a Sadeian divinity. This is not at all to say that what Robin Wood calls the 'basic sympathetic flow' is absent from Hitchcock's work; were it not he would hardly have the understanding of audiences which he has. But it lies along a certain wavelength, within a certain area, rather than others. Hitchcock is, discreetly, above it, ironically masterminding it, much as the Calvinist's God masterminds a sexual instinct with which he is in a gruellingly sado-masochistic relationship. In Hitchcockian sexuality there is much teasing, much dissatisfaction, much involuntary tussling for dominance, forced on one by situation rather than inclination. Perhaps its simplest yet most precise image is that in *The Thirty-Nine Steps*. Handcuffs pull your limp hand over the silk-stockinged thighs of the girl who wants to hand you over to the police.

In two interviews Hitchcock cites, and requests his interlocutor's assent to, Oscar Wilde's remark, 'Each man kills the thing he loves', and considers it 'a very natural thing really'. As, indeed, it is, whence the infestation of the human soul, and society, by so much that is tragic, squalid and perverse. His interviewers neither answer the question, nor follow it up, just as they ignore Hitchcock's various

references to psychoanalysis, whose view of the human being's emotional plight accords well with Hitchcock's citation. Truffaut claims
to be intrigued by what he rather hastily assumes to be a contradiction: (a) Hitchcock's claim to have been unusually sexually ignorant and
innocent, and (b) scenes in *The Pleasure Garden* and *The Lodger* might
just possibly be taken to have Lesbian undertones (e.g. one girl wears a
nightdress and another a man's pyjamas).[1] From this Truffaut gained
'a distinct impression' that Hitchcock was 'fascinated by the abnormal'
from his 'very first pictures on'. Hitchcock replies, 'That may be so,'
but adds that the interest was 'rather superficial'. But Truffaut seems
unduly discouraged by Hitchcock's disclaimer in this case. For
although he notices 'that handcuffs have a way of recurring in your
movies', he not only doesn't connect it with Hitchcock's fear of the
law, but sedulously avoids the subject of sexual abnormality, although
Hitchcock teases him: 'Psychologically, of course, the idea of the
handcuffs has deeper implications. Being tied to something . . . It's
in the nature of fetishism, isn't it? . . . There's also a sexual connota-
tion, I think. When I visited the Vice Museum in Paris, I noticed
there was considerable evidence of sexual aberrations through restraint. You should go there some time.'[2]

'In *Rich and Strange* there was a scene in which the young man is
swimming with a girl and she stands with her legs astride, saying to
him. "I bet you can't swim between my legs." I shot it in a tank. The
boy dives, and when he's about to come up between her legs, she
suddenly locks his head between her legs and you see the bubbles
rising from his mouth. Finally, she releases him, and as he comes up,
gasping for air, he sputters out, "You almost killed me that time," and

---

[1] A parallel misunderstanding occurred between Busby Berkeley and a film
aficionado at the National Film Theatre, who asked him what all those Lesbians
were doing in the sleeping berths in *42nd St.* and the showgirls' beds in *Dames*.
Berkeley was so taken back that he couldn't rally his thoughts rapidly enough,
and it's not surprising, to explain what 'bachelor girls' meant in the '20s: the new
freedom enjoyed by girls to move into the cities and towns, away from their parents,
and living with a moral freedom which Berkeley's good girls happily don't abuse,
but still thrill with *joie de vivre*. Between Hitchcock and Truffaut a similar generation gap exists. But it's possible to agree with them both; the spectacle of two girls
lively and cheeky and contrasted enough to set up their own sexual polarity, even
if they don't, is a delicious one.
[2] One doesn't have to be Sigmund Holmes to wonder whether Truffaut isn't
particularly tickled by the sort of para-Lesbianism indicated in the preceding
footnote (or even Lesbianism *tout court*) and Hitchcock by a sado-masochism
which is distinctly more benign than, say, the mixture of rape and violence
in *A Clockwork Orange*, and which would be an almost inevitable off-shoot of
Hitchcock's stock in trade as an entertainer, which is the provision of pleasurable
fear.

she answers, "Wouldn't that have been a beautiful death?" [1] Her answer is all the more mocking in its echoing everyman's ideal death, of pleasure in sexual intercourse (as per J. Lee-Thompson's title *What A Way To Go!*). The swimming pool is, of course, a favourite locale for school bullying.

But if Hitchcock's sexuality has its troubled streak, its variations from the norm are usually prudent, stylised and, if not exactly innocent, impersonal. The manipulating and teasing of slightly passive males by slyly overwhelming females looms large in his American period (of James Stewart by Grace Kelly in *Rear Window*, of Cary Grant by Eva-Marie Saint in *North-by-North-West*). These are deft little variations on a standard American theme (more fully deployed when, in Preminger's *The Man With the Golden Arm*, Sinatra gets Kim Novak to lock him up to kick his habits). Hitchcock remains, prudently, within the limits of the teasing game. If *Psycho* has successive identification figures (Janet Leigh, Vera Miles, Anthony Perkins), it is because it has no principal identification figure; it needs only a butt, a fall guy, that is to say, the audience, which thinks it understands the rules of the world, and of melodrama, only to discover that fate, and Hitchcock, have a few uglier tricks up their sleeves. Tricks which Hitchcock has often been too cautious to play. He would have liked to end with Joan Fontaine in *Suspicion* dying of the poisoned milk which her attentive husband has fed her, while he, whistling unsuspectingly, posts the letter which will incriminate him. *Shadow Of A Doubt* ends with the girl's disillusionment to be imagined—betrays it, indeed, by our relief. *Vertigo* ends ambiguously, with the spectator able to believe, *either*, that James Stewart will now plunge into his most terrible depression yet, *or*, that although he's temporarily shattered, his life has been freed from a lie, to his ultimate benefit—*or* any combination between these two positions. In a sense, Hitchcock is too mediocre to be diabolical: 'Stories they wouldn't let me . . . they wouldn't let me . . . they wouldn't let me . . .' Like a medieval gargoyle, his devil's face is built into the outside of the cathedral.

[1] As Hitchcock observes, the subsequent tightening of censorship would have precluded such a scene as late as 1962. Losey paraphrases some of its basic elements in *Modesty Blaise*. It may well be no accident that whatever prints Truffaut and the present writer have seen, lack this scene.

Our contention isn't that Hitchcock wasn't under enormous pressures against full expression of his deepest vision. But a sense of something withheld seems to have struck other English film-makers, as when Michael Carreras expressed his longing for a conjunction of Hitchcock and Hammer—implying, correctly, I think, that Hitchcock had evaded an aspect of his own genius, perhaps, indeed, because it frightened him.

In all this there seems to me little sign of Robin Wood's Hitchcock, who positively glows with Laurentian psychic health. There is a sense, certainly, in which *Marnie* asserts the value of 'a true order . . . very difficult and dangerous to achieve, but . . . the only order tenable . . . an order arrived at through empiricism, flexibility, a trust in instinct that has its source in a basic sympathetic flow, a rejection of all fixed rules, an acceptance of the necessary moral ambiguity of all positive action in an often bewildering world.' On the other hand, *Marnie*'s lacquered visuals betray the story's harrowing elements, while the marital spars which, within a sumptuous context, may seem adequate ersatz for katharsis or crisis, remain well below the level of many a routine Sunday dinner row, and are as agreeably unreal as Frank Sinatra's kicking the heroin habit one weekend in *The Man With the Golden Arm*. Those long oppressive kisses in *Notorious* come from some sumptuous mail-order catalogue of erotic behaviour (for Hitchcock they exemplify the lovers' refusal to stop spooning for life's little details; they might equally reveal the cerebral coldness which enables them to kiss and dial; the ambivalent interpretation seems to me the richest). How unreal, as Gavin Millar argues, is that scene in *Saboteur* in which the blind philosophical character divines an intruder's innocence from the honest resonance of his footsteps. One may blame it on rustic America. But it's no easier to find an artistic defence for the dapper badinage of Donat's Hannay in *The Thirty-Nine Steps*, one of the several matinée idols who move through ingenious nightmares to be only gently disturbed thereby. One talks easily of the Hitchcock nightmares, but often they are *ideas* of nightmares, alleviated by systematic comic relief, as Hitchcock makes quite clear in his discussion of the lessons he learned—artistically, how regrettably!—from *Saboteur*. Despite descriptions of his Jansenist severities, Hitchcock's happy ends allow his heroes, whether innocent or guilty, to get away with things while suffering rather less from the suspense than, say, the innocent hero of *Phantom Lady*, which, produced by Hitchcock's longtime associate, Joan Harrison, blends the Hitchcock formula with the *film noir*. The happy end has behind it, not the force of God or providence or fate, but the audience's preference for reassurance. And happiness is Grace Kelly, just as Hitchcock man, more often than not, is Cary Grant.

None the less, just as there is a temptation to react too far against the dismissal of Hitchcock as an entertainer for the masses who's a bore for the arthouse audience, so there is a temptation to react too far against the happy end Hitchcock and produce a merely depressed and nihilistic one, a Sade without the courage of his convictions (not that that is a particularly rare human attitude!). Even matinée idol heroism isn't without a certain human truth; if it weren't, it would be rarer, and disdained less than it is by those who feel menaced or disappointed by its acceptance of the surfaces of society, by the spiritual significance which etiquette, bluff and the maintenance of the pretence of complacency may possess. Often, Hitchcock's religiously absurd situations touch on these points of strength. There is the Hitchcock who, far from being preoccupied with the strictest possible morality, delights, as amorally as Ernst Lubitsch, in the 'demoralising' effect of good food and fine wine in *To Catch A Thief*, and whose acceptance of Grace Kelly as a moral norm in *Rear Window* implies a view of sensual pleasure, conspicuous consumption and luxury for its own sweet sake which comes as close to that of Lubitsch and Chaplin as that of to the *hommes moyens sensuels* who fill most of the seats in cinemas.[1] Many Hitchcock films are susceptible to a Social Darwinist individualism, and advocate a sturdy self-reliance at least as pointedly as they advocate a certain co-operation and rather more than they show trust in a 'basic sympathetic flow' between all sorts and conditions of men. The maintenance of contradictory moral systems is not, in itself, the sign of a profound or concerned moralist; it's the confusion which is the prerequisite for bringing the system towards a crisis point; sometimes Hitchcock goes a little way towards such a crisis.

Perhaps the key to the Hitchcockian philosophy lies, after all, in this balance of religiously practised absurdity and of a worldly but prudential order. It is the interaction of order and absurdity which

---

[1] One doesn't need to resort to an ideological tradition to explain Hitchcock's sybaritic streak. None the less it's worth bearing in mind that strange ability of Calvinist asceticism, once it has been secularised, to retain the assumption that pleasure is natural and that the natural is wicked; opening the way for the conception of natural vice as source of a rather pleasurable society. It's spelled out in Mandeville's *The Fable of the Bees* (Mandeville being a Dutch ex-Calvinist) just as clearly as in that well-known proverb, 'Heaven for holiness, Hell for company'. A parallel moral inversion underlines the Calvinist transition from economic individualism as a vocation required by God to a thoroughly perfidious conjunction of the notions of *laissez-faire* and enlightened self-interest, i.e. moral irresponsibility. David Reisman has observed a parallel reversal in the American transition from the Puritan ethic to 'fun morality'—a morality which Hitchcock has, it seems to me, espoused only guardedly, or as an entertainer. It's not surprising that Hobbes and Mandeville should be among the great outsiders of the European philosophical tradition; for that represents the thought of a minoritarian class ideology very quietly but firmly braced against the grosser concerns and more violent emotions of the essentially commercial society around and beneath it. On the effete complacency of upper-middle class liberalism/Socialism, Emanuel Shinwell and Alf Garnett are agreed.

produce the Kafkaian paranoia, where masterminds, police and Hitchcock's own genius conspire to give us that chilly sensation of being the quarry of every functioning system in a universe consisting of systems which are hostile to one another and which may casually, between them, grind an individual destiny into nothingness.

But this sense of the absence of a cosmic order is checked in a characteristically British way—by the influence of a kind of fundamentalist stoicism which may owe something to the stoicism of Calvinism, and to its disdain of friendship for the sake of conscience, but which, in popular belief, is often found as yin to the yang of an acceptance of injustice, and which does so much to give British films a tone rather dourer than American optimism. *Because* the universe is absurd, men must accept as valid a set of categorical imperatives with which it is extremely dangerous to tamper, absurd and unjust though close or logical inspection may show them to be. Here is the grimmer, darker side of the 'happy accident' theory of the English constitution. Against this structure of imperatives neither sentiment nor logic may be assigned any role as arbiter; for it is the function of a categorical imperative to oppose the fluctuations of sentiment. Even more dangerous is the combination of the logic of individualism and a resentment of social injustice, for it might dissolve, in violence, a social order whose injustices must be endured if life is to have any meaning at all. The celebrated British respect for law and order links with a Hobbesian fear of disorder, as it links with a Durkheimian fear of anomie, and profoundly mitigates the effect, on lower-class levels, of enlightenenment rationalism and Lockeian individualism alike. Enlightened self-interest becomes dread of anarchy, and aspires no higher than anarchy's avoidance.[1] In a cutthroat society, it's easier

---

[1] The question of the British fear of reform and anarchism as liable to dislocate an order which, however brutal, is reassuringly effective, is approached from another angle in *A Mirror for England*. One might say that the fear which the Civil War inspired in Hobbes was paralleled by the fear of the French Revolution, and reinforced by a sullen, smouldering, pervasive class friction, the very confusion and complexity of whose boundaries has rendered social snobbery so subtle, alert, and so full of self-deception as to make a signal contribution to the defensive insularity of the English individual. From another angle, our general thesis would run parallel to Svend Ranulf's *Moral Indignation and Middle Class Psychology* (Munksgard, Copenhagen, 1938, and Schocken Books, New York, 1964). Although American Populism has never lacked its ferocious aspect (whether its scapegoats are intellectuals, artists and people with foreign accents, as per Capra's *Mr. Deeds goes To Town*, or cyclists with long hair (as per *Easy Rider*), this was concealed, throughout the '40s and '50s, except in so far as Commies were concerned, by an optimistic belief in progress which, less marked in Britain, isn't absent either. This dismisses most social injustices as gently regrettable but not worth altering the social order

to fall than to rise, and its individualism is mitigated. Ambition, hope, happiness, are optional extras, luxuries almost, indeed, *hubris*. What gives middle-class complacency its profoundly satisfying quality are the intense, covert fears from which it feels only narrowly immune.

Rich and Strange, Saboteur and *Psycho* re-establish the agnostic mixture of pessimism and stoicism, of pain and prudence, which set the bounds of a cautiously and meticulously limited existence. This stoicism is not a by-product of the box-office Hitchcock, nor is it without its severity *vis-à-vis* the temptation to succumb to paranoia, to despair and all the other black complacencies. Hollywood, or the lowest common denominators of industry and box-office, contributed an inclination to take the best for granted and then introduce little 'disgrace notes', or more substantial undertones of asperity and imperfection, if suitably stylised, in a balance which is more authentic than Hollywood's mediocrities but not usually as good as Hollywood's best—from which Hitchcock's frameworks have regularly discouraged comparison, so contributing to the instability of his reputation. One might well argue that all but a handful of Hitchcock's very best films are really comedies of a new kind—comedies in a sense somewhere between the older sense of not being tragedies, and the newer sense of not quite being dramas. Hitchcock's films are not quite dramas, from which categories they are distanced by a fine combination of detachment, wishfulfilment and melodrama. But Hitchcock's hermetic universe, or ivory tower, is generously garnished with loopholes and windows opening on the world around.

It is perhaps this sense of a private domain which has contributed to the general acceptance of Hitchcock as a Master—but of what? In the course of despatching Penelope Houston to the bottom of the class, Robin Wood observes her assent to some 'general agreement that (Hitchcock) is a master; yet nothing she finds to say remotely supports such a valuation'. Maybe she means Master of Entertainment; or maybe she means Master of Aesthetic Effects? Characteristically, she makes no attempt to answer the question with which her little rumination begins. She quotes Henry James:

'. . . He gives me the pleasure so rare: the sense of . . . something or other.'

---

for, because the natural condition of the present order is a continuous improvement in which some improve faster than others, owing to their superior moral fibre. And only meanly envious or maladjusted characters would resent improving relatively slowly or merely marking time. But this forgets that relative position is what puts people in the power of others, and so is a legitimate source, not only of humiliating comparisons, but of well-founded fears.

'I wondered again: 'The sense, pray, of what?'

'My dear man, that's just what I want you to say.'

But James's phrase, 'that rare pleasure', evoking Aesthetes, Decadents and Symbolists, gives us a clue.[1] With the cult of pure sensation (emotional and even sensual) Hitchcock clearly has a great deal in common. His openly declared purpose is 'to put the audience through it'; to create 'pure emotion'. Of *Psycho*, which eventually secured his acknowledgement by the consensus of critics as a man of moral concerns, he stated, 'It was made with quite a sense of fun on my part . . . It's rather like taking the audience through the haunted house on the fairground. After all, it stands to reason that if one were seriously doing the *Psycho* story it would be a case history.'

A variety of factors may distract one's mind from the inner affinities between fairground and ivory tower, the candy floss of entertainment and lotus-eating. The cinema was long regarded as a coarse fine art incapable of affording anything so rare as a rare pleasure; its auditoria are gregarious, even though the darkness to some extent enwraps each spectator in his own version of the shared dream; while the varieties of exotica favoured by the Symbolists differed from those of the more demotic medium. One may be more immediately aware of the differences between, on the level of high culture, Xanadu and Byzantium, and, on the lower, the Astorias and Granadas and post-Tutankhamen Egyptian A.B.Cs. The language of ultra-refined ineffability favoured by the minor literati of the salons may seem altogether opposed to Hitchcock's succinct 'My films aren't a slice of life. They're a slice of cake.' But neither language, nowadays, is normally taken at its face value, and not only the Marxists, but writers like Mario Praz and F. L. Lucas, have emphasised the extent to which aestheticism was escapism. The entertainment cinema was the ivory tower of the common herd; not stately pleasure-domes, but High Street dream-palaces. How often and how carefully Hitchcock insulates his films, his careful continuums, from all those overtones which might trouble their orderly orchestration of sensation.

The Symbolist parallel is strengthened by Hitchcock's declared joy in aesthetics, especially 'pure film'. Since the cinema is traditionally associated with the lower social grades, a man who delights in perfectly wrought film form is likely to find himself referred to as a

---

[1] Given the general overlappings between Aestheticism, Decadence and Symbolism, we make no attempt, here, to distinguish between them, focusing instead on their common factor, a romanticism seeking an escape in art and analogous mental realms.

'master craftsman' and the full sense of his involvement with aesthetics missed. As to content, Hitchcock is as lordly as any Symbolist or epicure of *l'art pour l'art* of art as pure style: 'I only interest myself in the manner and style of telling a story.' A craftsman whose craft is aesthetics and who takes a deep pleasure in practising it as meticulously as Hitchcock does is an aesthete; and conversely the aesthetes took a special interest in the decorative, the ornamental, the aesthetic *crafts*, so long as they implied a certain kind of spiritual sensation which none the less was not to be confused with, and was if anything incompatible with, 'content'. Not that the Symbolists were able to dispense entirely with certain themes, as more propitious than others; Oscar Wilde's narratives are no more abstract than Hitchcock's. But Hitchcock, as an aesthetician, is an epicure of suspense, of terror, bringing us near the pain-pleasure ambivalence which, as Dr. Praz has shown, looms so large in the Romanticism of which Symbolism was an apotheosis: from Keats through Baudelaire to the fascination of Mallarmé and Wilde with Salome.

Isn't a certain Symbolism implicit in Hitchcock's repeated citation from Wilde, as in his reflections to Bogdanovitch on *Foreign Correspondent*: 'If the picture had been in colour I would have worked in the shot I've always wanted to do and never have yet. The murder in the tulip field. The assassin—say it's Jack the Ripper—comes up behind the girl. . . . Immediately we pan down to the struggling feet, in the tulips. We dolly the camera in on to one of the flowers, sounds of the struggle heard in the background. We go right to one petal—it fills the screen—and splash! a drop of red blood covers over the petal. And that would be the end of the murder.' Titles of the decadence flock to one's mind: *Le Jardin des Supplices, Les Fleurs du Mal*. . . . *Rope* is built on the juxtaposition of a crime whose motive is an aesthetic attempt at a moral emancipation with a Pateresque sense of meal as ritual. Hitchcock entertains those ideas so as to chasten them; perhaps, indeed, he takes them too seriously, as a fundamentalist might. For the argument can be extended. *Rope* is, after all, a crime of a type which might well have lent itself to imitation. And the inculpation of James Stewart, as the university professor who played with ideas, not realising they might be taken seriously, could be taken further. For James Stewart one might substitute two scriptwriters discussing, as Hitchcock enjoys discussing, questions like, 'Wouldn't it be fun to kill him this way?' And the tyrannical studio chief's delinquent son, who also lives in semi-fantasy, takes the point. Hitchcock is quite prepared to discuss the morality of his characters' behaviour, and in so doing he reveals a rigour which can be too easily assumed to be severity; it may be merely that of precision. As he observes, Robert Donat, in *The Thirty-Nine Steps*, is goaded to his dangerous investigations by his feeling of responsibility for the woman's death. But how far the spectator is supposed to feel that Donat is in fact seriously responsible is another matter altogether. It might be one mark of Donat's heroism that he feels himself to be seriously responsible even though most of us would absolve him of responsibility, since the woman's tale is so unlikely. And that in its turn requires a consideration of the extent to which characters in melodramas ought to take melodramatic stories seriously, i.e. ought they to behave by realistic standards, or by the rules of the melodrama which we know but they don't know this film will turn out to be, or by some compromise between the two? Until these questions are resolved, it is idle to dream up some invariable theme like a transference of guilt. And it is very doubtful whether these questions can be resolved, simply because various spectators in cinema seats will react in ways which, without lacking certain common conventions and understanding, will also vary from one individual to another. And films like Hitchcock's are intended to operate for just such a range of interpretations. One can understand why Hitchcock says, 'Clarify! Clarity!' It is necessary to insist on certain key polarities. But what emerges from this particular case is that it is not the objective moral aspects of Donat's involvement which are clarified. And while it's interesting to suggest that a man who doesn't believe a highly improbable story is as guilty of its teller's death in the same way as the people who actually murdered her, it's also necessary to insist that it's a moral nonsense. It's a moral nonsense also to suggest that a slight degree of responsibility for a major crime represents anything like a 'transference of guilt' from murderer to relative innocent. Though the relatively innocent often do feel a kind of conjoint guilt, it's often reckoned a pathological condition, explicable in, among others, psychoanalytical, terms, which are as prevalent in American popular culture as they are scanty in Rohmer and Chabrol. Our argument is not that morality in Hitchcock is insignificant or non-existent; but simply to insist that its existence in no way allows us to rule out the order of priorities which are implied by Hitchcock's remarks about his artistic purposes and which maintain the possibility that a Symbolist purpose is his ulterior, that is to say, his basic one. 'To me, the great art of the motion picture is by means of imagery and montage to create an emotion in the audience, and, therefore, the content is a means to an end.'

It's no accident, in the end, that Oscar Wilde and the dandies have so haunted the popular imagination as, finally, to lend their style to Christopher Lee's *Dracula*—just as the first vampire in English, Polidori's, was based on an earlier dandy, and decadent, Lord Byron. And isn't Hitchcock's sphingine, sinister pose a spiritual successor to a dandyism which, be it remembered, also aimed, blandly, to inculcate a certain disquiet? Although it's balanced, of course, by images of mock-fear . . .

Unfashionable as it may still be to say so, aesthetic pleasure is a prerequisite of the total experience of art (aesthetic pleasure in two senses: first, pleasure in experience as crystallised and clarified through the prism of the medium, in a situation where the experience is known to be fictitious or vicarious; and second, pleasure in the aesthetic and spiritual skill of the manipulation of the medium). The Symbolist insistence on art as a conclave within reality is, if shorn of a *jejune* or provocative extremism, not at all unfounded, even if it is incomplete, and it is certainly no more anomalous than the naive realism which supposes that art exists to offer simple tautologies of real involvement. The aesthetic of any artistic medium can afford to ignore neither the Symbolist pole nor the journalistic, neither Mallarmé nor Kracaeur, neither the concept of music as the abstract condition to which all arts aspire, nor any art's analogies with photography nor the extent to which art consists of a continuum of experience linking filtered reality, aesthetic actuality, and the spectator's mind. Musical comparisons for his control of a sequence come readily to Hitchcock's lips. And the ambiguities which his dramatic and moral structures allow might well bear comparison with the indefiniteness of interpretation which Mallarmé deemed to be of the essence of the highest art.

Not the least of the fascinations which Hitchcock exerts is this mixture of contrarieties: the Symbolism whose emotional key-signature is a delicious fear is also the petit bourgeois shopkeeper out of Orwell or Mass observation, whose stock-in-trade is Suspense. A precise moralist encounters an indulgent sybarite. The Calvinist God becomes an amiable Sade. A *petit maître* of the realistic vignette is also a master of escapist melodrama; and an aesthetic virtuoso is also a Hollywood conservative.

The Evidence

CHAPTER 3

The Pleasure Garden / The Mountain Eagle / The Lodger /
Downhill / Easy Virtue

The Pleasure Garden

Hitchcock's first two directorial assignments were executed for Balcon
in Munich, a locale less anomalous than it may now seem. In the
first place, silent films were more international than their talking
successors; only the titles needed changing, and audiences were sometimes unaware of the nationality of the films they saw. Co-productions
were therefore easier and more common. In the case of British films
there was a second reason: English production was so sporadic that
it often wasn't worth opening a studio for a single film.

How far did the Hollywood influence, on one hand, and these
European connections on the other, hinder British film-makers from
discovering Britain—or at least that vast majority of Britain which
didn't appear on the West End theatre stage? Perhaps the underlying
explanation is the discrepancy between a middle-class culture in
which so many of the British cinema's creative talents had been reared,
the unsubtle showmanship of so many of its producers, and the real
attitudes and experiences of an audience that was seventy per cent
working class.

Moreover, World War I had left its European victors tired. In the
'20s, France's commercial cinema limped like Britain's; only the
defeated and the virtually unscathed could adapt themselves to the
new artform. The American cinema, basing itself on the barnstormer-
and-vaudeville simplicities that suited her multi-ethnic immigrants, hit
on certain lowest common denominators of inter-cultural appeal,
quickly revved up to the tempi of Griffith and Sennett, and used
its vast home market to dump its product around the world, putting

every national culture on the defensive, particularly Britain's, which added a disastrous absence of cultural and linguistic barriers to the internal incoherence of its cultural islands-within-an-island. The German cinema found a firm basis in its theatrical traditions, its totalitarian mastery over studio spectacles, and state aid, and fought Hollywood for the European markets, finally foundering in Germany's economic crises. In a Bolshevik Russia whose spiritual dynamism briefly promised to rival America's, Eisenstein achieved his astonishing synthesis of American speed, Russian *avant-gardes*, and five hundred years of European culture. France eventually produced an *avant-garde* which, when joined with social realism and the Hollywood example, inspired the great French cinema of the '30s. Britain had its little line of patriotic documentaries. In an industry where, as usual, there was more young talent than opportunity, Hitchcock immediately imposed himself as a brilliant young director.

His *The Pleasure Garden* (1925) is a fairly typical '20s best-seller. For, despite the brand-image of the decade as a combination of the 'roaring '20s' of America's cities and the 'bright young things' of a tiny English minority, the period generally was stagnant, depressed, and very much more conservative and hesitant than one might have expected after the impact of such subversive and essentially Edwardian writers as Thomas Hardy, H. G. Wells and D. H. Lawrence. The film's scenario is concocted out of lower-middlebrow conventions of the time (as per H. de Vere Stacpoole and Hall Caine), and these also, alas, inspire the histrionics. But they seem to have suited contemporary taste, and Hitchcock found himself hailed as 'The Man With The Master Mind' with his first film. It struck Balcon and others as an American-styled picture; largely, it would seem, because Hitchcock had noticed the subtleties of backlighting (Hollywood practice to separate actors from their background), but perhaps also on the strength of its theme. The knowing showgirl (Virginia Valli) pals up with the waif (Carmelita Geraghty). All is set, it would seem, for an encounter of the worlds of de Mille (in his pre-Biblical, carnal era) and Griffith. But the waif turns out to be a bitch, the other wins through only after her grit is tested by a hard tussle with life's disappointments.

What now seems un-American is its tempo and shape. The American concern with simplicity and speed resulted in a highly disciplined 'streamlining' of every aspect of style, influencing not only acting but the succession of settings and scenes and theme. In their very search for slickness, the Americans had developed a sense of a film's overall orchestration—a kind of aerodynamic architecture, without excrescence or distraction. Not only the cutting, but acting, staging and screenplay enforced the rigorous reduction of a story to its storyline and its storyline to its theme.

The Pleasure Garden begins as the waif's story, then follows the two girls in parallel, finally forgets the waif-turned-bitch, and settles down as her friend's story instead. It's hard to tell, now, whether this unusual shape was a product of English primitivism or of Hitchcock's sophistication.

Even nowadays, of course, romantic dramas can accept a more diffuse shape than detective thrillers. Their subject matter imposes hesitations, separations, slower moods of languor or despair. Pre-war audiences were undoubtedly more spontaneous and less thoughtful than today's, and seem to have been readier to accept, and immerse themselves in, each scene, less inclined to worry about the rights and wrongs of every attitude involved. Hence a film could move more rapidly (as '30s movies generally move far faster than '50s movies), or, alternatively, take on a kind of shapeless shape (since the spectators experienced a series of 'absolute moments', rather than a variety of questions and answers which it took several scenes to answer). Plotted against time, the emotional graph was sharper, more jagged.

In this rather impersonal film, too steeped in period uncharm to be very bearable now, a few scenes and touches, in retrospect, at least, crystallise the future Hitchcock—or rather, future Hitchcocks. Hitchcock's somewhat remote view of happiness inspires the presentation of a blissful Riviera honeymoon in terms of picture-postcard views —although the device may also be part of Hitchcock's switching from hopefulness to indications of misgiving. Through the romantic material Hitchcock's shrewd sense of seedy intentions and mean indignities sends its tremors of uneasy truth. Miles Mander's too-ready smile, at once sharp and weak, sensitive and sulky, reveals him far more deeply than the plot, and catches the atmosphere of Denholm Elliott's best parts some decades later. 'A smile of gold but a heart of lead', the subtitle proclaims. By a stagedoor a man appraises a chorus girl with a grin like a nervy ferret. And Hitchcock seems more at home with middle-class life and show-business than with our upper crust, for a line of faces of the nobs goggling at the dancers abounds in sillyass Johnnies of a stereotyped kind. But the tracking shot against their variety of facial forms and movements is an aesthetically exhilarating one.

Already the Hitchcock touch hints at a saturnine view of human beings as easily opportunistic and exploitative. Invited to share a fellow dancer's bed, the waif blandly commandeers the best of the pillow. Later she humiliates her elderly millionaire lover, concocting, effectively, if none too intelligently, ridiculous *femme fatale* poses out of nothing more substantial then a guttersnipe callousness. This view of innocence as crueller than experience, while 'there's no fool like an old fool', is, in movies, a sardonic and refreshing brace of cynicisms.

The finale, with startling maturity, imbues a sequence of dramatic contrivances with a magic shock. As the film ends, the villain, delirious as depravity was still required to be, with drink and remorse, believes the ghost of his dusky mistress is inciting him to murder the heroine. In the nick of time, he's shot by the hero—and murmurs, with silly hypocrisy, 'Hullo, old chap . . .', before sinking to the floor. The ambiguity of this sudden pseudo-sanity gives his death-moment twist its barb. Between the stirrup and the ground, he hypocrisy sought and oblivion found—in a phrase which might have been every moment of a life which not a few barflies and salesmen and people have to lead.

As often in films from the age of innocence, the villain is distinctly more realistic than the hero, and indeed is the only character with whom a modern spectator can identify or sympathise. We can see him, now, as escapist entertainment's, and puritanism's, scapegoat for life's disappointments, which are explained away by his intervention and then denied by the happy end. But Hitchcock mixes pepper and salt with the sugar, and this patchy movie abounds in valid moments of unhappiness and pettiness. It would be interesting to exclude the inferior material, re-edit the realistic moments into a sort of kernel film, and see the result; perhaps when the cassette revolution eventually transpires, critics and others will be able to offer their variations on a theme.

It's possible also that the film's slipping from one story to another is connected with a resigned or sardonic view of life. Jean Renoir, whose vision of human attachments is often politely pessimistic or amiably evasive, once said that he'd like to do a story which 'side-slipped' from being, first, one person's story, then the story of some-one he meets, and so on. Ophuls, another pessimist, albeit a more romantic one, achieved precisely this form in *La Ronde*, and there are intimations of it in the episodic structure of various Duvivier pictures—*Carnet de Bal*, *Tales of Manhattan*, *Sous Le Ciel de Paris Coule La Seine*, *La Fête à Henriette*—about whose pessimism there can be no doubt. Perhaps a certain irony underlies the virtuosity with which Hitchcock can switch us from one identification or theme to another in *Psycho* and *The Birds*. *The Wrong Man*, with its miracle-or-coincidence big city encounter, has, unless it's an unequivocally religious film, a Duvivier-like sense of life's ironic precariousness.

The Mountain Eagle

Hitchcock's next film, *The Mountain Eagle*, has remained a very rare bird indeed, and the six frames published in the bumper Truffaut book may be all that remains of it. It starred Nita Naldi and Malcolm Keen. An English film produced in Munich, it was set in Kentucky among the hillbillies.

The Lodger

Hitchcock's first English film is the first Hitchcock thriller. *The Lodger* (1926), subtitled 'A Story of the London Fog', is a variant of the perennial Jack the Ripper theme. A kindly landlady (Marie Ault) comes to believe that the handsome young lodger (Ivor Novello) who goes on nocturnal prowls with an ominous black bag is none other than The Avenger, a sex maniac specialising in victims who, like her daughter (Daisy Bunting), have golden curls. Only after he has been all but torn to bits by a lynch mob is it revealed that his sinister perambulations resulted from his tireless attempts to avenge his sister on the man who killed her. The misanthropy lies not only in his murderous intent but in the film's study of upright citizens who like the heroine's mother and father (Arthur Chesney) and her detective fiancé (Malcolm Keen) jumped to conclusions and all but condemned an innocent man to death.

As in so many British films of the period, the men's playing survives the passing of time less well than the women's—contrary to a common assumption that the latter are creatures of flighty fashion in a way that the former are not. It is difficult to decide how far what may seem to us overacting derives from the West End stage of the '20s, or from a middle-class style of the time, which respected an uncool vulnerability in men, or from our merely contemporary conventions of 'cool' which are quite as artificial as the '40s stiff-upper-lip. One's decision isn't facilitated by anachronisms of another order—the clumsiness of the '20s facial make-up (which sabotages many a French film of the same era), and an idiom allowing heroes to look, at passionate moments, directly into the camera—poignantly, perhaps, to audiences then, as one looks full in their troubled eyes—but distractingly to us, even if we feel like embarking on some sort of aesthetic involving the director's direct relationship with the audience, or, more soberly, observing the same device used, so subtly and self-effacingly (as it were) in *Marnie*. Hitchcock forgets nothing, perfects everything.

He also cheats outrageously, contrary to what critical apologists here maintained. The lodger has only to pick up a poker to poke the fire, in a cosy scene where he has no sinister intentions whatsoever and where the heroine fears nothing, however fleetingly, for a virtuoso battery of angle shots, close-ups and screaming suspense.

Like *Blackmail* later, the film begins with a little 'Prologue', which today would be a pre-credits sequence. A brisk montage sequence shows the news of the murder spreading, by press, telephone and gossip. It affords Hitchcock splendid opportunities for bravura cutting and continuities, and, as often with Hitchcock, is less irrelevant to the body of the film than might seem. For the film's theme is panic as a social network—the angry crowd is its final, climactic 'crystallisation'.

There were to be deeper treatments of this mob-and-scapegoat theme, notably, Fritz Lang's *M* and *Fury*, William Wellman's *Strange Incident* (*The Ox-Bow Incident*) and Cy Endfield's *The Sound of Fury*. Yet Hitchcock's film stands up for itself, in its very intimacy, in its very concentration on the personal, on the doubts and fears and jealousies of ordinary people who are always, also, full of little friendlinesses and decencies that aren't just mannerisms or masks to be ripped aside. It's in this co-existence of decency and nastiness that Hitchcock's film is, if less immediately satisfying, more daring, spiritually, than Duvivier's equally intimate variation on a similar theme, *Panique*, after Simenon's novel *Les Fiançailles de M. Hire*.

Although the lodger is the victim of the film's big scene, the character in the most interesting predicament, dramatically, is the detective fiancé, who first loses his girl's affections to the lodger, and then his professional and moral self-respect. (One thinks ahead to *Vertigo*.) When saucy June ignores him for the ever so much better-mannered lodger, he's absolutely baffled by her preference for the weaker man, and is transformed, before our very eyes, from a pompous young brute to nail-biting torment which takes a dangerously vindictive turn. Deftly Hitchcock underlines those little details of callous treatment which make a strong man's life hell and twist him into ludicrous postures. Here, as in certain later movies, one has the feeling of a Hitchcock story hesitating at a crossroads. His real insights and sympathies lie with the frantic indignities of victims and losers, while the wishfulfilment formulae require him to follow instead either the winner in love, or the romantic tragedy, or the man who loses with a suave style and a gesture generous enough to hint that a splendid consolation prize must come his way before too long. But the most interesting moments of this regularly acutely observed film are those in which both men are betrayed, in their various ways, by their inner tensions, into absurdity.

Even into its happy little coda the same spirit pokes its little head. After her honeymoon, the girl's parents call on her in her new baronial hall, to bring, with fond solicitousness, her toothbrush. This reminder of old family days isn't enough to keep things straightforward, though. Overawed by her new station in life they bow and scrape and all but touch their forelocks. And it's hard not to feel that under the humour Hitchcock isn't sourly observing the indignity of deference (deference being closely related to something between hope and fear—a cringing while suspense is still diffuse)—a deference to the aristocrat which may perhaps be tails to the heads of their suspicion of the lone outsider.

The visual effects are more than stylish. The landlady listens to the lodger's footsteps and we look up at him through a specially constructed floor of plateglass. Hitchcock attributes the atmospheric shadows to the influence of Murnau. In these early days, a search for the vivid had yet to be subjugated by naive and dogmatic notions of the real; expressionism was in the air; and these effects, far from being gimmicks, as Hitchcock, regrettably, conceded, come as fresh and effective now as they were then. Ceasing to be invisible onlookers, we become involved. Novello's 'crucifixion'—handcuffed, suspended helplessly from railings, a mob clawing at him from above and from below—probably doesn't bear the religious parallel which it evokes; one thinks, as easily, of a Christian in an arena. Morally, certainly, any religious parallel would be absolutely outrageous, for Jesus would have sought The Avenger only to make him repent. But it is a classic masochistic dream, made, at least, by New Morality notions, more rather than less obscene in that it involves, not consenting adults in voluptuous privacy, but the unleashed moral earnestness of human society.

Hitchcock has criticised the film on the grounds that no audience in its senses would believe that a man with Ivor Novello's image and style could be a murderer (although he later expects us to believe that Cary Grant is, in *Suspicion*). Probably, in both cases, a half-belief is enough, if combined with suspense about what on earth he is doing if he isn't a murderer and what the consequences of other people's suspicion will be. For a natural consequence of Hitchcock's insistence on clarification is that the spectator is caught not only by one either-or issue but by batteries of corollaries. And the relative weakness of our suspicion grants fuller play to more straightforward dramatic involvements. We may brood on the overtone of fatalism implicit in the play of facial resemblances. We may wonder why this young man, with his delicate manliness, his sad jejune eyes and boyish keenness, should be so exiled, so haunted. As he shuddered away from the landlady's charming portraits of sentimentally yet saucily unclad ladies, all very poetical, I guessed, quite wrongly, of course, that he was a young clergyman striving to regain self-respect after having shamefully yielded to the importunities of the flesh. Whether Hitchcock intended things to be as precise as this is dubious indeed, but what's certainly worth noticing is the contrast between what seems to be voluptuous temptation but is really memories of his sister's evisceration. And that criticism would be misleading which, by deducing from the whole that the latter not the former was in the lodger's mind, analyses the naive spectator's reading out of the total meaning and loses a ghoulishly sensual contrast.

What does rule the Jesus comparison out of court is the implication that the lodger is out to avenge his sister on a murderer called The Avenger. The idea that two wrongs make a right and that one grisly crime deserves another certainly moves us towards a 'transference of guilt' from which the film shies away, precisely by its stress on the lodger as an innocent victim. Everything is set, indeed, for a plot which shows the sensitive idealist, in his hatred of hatred, becoming *another* Avenger, becoming harder than his tormented prey, as Captain Ahab exceeds even The Great White Whale in diabolism. Were Hitchcock a serious moralist preoccupied with the affinities and interchangeabilities between good and evil, the eventual encounter of the two men (not necessarily in terms of a direct physical confrontation; as obliquely perhaps as in *The Wrong Man*) would be the keystone of the moral arch. And how important it would be that the lodger be tempted to let another girl die (a lady of easy virtue and vicious temperament, perhaps) so that he shall have concrete proof of his quarry's guilt, and so that his 'lynching' is clearly half-deserved, for intention if not achievement. Certainly, to incline the film that way would be to run a correspondingly greater risk of audience rejection, although it is worth noticing that audiences would have had a great deal of sympathy with the lodger in his quest, even if they thought it was the wrong way of going about things—which of course it proves to be, since the murderer never gets caught. But the instincts which render the revenge motive sufficiently sympathetic—especially if it remains at the stage of intention—haven't altogether atrophied with the intensified efficiency of law and order. And, in London's fogs, this lodger, on murder bent, is almost as immune from criticism as he would be in the Western setting to which the story quite easily transposes.

Which way the moral balance dips depends also on the degree to which one is prepared to identify with the mob. For, on one hand, they are, literally, the men in the street, the men in the corner public-house, the folks in the cinema seats—in other words, you and me. But on the other hand their behaviour, in the context which we know, is so obviously wrong, that identification is impeded and all these common people become common in the other sense—'common', not like you and me, in a word, the rabble. This aspect of the film is ambiguous as to whether it intensifies the moral chastening of the audience (by extending lynchlaw mentality from one family to everybody and bringing it to a paroxysmatic intensity) or whether it mitigates it (by providing a collective scapegoat with whom we have no identification and whose style contrasts with the family's).

At any rate, the shift from the suspected guilt of the middle-class hero to the bestiality of the proletariat is only too familiar in the middle-class tradition to which the story belongs. Later, Hitchcock inclines to reverse the charge, and, beginning with *The Thirty-Nine Steps*, to develop a special line in rich, charming, gentlemanly villains —who don't exonerate the lower orders, however.[1]

---

[1] And by one of those ironies which popular culture owes to very real socio-historical origins, this refusal to take the established English gentleman at his face value appeals to a streak in American Populism. The three examples given in *A Mirror for England* (King Vidor's *North-West Passage*, Richard Fleischer's *The Vikings* and John Ford's *The Long Voyage Home*) can be supplemented by innumerable examples, such as the otherwise inexplicable extent to which, in Biblical epics, good Semites are played by American actors and Romans and bad Semites by English ones (cf. *Ben Hur, Spartacus, Solomon and Sheba, Samson and Delilah*). One should also, though, allow for that abashed, inarticulate yet widespread resentment of W.A.S.P. snobberies which finds a useful scapegoat in that specially intense American detestation of the rich, leisured aesthete and intellectual (cf. Preminger's *Laura*, Siodmak's *Phantom Lady*, Aldrich's *Kiss Me Deadly* (under protest, one hopes) and Hitchcock's *Rope*).

Downhill

One might have expected *The Lodger* to be followed by another
thriller. But what materialises is another romantic drama, whose
superiority to *The Pleasure Garden* may be linked with both Hitchcock's advancing expertise and its more sombre tone. The hero (Ivor
Novello, who also co-wrote the play with Constance Collier) takes
expulsion on the chin rather than sneak on his chum, who made the
mean little tuck-shop waitress preggers. Hitchcock, apparently in awe
of the public school spirit, or apprehensive about the audience's
respect for it, or under orders, or not liking the subject enough to
bother too much, takes it all uncritically, including a battery of prejudices which forty-plus years on all but take one's breath away. The
nasty working-class slut is followed by the soul-destroying degradation
of European cabarets, and the 'rats of Marseilles' come complete with
mockingly grinning big negro, lower than which one could hardly
sink.

In this prodigal son's progress from riches through rages to, *in
extremis*, repentant reconciliation, the enemies of the sometimes weak,
but also too decent, hero, are (1) an excessively stern father who not
only won't listen to explanations but expels his son from home for
being expelled from school, (2) women (respectively working-class,
theatrical, and foreign), and (3) money. If the second group of culp-
ables responds to the clichés of the British old-boy network, and perhaps to a diffidence which covers itself by exotic scapegoats, the first
and third show more promise.

The hero's silence before his headmaster is less conventionalised
than one might assume. The National Film Theatre audience laughed
knowingly at the hero's refusal to 'sneak', quite without realising that
apart from any schoolboy code it's reasonable enough. His friend's
whole life depends on his securing a scholarship grant, while his own
does not, and he has yet to realise just how unreasonably and
unpaternally severe his own father will prove himself to be.

In several scenes, certainly, Hitchcock indulges a partial reversal of
the obvious dramatic sympathies. Thus the elderly rouée who ruins
the hero when he won't be her gigolo is allowed a certain yearning for
love. And from time to time one suspects that Hitchcock is subverting
the pattern of sympathies, that he has a grim sympathy with the
hardbitten characters who have already learned, and not usually
comfortably, what the sheltered hero only, until the end, briefly

glimpses—that life isn't a game, but a struggle, and that no man can be a perfect gentleman without a gentleman's income. Because it isn't very strongly worked, it's difficult to tell whether this moral counterpoint arises from a radical counter-vision of his own (that rats, rouées and gentlemen are brothers under the bankroll and background) cautiously put forth, or from careful application of a useful dramatic formula. This is that every scene must at one moment tend towards the opposite of its ultimate meaning, so as to be dramatically strong and surprising. The consideration may be a purely formal one but has a secondary usefulness in making certain concessions, on the safety-valve analogy, to any spectator's conscious or unconscious or preconscious ambivalence about things. It also makes things very difficult for censors, who can never be quite sure exactly when the safety-valve is likely to become a catalyst. It doesn't make things easy for film-makers or critics either. But all criticism which implies that all the meanings of a work of art are self-evident is missing most of the game. And of the struggle.

Perhaps the greatest surprise, now, is the complete absence of recrimination by the son of the father who so harshly thrust him forth. The film's potentially picaresque form goes with a repudiation of the picaresque spirit. 'East West Home's Best' is its motto, and the youth's European tour is neither an opportunity to sow wild oats safely distant from his own doorstep, nor a pilgrim's progress, but more of an exile's imperilment. Its exoticism is somewhat escapist, not only in the continental low-life, but in the hero's starting-point —for an insignificant portion of the cinema audience is of public school background. By exaggerating the hero's downwards trajectory, and returning him to the upper crust, the film paraphrases that fear of social downfall which existed even more intensely during the economic miseries of the interwar years. The traditional association between financial ruin and suicide indicates the extent to which to become déclassé can be dreaded as a fate worse than death, by perfectly sane people, and de Sica's *Umberto D* approaches that equation from another angle. By no social group was this fate dreaded more intensely than by those whom George Orwell, borrowing the phrase from a music hall song, described as the shabby genteel, a class sufficiently conspicuous to loom very large in such films as *Separate Tables*, the Somerset Maughams, and Ealing England (particularly *Kind Hearts and Coronets* and *The Lady Killers*—not to mention the lad, who, give or take twenty years, might have been our hero's scholarship-winning friend, The Guinea Pig from Walthamstow, very near the Hitchcock homeland). The furtive little character who has the tables so tragically turned on him in *Blackmail* might also be on the slippery slope from a public school.

One's point isn't that *Downhill* would have been a sharper film if its hero had started from lower down on the slopes anyway, but that there was no need for the hero to go abroad at all. What Asquith's *Tell England* almost was for World War I, *Downhill* might have been for the peace which followed—had its story of a public school boy discovering life's gruelling seediness been related to the English social realities which Hitchcock knew exceptionally well (better by far than the slightly too fastidiously refined Asquith), had the lad who so hoped to play for the School against the Old Boys (and isn't that a natural enough aspiration, at sixteen?) graduated instead down through the worlds of *Keep the Aspidistra Flying*, of *Hangover Square*, of *Guignol's Band*, of *Down And Out In Paris and London*. Of course, to wish this is to wish that English producers of the '20s and '30s, had allowed Hitchcock's pre-war collaborators to be of the calibre of George Orwell, Patrick Hamilton, Gerald Kersh, James V. Curtis, Graham Greene, et al. At that stage of the game, or struggle, he might have been more responsive than, later, he was to be, in Hollywood, to Raymond Chandler—who arguably isn't of the calibre of the English writers anyway.

If the film is stilted in the public school scenes, and melodramatic about low life, it is lively in those milieux which Hitchcock knows best, the lower middle classes and the world of pleasure. It suffers from sets larger, it seems, than the lighting cameraman, or his budget, or the studio, can effectively cope with. All those baronial halls and Gothic fireplaces to express the solidity of tradition seem built out of grubby cardboard, while the cabarets have a flat and flimsy listlessness, into which the bright warm solid close-ups burst like intrusions from another film. In several shots the dramatic focus of the action seems quite casually plonked alongside an intrusive empty space, or a minor activity, or to straggle indecisively across the screen. It's difficult to tell, now, how far this is due to a residue of Cecil M. Hepworth editing, or an attempt to shoot faster by reducing the number of set-ups, or to a tentative pre-Renoir interest in life's little distractions. The last suggestion isn't gratuitously giving Hitchcock the benefit of the doubt, since such an interest fits his pre-war eye for asides and details. Technical indigence cuts into obvious climaxes also. A nightclub patron is taken ill; the curtains are pulled apart to give him air; whereupon a ray of startling sunlight affords the hero a hideous vision of bleary, sleazy, powdered and daubed female harpies. All of which demands a visual nuance way beyond the resources of the lighting; and if one feels surprise that Hitchcock didn't outflank the problem of lighting a large area by shooting off a close-up sequence, six rounds rapid, as it were, or resorting to expressionistic tricks, the answer is probably that these cost money too.

None the less Hitchcock, close-ups apart, comes into his own in a delirium sequence whose title is, 'Blind instinct saw him home'. Superimposed tracks, pans and shots of streetscapes and traffics create a visual bewilderment not unworthy of *Entr'acte* and more than deserving of the round of applause later earned by a montage sequence at the première of *The Ring*. It's still sufficiently effective to be of interest to students of abstract or psychedelic cinema and to the *aficionados* of Vorkapitch and Gance. It's rather more fluid, self-effacing and abstract than many of the effects found in the French 'impressionistic' *avant-gardes* of the time, and reminds us that within the ultra-professional Hitchcock there is always an avant-gardist never quite struggling to get out. Chabrol and Rohmer observe that 'the school is treated in horizontal forward tracks, the nightclub in a series of panning shots expressing stagnation, and the port of Marseilles in downwards vertical travellings'.

Easy Virtue

Hitchcock's career with Balcon at Gainsborough ended with *Easy Virtue*, an adaptation of a Noël Coward play with Isabel Jeans, Ian Hunter, Bransby Williams and Franklyn Dyall.

CHAPTER 4

The Ring

Hitchcock's period with John Maxwell at B.I.P. opened with *The Ring*,
described in *The Bioscope* of its time as 'the most magnificent British
film ever made'. Not only are the production qualities immeasurably
improved, the style more consistent, and the material more intelligent,
than under the previous regime, but we're parachuted from the flimsy
vapours of the upper middle class novelette to something more like
terra firma. For the picturesque settings of fairground boxing booths
no more rules out a certain realism than, say, the canal barge of
L'Atalante.

Hitchcock observes affectionately, but not too affectionately, retaining a balance of intimate asperity which is so propitious an artistic
attitude. The fairground scenes, by now, have picked up immense
interest, in revealing how recently this nation of now relatively passive
and apathetic television devotees had enough hunger and energy for
boxers to be able to count on volunteers stepping up from the crowd
to have a go at even the ominously named One Round Jack. Perhaps
they had more spirit; or perhaps a good fighter is a hungry fighter.
Certainly, until 1914 or even later, booths were not unknown in which
women boxers were prepared to take on any member of either sex of
their own weight class. Here, with happy accuracy, Hitchcock picks
out the variety of types who make a crowd; none, in themselves,
highly original or individual; but the whole is more than the sum of
its parts. The lantern-jawed sailors, the daintily-hatted ladies, the
unshaven faces all burst with a life which even in later documentaries
is a rarity. Hitchcock is winningly proud of such details as that the

card announcing 'Round One' is very grubby while the card for 'Round Two' is crisp and clean. He's quite right in observing how much atmosphere, and impact, lies in touches which critics don't notice (or which, when they do, they may forget, under a flurry of subsequent details, or fail to comment on, because words are a clumsy paraphrase of their brisk visual immediacy). Hitchcock's interviews abound in recollections of the observation of practical detail that distinguishes the films of his B.I.P. period. 'It wasn't the boxing that interested me so much, although I was interested in the shop, all the details connected with it. Like pouring champagne over the head of the boxer at the 13th round, if he was a bit groggy. You'd hear them uncork the champagne bottle and pour the whole bottle over his head.'

The opening sequence promises a welcome addition to the late '20s–early '30s wave of affectionate dramas and romantic comedies about ordinary people. The list includes, from the U.S.A., *The Crowd*, *Street Scene* and *Lonesome*; from Germany *Berlin Alexanderplatz* and *Ashphalte*; from Italy, *Prix de Beaute*; and from France *Marius*, *Toni*, *Sous Les Toits de Paris* and others. Shortly, however, Hitchcock's film slides up the social ladder to sheer off into a high life triangle which, laboriously rather than memorably, traces the involvement of the stolid, boorish, possessive booth-pug turned challenger, his flighty girl-friend (Lillian Hall-Davies) and the calmer, slicker champion (Ian Hunter). If the girl's a flighty silly, her boy friend has a glum insensitive simplicity recalling the detective fiancé in *The Lodger*.

The plot is built around a play on words—the ring referring to the boxing-ring, to the wedding ring, and to what one might call an adultery ring, a bracelet given by the champ to the wife. Finally he tosses it aside with a shrug—and it's this lazy, sharp, sensible, apathetic gesture which, retrospectively, gives the film its asperity. Since the affair didn't matter much to him, it shouldn't have mattered much to anybody. The last gesture, in effect, pulls the plug on the whole story. How much of our life consists of inconsequential fantasies?

A scene where Jack's girl mops his face while her glance caresses the torso of the classier champ opposite exemplifies the association of physicality and perfidy underlying the uninterrupted kiss in *Notorious*. The superimposition of the heroine's face in a second's bucket, recalling a happy riverside idyll earlier, ironically contrasts the sublime and the derisory. Occasionally the Hitchcock touch recalls the Lubitsch touch—a kind of emphasis by indirectness, the dramatic line being detoured through an unexpected object, detail or face. If the film's discursiveness represents Hitchcock's European side, the economy of the title-symbol indicates that he's still learning fast from Hollywood and that Hollywood as well as Germany is exerting its influence upon him. In the classic Hollywood style, already well-established, details tend to function primarily as terse reminders of simple feelings, contrasts and conflicts already stated in the plot. They are recalls, markers, rather than symbols in the fuller, European sense, whereby such details tend to draw attention to feelings or ideas which never come into the plot at all—whether *temps-morts* or some 'vertical', poetic, overtone or undercurrent. Thus, in an extremely American scene in *The Ring*, the boxer's hands put the wedding ring on his bride's finger—and the bangle which she knows but he doesn't know was a gift from her secret love slips down her arm from the top of the frame. In Anthony Asquith's *A Cottage On Dartmoor* (1930), an escaped convict hides out in a child's bedroom, and the mother finds him peering up at her from behind the bars of the cot. This sensitive, hysteric young man who loved and lost her, by cutting his rival's throat, is now at her mercy and, in a sense, a weak, passive child. The Hollywood symbol revives a previously overt idea in another context. The European symbol uses an earlier element (bars, prisons) in a new context to introduce a new idea. The Hollywood marker is conducive to swift sharp shocks on simple themes, the European symbol is slower, more reflective.[1] Something European certainly clings to Hitchcock's marker in *The Ring*, however; the bangle's serpent shape.

If some other touches seem less happy, it is possibly because they anticipate the eventual deflation, but not quite strongly enough, so that we take them as weak positives rather than preparatory negatives: e.g., champagne bubbles going flat, the face of the boxer's rival

[1] Our division between Hollywood and European styles is obviously a schematic one. Hollywood influenced the European cinema, while occasionally accommodating European style essays like, for example, John Ford's *The Informer*. And another dimension of queries is opened by the problem of the extent to which audiences are half-aware of, or take account of, the Freudian symbolism of father- and mother-figures which seems to be less conscious in *Rebecca* than in *Marnie*. Are these feelings felt to be part of the structure of motivations or are they felt more lyrically or discursively? But it seems to be true that Hollywood represented the main influence towards the deft use of the marker, just as the 'New Wave' was part of a reversal of cultural influence and preceded a degree of 'Europeanisation' of the American cinema. Hitchcock, talking to Bogdanovich, speaks dismissively of a discursive symbol in the English version of *The Man Who Knew Too Much*—the unravelling sweater is 'the thread of life that gets broken. One could still get pretentious in those days. It was also comic. You combine a little comic action with a break in the thread when the man falls dead.'

appearing on his punching bag. The film's structure is difficult, precisely because it is interesting. A potentially strong conflict (a boxer defeated by his rival, as a fighter, and as a lover also) is so handled as to avoid, for long periods, any easily climactic confrontation, and so produces something more petty, edgy, unnerving.

The Farmer's Wife

Meanwhile, Hitchcock's development seemed to be leading away from American slickness to an uneasy tiptoe along Gaumont-British's middlebrow shoestring. *The Farmer's Wife* is based on a rustic comedy by Eden Philpotts. A middle-aged landowner (Jameson Thomas) decides to marry again, and sets about selecting a suitable helpmate, with the aid and advice of his devoted housekeeper, Araminta Dench (Lillian Hall-Davies). He draws up a list of eligibles, all of whom feel, for very different reasons, obliged to reject him, and after several painful jolts to his vanity he realises that the woman whom he should attempt to please is his silent, devoted and ironic domestic.

The play is a pleasant enough piece within the rather parochial genre, the sensibly down-to-earth aspects of its comedy working within a myth of idyllic rusticity. It has its charm, and a certain wisdom, and Hitchcock respects both, while inclining the film towards a new mood, helped, perhaps, by a slightly substandard budget (making stylisation difficult) and by a company of knobbly character-players whose corners it can't have been very easy to round off in the interests of a cinematic rhythm. The film seems dominated by bulky, clumsy, rigid personalities knocking awkwardly against one another—pomposity against nervousness, blindness against timidity, a secretive irony against the social hierarchy. No doubt our sense of crusty exteriors is enhanced by our inability to identify with anyone—which isn't at all a defect, if the characters are interesting, although this point, again, is one on which American and European traditions show a certain degree of divergence.

Hitchcock seems to have made an effort towards catching the authentic feel of country ways. Old-fashioned mannerisms, faces and dress are lovingly observed, although with no sacrifice of matter-of-factness for calendar colours or Nature Notes or yokel picturesquerie or rustic innocence. The interest in practical things extends to iron kitchen contraptions and social etiquettte. Yet Hitchcock's dramatic dryness; or a certain detachment; or the fact that he is, after all, city-

bred, and alien to country ways, intrudes. And so the overall effect is
curious, as of a dutiful indulgence of quaint ways. And yet the film
acquires, unexpectedly, its homogeneity. A sense of clumsy contacts,
of loneliness, infiltrates the film, until every outgoing gesture, however clumsy, however stupid, seems cherished. The mixture of warmth
and solitudes, of pomposities and uneasinesses, of imperceptivenesses
and apologies, of deferential but firm rebellions, catch a kind of
finesse-in-oafishness which is a pleasure to watch. Minta's cool,
patient, passive style, seemingly content to let her man go if he will,
is quite as disturbing as the glamorous teases of his later films.

The visual style is penny plain, as appropriate for a rural backwater,
and here, as in other B.I.P. films, Hitchcock seems content, or con-
strained, to serve a middlebrow success which in its epoch doubtless
possessed the same aura of literary prestige, as did the Somerset
Maugham and Noël Coward films of the late '40s.

Champagne

Champagne, a lighter piece altogether, opens splendidly. Aboard the
S.S. *Aquitania*, a couple are demonstrating the tango at a cabaret.
Inexplicably, spectators trickle out, then rush in droves towards the
deck—the camera centring on the performers' discomfiture, as their
first fear, of flopping, switches into the greater, or lesser, fear that the
ship is sinking. But no; it's all right; nothing could compete with the
rival attraction, a seaplane which has touched down beside the ship,
in mid-ocean. Out from its cabin steps a lively flapper (Betty Balfour),
clad in flying kit from whose leather carapace she emerges, neatly as
an unzipped banana, to display her snazzy snappy Charleston gear.
The episode summarises all the magic and power of youth, wealth and
privilege; the poetry of the wilful romantic gesture, which, as we
gradually realise, is *hubris*.

After which, alas, the film goes, slowly at first, but steadily, downhill. Indeed, the two films run parallel, both being variations on the
theme of expulsion from the worldly paradise, and eventual return.
Champagne is keyed in a slightly erratic comic tone. To punish his
somewhat spoilt daughter, an American millionaire (Gordon Harker)
pretends to have lost all his money, thus condemning her to all sorts
of not-too-gruelling degradations. Her boyfriend (Jean Bradin) is
privy to the conspiracy too, and a third guardian angel appears in the

person of a private detective (Ferdinand Van Alten) who pops in and out of her life, disguised, threateningly, as a slick lounge lizard, with dishonourable intentions. Hired to play the role of tempter, so that, if she falls, she may safely fall, he reintroduces the theme, adumbrated in the final deflation of *The Ring*, and subsequently recurrent, notably in *Suspicion*, of paranoia turning out to be unjustified. At the same time, and paradoxically, the film depends, like *Downhill*, on a drastically stern parent, whom neither child nor film can bear to criticise. The father's cat-and-mouse game with his daughter's degradation suggests all sorts of intriguing theological parallels, the patriarchal trio comprising the American millionaire as God the Father, the boy-friend as God the Son, and the private eye as a mixture of Satan in the Book of Job and, if not the Holy Ghost, exactly, at least a guardian angel. Hitchcock does what he can to cover up for a story that's neither fish, flesh, fowl, nor good red herring, using bold details and emphatic confrontations to distract us from a plot which is not only improbable but creates a very tricky oscillation as between suspense and comedy. The idea is presumably that a certain fascinating be-puzzlement as to the oscillations between a certain suspense and a certain san fairy ann will rivet us to the superficialities and put the underlying logic in its proper place, out of mind.

But the American tycoon chewing an outsize cigar and shooting off nervous tics like a machine-gun is straight from stock, without the gritty sourness with which the same actor redeemed a 'Walter Gabriel' role in *The Farmer's Wife*. A myriad of sharp details falls on stony ground—the faces of old ladies in ships' corridors (already as studied and eloquent as the monstrous regiment of morbid ladies in the party scene of *Strangers On A Train*), a stress on meals (as befitting a sub-sistence story) and moments of seedy ignominy, prove Hitchcock's forte. The girl applies for a job in a photo agency, and the fat boss's lean sallow aide, standing behind her, lazily extends his patent leather shoe to lift up her skirt from behind. Her boss incessantly does the facial splits between snarling at his assistants and fawning on his patrons. If a great many scenes seem, now, mistimed, two elderly ladies behind me proved the film right for its time by reacting in ideal '20s style. At each lustful scheming glance from the lounge lizard they growled their disapproval, and, 'Oh, look at him!' they cried delight-fully each time the hero reappeared out of the blue.

All in all, the subject is the sort of scathing moral comedy needing the climate that produced Preston Sturges. It's a kind of playgirl's *Sullivan's Travels*. One doesn't need the clues afforded by the similarity of the plot's mainspring with that of Bunuel's *El Gran Calavera* to think of the mischievous version which the '60s would relish. The father would test the boy friend's love of his heiress daughter by keeping his real intentions a secret. The boy friend would promptly quit the girl. She would begin enjoying the thrills, the irresponsibility, the security of degradation (having fallen, one can't fall). On the proceeds of degradation she thrives, financially and otherwise. Her boy friend has to pay for her favours, her father *really* loses his money, and so on and so forth. Hitchcock began from the other end of the moral spectrum, it seems, the theme being that champagne helps girls get into trouble and that every bottle thereof means trouble for somebody. Even the film's final outline might have retained some kind of concern for, if not the victims of champagne, at least the victims of not being heiress to a million dollars.

The Lodger, Downhill and *Champagne* form a trilogy on the theme of the rich being out of their depth, and it's entertaining, though no more, to consider the lodger as a Comstock who comes under suspicion for peculiar habits whose motive is not to hunt down the Avenger but to hide his poverty from his landlady, his friends and family, who might find out where he lives. Since entertainment filmmakers regularly proceed by improving on life it's not altogether pointless for a critic to reverse the process and bring romance and melodrama back down to earth again. For the fears (as much as the realities) which a film denies are as much part of it as the latent content of a dream, just as a beautiful countryside owes much of its shape to subterranean strata which never appear.

The Manxman

Hitchcock's last silent film was *The Manxman*, with Carl Brisson, Malcolm Keen and Anny Ondra. Hall Caine's novel was first published in 1894 and was still best-selling in the late '20s. Its theme is the friendship between two childhood friends, resumed in adulthood when the inarticulate fisherman (Carl Brisson) sends the lawyer (Malcolm Keen) to plead his cause with the girl he loves (Anny Ondra), her father being an innkeeper who despises his lowly craft. Like a gentleman, the advocate silences his own feelings and speaks for his friend. Then comes false news of the fisherman's death, which excuses his declaration of his own real feelings, and her surrender to him. The girl is carrying the lawyer's child when, after all, her husband returns.

She attempts suicide, and the lawyer, by now a judge, finds himself required to sentence her. Instead he confesses his own involvement, and seeks, with her, to persuade her husband to leave them with the child whose father he believes himself to be.

The equivocations and entanglements which, in the '20s, the class aspects of such a story were likely to get themselves into, aren't too difficult to foresee. According to Chabrol and Rohmer the film was none too successful commercially, and Hitchcock remarked to Truffaut, 'The only point of interest about that movie is that was my last silent film.'

Blackmail

Then, abruptly, *Blackmail* asserts Hitchcock's maturity; in structure, in morality, in irony, in style.

An opening reel, silent against background music, shows the police using their very latest wonder, wireless vans, to track down a dangerous criminal, whom they duly apprehend, fingerprint, photograph and secure in custody. As Scotland Yard detectives disperse after their day's duty, we follow Frank Webber (John Longden) off to his evening date with little Alice White the tobacconist's daughter (Anny Ondra). He takes her to a restaurant where they have a tiff because she is reluctant to leave for the pictures until she has first given the handsome stranger who caught her eye a chance to take their flirtation a stage further. Frank moodily storms off without her and her intriguing new acquaintance (Cyril Ritchard) takes her to his elegantly appointed mansion flat. On its doorstep he rebuffs the seedy looking Tracy (Donald Calthrop) who approaches him with some kind of plea or threat. In his apartment he shows Alice his paintings and roguishly guides her hand into outlining a naughtily nude lady. He dares her to pose for him, and while she has slipped behind a screen, he embraces her. The struggle becomes an ugly one and she stabs him in the back with a breadknife, killing him. Appalled, she wanders around London, returning just in time to slip into bed and descend for breakfast, where she must suffer a gossipy neighbour raucously discussing the crime. Called to assist a senior detective on the crime, Frank recognises her glove, hides it, and comes to the shop. Meanwhile Alice has had a visit from Tracy, who possesses the other glove and means to extort at least a good breakfast and hopefully a lot more from her too. But Frank turns the tables on him by threatening to accuse him of the murder. After all, he too has the incriminating glove; and when the police are called the cowed blackmailer runs for it, falling to his death through the dome of the British Museum. Meanwhile Alice, petrified, goes to Scotland Yard to confess everything. But she is delayed by a friendly colleague of Frank's and various other formalities and Frank returns in time to prevent her. They return home together.

The final chase is a chase in reverse. For if the blackmailer is caught, he is very likely to bring up the issue of Alice's involvement, whether the lesser crime (blackmail) or the greater (murder) is pressed. Alice may well be exonerated by the court on the grounds of self-defence, and we know she ought to be, but her reputation will be blackened in public, and in any case she can be spared the whole pointless ordeal so long as Tracy is allowed to disappear into the shadows from which he came. One wonders, indeed, why Frank is so keen to have Tracy pursued. Is it a bluff that gets out of hand? Is he unaware of the strain Alice is under? Is he sure he can get his colleagues to help him keep things hushed up? The last seems unlikely, particularly given his stealthy way with the glove. Has he jumped to the conclusion that Tracy really is guilty and Alice altogether innocent of anything that might involve her in court? Is he a victim of his own policeman's reflex—not content with defending Alice, he puts the frighteners on Tracy so convincingly that before he quite realises it he's frightened Alice into betraying herself? Nor can one quite put that past him, given the way in which, by storming out of the restaurant, he left Alice alone with his fascinating rival in the first place.

It seems then, that the final pursuit of the blackmailer *endangers* Alice: and logically, we ought to want Tracy to get away, or, failing that, to breathe a sigh of relief when he goes crashing to his death. As if to remind us of this aspect of things, Hitchcock keeps the chase in long-shot, as if not to involve us in it too much, and he interrupts it with shots of Alice getting progressively more worried as the pursuers close in on the pursued. But there exists a powerful good guy-bad guy polarity between Frank as Alice's knight-errant and Tracy, which, together with the force of cinematic convention, whereby the good guy has only to chase the bad guy, and the cops to chase a robber, for us to hope they get him. And I suspect that for a great many spectators this thoroughly conventionalised logic virtually over-powers the real dramatic polarity of this particular situation, and that the excitement of the chase takes over, reducing the shots of the girl sitting with a glazed expression to nothing more than a static, tragic contrast which heightens the excitement and even the righteousness of the chase. We're not even sure whether Alice is driven to try to confess out of morbid guilt, or out of objective honesty, or because she's frightened that Tracy might get caught and spill the beans, or because she's frightened he might get caught and get hanged.

There's no doubt that Frank is a very wicked detective and that Alice ends up as his equally wicked accomplice. Rohmer and Chabrol, usually so severe, don't put the case against him half strongly enough. They speak of him proposing a 'rather ignoble bargain' with the black-mailer, but, in fact, he must *also* bear full moral and legal responsibility for concealing important evidence (the glove), and for exploiting the machinery of the law to pervert the course of justice, since Alice ought to be seriously considered as a candidate for a manslaughter charge. Furthermore, Frank is morally largely responsible for hound-ing a man who is innocent of murder to his death (which may be an accidental one, but certainly puts Frank in at least as bad a light as the coroner puts James Stewart in in *Vertigo*). In fact a better title for the film would have been *Manslaughter*, since, morally at least, both hero and heroine are guilty of it.

Were Hitchcock an unequivocally severe moralist, one might expect him to see Frank and Alice as each responsible for one man's death and each accomplice in the other's responsibility. Given the affective links between manslaughter and murder (links of which Alice, aided by her talkative neighbour's macabre monologue, is certainly con-scious), the logic of the transference of guilt ought to lead to the conclusion that the detective and his fiancée are spiritually guiltier than the rapist and the blackmailer. And Chabrol and Rohmer take at least one step on that path when they imply that a girl's virtue isn't worth a man's death. Thus, they're very severe where Alice is con-cerned, but relatively easygoing with Frank, and most lenient of all with the artist. The question of whether Alice used undue force in defending her virtue is a delicate one, at least as delicate as the question of when does a unilateral embrace become a criminal assault, and my own reaction to the minutiae of the situation is that Alice's way with the knife shows a certain ferocity which is not altogether necessary but also a natural response by a certain kind of (normal) temperament and a certain (everyday) moral code to the situation. The term 'a fate worse than death' may be dated but has a coherent moral meaning, and we can all understand the Western hero who devotes years of his life to shooting down the bandits who raped his wife. I wouldn't think it abnormal of a woman to threaten to stick a knife into a man who tried to rape her, and then do it. And in the case of *Blackmail*

Alice is in a physically very difficult position, she can't control what she's doing, she isn't used to self-defence and she shows so much remorse and moral responsibility that I should agree with Frank in taking her as morally innocent in the matter. And I think Hitchcock assumes that his spectators will, because the climactic suspense of the film lies in her attempts to give herself up to the law and being delayed by first one thing and then another until Frank arrives in the nick of time.

Of course, there's nothing to prevent one applying to the film another moral interpretation, whereby Alice was being unduly flirtatious, or unconsciously provocative, and that the artist, far from raping her, merely misunderstood her, and thought he was only relieving her of moral responsibility by using physical force in imposing his advances upon her, unwilling although she was pretending to be. I'm quite sure that defending and prosecuting lawyers, both using the very scenes which Hitchcock shows us, had it been filmed by hidden cameras (let's make the artist a voyeur too; he films his seductions!), would be able to present two altogether different moral interpretations of the case. Defending counsel would retort that far from being provocative Alice was being trusting, that it's no wonder that she panicked, and that my learned Jansenist friends are committing themselves to the proposition that a girl who trusts a man enough to go to his flat unchaperoned ought not to resist what looks and feels like rape in case they injure their attacker. According to their logic, the law allows a woman to defend herself only on condition that she does it ineffectively. Surely, ladies and gentlemen of the dream-palace jury, ought we not rather to praise the girl's spirited self-defence and only regret an accident to which he put himself entirely at risk? The case isn't even as clean-cut as that, because the film sequence which is the key item of evidence in our moral (not legal) court has undergone preliminary censorship, i.e. Hitchcock would not have been allowed to show incontrovertible evidence of rape even if he had wanted to, so there's room for doubt even on the issue of whether Alice is right in thinking she's being raped rather than merely forcibly embraced.

Or again, one can shift tack entirely, and say that the artist dealt with the blackmailer the right way, coolly and calmly, and Alice dealt with him the wrong way, by being terrified rather than insolent, and that Frank then swung too far the other way, being ferocious rather than prudent. The artist comes out of this best, especially if one argues that Alice feels guilty because of an unconscious ferocity which enabled her to kill the artist accidentally-on-purpose. The only snag is that both these arguments are reversible. The artist deals with Alice very badly, by getting himself killed, accidentally-on-purpose, no doubt, while Alice's very acceptance of moral responsibility proves that she's the sort of person who could only have killed the artist by accident.

The purpose of our little review of attempts at objective precision in the matter of defining the relative responsibility of the characters involved is to suggest that in this case it can't be done, and that therefore moral rigour isn't foremost in Hitchcock's mind. All one can say is that Alice and Frank seem to have some degree of responsibility in two accidents of which the victims are their assailants. If this is tragic for them, it's precisely because of their degree of innocence. That's why we understand Alice's fears and guilts at having killed the artist. And that's why we can be glad that she's spared the ordeal of a trial; and that's why Frank's hounding of the blackmailer doesn't put him, for us, beyond the pale, and why we don't feel that he's blotted his copybook so badly that we'll never trust a policeman again. It doesn't seem to me that Hitchcock goes to any trouble whatsoever to remind us that the artist and blackmailer didn't deserve to die, and I have a very strong suspicion that this is because he reckons that *l'homme moyen moral* won't be in too much doubt about the basic sympathetic flow, but will take as his moral baselines two points. First, Frank and Alice are the two people whom we get to know best and through whose reactions we will appraise the situation —not uncritically, certainly, but in dominant perspective. Second, there exists that cogent argument in playground, and vernacular, morality, 'Who started it?' To admit, therefore, that Frank and Alice are far from guiltless is not to admit to a transference of guilt, and to admit to a transference of guilt is not to alter one's polarity of hopes and fears in the way in which moral considerations would require if they were primary. Not for one moment do we want Alice and Frank to be punished for their sins, nay, crimes, of which we admit them to be guilty. In other words, we remain amoral. Chabrol and Rohmer try to get off this hook by supposing that 'by refusing to pay the price, Alice will be submitting herself to a *moral* chastisement' (though not, presumably, Frank, who, in their scheme, is far less guilty for, it would seem, framing an innocent man of murder, than a girl who defends herself from what they certainly accept as rape!). But it's just as reasonable to suppose that we heartily approve of Alice being rescued from her intention of paying the price, and that we are glad the couple remain united to find forgiveness and consolation in one another.

None of which implies that Frank's pursuit of Tracy is a psychological implausibility due to an ascendancy of the film's melodramatic aspects (situation dominating character) over its dramatic ones (character determining situation). If the situation dominates Frank, it is for good dramatic reasons, namely, that it is only too congenial to a side of his character on which Hitchcock has already a certain emphasis. He's a spiritual cousin of the detective fiancé in *The Lodger*. Just as Alice is so easily overwhelmed by guilt or fear or both that first she kills her would-be seducer and then seeks the expiatory ordeal of a trial (sadism followed by masochism), so Frank is confident in his own initiatives and in his own powers (sometimes rightly, he purloins the glove; sometimes wrongly, his tough tactics with the blackmailer endanger Alice almost as much as her own guilt, and probably adds to it). He has too little guilt, just as she has too much. Both are saved from the worst possible consequences of their follies by chances which may be considered the work of providence, or of life's inconsequentiality, or of a satisfyingly poetic justice whereby loss of innocence is sufficient punishment for the sins of innocent complacency.

Frank's complacency isn't derived only from the law which he enforces. He gets Alice and himself to a restaurant table by a quite irregular means, he conceals vital evidence from his superiors without a moral qualm (and maybe we should applaud him for his immediate loyalty to Alice right or wrong). If anything, his job as a detective is an outlet for, rather than a primary cause of, a temperament which is paternalist, authoritarian, not rigidly moral, and, under tension, prone to that little bullying streak which is far from uncommon in Hitchcock's heroes, as often to their profit as to their undoing (vide *Psycho*, *Marnie* and *Topaz*). Frank's wilfulness induces him to march heavily out of the restaurant in sulks even after Alice has apologised for an indecision of whose underlying interest in another man he's certainly not aware. If he were he wouldn't have abandoned her to the other. If one is interested in tracing patterns of guilt, then his begins, not only with his marching out of the restaurant in a huff, but with his managing to get into it although the pageboy has told him to stay out. And given his heavy style it isn't surprising that Alice finds the artist's light and laughing style a blessed and sensible relief and very intriguing (even though the '70s spectator can't be altogether sure that glances which he reads as a sensible sexual friendliness wouldn't be read by Old Morality spectators in the '30s as excitingly ominous knowingness).

To blame Frank for his wilfulness is like blaming Alice for her flirtatiousness. It's quite right but it doesn't justify that 'logic' which argues that if you're wilful you're guilty of sending blackmailers hurtling through the dome of the British Museum and if you're flirtatious you're guilty for being raped and if you defend yourself you're a murderer. Such logic takes its cue, and its air of plausibility, from puritanical and Freudian awareness of little symptoms as clues to profound tensions which might determine one's conduct in crises. And I've no doubt that a sense of such linkage is in Hitchcock's mind. But the amoral dramatic polarity is in Hitchcock's mind also, and this isn't necessarily an incoherence. For any theory tending to equate accidents with total depravity or unconscious crime must also accommodate orthodox distinctions between the benign wickedness and malign, between the lesser crime and the greater, between tripping over the kerb and kicking a blind man to death, between the imperfect saint and the Beast of Belsen: and not to do so is to make assumptions about human nature which also make it inevitable that everyone will decide to reverse the argument and decide to be hung for a sheep as well as a lamb. The moral of *Blackmail* is rather less likely to be that detectives who jump queues for tables will be fearfully punished through manslaughters committed by their fiancées than to be that the absurd is everywhere. I doubt if Hitchcock's prime interest is in blaming his couple, or his audience through his couple, than in contemplating the mixture of egoisms and loyalties, strengths and weaknesses, in both of them, watching them behave foolishly at one moment and shrewdly the next. They are an average couple, and a unique couple, a well-matched couple and an ill-matched couple, each beset by tensions within himself, by tensions between himself and the other, and by combinations and permutations of tensions which are absolutely unforeseeable, in just the same way as the weather may produce freak conditions due, not to root hidden causes, but to unusual combinations of all sorts of factors. This isn't to say that there aren't root hidden causes and consistencies also. But how morally simple life would be if they were all there was!

Something of the same irony, and humanity, informs Hitchcock's study of the two villians, and victims, even though his prudent dramatic polarities require him not to be too compassionate about them. Is the artist's easy manner that of a worldly, pleasant fellow who gets it as suddenly and shockingly as Janet Leigh gets it for theft in *Psycho*?

Is it that of a worldly, callous fellow who usually forgets he's raped as
coldly as he dismisses the blackmailer who maybe wasn't blackmailing
him at all but only asking him for another hand-out because they went
to the same public school or served in the same regiment? And maybe,
where there are alternatives like this, it's reasonable to accept them
both, as outside limits, illustrating the extent to which none of us are
very consistent anyway. Sometimes we behave very badly, get away
with it and sometimes we genuinely meant no harm and get the knife
thrust in. Ambiguity, far from being imprecision, is of the essence;
and it's to the credit of Hitchcock's movies that they solicit this sort of
response even though one would not allow it to entertainment movies
in general. The blackmailer, certainly, is vastly more interesting than
almost any of the small-part villains of Hitchcock's thriller sextet.
Neither suave nor eccentric, he brings with him all the seedy reality
of a character from Grahame Greene or George Orwell or Simon
Raven. If not a public schoolboy then a counterfeit of one, he is now
hungry enough to snatch a quick breakfast, and wonder whether he
can squeeze some money from a tobacconist's daughter. Whether we
allow pity or contempt to predominate is up to us, but an individual
and a type is there.

The 'American' symbols inaugurated in *The Ring* are here developed
and refined. They feature as straightforward 'props' in the overt action,
but in so structured a way, that, one suspects, some, at least, dominated the structure of the film, by virtue of the possibilities they opened
in linking separate actions. Obsession and precision seem to be yin
and yang of Hitchcock's creative processes, whence the mixture of
ambivalence and clarity in his structures. Nothing could be simpler,
or ramify into more intricate intersections. Alice half-undresses.
Among the things she removes are her gloves. The blackmailer finds
one glove. The detective finds the other glove. What do gloves call for?
Hands. First the girl, and then the detective, and then both together,
notice the laughing jester with the pointing hand. Alice remembers
the corpse by a close-up of his drooping hand. The artist's hand closed
over Alice's hand as she drew her sketch. What do hands hold?
Knives, and if, at breakfast, Alice's hand is unable to pick up the
breadknife it's because the knife and the corpse's hand in the artist's
studio are near a loaf also. Behind the picture of the exuberantly
laughing, accusing jester is the little sketch which implies her nudity
(in an invitation to jealousy which Frank, loyally, or stoically, or
aided by his pomposity, resists). The theme of gloves is the tip of the
theme of clothes. She undresses behind a screen. Hardly has she

returned home before she must hop fully clothed into bed, and then undress again, and then dress again to descend in her day clothes. The jester has his counterpart in the droll-faced gossip who turns up at breakfast and whose dress recalls convict's stripes. A coster comic type, she is equally accusatory, in another (unsuspecting, macabre) way. The accusatory jester is balanced by a jolly policeman. The portrait and the sketch in the artist's studio are matched in Alice's bedroom by the film star faces who gratify her flighty, dreamy streak. But Fred in his helmet is there too, normally, no doubt, comforting if a bit boring, but, in this context, rather menacing, his normal meaning thus reversed, just as the jester's is. There are two remoter faces on walls. A mask hangs on the wall of the artist's studio, small but conspicuous because isolated. It might be a primitive God or a death-mask. And in the British Museum the blackmailer flees past a vast stone countenance looming as large, seraphic and cold as the moon. Through the studio window Alice looks down to see a helmeted policeman stroll by. Very simple and obvious; but he is at once an ironic reminder of the boy friend whom she may yet be seduced into betraying, he is too far away to save her from rape if the artist turns ugly, yet he is near enough to be a threat once she has become a murderess and has to sneak her way out.

Before Alice accompanies the artist up to his studio, the screen is divided by a shot in which the lower staircase fills the left, and a passageway leading to 'below stairs' on the right. A matching composition introduces the stairs up to Alice's bedroom in her own home, alongside the ground floor passage. This puts her parents, whose kitchen and shop, where we have seen them, is on the ground floor, on the same level as the artist's maid. There are two large temples. Joe Lyons' Corner House, which in its pre-war heyday was just as much the grand life for the masses as the Astorias and the Granadas, with its gypsy orchestras and oceans of tables and marble walls and thousands of maid-type waitresses, is introduced by a little sequence of impatient dodging in a doorway with pageboy, as at the entrance to Destiny's labyrinth (and maybe if Hitchcock's budget had permitted he would have remembered the revolving door in the Atlantic Hotel in Murnau's *The Last Laugh*, with its rhythm and shine). And there is the British Museum, with its emptiness, its God, its domes, accommodating a little scurry of humanity which leaves a window broken but hardly affects its timelessness.

The film's involvement in the changeover from silence to sound doubtless encouraged, not only Alice's psychologically distorted hearing of gossip about the 'murder' (the neighbour's voice becomes an indistinct vocal buzzing, from which the word 'knife!' intermittently jumps forth), but the obscure burble of detectives' voices in washrooms and corridors as they stroll home after their day's work.

As Alice drifts dazedly through London after the artist's death, Hitchcock cuts to an aerial photograph of the capital, an effect whose meaning is almost impossible to state precisely, like meanings in art of all kinds, including literature, where words suggest or describe but rarely define (definition being difficult enough in philosophy and law), and, where they begin by defining, go on to multiply or intercross definitions out of all precision. It isn't always easy to indicate the difference between an imprecision which is richly suggestive, or provocative, and the imprecision of emptiness, and it's evident that, here, a photograph which, in itself, has no conceivable intrinsic connection with this or any other drama is being given one from the invasion of a variety of preoccupations from the context. 'Montage' is not normally a matter between two shots each with one meaning, and certain Bazinian and semiological criticisms of Eisenstein's theories cease to apply as soon as this quite unnecessary limitation is removed. Maybe, indeed, 'montage' finally comes to mean the influence of everything on everything, as the dialectic can become a block universe. The leap in viewpoint, the generalisation, and the immobility, suggest a continuation of the previous action through indefinite time. The photograph's impersonality suggests Alice's loss of her sense of self. It makes of the familiar capital a labyrinth. It suggests that God can't see her, that she's lost, although it also suggests that wherever she goes, God sees her. It suggests that this black maze of stone is all there is. It suggests that her anguish is only one strand of a tangled web of sufferings and destinies. It suggests that everything's dead. The most resourcefully reproductive of media is hardly more definite than music.

She strolls past a placard with a prayer and a poster proclaiming 'Gordon's Gin For Purity' (a very common '30s poster). Both touches extend the story's branches, or roots, into areas where the overt drama doesn't enter. Had the story dealt with, say, religious issues, or seduction by alcohol (which Hitchcock had in mind for *Champagne*), the posters would have been, at best, tautologous, or, at worst, implausibly pat (not that that worried people so much in those days). One might see some ironic contrast between the opportunity for prayer and repentance and the unseeing God in the British Museum, just as one might see a contrast between the mask on the artist's wall and his seductive little song, 'Miss Up-To-Date'. But the gin advertisement clearly exists across some borderline of the relevant and the irrelevant. 'Purity' is relevant (you stick a knife in a man's back for treating it lightly), and maybe 'Gordon's Gin' has a more diffuse relevance, in so far as the Misses Up-To-Date of the '20s and '30s were drinking it, with a sense of emancipation, in madly fashionable cocktails in Mayfair bars, or in hipflasks in Prohibition America. And Miss Up-To-Date is just what she, and the artist, have both, shockingly, found she isn't. But, by and large, this first phrase indicates the relevant use of irrelevance. We are all surrounded in life by irrelevancies which we may feel as stimulating, neutral, ironic, or absurdist, and in moments of crisis some meaninglessnesses may obtrude, perhaps as a refuge from meaning, perhaps as an example of the outside world's mocking indifference. Obviously it would be easy to find in the film details which have no such meaning and are only there because they'd be conspicuous by their absence. Even if they have to look right, they contribute nothing to the meaning, scarcely indeed to the general atmosphere. It would be absurd to read every name on every truck that passes in the street, or to count their number, even in those cases where their rhythm and pace are of importance. (A problem for semiology being that every sign carries a battery of meanings which context can reverse or subsume under different selective processes.) And a certain quality of absolute irrelevance may be necessary, not simply to preserve our normal awareness of life as full of irrelevances, but for the purely negative purpose of obviating the futile challenge which a universe of a hundred per cent relevance would pose to our credibility. After all even when due allowance is made for the extent to which our preconscious perceptions and unconscious emphases surpass our conscious selections, a universe requiring a hundred per cent interpretation of significance would be like Borges's Library at Babel, and the artist normally helps us along by a great deal of repetition (so that what you miss in one idiom at one moment you get in another idiom at another; you don't have to interpret the entire structure to get the overall meaning; a selection of details will often give you that; it's surprising how some novels have all their dramatic and atmospheric elements implicit in the landscape descriptions in the opening chapter). A director may give very clear indications of significance, particularly when it's of a type which, like a given character's reaction to a given circumstance at a given moment in a story, can be seen once and once only; thus he may track in to close up. Or he may be less emphatic, e.g. by locating a usefully atmospheric object along the line of glances

which two important people are exchanging; the spectator will keep
seeing it as he looks from one face to the other. Or such an object may
have no significance in itself, simply functioning as a marker to help
create a space which does have an important meaning; if the marker is
too interesting in itself, it may disrupt that space.

High culture is currently much given to amiable deliriums of interpretation which sometimes impede rather than enhance understanding; Barbara Hardy's favourite example, a genuine question from a
intelligent student, being, 'What is the meaning of the handkerchief
which Fagin gives Oliver?' Sometimes such questions are profitable,
but the list of analogous nonsenses is hilarious, e.g., 'What is the
meaning of the knife which Alice plunges into the artist's back?',
'What is the meaning of the third bubble of air escaping from the
mouth of the boy held underwater between the girl's thighs in *Rich
and Strange*?' 'In what ways does its meaning differ from the second
and fourth bubbles of air?'

Conversely, meanings which are conspicuous by their absence on the
screen may be provided by the spectator. Frank and Alice sit at a
restaurant table which is placed before a thick pillar, and at a considerable distance from it a waitress walks, in the right-left plane, to
and fro. It's quite obvious that she's there to indicate the existence
of a vast expanse of space which the column saves the studio from
having to fill. Anyone who can remember the great days, or even the
decline, of Joe Lyons' Marble Halls on a Saturday night will recall, or
can imagine, the sea of tables crowded with people enjoying the happy
sense of a night à la Savoy. Maybe the scene can't work for the unsuspecting, but it's worth remarking that this kind of demotic grandeur,
crushed and convivial, vulgar and pretentious, hectic and delightful,
contrasts with the artist's cosily-ensconced flat with its pseudo-baronial
fireplace. The hero of *Downhill* is no more out of place than Alice
when she goes Uphill; and it's no more, and as much, her fault than,
and as, it's his.

Blackmail has one of the most intriguing structures possessed by
any Hitchcock film until *The Birds*. The characters are conspicuously
separated much of the time, and it is curious that no critic has commented on the fact that, in normal narrative terms, the film's long
opening sequence has little or no connection with the subsequent
story. It might, itself, be a one-reel film, or introduce any police crime
story, much as some of Busby Berkeley's production numbers could
have appeared in any musical comedy Warners happened to have on
the stocks. Chabrol and Rohmer are clearly sensitive to this irrele-

vance, its moral implications particularly, and suggest that it exists to indicate the sort of punishment which Alice will have to undergo if she's arrested. This is quite correct, particularly in view of Hitchcock's original ending, which of his own volition apparently, he put aside, whereby Alice was in fact arrested, and had this routine to face. But what this explanation doesn't explain is why this prologue is quite different in style from everything which follows. For it is, in effect, an exposition and a happy assertion of the efficiency of, police procedure, and corresponds in every way to the canons of 'semi-fictional' or 're-constructed' documentary which the thriving school of pre-Grierson documentary film-makers had used from the war years on and to which the Grierson school was to adopt for such films as *North Sea* and *San Demetrio London* (with, as usual, no acknowledgement that the British commercial cinema had been there ten years before). This sequence, which nowadays would be a pre-credits affair, as in *The Lodger*, shows the police apprehending a wanted man, a mean, weasel-faced character whom they catch in bed and who can't quite get to his revolver in time (a weapon which makes one doubt just how much it's a trailer for how the police will handle Alice). In every way the crime, the criminal, the type of pursuit and the social setting contrast with the far more complicated story which is subsequently recounted. The solitary man in the slum district compares with the respectable middle-class shopkeeper. The gun about to be drawn on the unarmed police marks a vicious professional criminal, as against Alice's neighbour's remarks to the effect that although there's something British about bashing somebody's head in with a brick, there's something sneaky and un-British about a knife.[1] He has his moment of cheeky ascendancy over the police officers. They're so apprehensive of some counter-move by him, such as having more guns stashed away in his chest-of-drawers, that he can send them to fetch him his trousers, i.e. make his manservant of them. This is one of those concessions with which the anarchic human spirit can infiltrate the most efficiently routinised relationships. Much is made of the general unpopularity of the police in this very poor district. The camera warns us that the criminal may plan to make a daring leap for freedom through the window, and a police-officer places himself between the window and the bed—only to be narrowly missed by a stone thrown up from outside. (The contrast is characteristic of

[1] The neighbour assumes the murderer was a man, Italian no doubt, not realising that the knife in the back was desperate rather than sneaky and that Alice's ability to plunge it in was a product of British womanly grit, not of sneaky Wop ways.

Hitchcockian syntax, which determines such details as impeccably as it redirects plots. You worry in case a man jumps out of a window, and what you get is a stone thrown in. It's a worrying world.) This easily pierced lowlife window contrasts with the highlife window which suavely isolates Alice from the policeman in the street below. The heavy archway which, blocking off the slum street, presumably a converted mews, almost like a ghetto, has no strong architectural counterpart until we find our characters running over the top of the dome of the British Museum. This dome carries a steel gangway (the staircase theme). The blackmailer crashes through its glass (the window theme).[1] The armed man dresses whereas Alice undresses. Both the 'little film' and the 'big film' are linked by the wonders of the flying squad and of radio-telephony in the service of Scotland Yard (for good measure, Hitchcock's police career about London in a deceptively ordinary looking van, which is presumably Hitchcock's fictional improvement on an already publicised innovation; the idea could have come from the Q-Ships of World War I).

One might schematise the connections thus. The British Museum, arcanum of timelessness and omniscience and eternity, is the absolute, and the face of its God exhibits indifference to the lot of the individuals whom it doesn't condescend to see. In the curtain-raiser, the police are, if not infallible, at least firmly in control, their operation goes reasonably smoothly, because of their courage and firmness, and the rights and wrongs are an open-and-shut case; they don't let their unpopularity shake their resolution. They're hard and have to be. But in the intermediate area, of Frank and Alice, the operations of justice are confused by a thousand human and moral contradictions. After the efficient routine of the opening reel comes a final reel in which Alice is trying to confess the truth but can't because a friendly policeman feels she's one of the family and in so far as she isn't everything

---

[1] Maybe this architectural structure does carry a certain charge of meaning—as of society transmuted into dreamlike terms. There are two absolute bars; one runs across the top of the slum street, the other runs under the dome which is infinity, or destiny, at any rate, a realm of the absolute. The staircases at the artist's and at Alice's produce the hierarchy: Mr. and Mrs. White (lower-middle class); Alice (socially mobile, easily lured uphill); and the artist (upper class). The artist's maid, from below stairs, is above the slum bar. On the level of the absolute, accident rectifies everything (although maybe only accidentally, since this clearly isn't a Christian realm, its presiding deity being unseeing and pagan). The police operate at every level. The areas linked by staircases are all reasonably comfortable if you're contented. Below and above are very, very dangerous. The poor are the damned; the unfortunate and the vicious. The rich aren't safe. Nobody's safe. The complacent are ignorant. Maybe, given the spiritual nastiness of blackmail as a crime, the blackmailer corresponds to the armed criminal on his level.

is slowed down by very inefficient bureaucratic form-filling. The communications which work so exhilaratingly in the beginning begin going wrong when the woman trying to report the murder is consistently misheard by the man at Scotland Yard. The opening sequence features a discreet montage effect in which the prisoner's face, posed for a mug shot, is succeeded by a matching big close up of a fingerprint. The meltingly easy transposition, and depersonalisation, is turned inside out when Frank's interest in fingerprinting is followed by his spotting the glove and so helping him to disrupt the machinery of justice, or of course injustice, in the interests of his beloved. And so he should, since it's love that makes the world go wrong, that is to say, remain bearable. The underlying contrast—the law's smooth handling of a prisoner, followed by an anomalous event which puts things right—is that of *The Wrong Man*, only this begins with the right man, and the couple conclude united even though they're doubly guilty instead of tragically disunited even though they're innocent.

The rabble's active hatred of the police contrasts with Alice's fearful masochism and the apparently foolish Frank proves robust and sophisticated, for he is a policeman, and probably a pretty good one, and wastes no time in saving his beloved from everything he stands for as well as from nasty little sneaks who might tell the truth. He certainly incarnates what Robin Wood describes as 'an acceptance of the necessary moral ambiguity of all positive action in an imperfect and bewildering world', although I'm not quite sure how far Robin Wood means this statement to justify crooked policemen, nor whether we would agree where psychic health begins and moral cynicism ends. At any rate, Alice's fear of the police might at first sight seem at odds with the theory, referred to in the introduction, about middle-class insistence on law-and-order, but Puritanism itself reminds us how an insistence on efficacious severity may lead to the bewilderments of masochism. At any rate, the danger to Alice doesn't come from the rabble, with their volatile violence, but from those above her in the social scale. Hitchcock, discreetly impassive, gives us no clue as to whether we should pity the slumdwellers and admire their revolt, even though in this case it's misguided, given the criminal's gun, or whether he means us to condemn them and fear it and admire the police all the more for braving an ugly mob who might unintentionally or otherwise protect vicious elements, or whether he means us to pity the slumdwellers *and* admire the policemen, law and order being a necessity even in an unjust society, although, conversely, it's just as well if Frank tricks it for Alice. During the opening sequence there is a slight danger that we'll reverse our sympathies, whence the importance of the criminal having a gun—some of us might otherwise be mischievously delighted if he got away.

Although the film, if taken as a whole, is distinctly ironical about law-and-order, and probably wouldn't have been allowed by the Hays Code a year or two later, nor by the English censor who regularly followed the American principles, very few spectators seem to register its anarchistic side, perhaps because the opening sequence is so strong, firm and self-contained that its image of the police survives the ironies which follow. It may be that that was one of the reasons, conscious or unconscious, for the prologue existing as it docs. It encapsulates any indulgence of disorder within a strong general affirmation, at least for those spectators for whom law and order is sacred, as well as for those, more numerous between the wars than since, who deplored the political aspects of the police, while admiring their personal bravery.

The importance of the window through which the criminal doesn't get a chance to jump, and the fact that the throwing in of the stone can work as a contrast against an expected non-event, reminds us of the extent to which film suspense depends on events which never materialise, and so can't be shown. And when one thinks of the extent to which not only melodramas but dramas also depend on hopes and fears of things which don't happen, it's evident that the mainstream cinema is not only less exclusively a visual medium than silent era theorists thought but it's also less exclusively an audio-visual medium than is sometimes assumed, and depends on all sorts of invisibles and inaudibles. It isn't merely that what isn't seen exists in some sort of subjunctive of possibility; what isn't seen may be the motor of what is, and everything which is seen is referred to it. It's because of the extent to which the cinema isn't a visual art that Eisenstein defined montage in terms of the intersections between the suggestions of separate shots (or meanings within a shot), and that Hitchcock insists: 'Clarify! clarify!', for the film's suspense backbone is often a series of possibilities and deductions. Theorists traditionally speak of the necessity to make everything visual, forgetting how often movie characters discuss the past, or the future, or something which might be happening elsewhere. And how can one make, say, the abstract idea, or invisible emotion, of 'love' visual? All one can show is some concrete object, say, a face, and hope that the spectator interprets its expression and atmosphere as love rather than, say, infatuation, or indigestion. And as Hitchcock, who isn't sparing of reaction shots, observed, our faces rarely reveal any precise emotion (which Kulyeshov's celebrated experiment also implies). What we frequently do is infer an emotion from the range of possibilities implied by a reaction and from the situation as a whole. Not only are all human feelings as abstract as that, but so of course are all abstractions and general processes, creating the difficulty that a film is like an iceberg; one-tenth of it exists on the screen, the other nine-tenths in the spectators' minds, which are likely to be far from unanimous on many crucial points of idiom, experience and response. Conversely, suspense can only exist insofar as things go on in the spectators' minds which don't exist on the plane of the film, a simple example being the 'Look behind you, Mister!' response as Melanie in *The Birds* doesn't notice her feathered friends massing behind her. Some semiologists have pondered long and deep over problems of tense and other grammatical and synthetical markers in films, without realising that films have gradually shed them all because they don't need any. If one shot looks as if it might follow the spatial-, temporal-, or activity-group of the previous one, then we assume that it does, and we decide it on the basis of what we know of the space, the time, and the activity, and how we would expect them to continue, partly on our knowledge of time, space and activities, and partly on the analytical pace and purpose which a film has shown so far. In this respect the film is typical of the theatrical arts to which it belongs.

The derisory nature of movie realism may be exemplified by movie meals, of which *Blackmail* offers no suitable examples, since they're all interrupted by the dramatic action anyway. But *The Lady Vanishes* offers two useful examples, in which the heroine and a companion enter the train dining car, talk continuously and leave, having supposedly eaten a complete meal in about one mouthful each and less than a minute of real screen time. The outrage against realism could hardly be more obvious, yet no spectator notices, simply because he's attending to the faces and words and more important matters, and has been distracted from thinking about the meal qua meal. He's quite happy to accept one spoonful as a three-course meal. The spectator doesn't ask to believe; he asks to be interested; and if he's interested, belief will follow where it needs to, and respect will maintain participation where belief isn't necessary.

Another disparity between realism and response is exemplified by a short sequence in *Blackmail* in which the artist persuades Alice to trust herself with him in his apartment. All we see is a brief, bland, banal conversation, but the responsive emotion of the audience is a rising curve. We know something must happen, or there'll be no film, and we want it to, although at the same time we urge her, 'Don't go, don't do it, don't listen to him!' because we don't want her to suffer. Once the course is set, we level out at acceptance again, but one stage deeper in foreboding. Why does Hitchcock make no attempt to present this 'rising curve' 'filmically'? Because the conversation does so much of the work itself, that to reiterate filmically, at the same moment, would be too strong a climax at this stage of the film.

But he goes straight on to some effectively ominous shots of Alice and artist ascending the stairs, including a very beautiful shot of them in profile, with the camera watching them 'through' a wall which ought to be there but isn't. And the visual effects occur here, not in the preceding scene, because the tension of decision is over and this is a relatively 'dead' scene, a mechanical continuation of its predecessor. A less resourceful director might give us a boring trek upstairs. Or he might decide to avoid a sag in tension by cutting the ascent out and moving quickly on to the room. Hitchcock, confident in his resources, can afford to dwell on this scene, gaining a variety of advantages, notably: (1) the girl, and we, are curious, and it's natural to show the experience as a continuous whole, (2) this staircase, if made memorable now, can be echoed by, and contribute its tragic irony to, later shots of the girl's staircase, which also threaten to be a flat moment, and (3) he wants to maintain the tension in the scene, but to maintain it he needs a variety of emotional stimuli, for which he calls on the visuals for aid.[1] Within certain limits, one may reckon, schematically, that the lighter the dramatic content of a scene, the more visual rhetoric must provide the mood, with a combination of the two restricted to climaxes. It's interesting that the change in style doesn't disrupt the continuity of the tensions; partly because situation and personalities are continuous, partly because of Hitchcock's rigorous control of effect, partly because the film has already asserted a flexible style, so that this change, being one of many, discreetly maintains the pulse and energy of that variety rather than breaking abruptly into an established idiom. If one denies expressiveness to whatever isn't communicated through startling visual effects, then, of course, the doorstep scene will seem weak and flat and the staircase sequence enthralling, so that a Hitchcock film will come to seem a matter of mere 'touches'. But both a more naive involvement with the characters and a more sophisticated appreciation of style will sense that admirable orchestration of the whole, through contrast and con-

---

[1] For the sake of simplicity, I omit the conversation with the maid, which opens up a new branch of interest, albeit relatively quietly here.

tinuity, which now seems so conspicuous a source of the aesthetic pleasure in Hitchcock's work.

And powerfully reinforced, in fact, for the film is also among the tenderest of a period when Hitchcock was more open than he was ever again to be to the poignancies of the human detail, to drama uncircumscribed by suspense, to everyday setting as life lived rather than calculated intrusions to enhance the melodrama. For the first time since *The Lodger*, Hitchcock seems fully at home with story and background. A lost era comes flooding back more eloquently than from any of the documentaries which it precedes as one watches again the policeman who, at 20 years of age or so, already has the stolid certainties of a young old-fashioned heavy father; or the artist's hands-in-pocket, broad-trousered, jaunty, fireplace-spanning stance; his mixture of roguish ogling, calculation and odd little quirks of vulnerability; or the old lady scared out of her wits by questioning from Scotland Yard but doing her scatterbrained best; or the slumkids, hurling stones at coppers; or Alice's cool, childlike intonation, 'Ooh, you are awful', and her forlorn, weary, 'Don't let's have a row, Frank'. For once Hitchcock's films take us to the centre of the spiritual stress, instead of restricting us, as the mystery aspects of the thriller format so often do, to loiter, on its periphery; and the spiritual stresses and the everyday fuse into one.

Here, too, Hitchcock identifies, quite straightforwardly, with both the man who bullies (or fears) a woman, and with the woman who, as usual, suffers the most intricate spiritual stresses. There is no mystification. The beauty of detail is all the more surprising in that Alice White is played by a German actress who mouthed to a simultaneous reading of her lines by Joan Barry. Discrepancies and all, the effect is as beautiful as some of the curious cross-casting in Renoir. The sparse, faint restraint of the delivery express *lostness* rather than stiff-upper-lip, which in any case the face belies, creating, in itself, a kind of gentle, ineffectual duplicity. With the actress's slight hint of expressionism (a doll-like amazement), firmly absorbed by Hitchcock's firm sense of structure, it coheres into something at once realistic and dreamlike. Such modes weren't rare in the Populism of the time, whether one thinks of the German films, or Clair's. Linked with, and interconnecting through, the drama, these details cease to be 'touches' and become a continuity, more important, in the final reckoning, and difficult to describe, than the motifs which we have observed. They catch something of the times with a fidelity of a kind which comes somewhere between the poetic vision of Graham Greene, the diligent prosaism of Mass Observation, the charms of England's little Hollywood and something which is true enough in the *News of the World* philosophy. Hitchcock is still fascinated by the small change of human contact, for its own sake; increasingly, later, he will dedicate his keenly ironic eye to the lesser cause of dapper badinage or to intimations of a melodrama which flattens out that reality.

A recent article in *New Society*, lamenting the decline and fall of the small shopkeeper, predicts that we won't much longer see those little backstreet home-shop-cum-social centres owned and run by a couple who take their meals in the room behind the shop, making a leisurely and dignifiedly unhurried appearance in response to the bell on the door, or a polite but loud cry of 'Shop!' Just this scene—and a breakfast—is the background to the famous 'knife' effect, and, perhaps, quite as important as it, in the overall and unique ambiance. An errand boy on a bicycle comes whizzing round the corner with a slant, a speed and a parabola which, impossible to describe, catches so much of the cheery cheek of a once prevalent Cockney style, that it cuts like a knife. And the gossipy neighbour, with her Gus Elen face, her jocular but disquieting discussion of the nuances of violence, is another notation of a generation all but gone—not quite coster-comic, not quite '20s.

With an intimate mixture of affection and sadness Hitchcock observes two of the millions like us in a situation which makes nonsense of commonsense and brings two everyday people so near being their own executioners. And this intimacy endows the film with its delicate and precious balance between qualities so diverse one can hardly bracket them without a faint sensation of incredulous hilarity: the spirit of Mass Observation, a Dostoievskian, or Jesuitical, awareness of the moral masochism which, redeeming our egoism, underlies us all, and a kind of plodding, constabulary, effective resistance to it. Their very incongruity is of a piece with Hitchcock's religious absurdities, and creates an emotional forcefield sufficiently strong to allow a masterly emotional orchestration which only the needs of verbal description may seem to disintegrate into details: the isolation of, and doubleness within, each phrase of dialogue; the separation of the prologue and of the characters for long periods within the story; the recourse on linking motifs; the Hitchcockian clarification leading to an emphasis on each narrative point in a situation; the consistent division between the actual situation and its distinct, opposed possibilities; the intermittent alternation between objective narration and an optico-acoustical 'expressionistic impressionism' about which the

French avant-garde had so prestigiously theorised while rarely contriving much more than rhetorical concoctions or wildly slapdash flurries. How simple, sharp, exact is that distortion of sound: 'mumble mumble *knife*! mumble mumble KNIFE!' Not only the sudden jerk and squawk of phrase within the syllabic fuzz of faintness, but the whole sensory gestalt achieves a perceptual *rightness* which distinguishes from the touchingly earnest formalism of the avant-garde an authentic stream-of-consciousness. For that, simply because we live in, after all, a substantially intersubjective world in which relationships and action have sufficient significance, permits—indeed, requires —rapid, flexible, definite alternations between internal and external realities.

Elstree Calling, Juno and the Paycock

After directing Gordon Harker in a sequence of *Elstree Calling*, Hitchcock went on to another eminent literary adaptation, *Juno and the Paycock*, which he describes as 'a photograph of a stage play. . . . The camera was encased in what looked like a telephone booth in those days for reasons of soundproofing.' The cast consisted almost entirely of the production's original Irish actors, and this transliteration of Sean O'Casey's most popular play was highly regarded at the time by, notably, James Agate, as well as by others whom one would have expected to be very sensitive to any infidelity. Retrospectively, and to anyone sufficiently attuned to film form, the film's very fidelity lies in its infidelity. It's not particularly a matter of opening out in time and space. There are, by now, examples enough of films quite as 'enclosed' as this one is, to vindicate the medium from the imputation that it can't remain within narrow bounds. And in any case it's obvious that any living space offers a multiplicity of subspaces, reverse-angles and varied configurations, particularly if you allow for changes of lighting, contrasted rhythms of cutting, and so on. It wouldn't be a very great *tour de force* to make a half-hour film whose hero never moves outside a telephone-booth, and even easier with perfectly organic and natural interludes like leaning against it outside waiting for the irascible old lady to make endless calls or to scan the bend in the road for the first possible sight of the expected automobile. The key lies in the phrase, 'natural and organic'. Where the stage-play's restrictions start to cabin, crib, confine, bind in, is when the play can't expand to take in action which it would be relevant to see and when unity within the scene requires a stylised concatenation of events. Here again, the distinction is far from clear-cut. The mainstream theatre has subsequently absorbed, from a pre-cinematic avant-garde (and the popular Victorian theatre!), a sufficiently fast and fluid staging. The difference lies not so much between stage and screen as media as between the rules and conventions of the naturalism within which Sean O'Casey worked, and what was required of the mainstream cinema at the time of Hitchcock's adaptation. Even here, it's worth remembering that, at about this time, Lewis Milestone with *Rain*, King Vidor with *Street Scene*, and Jean Renoir with *Boudu Sauvé des Eaux*, were all solving the problems of endowing the enclosed, naturalistic play with appropriate movement and rhythm. The real problem, one suspects, was more specific. On the one hand was the relationship between this particular play's form and the events which it describes. On the other, were the technical and financial limitations of the company and the studio for which Hitchcock was working.

Perhaps, as Agate's remarks imply, the film worked well enough within the filmic conventions of its time, when, mainly for reasons of cheapness, 'stagey' general shots were much in use. Perhaps *aficionados* of the theatre and of literary texts are not the best judges of whether a film adaptation thereof works well as a film. In any case, the film offers the modern spectator a variety of problems.

In the first place, of course, a spiritual, rather than purely conventional, problem is offered by O'Casey's 'well-constructed play' with its 'great moments'—which are all the more awkward in view of the play's constructional clumsiness, at least by the standards of Ibsen and Strindberg. Second, the film relates to an older cinematic idiom and rhythm, geared partly to the excitements of the Americans and the Russians, and partly to relatively simple, fast, full-hearted reactions to events. Today's intellectual spectator is likely to be more at home with the slower, smoother, heavier, more brooding style of, say, Wyler's *The Little Foxes*, and to require more time to catch, and then to think through, his more cautious and nuanced feelings (whence the relative slowness of Henry King's films for Fox through the '50s). *Juno* moves too fast; climaxes appear too suddenly, are cut across too drastically. In a decade or so fashions may have changed again. The spectator may find the smooth slow pace of the '50s and '60s tedious in the extreme, and feel only repetition whereas in fact the spectator was groping for attitudes so that his mind was moving even though the film wasn't. *Juno* seems particularly lacking in dolly-shots, and tends to restrict any depth in groupings to long-shot, which suggests problems with sound equipment and shallow-focus lenses analogous to those with which Renoir was grappling. But whereas the French situation gave the director and his creative *équipe* an ascendancy over the technicians, in England the balance between the system and the artist was less favourable to the innovations required to master the new techniques, and for once Hitchcock the redoubtable technical thinker was unable to impose himself.

A third problem lies in changes of behaviour. It's one that has to be thoroughly clarified, now that the cinema's existence stretches back through three-quarters of a century characterised by rapid and continuous cultural, and therefore behavioural, change. The problem has appeared already in literature, of course, although there too a kind of uneasy avoidance of the problem exists as between those who claim that art is great in so far as it transcends local differences of behaviour (so stressing, with pleasure, the fact that it lends itself to different interpretations in every age), and those who claim that art is valuable also in showing other, different, mutually exclusive, patterns of thought and behaviour, thus widening and deepening our sense of historically real human possibilities. Although it's not too difficult to combine the two propositions, there is a great deal of tension between them, particularly as regards the usefulness of minor works of art, which, precisely because they are tied, albeit intelligently and sensitively, to their time and place, force us to adapt to them and don't allow us to bring to them assumptions with which we are already more than sufficiently familiar. It can certainly be argued that intelligent minor works are a necessary commentary on major works of their epoch, precisely by making it easier for us to see the meaningful differences as well as the similarities, many of which may well be taken in a shallow and sentimental way unless their complex interaction with dissimilarities is grasped. In consequence, many semi-alien works of art tend to get unjustly consigned to nostalgia or camp. And the importance of honouring, rather than dismissing, many intelligent minor movies remains. The problem is particularly acute for the cinema, not only because of the particular severity of judgement mentioned in the preliminary chapter, but because the ciné-camera with its very detailed recording of external behaviour, depicts every aspect of human style, from ways of standing to the slightest mannerism, far more precisely than the merely evocative paraphrase which is all that words can provide. The less thoughtful men of letters sometimes point to the fact that films seem to date more rapidly than the written word as indicative of some lesser level of achievement in the film medium. But one important reason why films seem to date more rapidly is because they record everything external more exactly. And it's impossible to dismiss what it records as mere ephemera. One doesn't need to be a psychologist to understand that gestures and postures may reveal states of soul, or complex psychological attitudes and progressions, while also (to provide a further degree of refinement) requiring, for fuller understanding, some sense of the conventional, the normal and the ideal, kinds of physical existence. All the nuances which so often filter through the meshes of verbal description are not too fine for the camera eye.

Just as the Cockney accent has changed profoundly since its—stylised and approximative—recording by Dickens—and is still changing—there's every reason to suppose that the language of the body has changed no less profoundly. In the 1930s Pathétone film clips of the coster comic Gus Elen, reliving his heyday of twenty or so years earlier, not only the accent, but the facial expressions and every gesticulation frequently strike those born after 1940 as being quite as alien and incomprehensible as a Zulu's, being adapted to the more specialised world of the old East End. The differences between them and us are so striking as to make it immediately obvious that spontaneous responses aren't enough and that the critic can't 'judge' the performance as false or true at all. He can enjoy learning from it, though, quite apart from the great deal that remains of its contemporary entertainment value. The problem becomes much more complex when the difficulties are less striking, as when behaviour is in a kind of transitional stage (although all stages are transitional!) between a familiar style and an unfamiliar one. The spectator is jerked, often rapidly, between what he immediately recognises as authentic and strangenesses which he may too rapidly assume are inauthentic. What's even more difficult is that very often these semi-alien styles of behaviour were observed and reproduced by people to whom they were semi-alien, stage Cockney and Stage-Oirish being celebrated instances. As if all that weren't enough, much that is spiritually authentic in high culture art responds to a tradition of attaining the larger than life which may seem false to temperaments steeped in the current combination of documentary realism and cool underplaying, but which responds to a natural and logical intellectual process whereby the extraordinary clarifies or comments on the ordinary.

One might have anticipated difficulties in adapting distinguished stage performances for the screen, but as it happens the smoothest and most cinematic performances (Sara Allgood as Juno and Sidney Morgan as Joxer) come from the actors who had played those parts on the stage, while Edward Chapman, who didn't play the Paycock in the theatrical production, plays in what looks to me the stagiest way of all; seems, at times, almost beyond Hitchcock's control. Otherwise the film's merits and artifices make for a blurred but legible carbon copy of the play's, and moving as Sara Allgood is I wouldn't myself want to say that its humanist fundamentalism as to poverty, suffering, family feeling, treachery, irresponsibility, divided loyalties and the horrors of Civil War survive without impairment the contemporary preference for irony, coolth and moral scepticism. It may well be that the loss is largely ours.

An act division is marked by a burst of fire and the appearance of a row of machine-gun bullet-holes. The effect precedes the analogous one in Howard Hawks's *Scarface*, although Hitchcock, like Hawks, may well have got it from Von Sternberg, who had used it in *Underworld*. A few years later and Hitchcock or B.I.P. might have been tempted to open out the play in such a way as to give it something in common with the gangster film, in which, at this point, immigrant-class families and mothers did loom large. It's ironical to think that a few years later Hitchcock might thus have found an extensive American audience and enjoyed a success which would have set the British film industry a valuable counter-example to *The Private Life of Henry VIII*. The encounter of O'Casey, and Hitchcock's adaptation of the gangster's film expressionistic opportunities would also have been interesting, quite apart from the resultant parallel to John Ford's *The Informer*.

Murder

Hitchcock has spoken of the expressionist influence on his next movie, *Murder*, which was simultaneously shot in a German version entitled *Mary*. He describes it as 'the first important who-done-it picture I made'. This presumably excludes *The Lodger* and *Blackmail*. The murders in the former aren't solved, and the emphasis doesn't lie on who-done-it, only on who-never-done-it. In the latter we know who-done-it, it's only Scotland Yard what don't know who done it. The basic material seems dated, although it might have made an effective play on stage, since it's about murder in a rep company.

Actress Nora Baring is on trial for the murder of her fiancé, and, as if honour-bound, holds on to her secret while a jury condemns her to death. The lordly amateur detective (Herbert Marshall) who has interested himself in her case is constantly on the verge of giving it up, owing to feeling tired, or peckish, or nonchalantly uninvolved, and it's his N.C.O.-type sidekick who keeps the aristocratic nose to responsibility's grindstone.

The theme of a girl's fate depending on the whims and fancies of her quasi-anti-knight errant leads naturally to the film's particular interest in superficial detail, and so renewed stream-of-consciousness effects as trivial stimuli loom ironically large. Without having researched the matter, I have a suspicion that the reasons why the film didn't repeat the critical success of *Blackmail* or become, like that film, a standard critical reference, are (1) the film doesn't sit so easily in the stream of populist realism, (2) subsequentially influential critics, not being too bright, couldn't grasp that the superficiality of the distractions is the basis of the irony, and not just a touch for the sake of a touch. Years before Resnais and Truffaut, there are subjective shots (whether flashbacks or flashforwards Robbe-Grillet and his ilk could debate to their hearts' content) of such vividly remembered (or anticipated) delights as cheese and Guinness when Sir John's internal economy begins to feel it's lunch-time. An interior monologue before a shaving-mirror is superimposed over a wireless-broadcast. The question of what to do with the cherry in one's drink looms visually large—all to somewhat bitter effect. And a parallel psychological distension of the objectively obvious continuity pervades the décor, through which runs, discreetly but palpably, an expressionistic shudder. Without doubt the slum in which the policeman's widow lives is meant as a comment on the poverties of the deserving poor—'homes fit for heroes' widows to live in'—distilling a great deal of interwar disillusionments and anxieties.

The sense of mental worlds is strengthened by the use of two plays-within-a-play, as by the deliberations of the jury. The ironies of the former hardly need comment, in these days of acute consciousness as to the metaphysics of aesthetics, the reality of illusion and the illusion of reality, but Hitchcock is still ahead of the field. One play is a tragedy, and the other a farce involving comic bobbies. The jury's arguments explore that perennial, and revealing, conflict between penological theories. Hitchcock observes, with irony, the independent-minded intellectual who astutely senses and argues for the heroine's innocence, but then weakly capitulates, whether because he's worn out by years of being odd man out and resigned to failure, or because he's an intellectual for the same reason that he's a weakling. The other partisan of the heroine's innocence is a society sentimentalist of whose fashionably optimistic ideas Hitchcock seems rightly suspicious. It's difficult to tell whether Hitchcock is performing the intellectual feat of showing a jury wrongly convicting an innocent woman to hang while making no concession to progressive penological theory, or whether he's simply creating one of those paradoxes which do so much to make the spectator hang on every word and detail, thus adding intellectual suspense to an emotional one. If the film's structure fails to complete itself, and remains something of a broken arch, it is principally because the heroine's experience remains, on the whole, an enigmatic gesture, seen from outside.

As often in Hitchcock, the dramatically and psychologically most interesting character is the one of whom we learn least. He constitutes an enigma, a mystery, towards which the detection moves, but into which it scarcely penetrates (except in a rather schematic fashion—summary revelations of motive, brief notations of mood, with all sorts of circumstantial detail as to train times and such all but smothering any profound exploration of the motives and experience of a murder). This limitation is a natural one for the whodunit genre, and explains why it tends to be a minor one.[1] But in so far as Hitchcock assents to stories which don't find ways through these limitations (as does, for example, the Simenon story which is the basis of Jean Renoir's *La Nuit de Carrefour*), one can't pretend he doesn't, particularly since in other ways he distends or junks the whodunit formula with an expertise which in the end looks like consummate ease. Were Hitchcock the penetrating moralist and psychologist he is sometimes alleged to be, he would turn these films inside out. In *Murder* we would look out at the world through the eyes of the silent suspect, and suspense would be created by whether its responsibility, concern and acumen are sufficient to save this woman from herself. Like a sphinx, she would sit in judgement on individuals, the social consensus and its processes, her own aloofness complicated, in its turn, by her desperate and masochistic inner struggle about the quality of her fiancé's love for her, her love for him, and the waste of her own life.

[1] A limitation of which Hitchcock is quite aware. Discussing *Psycho* he maintains that if it were a serious story about Norman Bates, it would be a case-history, and essentially that's quite right. As to the film's seriousness, though, this is one of the cases where the present writer would incline to agree with Hitchcock's admirers rather than Hitchcock, although Hitchcock is quite right in so far as the film isn't at all a psychological study of Norman Bates.

The film has something of this accusatory quality, of course, although only in so far as the tension implicit in any murder trial belies the cliché faith in British justice. And that often isn't very far, since the very people who most love reading tales of near-miscarriages of justice often combine their taste with 'happy accident' theories about the impossibility of bettering the *status quo* (unimpeachable exceptions being a matter of life's ineluctable tragedies and nothing to do with anything so matter-of-fact as the imperfect operation of an imperfect system which a society which passionately cared about justice would passionately care to improve, even if improvement always fell short of perfection). Equally, Hitchcock criticises the dilettante streak in the gentlemanly amateur. You can't trust the super-privileged too far either. And yet, in the end, the film allows the complacent spectator to maintain his complacency undisturbed. The girl gets off; one of those happy accidents which make this the best of all possible worlds. . . .

The dénouement depends on the murderer's weakness of will. And on an intriguing ambiguity. He killed the girl who was about to reveal his dreadful secret to his fiancée. 'He's a half-caste!' One suspects that Hitchcock in 1930 might, like his audience, have had a great deal of sympathy for the Alf Garnett response, which is hardly negligible forty years on; that though murder is never justified, a secret like that makes it rather sympathetic, although it's also typical of jungle-blood to be prone to murder people, which makes them very dangerous and contemptible, and shows why the number of half-castes should be kept to an absolute minimum, in Anglo-Saxon countries above all. And if you think I'm exaggerating just think about Herbert Lom in *North-West Frontier*, a film rather unfortunately timed to coincide with the arrival in England of Indian and Pakistan immigrants in appreciable numbers. The logic might then continue along lines whereby the girl's motive for silence is that though she still loves her lover and wants to protect him she can't bear the thought of running the risk of pro-ducing babies which might have more than a touch of the tar-brush about them and might even be as big, black and buck as those things that you catch by their toe; so that dying for him rather appeals to her as a noble solution to her dilemma.

All the same, the obscenity with which 'half-caste' is uttered seems to me to have a special edge, and since it's coupled with the assassin's feminoid edginess, hardly a big buck half-caste trait, and with his transvestite circus garb, it leaves us, sophisticates of 1970, in little doubt that 'half-caste' means 'left-handed', which means bisexual or homosexual. The play-within-the-play involves not only cops and drinks but a man in drag tied up and a lovely girl in jodhpurs and riding-boots, completing a common enough collection of symptoms, and even if pre-permissive society spectators might not have been able to spell the Kraft-Ebbing words for it there's a chance and a half that something communicated without being understood. In just the same way (and particularly given this film's recourse to the play-within-the-play as revelatory of reality), the idea that a play-within-a-play, or fancy dress, or party games, are a kind of double fiction and therefore poetically or profoundly true, 'lies like truth', is in the air as well. We don't have to read Norman Bates-as-Mom for the assassin-in-drag and Grace Kelly for the horse riding (i.e. cool, classy, domineering) young lady to feel we're in the presence of two favourite Hitchcock themes. But the interest lies not in the fetishes *per se*, at least nowadays when they're almost too well-known to be fashionable party chit-chat, but in the skill with which Hitchcock translates their psychological concomitants—embarrassment, passivity, hysteric apprehension—into, not only melodramatic suspense, but personal relationships (at their most superficial: the badinage of *The Thirty-Nine Steps*, at the more profound, the transmogrification of *Vertigo*). One may prefer the pre-permissive dissimulation to a post-permissive banality, which reduces a complex psychological predicament, abounding in nuances and half-tones and hysterias, to a label which is half-clinical, half-contemptible, yet misses all the 'atmospheric', i.e. subtle, tensions which Hitchcock's film retains.

Whether or not one substitutes another meaning for 'half-caste', the girl keeps her silence to protect a lover who is too cowardly and ungentlemanly to admit his guilt when doing so might save her. And although the paradoxes of masochism and indulgence and/or pride in that are of a kind familiar to addicts of famous trials, that very fact seems to me to dispose of two assumptions commonly made by Hitchcock's admirers, (a) that the British films don't have the psychological complexities of the American ones, and (b) that psychological complexities are rather rare at the low culture level. If anything, traditional British low culture is more aware of them than American, even though it more often checks and stunts that awareness by a fundamentalist disapproval. But I should expect that women in particular, identifying with the heroine, might wonder, during and after the film, about her mixture of motives.[1]

[1] The notion that spectators might wonder about some films sometimes isn't merely a critic's pious hope (*vide* King Vidor's absolute agreement with David

All the same, the apparently outrageous substitution of homosexuality for miscegenation seems to me to improve the film. May we
not believe that she also knew, and forgave him, his shameful, as they
both seem to believe it to be, sexual secret? Is she not giving even
her life for a man who cannot but love something or someone or a
succession of people other than her? Or were her motives icier, more
superficial, connected simply with protecting her honour, and his,
from so sordid an involvement? In the former case, the murder was
unnecessary, and was the result of the murderer's incomprehension
and paranoia (often, in Hitchcock, a temptation). In the latter case,
the film hinges on a double hypocrisy, perhaps noble, perhaps ignoble,
perhaps both—his hypocrisy towards her, her hypocrisy in obedience
to a morbidly ultra-refined notion of honour.

Although the association of transvestism with homosexuality is
a fairly easy one, and is the only one, so far as I know, to have been
suggested by critics, it is also worth remembering that it is quite
possible for the visual overtones to imply nothing more than transvestite and passive predilections or compulsions; which perhaps alters
the moral pattern again, and certainly strengthens another latent
paradox; the strong woman as victim of the weak man.

With its subjective shots, its interior monologue, its play with
social detachment, its expressionism, its camouflaged sexual problems,
its sense of pervasive prejudices intense enough to drive a sufferer to
murder, produce a kind of exteriorised introversion, a preoccupation
with mental anguish, pointing towards a universal malaise, of which
trivial and superficial details are ironically part. And it's in this
alertness to the superficial that Hitchcock can sometimes open our
eyes to the life around and within us more sharply than many an
arthouse artist, for whom the superficial is the 'merely' superficial, or
who moves in a closed circle of harmonious lyricism.

The defect of the quality is, of course, that Hitchcock often indicates,
but rarely explores, the deeper layers of existence. This makes his
films highly convenient specimens for critical detective work about

Selznick about what the latter called 'the icebox element'—the points which a
family can discuss and disagree about on returning from the film to take a midnight
snack from the icebox). The question of *whether* the average uneducated unthinking
spectator notices subtleties isn't worth discussing. What is extremely crucial, and
difficult, and therefore never discussed, is the question of which sorts get noticed,
because educated spectators don't notice them all either (which is why they
discuss films and read criticism; not to get 'the whole truth', but to be offered
some interesting and plausible ideas some of which they can accept, so adding another person's insights to their own).

motifs, undertones and patterns, and all the more so by virtue of their high degree of ambiguity. In terms of lived and fully apprehended experience, however, they may remain, not so much Potemkin villages, as Potemkin submarines—a fleet of periscopes without hulls.

The Skin Game

The Skin Game is another photographed play, less enclosed than *Juno and the Paycock*. To write about it is to find oneself writing about Galsworthy rather than Hitchcock. Class is the only theme they have in common, central in one and reticent in the other, perhaps because downhill for Galsworthy is uphill for Hitchcock. Like the O'Casey, the play is particularly interesting in its record of an era whose particular style has passed, so that the film is particularly interesting in its record of a period conception of the play.

This may seem an ominous justification, so often advanced in connection with cinematographically passive or ham-fisted adaptations of edifying, i.e. extinct, classics, by prestige-bound theatrical companies. The implication is that one is somehow helping the cinema and its spectators gently up the slopes of Parnassus by entrusting to it the performances of theatrical knights; and honouring posterity by recording them for its edification.

But if past experience is any guide, posterity will be rather more disrespectful of the present than the present expects, or will be impressed for reasons which we'll be unable to understand, let alone anticipate. One can be a witness before posterity, but as posterity is only a series of presents it's as subject to whims and injustices as an artist's own time. It's a series of alternative courts of appeal, but hardly an oracle.

Hitchcock's film seems to me to be of the greatest interest, not only because Galsworthy's play can still involve us in its drama and carry us along, but because the film reproduces so many attitudes of a period roughly contemporaneous with the play, and quite without the falsities of cultural elevation. Indeed, Hitchcock slightly alters its social perspective. Galsworthy, a Forsyte by class, began by trying to criticise his kind, but ended up by admiring them; after Soames dies, what is there? And what he constantly opposes to their middle-class money-consciousness is the gentlemanly responsibility of the upper classes. He insists, also, on the restrained, but lurking, brutality of the upper classes especially when they're at bay. But to be at bay is a considerable extenuation. And what Galsworthy, a middle-class idealist, and innocent, never quite realised, although he almost realised, was that gentlemanly responsibility was imposed on the court and the gentry by, principally, a combination of factors, first, the challenge which the Forsytes' wealth and influence posed, second, the humanitarian side of a nonconformist conscience, and third, various strategical considerations very schematically outlined in *A Mirror for England*. Hitchcock can be ironical about this kind of moral deference, and rather less trusting than Galsworthy.

The Skin Game shows Hillcrest the gentlemanly landowner (C. V. France) at bay against Hornblow the coarse pushing industrialist (Edmund Gwenn). The names couldn't be more appropriate: lyrical rolling countryside, essentially modest—hills not mountains, versus the clamorous and militant bragging of own-trumpet-blowing. One might well suspect that in socially more accurate terms, Hillcrest had long ago sold large tracts of his estate to buy Hornblow shares, and had become his co-director, and that Galsworthy is transposing into the idealistic terms of a radical socio-moral conflict what is really a sharp but minor readjustment between fellow-travellers. He hints as much by the eventual marriage of the second generation (a cynic might comment that Montagu-and-Capulet true love is an emollient euphemism for the phrase 'thick as thieves'). Hitchcock, albeit cautiously, shifts to a slightly new perspective—to a worm's-eye-view. A special intensity invests the vignette of a lowly old cottager who mutters, to Hornblow's credit, 'They're putting electric light in the village now'. The Hillcrests claim to be on the financial ropes, but their Rolls-Royce is bigger than the Hornblows'. Lady Hillcrest is that much less concerned with her social responsibilities than her husband, and that much more of an honest bitch. The cottagers' obsequious gratitude to the Hillcrests, whereas it's Hornblow who's bringing them the electricity, is more than a little ambiguity—are they displaying a touching loyalty to the best in Olde England, or just biters of the hand that might feed them? With the same prudence as evidenced in *Downhill*, we're edged towards a reminder that the 'third world' whose fate the Hillcrests and Hornblows are deciding, is not a few doddering old yokels, but the other ninety per cent of the English people. The absence of lyrical countryside shots may well have been dictated by productorial thrift or indigence, but Hitchcock makes no effort at all to present the Hillcrests' love of their view as anything more proprietorial, and refuses to relax his focus into any sentimental fuzziness.

In some of the stagier scenes one may suspect that Hitchcock has let his actors run away with him—or are we confronted with bold personal styles appropriate to era and type? He has to deal with undoubted contrivances, like split-second entries and exits through the French windows, and characters dodging behind curtains just in time to overhear vital conversations. It's not surprising that he tends to vary the drama by setting several scenes, which are really interiors, in and around motor-cars. The bunching of the actors is often somewhat ungainly. (One wonders if the alterations in the screenshape which occurred around the time of the introduction of talkies were giving the same problems with composition which later recurred with wide-screen ratios.) He certainly scores some cinematic six-hits—notably the auction, with the cutting flashing and the camera zip-panning from one bidder to another; certain close-ups of George Bancroft's face smashing into close-up; and the cinematisation of stage dialogue by overlaying the pain-inflicting voice on the listener's silent face (which, after all, is a very logical way of doing things). It's an edgy, erratic, yet involving film, tattier, no doubt, but of infinitely greater interest, than, say, *The Paradine Case* (another 'talkie') twenty-odd years later.

Rich and Strange

Rich and Strange was a throwback to Hitchcock's romantic period, and, apparently, a box office flop in its time. In retrospect, it appears as one of his most thoughtful films. It centres on a suburban couple (Harry Kendall, Joan Barry), who are calmly bored with their life's routine and with each other. They come into a small inheritance and go on a world cruise, to taste a little high life and adventure. She is courted by an English gentleman (Percy Marmont) whom she doesn't treat too kindly (the meanness of the 'innocent' towards the more worldly provides another variation on the waif-bitch heroine in *The Pleasure Garden*, and, perhaps, the stabbing of the seducer by the virgin in *Blackmail*). The too complacent husband has a romance with an exotic Princess (Betty Amann). But she's merely an adventuress exploiting the gullibility that goes with his vanity, and runs off with all his money. His wife, offended rather than hurt, is easily able to forgive him. They're shipwrecked, menaced by Chinese pirates, confronted by death, and, while confronting it, find something more than companionship: comradeship. They return at last to their familiar sitting-room in their cosy semi-detached. They settle in their arm-chairs by the open coal fire once more, and switch on the wireless. The gale warning reminds them of the shipwreck, and they briefly shiver reminiscently. But that's all. They have settled again into their cosy old rut, a little more disillusioned with each other, but just as bored, and certainly no wiser about life, love, death, existence. They've gone round the world in a grey flannel bathysphere.

The same story, with the characters suffering from, rather than expecting nothing other than, this meaninglessness, would bring one right into the Antonioni world: *The Ship Wreck*, instead of *Blow-Up*. As was suggested in *A Mirror for England*, a book whose themes, this, for obvious reasons, intermittently approaches, English enter-tainment shows an early awareness of the absurd, and it isn't difficult to moralize over *Rich and Strange* (as, later, *Vertigo*, *North-by-North-West*, etc.) in a Sartrian way. The couple are immured in the bad faith of 'invincible indifference', the iron curtain of complacency lifting in an extreme situation and dropping imperceptibly and herme-tically once more. And each will die without having 'suspected what the other is'.

One can imagine a film which saw such realities, without melo-drama, in the exotic, or perhaps even without it; in which the world's cruelty found, as scapegoat, not a cat skinned and eaten by Chinese pirates, but something more diffuse and nearer home. Yet the com-parison of contentment's grey blur and alternatives which, by impli-cation, exist beneath as well as beyond, is effective, and the mean vanities of the denizens of semi-detachedom are only the one-tenth of the iceberg. It's a thousand pities that the critical consensus fastened on a minor amusement like *The Thirty-Nine Steps*, rather than this, as their notion of a good Hitchcock movie.

No. 17

After *Rich and Strange*, which was neither a critical nor a commercial success, Hitchcock was perhaps under productorial and other pressures, and has since accused himself of a certain lack of dis-cipline in response to a subject confronted with which he might well have felt his heart sink a little. None the less, he makes a very free adaptation of an ingratiating comedy-thriller by J. Jefferson Farjeon, although little but the title, a tramp and the idea of continent-bound trains passing a deserted house and being handy for smuggling links

No. 17 with its original. The novel, by now, is an amiable curio
about a comic Cockney tramp who's frightened of his own shadow
and wheezes obsequiously in the 'Corluvaduckguv' idiom. It seems a
little less amiable when one matches it with another detective thriller,
Tiger in the Smoke, with its sinister band of ex-service tramps. Farjeon's novel appeared at a time (1926) when the kerbs were littered,
so to speak, with thousands of injured, or healthy, ex-soldiers unemployed through no fault of their own, but simply due to the stagnation of the economy. Farjeon's tramp, rascally but happy, makes
everyone feel quite a bit better.

Hitchcock seems relatively bored by Farjeon's old Ben, 'the glory
of the Merchant Service . . . late of the Merchant Service . . . of the
Merchant service', who 'was not in love with work. The stomach,
however, drives.' He's lumbered with him, as incarnated by Leon M.
Lion, on whose joint stage adaptation Farjeon's novel was based,
and he has to devote a fair amount of preliminary footage to him, but
he doesn't seem very interested, maybe because he's a distinctly
problematic identification figure by conventional movie formulae,
maybe because the problem of deference seems beyond redemption.
In retrospect the most vivid enjoyment of all the scenes in the scarey
empty house, quaking as the trains thunder by, is a jocular but really
rather lyrical touch of bondage, with a girl and a man left tied by their
wrists to hang, in the dark, from creaking first-floor banisters, in a
deserted house, climaxed by, later, a girl handcuffed and nearly
drowned in a sinking railway wagon. A sinking railway wagon!?
Hitchcock has thrown the whole second half of the novel out and
substituted a spirited cross-country chase between an eventually altogether out of control goods train and an abducted Green Line coach
packed with variously meek or outraged fare-paying passengers, until
eventually locomotive, tender, and wagon after wagon go thundering
wildly on to the cross-channel ferry, sinking it, in one of the most
sustained, varied and exhilarating disasters in movies. That train,
coach, ferry and all are clearly models doesn't spoil things in the least,
our natural preference for large-scale and genuine catastrophes being
compensated for by nostalgic references to Hornby Trains and Dinky
Toys, all taking on the curious artificiality of a dream, like a Trinka
puppet film. The movie has all it takes to become a camp cult, and
something more, something strangely precious, distilling a kind of
essence of childhood pulp, producing an effect which isn't precisely
capital-P-Pop art and isn't quite capital-Quaint-Camp, but something
much nearer the pleasure of *The Penguin Book of Comics*, where the

question of what's good small-p-popular art is counterpointed by its affinity with what is cheapjack but alive, and one can relish a semi-participative enjoyment of past pop art. What isn't very good is far from all bad, and a kind of vivid mediocrity can have its charms—and by which one needn't be abashed of being charmed.

Lord Camber's Ladies

No. 17, a conspicuously low-budget production, in accordance, apparently, with B.I.P.'s failing fortunes, was followed by a production credit on what Hitchcock describes as a quota quickie, although its stars were Gertrude Lawrence and Gerald du Maurier. *Lord Camber's Ladies* was 'a poison thing. I gave it to Benn Levy to direct.'

Waltzes from Vienna

Hitchcock's last film before moving to Gaumont-British was *Waltzes from Vienna*, and he described it as 'my lowest ebb. A musical and they couldn't really afford the music.' The operetta story pits Johann Strauss the Younger against Johann Strauss the Elder (Edmund Gwenn) in Old Vienna. The stylised operetta-musical comedy form had displayed splendid filmic potential in such films as Erik Charell's *Congress Dances*, René Clair's *Sous Les Toits de Paris*, and Ernst Lubitsch's *One Hour With You*.

Hitchcock's style has some odd affinities with Lubitsch. Both have a 'touch', that is, a fondness for emphasis by symbolic detail or sprightly ellipse, both relish artificiality, both achieve a linear clarity of style, a clear melody, with subtleties boldly centred in a smooth continuity. If Hitchcock isn't really successful in light comedy unless it also involves suspense, it's perhaps because his light touch entails a dryness which needs continuing undertones if it is not to sag. It's interesting to consider Lubitsch's one Hollywood drama, *The Man I Killed*, and his black suspense comedy, *To Be Or Not To Be*, as Hitchcock might have handled them, and Hitchcock's one bright comedy, *Mr. and Mrs. Smith*, as a Lubitsch film. Where Lubitsch infected his actors with a light, smooth, rippling buoyancy, *Waltzes from Vienna* prefers heavy exterior jokes, e.g., Strauss deriving inspiration from the sounds of pastry-making; a slammed door replacing the blare of the orchestra beyond it by the warble of the lady soprano on the nearer side, or mischievous mannequins taking their cue from the sound of a military band in the street below and marching instead of mincing in.

The camera is extremely mobile, as often in the early '30s. Thus two men separate after a conversation, and the camera tracks back with the man walking towards us while the other walks away into deep focus. The effect isn't of his being forgotten, but of a symmetrical, patterned splitting. The film enjoys bold clear sets, creamily-lit cleavage, and Jessie Matthews's spirited middle-class miss, while Hitchcock maintains his intimations of surliness, sycophancy or smooth independence on the part of the lower orders. Domestics kiss while conveying orders (foretaste of *Notorious*). A 'chorus' of charladies lift their heads to watch a kiss (premonitions of *Rear Window*?). And a flunkey asks 'Will that be all, sir?' after being kicked downstairs. In fact a variety of Hitchcock motifs amble, rather than waltz, about, looking for a context, like the duelling Count saying 'I killed my man!' as he opens his fist to investigate a fly which he's just snatched from the air (*Psycho*).

CHAPTER 5

The Man Who Knew Too Much / The Thirty-Nine Steps / Secret Agent / Sabotage / Young and Innocent / The Lady Vanishes / Jamaica Inn

The Man Who Knew Too Much

Hitchcock's first Gaumont-British film, although his second for Gaumont release, inaugurated the group of characteristic suspense thrillers. *The Man Who Knew Too Much* is the first Hitchcock film to involve gangs and spies and picaresque pursuits, a mixture which became his trademark for a while. Its similarities and dissimilarities with the later version make a handy battleground for 'early' versus 'late' Hitchcockians. Or it would have done if the former had got around to discussing anything with the latter. The first is faster, more irrational, and sports a poetic flair for the bizarre, while the latter is more elaborate, not to say plodding, in its identifications and its tourist appeal. Hitchcock told Truffaut that he was attracted to the first version because of its contrasts of background—white ski resorts and black slums, Alpine peaks and back streets—while, for the American audience, he reinforced the sentimental aspects. He claims to prefer the remake because the original is structurally slipshod and less 'professional'. For which very reason I prefer the original, as more humorous, spontaneous, poetic and avant-garde.

Given the chopping and changing of locale, continuity certainly isn't its strong point, and its suspense veers erratically from the intense to the inexistent, when humour takes over. Will the nice English couple recover their child from the kidnappers who are holding him hostage to ensure her silence about an impending political assassination during an Albert Hall concert? Understandably, from the entertainment viewpoint, the moral dilemma—child versus history versus morality—is, if not quite obliterated, at least left to linger under a mixture of suspense, humour and an inspiriting heartiness. Bulldog Dad (Leslie Banks), hot on the track, achieves several of the zany turnabouts which real life denies us. The menacing dentist is forcibly anaesthetised in his own chair. In the Tabernacle of the Sun, a thinly cranky disguise for the drab piety of back-street nonconformism, the sleuthing hero and his pal do all the things our childish irreverence dreamed of during those long and dingy services. They sing burlesque words to the hymns, they put their hat on top of the Holy Bible, start a fight and hurl the stacked chairs at the deacons. Of course, they have to pay the wages of sin—the crab-mouthed old lady makes them drop their guns into the collection-plate—but at least the labourer is worthy of his hire.

The intercutting of a man's death with the heroine's knitting breaking a thread seemed to Hitchcock, in retrospect, pretentious ('It's the thread of life breaking'). Yet its juxtaposition of the domestic and the sinister, with a young mother as the fates, recalls *Rich and Strange*, and in its context has that callousness of triviality which is a recurrent Hitchcockian motif. The final shoot-out, inspired by the Sidney Street siege, takes us in and out of shabby little homes as the police take up their positions. And Hitchcock's eye for details looks forward to Jennings's—the mattresses, the wallpapers, the backchat—'Bed's still warm'—acquiring the dour intimacy which becomes central to *Sabotage*.

It's just a little too obviously a fun film to make the most of its darker, more terrifying—and therefore its human—side. Nova Pilbeam and Peter Lorre attain, at moments, a deeper intensity. Its broken family—mother one place, daddy gone a-sleuthing, child a prisoner—creates constructional and dramatic problems also, which Hitchcock doesn't quite manage to solve, and which all but prohibits the paradoxical relationships of *Sabotage*. A useful test is to consider it as a Western; and then its story becomes rather a run-of-the-mill affair. Obviously the story, thus isolated, isn't the whole story. Hitchcock declared that much of its inspiration came from the interplay of backgrounds and the interplay of the story, the social setting and the backgrounds, which have a Populist poetry to them, makes out of what might have a melodrama a poetic melodrama—which is an altogether more poignant and beautiful thing. But artistically, I should consider it a rough sketch for *Sabotage*, where a child is also at risk, and threatened from a very different quarter.

It seems to me that the theme for which the film gropes, perhaps intuitively, perhaps despite itself, is that of private anguish versus public lies. A similar theme reappears in *Sabotage*. Both films recall, in one way, the pre-World War I anarchists, and in another, contemporary spies, mirroring the rise of European Fascism. Hitler had come to power in 1933, probably a little after Hitchcock wrote the original story, but Hitler's threats were already headline news, Mussolini's menaces were inflating, a sense of intensifying European hostilities was already in the air, and the aftermath of the General Strike had sustained the Bolshevik bogey. From one angle, these foreign spies are a kind of non-controversial scapegoat to decontroversialise the contrast between (a) a middle-class couple who have affluent holidays in Switzerland or Austria and buy expensive toy-trains for their child to run on an expensive carpet, and (b) some maleficent atmosphere arising from back-street chapels, cells and plottings. The visual contrast of the settings is craving to become a social contrast also. From another angle, foreign spies offer a highly plausible, and not altogether irrelevant, alternative explanation, since assassination wasn't exactly unknown in European politics; and just to make everything more plausible, the Sidney Street siege had thoroughly embedded itself into popular folklore, so that people who were unworried about Europe had that to fall back on. A mixture of references like that is sufficiently common in entertainment. Lilian Winstanley has suggested that Shakespear does exactly the same with certain conspicuous details surrounding the murders in *Macbeth*, some being reminiscent of the Gunpowder Plot, and others of the St. Bartholomew's Massacre. Obviously such reminiscences both thicken the asssociations and lend a familiarity like historical authentication, with, in Hitchcock's case, a further advantage; every spectator selects only those analogies which he cares to see. To select certain reminiscences as rigid analogies is to misunderstand them, even though the film-makers may be quite happy for spectators to do so, provided that their readings don't get them into trouble with censors and controversies. Sometimes again, a film-maker may wish to point a moral, even if only in the negative sense of confirming the attitudes of those sufficiently in tune with the film's message, without obtruding on the enjoyment of those who would resent it. In the case of *The Man Who Knew Too Much*, any disruptions of sympathy introduced will be overwhelmed, if they are not first averted, by the combination of the patriotic, the middle-class ideal (which is also accepted as a symbol for ordinary Englishness), the most dashing, sensitive, generous and suffering characters, and our most continuous identifications.

All the same, the semi-detached couple of *Rich and Strange*, who go round the world and learn nothing at all, are replaced by the tourist couple who come home to find that European political intrigues have taken their child. Ask not for whom the cymbals clash; they clash for thee. In *Sabotage*, two years later, the division strikes home. The menaced child is killed, and husband and wife find themselves on opposite sides of the terrorist fence. The earlier film sails, at least, into a political atmosphere. The assassination is a political one, and the plot involves us in deceptive places of assembly (the Tabernacle, the Albert Hall). The climax, based on the Sidney Street siege, also suggests a militarisation of the civilian atmosphere, and in the years of Oswald Mosley's marches the censor was, as Hitchcock recounts, so extremely sensitive to the political overtones of the arming of the police that he insisted they be shown as unfamiliar with firearms.

It's easy to imagine a *tragic* version of *The Man Who Knew Too Much*. The couple, like Britain in the early '30s, put domestic matters before European involvements. They allow the spies to assassinate the statesman, just as Britain allowed Hitler to assassinate Czechoslovakia. And they lose their child anyway, because no man is an island. All in all, Hitchcock shies away from such grim possibilities, and even from the story's obvious focus, family and conscience. The result is that the film never quite finds the theme for which, via an intense atmosphere, it none the less gropes: the theme of private involvement in apparently remote politics, bringing civic anarchy in their train. But it is possible, after all, that the wife's cry of warning was meant as exemplary, and that Hitchcock, or his producers (one of whom was the Communist Ivor Montagu), sensing that England was sinking into dispirited appeasement, intended the film as a self-falsifying prophecy.[1]

The Thirty-Nine Steps

Meanwhile, however, Hitchcock turned to a novel by John Buchan, whom he regards as a master of narrative. The screen version of *The Thirty-Nine Steps* relates to its original even less closely than *Joe Macbeth* to *Macbeth*, and should perhaps be described as '*un hommage à John Buchan*' rather than an adaptation of him. As often, Hitchcock, here confiding to Peter Bogdanovich, is his own best critic: 'What I liked about *The Thirty-Nine Steps* were the sudden switches

---

[1] A function, and a category, which pose considerable problems to the common equation of social or ideological commitment with realism.

and the jumping from one situation to another with such rapidity. Donat leaping out of the window of the police station with half of a handcuff on, and immediately walking into a Salvation Army band, darting down an alleyway into a room. "Thank God you've come, Mr. So and So," they say and put him on to a platform. A girl comes along with two men, takes him into a car to the police station, but it's not really to the police-station. . . . You know the rapidity of their switches, that's the great thing about it. If I did *The Thirty-Nine Steps* again, I would stick to the formula, but it really takes a lot of work. You have to use one idea after another, and with such rapidity. . . .'

The price of such rapidity, here, is superficiality. The corners Donat's in are tight enough, but his manner's distinctly 'Anyone-for-tennis?' with just a touch of dapper grit. In post-war thrillers Richard Todd is his successor, and our reference is to the roles rather than the actors. But just because it's so light and easy, this has among older critics a king of unofficial reputation as 'the' Hitchcock film, maybe because of the direct cut between a woman's scream, as she discovers a murdered body, and the locomotive's whistle bearing the fugitive away. It's worth looking at the relationship between this film and the more authentic tensions between a tragic-paranoid vision and its antithesis which are Hitchcock's profounder inspiration. In *The Lodger* and *Blackmail*, the stress lies on the apparent or hidden guilt of an ordinary person, in intimate surroundings, and in this respect the later Hollywood films mark a *return* to these pre-spy thrillers. The stress on secret agents appears only with the escalation of the Nazi threat in Europe. The spies here wear leather (Gestapo) coats, their network interpenetrates the English scene (fifth column scares), and their agents include both a squirearchical character almost as charming and gracious as Sir Oswald Mosley and an old-fashioned drill-sergeant type character who might be seen as an extremist combination of Populist militarism and the classic right, groups which in France were succumbing to the Fascist lure.

There's no reason to suppose that any of this is accidental or innocent (words hardly applicable to Hitchcock's artistic procedure). Maybe he's merely evoking topical imagery to make his villains plausible and frightening without having to dwell on them at length and slow the pace. But it's quite on the cards that all this was meant as a (badly needed) nudge to the effect that Nazi nastiness might even happen here, from a combination of inside and outside influence—making, in this respect, a sharper point than *The Man Who Knew Too Much*, whose crooks are cranks. The sinister range and influence of the agents here take on a sharper contrast, fortuitously perhaps, with the political meeting at which Donat, hiding his half-handcuff, has to speak. Having no idea of which party or candidate he's supporting, he improvises, desperately, stirring generalisations of the utmost ambiguity and uselessness. He is loudly applauded, the scene thus commenting on the idiocy of political rhetoric, and of the political process, in this democracy. *The Lady Vanishes* and *Lifeboat* go on to make, more explicitly still, similar points about the confusion and vapidity within the democratic creed.

It's a thousand pities that some such meaning, of unity-and-disunity, wasn't extended to the film's admirable central idea, the handcuffing of hero (Robert Donat) and heroine (Madeleine Carroll). As it is, his unfortunate fellow-traveller suspects him of being a murderer, fears for her life and wants to hand him over to the police, forcing him to a little gentle terrorism in her direction. And their plight offers a perfect image for democratic dissent—they're very equal, they have free speech, they're both in the same (life)boat—and their interests are antagonistic, it's pull-devil-pull-baker. Each is tyrant of the other. Unity is paralysis. All it needs, to arrive at a political equivalent of the racial theme of *The Defiant Ones*, is to convert the hero into a miner's son and the heroine into a Mayfair playgirl who under the influence of her beloved uncle thinks she's a Fascist, until she learns he's a Quisling. And a minor enigma begs to be explored in a way which leads us to the same situation. The complex technical details of Britain's secret McGuffin are transmitted to the enemy via the perfect recall of a music hall artiste, Mr. Memory. A classic Edwardian regular soldier, his style was formed in the days of wax-tipped moustaches; and how did he come to be working for foreigners whose treasonable intent he could not but suspect?—indeed, as he lies dying, he murmurs, 'It's a load off my mind, sir.' Is his a tale of desperation in unemployed old age? of bitterness about 'homes fit for heroes'? of simple loyalties misled by ultra-Empire Loyalists? Like the most interesting stories in Hitchcock, it's just the story that Hitchcock's mystery story approach hides from us, and I don't think it's an accident that it could be wrapped up very neatly. Before the war he was influenced by the preparations for the Ulster Rebellion. In those days he stood firm, neither aiding the conspirators nor, since they were his senior officers, denouncing them. But the idea of subversion against the Crown lost its horror for him. During the War he was R.S.M. to the regimental adjutant, who was the Squire. And when retirement and unemployment came, it was easy for his commanding officer to help his family financially and promise him a Britain purged of slackers and Bolshies, a Britain where strikers would be drafted into the army, to the nation's and their own benefit, while hiding from him the influence of foreign agents and foreign ideas. Thus this Sergeant Pepper became a Nowhere Man. . . .

The sexual overtones, too, are strengthened rather than weakened if one uses hero and heroine as images for different classes, with the upper-class girl having to steel herself to side with the offensive, 'criminal', lower orders against the authoritarian principle which, in Germany, had come to the support of Nazism; one then arrives at the lady-and-the-groom relationship which was to inspire *The Paradine Case* and *Under Capricorn*. Evidently the cool, aloof, 'Grace Kelly' type, ice above and fire below, relates, it seems, to the image of the superior lady. It's not only in *The Skin Game* and *The Manxman*, in *The Lodger* and *Blackmail* that class rears its hydra head.

In *The Thirty-Nine Steps*, however, a conflict of social values is adumbrated only in safely non-controversial terms, in the encounter between the London sophisticates and John Laurie as a righteous crofter and his lonely wife. There's social comment, in the broadest sense only, in such asides as the commercial travellers and their scatological chat, the aged clergyman peering at the bra they're peddling—familiar jokes given a seedy reality. They and the crofter's home typify two contrasted creeds, the old, rural, thrifty Puritan ethic and the matter-of-fact mixture of Mammon and titillation later to loom rather larger everywhere from underground escalators to Bunny Clubs. Misplaced trust in the apparent values of public places (political meeting, music hall, fete) is played off against, this time, more intimate mistrust (between hero and heroine); while the commercial travellers and the crofter's home typify the smaller furtiveness, hypocrisies and ignominies of settled private lives. The truth is told by a German refugee whom the hero, like the audience, might be inclined to distrust; and the hero, unlike the woman who knows too much, doesn't save her: the locomotive whistle cancels out the mother's cry. Later, the fifth columnist's ladylike wife looks in to announce dinner and splendidly doesn't notice the gun her husband is pointing at their hapless guest. It's sufficiently 'English tact', or rather, English not-noticing, to suggest something about *sang-froid* being bad faith rather than English wonderfulness. 'You must trust those "hysterical" German Jewish refugees, not your squire-and-his-lady!' All the same, Donat-Hannay's smooth brio finishes by vindicating what Hitchcock briefly queries.

The film has a relatively weak thematic unity, artistically, since the different sets of values implied in the different confrontations convey nothing to the hero as he goes along and hardly comment on one another; if they did they would balance one another in such a way as to cancel out. It's true that the bible which Donat gets from the Scottish crofter stops a bullet and saves a life. But the irony could work either way. The Bible belt moral would be, 'Ah, you see, the sophisticated man-about-town owes much, after all, to rural fundamentalism, whatever the latter's faults and sufferings may be; because where God is involved there's no such thing as accident or coincidence or chance.' A more worldly moral might be that if God's Bible saves the sophisticated man-about-town it must be because God helps those who help themselves and doesn't think men-about-town any less worthy of little miracles than Scottish crofters. Or the moral might be be felt that since Donat's attitudes are closer to our identification, then little checks to his assumptions count for more than the objectively speaking thoroughly unhappy life the crofter leads his wife. How many moral meanings can dance on the head of a contrast? Almost as many as there are spectators.

With only a little more moral seriousness to connect his tactfully separated touches, and topped by some gradually accumulating *crise de conscience* in Hannay himself, Hitchcock might have produced a caustic insight into the British character *circa* Munich. But all his films, up to and including *Jamaica Inn*, renounce a kind of psycho-cultural relevance which it is not too much to expect from entertainment, let alone art. For all that, Hitchcock's Britain wears a great deal better than Ealing's, perhaps because so much slicker, less pretentious, and less complacent. One need only compare the vigorous and bleak music-hall atmosphere here with Ealing's *Champagne Charlie* (1944). Hitchcock's have a first-rate journalistic, and perhaps artistic, weight and sharpness compared to which Ealing's *ersatz* gusto is a thin, watery, pasteurised middle-class beverage. Equally, Ealing's confirmed celibacy (with domesticity a sort of celibacy for two, and courtship a tiff-but-no-tickle no-man's-land) says vastly less about the tensions of English togetherness than this film's ironies of imposed sexual intimacy.

Those handcuffs convert togetherness into a reciprocal restrictive treatment full of Siamese twin torments. Each time he gestures at her he waves her hand too, in limp, idiot mockery, and although he can't get rid of her he has to show her every consideration. She adjusts her stockings and his hands follow hers; Tantalus never had it worse.

Scenes omitted on the screen, but not necessarily in our minds, concern their toilet arrangements, and their nights—when either wants to turn over in bed the other has to roll over him. Ah, sweet pain.

The establishment of recurrent motifs is a prevalent concern of *auteur* theory, and suits Hitchcock's work almost too well; for there's a sense in which all his situations are permutations of one another. His movies interlink like paper-chains, or, if the idea of progression is made too emphatic by that metaphor, that of rings that can be shuffled around a ring, may serve to counter-balance it. His remark to Truffaut, that one makes the same film again all the time, shows that he is perfectly aware of this, and corresponds to a remark of Renoir's. In his almost unique mixture of tragic-paranoid themes and picaresque genres, he creates a kind of sub-, or neo-, or anti-Surrealism, in which persecutory fantasy and concisely summarised reality intriguingly interpenetrate. The nun and the village square are enemy agents, the lounge lizard is your guardian angel, Green Line coaches are commandeered by smugglers, and even those who aren't villains will betray you to the injustice of justice; because the devil's at your heels but the hounds of heaven are just as ferocious and they're not just sheepdogs rounding you up to safely graze. One says sub-, or neo-, or anti-, Surrealism, because the predominance of chance and terror is such as to counsel prudence. The bourgeois order isn't absurder than any other and it's less absurd than some. Hitchcock bets on it in the same way as, and with the same intensity as, Pascal bets on God. Occasionally this intensity comes through, but rarely with the awful clarity of its appearance in, to take only two of an infinite variety of ways, Asquith's *A Cottage on Dartmoor* (1927) and Clouzot's *Quai des Orfèvres* (1947).

Asquith's tender little piece enshrines the extraordinary sequence where a barber's assistant shaves his boorish, well-to-do and successful rival for the girl he loves—Comstock shaves Hornblow—and gradually surrenders to the temptation to cut his throat. A brilliantly edited sequences makes every gesture, every detail, a revelation of the nightmarishness held at bay within the sensitive, underlines the terrible necessity of self-respression and the utter precariousness of trust. Suavely the sequence indicates the romantic sentimentality underlining the hope of a truly Surrealist life, as of the '60s' sentimental toying with the notion of violence as freedom. For in the world advocated by the hero of the Marat-Sade (who is not Marat but Sade), you couldn't even go for a shave in case the barber disliked the shape of your nose, and anyone who says that Sade didn't mean to extol arbitrary violence relished for its own sake is reducing him to an impenetrable rhetorician who is a Tolstoy at heart. The scene in *The Man Who Knew Too Much* between dentist and patient is a melo-dramatically escapist, and morally far weaker, equivalent of the Asquith scene, which not only anticipates the characteristic Hitchcock, but is ultra-Hitchcock in its perfect and devastating integration of everyday realism, emotional sobriety, and nightmare.

In *Quai des Orfèvres* the mediocre, dull, consciously inferior husband of a glamorous and flighty wife follows her to a rendezvous with a lecherous producer—finding his wife flown and the producer dead. Thus mistrust leads to relief and a deeper danger—in, if you like, the Jansenist tradition. Clumsily endeavouring to protect the woman whom he believes guilty of murder, the husband manœuvres so ineptly that eventually the blood from his cut throat flows under the door of his cell while Christmas bells ring and an amiable tart reminisces in the adjoining cell. The shift from the everyday to life's hideous potential is made without recourse to melodramatic clichés which are at best abstractions—artistic McGuffins—and therefore distractions, and at worst banalities.

Secret Agent

The dapper heroics of *The Thirty-Nine Steps* offer, however, another aspect, which Hitchcock's next film sets out to find (or just finds). What if heroism is shorn of its easy levity, and is a little more sensibly less willing; if it had to be, not passive (flight from murder) but active (murder), and concludes by an incomplete expiation of its guilts? *Secret Agent* (based on Somerset Maugham's *Ashenden*) goes through the looking glass of first-class tourism into an espionage world which resembles it as 'la zone' resembles the real world of *Orphée*. In a few scenes, and moments within the scenes, a black hard mood catches this eerie and unwelcome alloy of freedom and guilt. The love-hate badinage and the pursuits which once offered audiences thrills leavened with comic relief have now, perhaps, mellowed, and softened; for, more sophisticated now, after World War II and saturation by television, we know villains never catch principal heroes, except in *Psycho*, and, even since *Psycho*, no villain has ever caught a dapper principal hero unless the hero was a villain too.

None the less, Hitchcock's film has its quieter, internal movement, from espionage as patriotic fun to espionage as sickmaking duty. Ashenden (John Gielgud) reports for duty and finds himself looking down into his own open coffin. This introduces his preliminary briefing, and Jean Douchet might have made rather more than he does of this posthumous, Orphic preliminary. His mission is to find an enemy agent, to which end he is offered a smart Alpine holiday, and, as cover (purely), a pretty young wife, Madeleine Carroll, whose connubial duties are to be apparent but not real (Tantalus again). A second colleague, or accomplice, is professional assassin Peter Lorre (surely some subdemon being offered a chance of self-redemption by the powers of good?).

After the delicious torments of false intimacy (that recurrent Hitch-cock theme), Ashenden finds his quarry, an amiable English gentleman (Percy Marmont). And once dead, he turns out to have been innocent indeed. The chase begins again, and the agent turns out to be the affable American (Robert Young), whose love for the 'wife' is, it would seem, not false. (Here, clearly, Hitchcock's agent has no poli-tical overtone, and it's entirely up to the critic whether he chooses to see in the idea of an ugly American an apolitical but effective surprise or Hitchcock's affirmation of Macchiavellian mistrust as the political, and, perhaps, personal norm. The switch must have been particularly piquant for American audiences, although without any major spiritual sharpness, given their countryman's secondary or tertiary position in the hierarchy, or perspective, of identifications. Presumably the over-all impact of the twist is that surprises never cease and you can't be too careful and you never know who to trust and complacency is debility, and just when trust becomes complacency is one of those agonising questions where neither intuition nor rule can be, and the circle is vicious, trusted). The assassin looks forward to killing him with a happy humour which doesn't leave us easy, even though Peter Lorre is a very un-British British agent, his quarry is treacherous, and the usual thriller ending supervenes.

The 'teaser' opening (a mystified man-about-town peering down into his own coffin) prefigures *The Avengers*, and the movie occupies an odd spiritual territory between that and Asquith's *Orders To Kill* (which is its dramatically profounder late twin; the titles interchange perfectly). The emotional network is rather more profound than in its two predecessors. Ashenden, the assassin, and the real villain, all hanker after the girl. The girl spares the villain, who mortally wounds his assassin. Thus the too-sentimental girl spares her smooth enemy to destroy her bizarre friend. Just as the villains in *North-by-North-*

West are, as Hitchcock said, one man split into three, so Peter Lorre's anxiously ingratiating little wog or greaser sadist is the other face of His Majesty's Secret Service. The quality of moral doubt might have reached the intensity of Jack Lee's *Circle of Deception* or the Asquith film *if* (to invent one of many different possibilities) Percy Marmont had expressed horror at his younger fellow-Englishman's readiness to kill in cold blood even before realising he himself was the designated victim; if the Mexican had been replaced by a typical British type of sadist; if Ashenden had felt himself being, not merely an easy accomplice of the crime, but, vicariously, its perpetrator. As it is, the film's atmosphere has something of this effect, even though the storyline doesn't, because Truffaut and Hitchcock, in discussing it, both forget that the villain is shot by the Mexican, and not, as they agree, by Ashenden himself (unless the admittedly imperfect copy which I saw was misleading in this respect too).

Hitchcock remarked to Bogdanovich, 'You can't root for a hero who doesn't want to be a hero. So that's a negative thing. I think that's why it didn't really succeed.' In the longer Truffaut interview, he added, 'There was too much irony, too many twists of fate . . . when the hero finally agrees to do the killing, he botches the job by killing the wrong man. From the public's point of view, that was bad.' And maybe Hitchcock is right; but it's interesting that it's just those points which we select as marking the film's superiority to the immensely popular *The Thirty-Nine Steps*, and that they turn up as the central dramatic issue, intensely and frankly handled, in the post-war films by other directors. One may well experience a certain surprise that these didn't interest the devotees of Hitchcock the 'chastening' moralist. A hero's chastening in relation to melodrama is a sign of spiritual mastery, but his chastening in relation to reality is simply ignored. As so often, critical opinion aligns itself with the least thoughtful sectors of public taste.

The patterns of object-symbolism which the French occultists praised in the Hollywood Hitchcocks also appear in the English Hitchcocks, as we saw in *Blackmail*, and shall see again in the case of *The Lady Vanishes*. Meanwhile, let us refer briefly to the fact that in *The Thirty-Nine Steps*, the hero is afflicted with handcuffs and a woman's hand while the villain identifies himself by holding up a hand devoid of one finger. Were one to open out the symbolism into something less cryptic, the contrast is intriguing between, on the one hand (so to speak) monogamy, heterosexuality and single-mindedness, and, on the other, megalomania, impotence and two-facedness. Alas, the code is too cryptic. You only understand the symbolism if you understand what it symbolises already, so that the symbolism tells you nothing, merely offering you a chance to interpret things and tidy them up, which perhaps helps to explain the popularity of such symbolism among critics. In *Secret Agent* the baying cry of the innocent man's apparently telepathic dog, as he plummets to his death, is echoed by the sustained organ note from the Alpine chapel as his corpse slumps against the stops. Once again, Douchet might have come to our aid had his attention not been pre-empted by the Hollywood movies, for the interconnection of the animal, the musical and the telepathic, at the point of death, must represent climactic transcendence within the Orphic rites. More probably Hitchcock was thinking about the English fondness for pets, and about that ecclesiastical irony, whereby churches, which in a sense are associated with death, are also associated with sentimentalities of goodwill, in contrast to which murder strikes its absurdist (so to speak) *note*. And it may well be from the latter, vernacular, sequence of associations, in connection with the complete dramatic pattern, and the dramatic and visual mood at any point, that this sequence, with its powerful and mysterious mood, symbolises nothing other than the mood which it exists to create— a mood which is far from simple, and deserves analysis, but in terms of its components, not of a subjacent level.

Alfred Hitchcock, Graham Greene: the comparison can't be evaded for long. The very title, *Secret Agent*, anticipates Greene's *Confidential Agent*, and the meta-version sketched above might have borne the title *England Made Me*, or substituted some other city for *Stamboul Train* (its climactic train crash being beautifully visualised). Hitchcock's sense of the seedy might have produced something more intricate than the Boultings' version of *Brighton Rock*, while those for whom Hitchcock is essentially a religious moralist might have made much of Greene's title *The Ministry of Fear*. Our meta-version of *Secret Agent* offers the Greeneian syndrome of public school Britons exiled in settings which, conventionally exotic (and Europe could still seem exotic in the relatively insular '30s), turn out to be spiritual slums, and find themselves involved in intrigues revealing establishment morality as a whited sepulchre.

But whereas Greene, as early as *Stamboul Train* (1932) and *England Made Me* (1935) was essentially subversive and indignant, so that, in Paul West's phrase, 'Greene's triumph is that he has always tried to make the simplicities of the thriller condemn themselves', Hitchcock has by and large been content to remain an astonishingly ingenious craftsman—reducing the potential contradictions within a thriller situation to passing tones. He's a clockmaker whose pendulum swings inexorably, mesmerically, from one hypothetical extreme (subversion) to the other (nihilism), but only to insist on the relentlessness of order and to come safely to rest in the middle where the spring uncoils and the clock winds down.

This is not to accuse him of soullessness any more than it is to accuse conventional opinion of soullessness merely because it is conventional. If clockmakers, like cobblers and tailors, loom large in romantic tales, it is because they typify a pattern of soul, mechanistic, no doubt, rather than biomorphic, but conflating (a) the sense of control as potentially demoniac, (b) the meticulous diligence of the Protestant ethic, (c) the ideal of devoted, myopic, craftsmanlike diligence which the petit-bourgeois share with the labour aristocracy, and (d) the industrial revolution's subjugation of the world to mechanical time (rather than the agricultural year). The mind jumps rapidly from clockwork mechanisms to clockwork men and then to puppets and dolls that come alive (technological Liliths). It only needs *Rich and Strange* and *Vertigo* to remind us how much in Hitchcock springs from a saddened scepticism about the romantic quests for other places, other times. This scepticism, in turn, remains in his work as a subordinated, yet never altogether silenced, existence, under an acceptance of all which conformity borrowed from the Victorian mixture of 18th-century rationalist optimism (God the great watchmaker), gruel-and-water romanticism, and the evangelical transformation of Puritanism. The cobbler bends over his last, not looking out of his window, and dreams of Cinderella; the tourists of *Rich and Strange* become the private eye of *Vertigo*.

The paradox is only apparent and only too typical. Greene, the upper-middle-class writer, can afford to exteriorise a relatively black vision of society's moral climate. The lower-middle-class director is sufficiently cautious to kiss the box-office rod, or to bend his neck to its crook, and to accept, whether through fear or duty, an optimism which is none the less faintly redolent of a hard-edge stoicism and a certain pitilessness. The comparison between Greene and Hitchcock can be maintained, if one considers the affinities and antitheses between Greene's Catholic novels, with their peculiar mixture of the sensitive and the mechanistic, and Hitchcock's *The Wrong Man* and *I Confess*. Curious how, in both artists, a sardonic attitude to back street nonconformism goes with a somehow external Roman Catholicism. Obviously, Hitchcock is a Cockney where Greene, with his genial graft of poetry and journalism, exists, spiritually as well as chrono-logically, in an area between a romantic fascination with low-life exoticism and the spirit of Mass Observation.[1] Greene sees melan-choly where Hitchcock sees fear; Greene sees as tatty even that lower-middle-class dichotomy, whose essence is distilled by the overall atmosphere of Hitchcock's English films. Perhaps Hitchcock's pre-occupation with suspense paraphrases that fear of falling—socially—which led Orwell to describe the semi-detacheds as 'cells of fear'; yet prudence senses its own limitations in *Rich and Strange* where the semi-detached is a 'cell of complacency'.[2]

Hitchcock and Greene reveal affinities also on the level of style. Both combine an astonishing expertise at rapid narrative with a sensi-tivity to atmospherics and details which it is not at all absurd to see as an adaptation of the stream of consciousness tradition, in Hitch-cock's case as much as in Greene's. And in both cases it is a creative one, since stream of consciousness, in focusing on perceptual detail, often has the greatest difficulty in eliminating detail sufficiently to deal with the articulation of significant dramatic events. It's quite possible that Greene's reconciliation of stream of consciousness and main-stream narrative was influenced by the cinema, although it need not have been, since Hardy was virtually at such a synthesis, although his prose proceeds at a slower tempo and is sometimes lumbering, and although the perceptions which Greene notes aren't particularly visual ones. The nearest Hitchcock comes to a Greeneian style is in *Murder*; and, thereafter, although he never quite loses his European discur-siveness, his style increasingly crystallises, or fossilises, into a pen-chant for bizarre contrast, whereby what might be read as 'absurdist' also conceals this relatively sophisticated attitude from minds which might find it chilling or perplexing and offers instead the intensifica-tion of melodrama into drama by detail which is both realistic (in the interests of plausibility) and fine (once a finer perception or hope is stimulated, the blow cuts more keenly). One can't describe either as a pioneer; but their development is their own; it is a re-creation, not an imitation. One might of course prefer to run, in one's *cinéma imagi-*

[1] Briefly indicated in *A Mirror for England*. Hitchcock's admirers regularly for-get Hitchcock's social origins, which can still be heard in his voice. But to forget that Hitchcock is a quasi-Cockney is like forgetting that Losey is American or Fritz Lang German.

[2] The contrast between fear and complacency isn't particularly paradoxical. It's natural enough to be very frightened if your job isn't secure and very complacent if it is. The Marxist influence has regularly led to an excessive characterisation of classes in terms of one particular attitude or ideology rather than a tension between two positions; of which a dialectic attitude ought, above all others, to be aware.

naire, the Pabst version of *The Man Who Knew Too Much*. But that is another story . . .

Sabotage

None the less, the movement, through *Secret Agent*, to a certain grimness, is accomplished in the profoundest film of Hitchcock's thriller period, and perhaps of his career: *Sabotage*. This is *Secret Agent*, from the other side of the fence. And since it is England's enemy who incurs remorse, the portrayal of moral tragedy can be almost untrammelled by caution. Appropriately enough, the film is based on a novel of Joseph Conrad's bearing the title of Hitchcock's previous film. Oscar Homolka plays the manager of a London fleapit, a foreigner, who is prevailed upon by his compatriots to plant terrorist bombs which will shatter the capital city's morale. His first attempt, on a power station, merely blacks out the West End; newspaper headlines proclaim, 'London Laughs'. The agents warn their man: 'London must not laugh again tonight.'

The theme illustrates a characteristic melodramatic process which Hitchcock uses more sharply than most. Just as *The Man Who Knew Too Much* harks back to the siege of the anarchists in Sidney Street before 1914, so do the bombs of *Sabotage*, and the events to which Conrad's novel refers. On the other hand, Oscar Homolka's heavily Germanic style suggests the Nazi Fifth Column. And newspaper strategists were already discussing the effect of aerial bombing on civilian morale, relatively light, by subsequent standards, bombings of London by German Zeppelins and Gothas having given some grounds for predictions of panic. Meanwhile, experts were talking of Air Raid Precautions and anti-bomber blackouts. Thus the film catches a dreamlike overlap between memories of the anarchists, depositing bombs, and the blackouts and terrors which were later to materialise in the blitz. A sequence in *Things To Come*, made in the same year as Hitchcock's film, makes an interesting comparison with it.

The film followed rapidly on the heels of *Secret Agent*, and it is interesting to speculate whether it was under way before Hitchcock had decided, from the earlier film's relatively disappointing reception, that plots must not be too negative or too cruel. For this is both. Its central protagonist is not only a negative hero but a negative villain, and the killing of the innocent gentleman is exceeded by the killing of an innocent boy. The plot's cruelty is unmatched until *Psycho*, and, perhaps, even by *Psycho* (and one can see why so often Hitchcock films have their strongest scenes in the middle. They are strong because they are outrageous. The audience is then desperate to see a moral order re-established. The climaxes have their strength, and a grim satisfaction, but not that moral shock, for they reassert order). Although Verloc (Homolka) is reluctant to kill innocent civilians, his countrymen are adamant, and he gives the bomb to his wife's young brother to deliver. The boy stops to watch the Lord Mayor's Show, and the bus on which he's riding is delayed by traffic. The bomb kills him, and everybody aboard the bus, including the jokey conductor who good-naturedly let him on. When his wife (Sylvia Sidney) discovers the truth, she, blindly, kills him, as he almost wills her to. Then she wants to give herself up; but the detectives don't understand her, and the evidence is destroyed.

'Oh, that was a big error,' says Hitchcock, penitently. 'The bomb should never have gone off . . .' He explains his miscalculation to Bogdanovich in slightly heartless terms: 'If you build an audience up to that point, the explosion becomes strangely anticlimactic. You work the audience up to such a degree that they need the relief.' To Truffaut he offers the contradictory explanation: 'The boy was involved in a situation that got him too much sympathy from the audience, so that when the bomb exploded and he was killed, the public was resentful.' Both considerations are valid, which is why the normal procedure would have been to spare the boy and substitute some perhaps more spectacular but less painful catastrophe. Again, it can be argued that the boy, in himself, is too sympathetic, too innocent, to be an easily bearable victim; he showed every characteristic of the good luck person who was likely to be miraculously spared. (A Hollywood rule of thumb is that victims have to be, in some way, victim types. Not so clearly that they're quite obviously for it, for in that case a substantial sector of the audience would be quite likely to withdraw its sympathies from him altogether, even assuming that they had first agreed to identify with him; yet clearly enough for the audience not to have pinned its main expectation on to their living. A hero, can, of course, die, so long as his death asserts something, and even fail and die, so long as his attempt asserts something, and he can be inadequate, sin, fail and die, so long as his sin has a certain liberating scandal about it; in this case his guilt will forewarn us that he must die, and help us to adjust our hopes accordingly. In the case of secondary characters, there's a marked tendency for them to telegraph their victim status— maybe they're rather nervous, or subtly pathetic, or none too attractive. If one bears all these points in mind, it's impossible to avoid spotting the loser in any Hollywood movie—alas.) Hitchcock, in *Sabotage*, has hit us as hard as in *Psycho*—for we identified with that cheery kid—and in this case the victim isn't even mildly guilty and the murder isn't even sex fun and a bus-load of innocents go with him. Hitchcock is very repentant; yet the spirit behind that tragic outrage, permeating the film, enables it to sustain comparison with a film which in other respects also resembles it (immigrants in London, bombs, families), that boldest and least typical of Ealing films, Thorold Dickinson's *Secret People*.

A later sequence offers images, worthy of Bergman at his best, whereby show business becomes eerie, unnatural, perhaps even diabolical, in its competition with reality. Distraught with grief at her young brother's death, the wife hurries through her husband's cinema. Delayed for a few seconds, she finds herself watching the Walt Disney cartoon—and she begins to smile. In this extraordinary yet absolutely plausible disjunction of the stream of consciousness, which does more than find a topical pretext for traditional hysterics, Hitchcock anticipates that sense of city existence—and of the mass media's so-called 'global village'—as an onslaught on the integrity of the individual, and on the continuity of his emotional consciousness, which a quarter of a century later was to determine the distraction-cluttered styles of Alain Resnais's *Muriel* and of Dick Lester's *Petulia*. The stream-of-consciousness reaches its internal antithesis, its point of paroxysm and protest.

Sabotage is consistently what *Secret Agent* is intermittently, a Greeneian film. The masochistic pet-shop owner disguises his explosives as tomato ketchup, while commenting portentously, on his daughter's illegitimate child: 'She is her cross, and she must bear it.' The remark is all the more meanly puritanical for the mother's bitterness and for the little girl's fresh, pert way; we glimpse the impending and relentless inculcation of shame which will crush her, as she will be meant to, for the vicarious sin of being alive; a transference, not of guilt, but of punishment, that is to say, an injustice—the notion of the world's injustice being one which rarely enters the remarkable morality of Fathers Rohmer and Chabrol (but they were young at the time, as were we all). The details of inter-war London types and life dovetail impeccably with a suspense structure sufficiently unconventional to take on a metaphysical overtone which is a subtler development of the canine telepathy in *Secret Agent*.

Says one of the two detectives: 'Funny—Mrs. Verloc must be

psychic. She said—"He's dead!" ' And his less perceptive companion retorts, 'You don't need second sight to see that, man!' 'But', the other muses, 'she said it before . . . or was it after? I can't remember . . .' Injured in the final explosion, a bandage is being wound round his head, and we think of Mr. Memory, of a kind of stealthy, yet benign madness, of the dislocation, at last, of the due process of law and order, a dislocation which, as in *Blackmail*, is a blessing.

Nor is the boy's death merely an accident; or rather, the accident is a trick of fate; the arbitrary expresses the implacable, the uncaring, and should warn us not to impute the final sparing of Mrs. Verloc to the intervention of a higher order (or of what sin is the boy guilty that she, a murderess, is not?). Verloc terrorises ordinary people; his wife and her brother are ordinary people; he destroys one, provokes a retaliatory violence in the other; achieves nothing.

Sabotage, atmospheric in detail, ruthless in plot, achieves a hallucinatory quality matching, in its own way, that of Lang's *Fury* and Welles's *The Lady From Shanghai* (which it anticipates by having a furtive conversation in an aquarium). Again though it's not difficult to see how a dedicated moralist (a Graham Greene) might have given the moral tensions several further twists of the screw. The illegitimacy theme suggests certain possibilities in the way of changing Mrs. Verloc's little brother into Mrs. Verloc's illegitimate son, by a callous, sly and brutal, or priggish and thin-lipped, Briton, such that we feel, with her, how much gratitude, indeed love, she owes to the genuinely kindly Verloc.

One must remember, of course the Anglo-Saxon censor's stranglehold on the cinema's largely theoretical freedom of speech. The parallelism between German disorder and the Fascist threats abroad resulted in the usual ironies of censorship. Fritz Lang's contemporary *The Testament of Dr. Mabuse* was banned in New York, of all places, as tending to encourage 'crime, chaos and the overthrow of civilisation'. And while the English censor let Mrs. Verloc's crime through (relenting, it seems, on his usual adherence to the Hays Code) one may well doubt whether he would have been so forgiving had Mrs. Verloc been guilty of something much more serious than that significantly favourite movie crime, murder-cum-manslaughter-cum-self-defence-cum-hysterically-mistaken-self-defence.

Young and Innocent

Perhaps because of the objections to *Sabotage*, *Young and Innocent* is a lightly-and-sprightly piece, a reversion to *The Thirty-Nine Steps*, done with, perhaps, a little less dash. This time the hero (Derrick de Marney) is on the run for a murder he didn't do, and the girl he picks up (Nova Pilbeam) is the police chief's daughter. Underneath some fairly conventional, if agreeably misanthropic, caricatures of dangerously incompetent lawyers and policemen, an underlying pattern of ironies cries out for development in dramatic, as well as melodramatic, terms. At any rate, the film registers as little more than an entertaining prologue to its denouement, when, at last, it touches the heart.

A matchbox inscribed 'Grand Hotel' has directed the sleuthing couple to its foyer. A friendly tramp (Edward Rigby) helps them scan the guests for 'the man with the twitch'. The camera finds him for us. He's not one of the rich and pompous guests, as we naturally expected, but one of the menials, to wit, the drummer with the orchestra, in blackface. And as he sees the tramp demonstrating the twitch, he begins twitching worse than ever. And this is hilarious. But as, alongside the twitch, we become increasingly aware of his miserable fear, our hilarity switches to a share in pain on his behalf, and we weep as we laugh as he confides to a colleague, 'This twitch is getting on my nerves.' And eventually distraught with terror, he goes over the top with masochistic hysteria, and begins drumming, drumming, crazily drumming, drawing every eye in the ballroom to his frenetic facial spasms.

And if one unfolds the plot, there is, indeed, a sense in which he is the hero's victim. His wife, whom he murdered in a fit of wretched jealousy, had her gigolos, of whom our young boy was one. Well, maybe he wasn't, and maybe the money she left him in her will had some other explanation. If it did, I forget it; but we never quite forget the *apparent* one.

Of all Hitchcock's post B.I.P. British thrillers, it is in *Young and Innocent* that the undercurrent of dramatic uneasiness and moral dissent is weakest. It became his greatest American success, and provoked the overtures of David O. Selznick. Meanwhile, he began preparing a film for which we have less admiration than other protagonists of English Hitchcock have had, and a more detailed analysis of it may serve to explain why.

The Lady Vanishes

After two of Hitchcock's spiritually most troubling and commercially least profitable films, *The Lady Vanishes* is the second of two more superficial and successful efforts, and, indeed, his least substantial thriller since *No. 17*. But it has acquired almost as special a place in critical esteem as *The Thirty-Nine Steps*, both as the last of the characteristically English thrillers, and for its resonance with the mood of Munich, when the British, whether or not they accepted Chamberlain's assurance of 'Peace in our time', had war on their minds.

During a holiday in a Central European resort, smart young Iris Henderson (Margaret Lockwood) is exasperated, and secretly attracted, by Gilbert (Michael Redgrave), a sharp-tongued fellow-countryman who is busily, and noisily, recording the hotel servants' folk song and dance. During the journey home, she gradually realises that dear old Miss Froy (Dame May Whitty) has disappeared from the non-stop express, while even the passengers who shared their compartment deny having seen her. A friendly brain-surgeon, Dr. Hartz (Paul Lukas) assures her that she must be suffering hallucinations from her subconscious, caused by the flower-pot which fell, or was pushed, on to her head on the station platform. Gilbert, initially facetious, gradually comes to take her seriously; and a rather unconvincing double of Miss Froy appears on the train. Eventually the two young Britons turn on the nursing nun with the high heels showing, and find that her bandage-swathed patient is none other than poor Miss Froy, who, freed, explains that she is really a secret agent smuggling vital information back to England, home and beauty. At the border station their coach is shunted on to a siding, and Iris and Gilbert have to persuade their fellow-tourists that there's an emergency on and that they must fire back at the militia and make a dash for the border.

The vanishing lady is a conjuring trick, and, more deftly than most comparable films (Hitchcock refers to *So Long at the Fair*), gives the simple notion of a missing person a special cachet by simultaneously persuading us that she must exist (because Iris and we saw her) and that she can't have (because everything else rules it out). The film is a mystery, that is to say, a cluster of riddles, activated by another source of suspense, which is our concern for two central characters, and, to a lesser degree, for a variety of others who are related to them, not only by being part of the same situation, but by constituting variations on their theme. The structure of variations isn't logically compelled by the common situation, but it is suggested by it, and the requirements of speed, i.e., economy, make some such symmetry virtually ineluctable in a film of this type. Even in their absence, a common situation would tend to emphasise, or to induce us to notice, the similar or related aspects of diverse characters.

Curiously enough, what might look like the simplest plot link isn't used. This is the theme of music, or, more strictly, the appreciation of music. A, the secret is in the music. B, our hero is a musician. But we don't know, or even suspect, the first point until well on into the film, and our primary narrative pick-up is not through Gilbert but through Iris, whose only connection with music is that she objects to Gilbert's, and his music in its turn has nothing to do with the secret message either, except as part of the musical scenery which is used to hide from us the fact that a completely different character's music has a code in it. Towards the end Miss Froy asks Gilbert to memorise the vital tune, which he does, only to forget it, but it doesn't matter, since Miss Froy has got through, and remembered it, anyway.

Ironically, the common theme contributes nothing at all to the logic in the narrative. But it is extremely useful for the structure of atmospheres. For while Gilbert and Iris are quarrelling over folk music, sung and danced by the hotel staff, Miss Froy can seem to be whimsically appreciating the strains of a guitar serenade, and everyone is establishing and characterising himself in terms of a theme which links them and which won't have to be replaced by another when the knot of the climax is tied. Thus the climax can retain the strength of all the associations and affect which the film has built up; it completes them and includes them; simultaneously, they link the film as it goes. At the same time, the theme of musical appreciation carries a certain variety of both form and mood. Gilbert makes the reluctant domestics go through dance routines whose rustic nature seems rather to embarrass them; not only that, but he is playing *their* music on *his* recorder and *making* them dance to his/their tune; and not only that, but at every few notes he makes them 'freeze', in a ridiculous tableau, so that he can record their steps. The obvious, flat presentation, which is all that logic *per se* requires, is pixilated by all these little switches. The embarrassing, laborious and tyrannical atmosphere, is piquantly contrasted with conventional notions of school folk-dance, and it's just as well, for it makes Gilbert a strong and lively character, enough of the music-teacher to be familiar, but imbued with the energy needed to turn order into disorder and make him fun. In the bedroom below, the music becomes an infuriating noise, while in a room adjoining Miss Froy's apparent air of school-marmish rapture is relieved by a faint sense of her loneliness, her unselfish pleasure at someone else's loves. Eventually, two hands then grab the guitarist by the neck and strangle him, satisfying just that berserk rage which schoolmarmish raptures about art are likely to provoke in us, and moving us smartly out of the schoolmarm orbit into something more interesting. The moral logic applied to later Hitchcock films ought to require us to see the remainder of the film's suspense as a purificatory punishment imposed on us for those fits of rage which music can induce in us when we're trying to sleep, and, or also, as an initiation into certain Orphic rites whereby Gilbert, with all the arrogance of a Western musical education, fails to become the heir of the Orphic mysteries, until reinitiated by the, as we shall see, mystical-minded Miss Froy. At any rate, the music's final forms ring two new changes on it, Gilbert's worried and hesitant whistling being capped by Miss Froy playing it on a grand piano in Whitehall.

Thus the symbol changes as it goes, partly by context, partly by internal transformation (from Ruritania to Whitehall; from guitar to whistling to grand piano). And this sort of development is even truer of the characters, who, whether or not they profoundly change their character (as no-one does here, except in so far as Gilbert and Iris soften towards one another), certainly reveal new sides to their character (like Miss Froy and Hartz), or adopt significantly new attitudes. Either way they manage to be the same character and a different character, and they remain the same even when they change what might seem to be their most salient characteristic. Thus Miss Froy changes from being a whimsical old spinster to being a resourceful secret agent; from life all but lost to life at its most intense; from hysteria to calculation; from someone to be easily dismissed to the centre of absolutely everybody's attention; and so on and so forth. In fact, of course, although Miss Froyness and spying are atmospheric-ally and presumptively contradictory, there's no contradiction between them, since it's quite plausible that she should be both a senti-mental old spinster and a spy. It's on just this sort of introduction of unexpected possibility (contrast) that melodrama and the simpler kinds of drama rely. Logic becomes misleading in so far as it forgets just how many aspects go into the idea of a 'whimsical old spinster', and it's quite easy to combine contrasts along the axes of one aspect while retaining all the others as a continuity. Similarly, one can climax everything by reversing the hierarchy of sophistication as between the knowing Gilbert and silly ducky old Miss Froy. Since people with the knife-edge keenness of Gilbert often show a certain nervous tension with it, it's a contrast, but it's not out of character, that we should complete the reversal of hierarchy by having Gilbert forget even the simple little tune which Miss Froy entrusts to him and which she doesn't. In fact this sort of contrast isn't at all out of character whereas a sudden irrelevance would be. Given reasonably accessible intuitions, contradiction is easily seen as a form of continuity, and in this respect the similarities between drama, the Hegelian dialectic and the Freudian sense of conflict as intrinsic to the formation of human character and sensibility explain why so much interpretation of symbolism in art rings false. It's not that it's over-subtle; far from it; it's just not flexible enough, and tries to impose rudimentary one-for-one values instead of acknowledging all the interactions of context, continuity and contradiction. Writers with less sense of structure than Hitchcock's might well have felt obliged to do things the obviously logical way, i.e., because Gilbert is a musicologist, he would sense that the music is a code, and explain it to Miss Froy, and she would try and get through, and forget the tune. And what's wrong with that isn't that it's too logical but that it isn't logical enough, ironing out all the paradoxes.

The theme of Englishness appears in so many guises that the film is clearly a forerunner of the 'omnibus' form so common in wartime and post-war British films. (In fact if you substituted a Green Line coach, as per *No. 17*, or a freedom bus, as per *Torn Curtain*, for a train, you would literally have an 'omnibus' film; the difference between this and those being its sustained stress on the form.) There are two sexual couples: Gilbert and Iris (who are clearly meant for each other because they keep quarrelling), and Mr. and Mrs. Todhunter (a very respectable lawyer and his popsy, returning from a dirty fortnight). And there are two sets of English couples who conspicuously aren't sexual couples, but celibates instead: the two clubmen (whose overriding interest is the Test Match), and Miss Froy (who maintains the idea of a couple because she's a lonely spinster, and explains to Iris how it is that her life isn't too lonely to bear). The equivalence of clubman celibacy and potential sexuality is neatly turned in a series of jokes which have no great narrative importance, if any, but form the substance of a scene. The screen is filled by the alarmist headlines on the front page of a newspaper, the contents of whose back, sports, pages are discussed by two languid English voices. This 'screen' is lowered to reveal Charters (Basil Radford) and Caldicott (Naunton Wayne), crammed side by side into one narrow bed, one of them stripped to the buff. It's clearly a case of the hazards of holiday accommodation, and of overgrown schoolboy innocence, but even if we haven't already laughed at this parody on the physical intimacy of a honeymoon couple Hitchcock gently sexualises our associations. First a pretty maidservant appears, and tinkles with laughter in a way which more dashing holidaymakers might have thought rather promising. Then the pompous man nonchalantly extends his arm to shield the other's bare chest from view. Then after the maid has left he gets up to bolt the door, but turns out to have no pyjama trousers on (hazards of holiday baggage; no doubt they're sharing the pyjamas with the same rigorous fair-mindedness as the bed). And then before he can get to the door the maidservant reappears to titter afresh while he just freezes into immobility. And he does just this in front of a wooden upright whose form discreetly parodies his carefully keeping his legs together, as well as whatever secret sentiment might lie between them.

The scene certainly has an atmospheric function, as one of two variations on the theme of accommodation mix-ups, the second involving squabbles and shifts between Iris and Gilbert, Iris having Gilbert turned out of his room directly above hers because of the noisy dancing going on. Thus a united celibacy contrasts with a potential sexuality camouflaged by quarrelling, and the two atmospheres are in a polyphonic relationship, rather adventitiously, since the function of the bachelors scene is to abbreviate the other. The Iris-Gilbert affair is relatively complicated, in time and space, since it involves Iris complaining via the hotel manager, the manager being repelled by Gilbert, the manager returning to Iris to be reinvigorated by a bribe, and trekking back to, this time, throwing Gilbert out. Of all this repetition Hitchcock, surprisingly, goes on to omit the key scene in which the manager throws Gilbert out. Why the key scene should be omitted is presumably that unlike the earlier scene it goes against rather than with the grain of Gilbert's forcefulness. (Of course, this forcefulness could have been shown by detailing Gilbert's recruitment of his dancing-team, but that would have been less relevant and much less interesting than this gradual movement of our two identification figures towards one another.) After the cutaway to a preliminary variation on the theme of irruption and sexual defensiveness, Gilbert comes storming back, in the active voice again, barging into Iris's room, asking which side of the bed she likes to sleep on (she refuses to reply so he says, 'In that case I'll have the middle'), noisily brushing his teeth, and threatening to tell all and sundry that she invited him down. Thus defeat becomes victory and a strong polarity with the clubman's conventional passivity is set up. The scenario has a second, internal, source of suspense. As Gilbert enters, we don't know what his intentions are, and even when they become apparent, we don't understand his tactics, i.e., what will he do if Iris calls the manager as she just has done about something much less offensive than this? So the scene has the quality of successive riddles, thus combining rapidity and suspense and observing the classical rule of beginning *in medias res* and putting the beginning in the middle.[1] As Montaigne remarked, the art of good writing is to jump the intermediate ideas.[2]

In brief, the art of dramatic effectiveness is the combination of contradictions and consistencies. The major contradictions are the big surprises of the plot; sometimes they work against, not only the pre-ceding state of affairs, but against expectations as well, forming, as it were, a three-cornered shock rather than a simpler change. But the minor contradictions and the small surprises are all part of the mosaic of style which makes up content. Thus Dr. Hartz explains to Iris and Gilbert that their drinks have been spiked with a strong sleeping dose. We are shown a two-shot of his two victims listening, already, it seems,

[1] This anticlockwise rule does have innumerable advantages, notably (a) in so far as everything is what it is because of what happened previously, so one has to begin at some convenient point rather than at the Creation, (b) a scene beginning near a climax both emotionalises and abbreviates any necessary explanations, the action being a partial explanation, (c) the scene in full would involve a repetition of weakly-made points, and (d) one can chose a convenient and striking starting-point. The interruption of the Gilbert-Iris squabble is, in effect, a way of jumping to a new middle at which to recommence the story. This need for brevity isn't incompatible with the other rule-of-thumb, applicable to gags and stories alike, 'Tell 'em you're going to do it, tell 'em you've done it.' On the contrary, it explains how the latter can be applied, fulfilling the normal form of intellectual apprehension, expectation-exposition-confirmation, without unnecessary repeti-tion. One suggests something will happen in one way; one shows it happen in a slightly different way; and the confirmation is effected via the character's response, or some other character's response, in either case giving the event itself a different emotional colour. One's repetition is diversified with variations.

[2] One reason why good novelists are not *ipso facto* good scriptwriters is that thinking along an informal flow of words where time and space unities are of no importance is rather different from the selection of one or two strong, simple yet many-faceted ideas, and the mixture of emphasis and ellipse involved in concen-trating scenes. Obviously it isn't impossible to think in both terms at different times, and some novelists write like this anyway.

Montaigne's recommendation obviously can't apply to all kinds of thinking and writing, e.g., geometrical theorems, whose nature it is to never miss a step, or critical exegesis, which may depend on demonstrating how many jokes may dance on the point of a gag. But it describes an aspect of good writing in terms usefully complementary (and sometimes contradictory) to the usual critical-academic stress on detail as opposed to ellipse, reminding us how much of the text isn't in the text.

showing signs of drowsiness. Then Iris's head slumps forward, seen from such an angle, and in such a composition, as to leave space for Gilbert's head to slump forward beside hers too. The neat, pat, temporo-spatial symmetry, when it comes, will be faintly comic (two snoozing prisoners), and our suspense is already leavened with a little added light-heartedness as our very strong expectation leads us to 'see' it. And so, after Hitchcock has cut back to Dr. Hartz, he returns to his prisoners, to show them from a rather different angle, which leaves space for Gilbert's head to fall backwards instead of forwards, as it in fact does. There's no real narrative point to the change, except that (1) while the idea of two meekly quiescent heads is just funny enough for the film's tone, such unanimity in helplessness, if reiterated by actually materialising, would run a risk of cheering us up too much, or compelling disbelief, (2) a head falling back when we expected it to fall forwards is a compositional surprise, just as the shift in view-point adds emotional tension by visual means, and (3) two people sitting slumped with heads forward would slide to the floor; the other group is more stable, and so finishes the scene more neatly. Given the long critical emphasis on camera-angles and camera-movements, it may seem strange that Hitchcock should shift his camera about simply to render both smooth and emphatic the surprise involved in the drooping backward of a head. Yet there can be little doubt that here, as so often, it is what happens within a scene, its internal relationships, temporal as well as spatial, which determine the moments of cutting and the angles of the shots, and that any analysis of the basic elements of the scene would consist of an analysis of the relationships between the elements within the scene (as on an, admittedly rather peculiar, form of theatrical stage, or as in a painting, or for that matter a real-life event).

The sleeping-draught sequence helps to prepare a more substantial twist when Dr. Hartz, watching his adversaries steam safely away across the border, calls off the chase and says half-admiringly, 'Jolly good luck to them!' Just because he is as smoothly polite to Iris as he is, we expect him to be a ruthless villain, and a certain coldbloodedness is emphasised when he predicts that his operation on Miss Froy will be a failure. This remark probably conjures up pictures of an anaesthetised old lady being cut up with scalpels in some very nasty parody of a hospital's normal purposes, and we probably don't have time to reflect that she'll probably just be sent smoothly off in what is, after all, one of the pleasantest ways to go. In the same conversation he informs his prisoners that the sleeping-draught which he has just given them causes death in large doses, followed, although only after a suitable pause, by, 'But I give you my word of honour that you have been given the normal dose.' Surprisingly, perhaps, this doesn't drastically deflate the tension. We're inclined to believe him, because he probably wouldn't bother to lie if they were already dead, unless he was gloating, which he isn't. Second, if the dose had been fatal, it would be obvious to us that Iris and Gilbert hadn't taken it, and all hopes would be possible; but given a normal dose, it's very probable that things will get worse before they get better, especially for Miss Froy. Thirdly, his more complex mixture of ruthlessness and 'minimal' force' adds a complicating tension (although this last point goes rather weakly). While Dr. Hartz has perforce to be absent from the action, his mixture of menace and apparent chivalry is maintained by a younger officer, who, physically, has his lean, dark look, and is obviously intended as reminiscent of him, although his style is more restrained, so as not to eclipse him. The latter's sporting farewell might establish him as a counter-hero (rather than a villain), who is just doing his duty for his country, much as another crypto-assassin, Ashenden, did his for his. Although its impact in its time is now difficult to ascertain, the brief shock, climactically placed although it is, hardly survives (a) our renewed upsurge of affection for dear Miss Froy at the end, (b) the fact that his victims are a dear old lady and a Briton, (c) the false-nun's denunciation of his past dirty work and now murder, (d) the calm way in which he contemplates murder, as to the manner born, (e) his conventional villain appearance, (f) the overwhelming firepower finally deployed against a scratch squad of holiday civilians, a sort of Dad's Army Abroad, and (g) our assumption of his suave ruthlessness throughout, particularly given all that being a brain-surgeon implies, in the paranoid logic appropriate to spy melodrama, even though it eventually transpires that he may only have been pretending to be a brain-surgeon.

A similar series of twists determines our discovery, through the course of the film, of the nun. Merely by appearing in a spy story, a nun is herself a surprise, a twist in the atmosphere. Second, Iris notices that she is wearing high heels. Third, she indicates that she is deaf-and-dumb, thus balancing her arousal of our paranoia with a plea for our pity. Fourth, she reveals herself as English-speaking, and, moreover, with an accent which we haven't heard before in the film, a lower-class, criminal-type accent, and what she says is, 'You didn't say the old girl was English.' And this altogether new identity introduces, not just a new fact, but a whole new flock of possibilities and, be it noted, balance of conflicts, all those within her. She's a crook *but* she has a patriotic streak *but* she's an old accomplice.

We can all think of ways in which all these pretty filthy things including murder square with Hartz's eventual sportsmanship, and Hitchcock counts on our doing so, but what matters is not so much how all these elements can be reconciled against one another to produce one eventual truth, but how each shocks against the immediate context of the story so far (including its imminent possibilities), which is how we experience it, certainly in the first, and probably in the only, instance, since although many spectators will think back to, and retrospectively resolve, certain outstanding near-discrepancies, they certainly won't remember the film well enough, or probably have the time or inclination, to do the same for details which otherwise deserve it (as Hitchcock says, one ought really to see his films twice). Later, the nun is gagged by Hartz and his henchman, which can be taken as a variation on the pretence of dumbness (Chabrol and Rohmer would probably describe it as a *punishment* for pretending to be dumb), and finally she appeals for our compassion while preserving our moral assurance by dying a punitive and/or sacrificial or merely poetic or ironic, death, i.e., being shot by her ex-allies just after switching the points (and a nun as railroad hand is another twist). She dies hanging between two men who are trying to lift her up into a locomotive cab, and the crucifixion isn't at all irrelevant, and all the more poignant because both her sex and her past prevent her from being Christ. Indeed, the crucifixion symbol in art regularly draws its meaning from *incompleteness* of the identification, i.e., from all the elements of *inappropriateness* in the symbol, which is another instance of contradiction as continuity. Strictly speaking, the nun has a double motive for turning against her foreign companions (Miss Froy is English, and this is murder), and double motives make precise psychological analysis impossible, since it's just as perfectly possible that neither motive would operate without the other, which makes it impossible to say which motive is operating, or, if they're each necessary and sufficient, what their relative balance is. It's for just this reason that double motivation is popular in melodrama, each motive appealing to spectators who wouldn't respond to the other, and triple, quadruple or quintuple motives are common, not without reason, for multiple motivation is the normal state of man, and people with only one good reason for detesting someone else are often tempted to invent a good few others if they don't exist, resulting, finally, in paranoid-scapegoat, soot-and-whitewash morality. The point is that one-action-one-motive, a kind of rationalist equation often assumed by critics, is extremely rare in art, and rigorously 'psychological' artists have to go to considerable lengths to distinguish various motives which are then often regrouped into a combination of motives. To select one motive from a battery makes pattern-making very easy, particularly since it has a legitimate aspect, whereby context is intended to affect our interpretation of particular details and configurations. My own feeling is that Hitchcock's film operates in the same moral force-field as *Secret Agent*, and that although it's wicked of foreigners to kill our side, it's altogether forgivable, and even desirable, if our side kill foreign agents. The underlying polarity would then be patriotism as opposed to moral objectivity, and the nun represents another variation on the same theme as Mr. Memory in *The Thirty-Nine Steps*.

The motive for her sins may be purely mercenary, but it may also, given her bitter voice, arise from moral disenchantment with the world. Hartz, however, underestimates her morality, remaining quite oblivious to the force behind. 'You didn't tell me the old girl was English.' His retort, 'What has that to do with it?', might be that of a purely objective moralist, although it also suggests the innocence which cold logic is apt to possess about the sentimentalities which for good or ill are the stuff of ordinary human conduct. Given the reinforcement of British xenophobia by melodrama, the touch possesses an overtone to the effect that even a crooked Briton may possess quirks of decency in which foreigners are curiously deficient, although, in itself, it might only suggest that Hartz is a rigidly moral patriot (or a chauvinist) who doesn't understand the residual decencies of the criminal mind and thinks that a girl who's done his filthy things for her own motives instead of his patriotic ones must be beneath consideration. Either way, what he doesn't bargain for is the rich untidiness of the British character, an untidiness which often enables them to lose every moral battle except the last. It's equally difficult to determine whether anti-xenophobic tendencies or self-criticism or both underlie Miss Froy's smilingly effective rejoinder to the High Tory clubmen. As she enthuses over simple rustic foreign ways, they remind her that this country's dictatorship is pretty nasty, whereupon she observes, 'One mustn't judge a people by its politicians. After all, we British are very honest at heart.'

A favourite critical procedure is to consider every point in a film (or rather sample points in a film) in the context of other points in the film, and then deduce from the two a critical attitude. The justifications of such a procedure are obvious, and many films require such an interpretation. Narrative is itself a *relating* device, and the search for a coherent reconciliation of contradictions is quite as natural as the human fondness for order and the general rules that go with it. But the procedure can be applied obliviously, as if all contradictions of any sort were intended to be resolved in one way or another. In fact, of course, many contradictions are left unresolved, perfectly happily, and a state of ambivalence is a perfectly natural one, whether or not a general rule is supposed to be valid. In the first place, it may co-exist with a general acceptance of the rule, the acceptance being based on the balancing of two equal and opposite attitudes neither of which is altogether abandoned. In the second place, the ambivalence is maintained because in the absence of a general rule it's the only position which isn't a partisan preference for one attitude and an anxious suppression of the other. Thus, on the problem of the balance between patriotism and objective morality, which is obviously involved in *The Lady Vanishes*, relatively few people would be prepared either to allow or to deny all the claims of patriotism (even 'my country right or wrong' tends, in the end, to allow degrees of wrongness) or all the claims of moral objectivity. And it's certainly as possible for a film to elicit contrary responses during its ninety minutes as for any other sequence of ideas to do so. It may controvert our xenophobia at one moment and appeal to it at another, and the state of contradiction may remain altogether unperceived, or perceived but unresolved.

Even the notion of a nun is, in itself, morally synthetic, allowing a variety of axes of interpretation. For it possesses a whole range of associations, e.g., a nun is very good; waspish; kind; strict; devoted; perverted; un-English; above nationality; exotic; reliable; as per *The Sound of Music* as well as *The Devils of Loudun*. And many of these associations are contradictory, so that the notion is not only synthetic but internally inconsistent.[1] It's true that all the other factors

---

[1] Thus, in relationship to its context, the notion of 'nun' is a collection of contrasts-and-twists, analogous to a collage, or to Eisenstein's use of shots in a montage. And the further reflection that the notion 'nun' is in itself quite as complex as the content of a particular shot. Thus a series of shots of the same nun would be likely to differ less in meaning from one another than one shot within which a nun was placed against some counter-symbol, whether a shop window of ladies' lingerie, or a waterfall, or a crucifix, or a housewife encumbered with much serving. Whatever the unit of film meaning may be, the shot it most certainly isn't, and any attempt to relate what is specifically cinematographic in film form to the basic unit of cinematic meaning would seem ill-founded, for the quantum of cinematic meaning is each individual association of everything present in or suggested by the sequence of images. In a series of shots of the same nun, e.g., a cut from full-face close-up to left profile to right profile and so on, the meaning would not be the sum of the shots but would be transformed by the visual shock of the impacts of the similar but not identical shots against one another.

involved in the film may be so deployed as to strengthen some associations and obliterate others, but it's equally true that without some
degree of internal complexity we begin to complain about soot-and-
whitewash morality, platitude, facile responses, and so on, and often
with excellent reason. Other connections may strengthen the internal
tensions, however. Thus this woman's mixture of human loyalties and
the supernatural affiliations suggested by her disguise might well be
Hitchcock's symbolic or poetic shorthand for the familiar argument
that religious absolutes, however arbitrary, are the natural and necessary foundations for an imperfect decency. Or the meaning of her
unveiling might be that religion is merely a hypocritical cloak for
whatever happens to be going on underneath it, whether mercenary
treachery as at first or a self-sacrificial patriotism and/or remorse at
near-murder at the last. The very ambiguity may or may not reflect
Hitchcock's own ambivalence, or it may reflect the happy-go-lucky,
unembittered down-to-earthiness of Frank Launder and Sidney Gilliat
who were largely responsible for the script and for whom the crooked
nun was a forerunner of their St. Trinian's girls, sweetly innocent in
their uniforms and up to all sorts of mischief underneath. And is there
a religious reference to Roman Catholicism, or to Christianity, or to
all religions? Does the footplate crucifixion represent some kind of
private transcendence by the 'nun', or a generalised Christian redemption of the profane world, or the notion of sacrifice and atonement as a deep human reality altogether independent of specifically
Christian belief? or a theology of handsome-is-as-handsome-does? or
a theology of 'between the footplate and the ground' . . .?

Similarly the film's political meanings are a little less straightforward
than they may seem to be. It certainly mirrors a British mood immediately after Munich, but that mood isn't one single simple thought.
It's probably fair to say that if the scenery has shifted from England
in *Sabotage* to MittelEurop it's because the fear of internal disorder
has given place to the question of English intervention on behalf of
Czechoslovakia and then Poland, and people are thinking either in
terms of an expeditionary force or self-extrication from Europe. In
military preparedness Britain lagged so far behind the Axis that her
plight was well paraphrased by that of so many sleepily complacent
tourists suddenly shocked to their senses by an ambush abroad.
International politics seep into the film by every pore. These innocents abroad may be divided into internationalists (Gilbert, Miss Froy)
and insularists (the clubmen, the Todhunters), with Iris as a don't-
know neutral in the centre, until gradually she does know, and that's

the way the film's urgings go. Miss Froy rhapsodises with clasped hands over simple peasant customs, while carrying secret messages, which goes to show that she's both more sensitive and tougher than the crustily aloof clubmen, who think the country's dictatorship is a jolly good reason for dismissing it from one's mind. Gilbert collects folk-music (and Iris), while Todhunter lives in the fearful seclusion of the ultra-respectable, and hypocritical, with 'Mrs. Todhunter'. And a variety of cracks about the empty-headedness of British politicians (particularly one shared by Gilbert and Hartz) are clearly aimed at the Chamberlain era. The clubmen live in a curious circularity and confusion of their own, compounded of monosyllabic conversations, an obsession with cricket, and prickly glares at any invasion of their privacy, even by Miss Froy. Caldicott, still resolutely unsuspicious, eventually peers out of the window to see militiamen blazing away at them (twist 1), and scarcely raises an eyebrow (twist 2—actually ambiguous, for while there's something admirably cool about this response, it's still also possible that he's going to say, as Todhunter goes on to do, that there must be some ridiculous misunderstanding, and remaining stupid). The matter is settled for us by twist 3, when he silently shows the others the painful-looking wound in his arm, not in complaint but as proof; and there was the real meaning of his scarcely raised eyebrow (twist 4). Later, the two club bores turn out to be crack shots (twist 5), and one says of the other, 'Don't let his modesty fool you, he's a crack shot,' while himself bringing an enemy down with impeccable precision (a very neat little crossover, twist 6). Todhunter's egoistic fears for his own respectability (a preoccupation with domestic politics) survives even the outbreak of hostilities. He ventures forth with a white handkerchief fluttering, only to be shot down, and crash down from the wagon step like a felled trunk. Impressive personality though he was, he dies still babbling in the dust that all this is nothing to do with him. Todhunter (Cecil Parker), an authoritarian judge-to-be, is a diehard appeaser, yet Blimpishly apoplectic at the thought of being taken for a pacifist, i.e. confused with one of those ghastly lefties. The ossified style of the bores and the hypocrites is clearly High Tory, although two of the three amply, albeit tardily, redeem themselves.

Their style compares with Gilbert, who, as an impoverished upper-middle-class musician, is free from most British constraints, i.e. traditions. With his cosmopolitanism, his artiness, his bowtie, his interest in foreign folk, his intellectual arrogance, he's the best in a sort of Whiggish-radical intelligentsia, although he's carefully given no clearly

political label, or any feature which might alienate those who prefer
to see him as just a sort of trenchant squire ruling the European roost
as Great Britain ought. And the concern with Miss Froy (rather than
with, say, a foreign woman acting on Britain's behalf, like Lucie
Mannheim dying on Donat's bed in *The Thirty-Nine Steps*), ensures
that political concerns remain a patriotic matter, so that the film was
non-interventionist enough not to annoy those who would have been
annoyed by or lost interest in anything less than direct danger to pure
Britons. All the same, there's sufficient force in the film for even anti-
interventionists to sense a message which is not so obstreperous that
it can't be put aside for the purposes of enjoying this patriotic film. In
fact its propaganda force lies in the skill with which it equates a
general atmosphere about dictatorships with urgent dangers to
Britons, so tempting even diehard appeasers to start reading dictatorship as dangerous. The film's efficacy, as well as its limits, as persuasion, are dependent on this double reading which, as we've seen, it
isn't hard to remain ambivalent or placid about; whence, perhaps,
those relatively pessimistic (or optimistic) suggestions that far from
being a potent propaganda force an individual entertainment film
can't normally expect to do more than persuade a few waverers and
encourage those who see their own convictions reflected in it more
than it can encourage those who don't or who approve of it because
they've misunderstood it.

None the less the film attains its sharply accusatory moments, as
when all the insularists, who have certainly seen Miss Froy, and
whose testimony would encourage Iris and Gilbert and maybe save
her life, lie, thus allying their fellow-Briton with all the sinister
foreigners in Iris's compartment. The clubmen lie because they reckon
that the outside world is inexplicable and best kept out of and they
want to catch the last day of the Test, while Todhunter lies because
he doesn't want any trouble which might lead to a scandal. 'Mrs.
Todhunter', a determined little social climber, plays an interesting
role. A certain decency seems to have a freer rein in her than it does
in the lawyer, but it's got a selfish motive too: she wants to scare
Todhunter with the prospect of scandal. But after Todhunter has
pointed out that any scandal which smashes his career will wreck her
ambitions also, she supports his lies. Thus, as a force for truth, a
merely mercenary independence eventually cancels itself out, although
scandal represents what is objectively its healthier aspect. But if that's
Hitchcock's moral it's not one of those morals which couldn't just as
easily be countered by some such proposition as that even though

responsibility is hypocritical it's preferable to mercenary egoism. It's a cynical meaning rather than a subversive one. Although the indictment of all the Old High Tory liars is clear and repeated, hardly anyone remembers it; everything moves too fast, and the final assertion of Hartz's chivalry introduces another ambiguity. It could be a reminder that not every Fascist is the devil incarnate, or a suggestion that Fascism is an honourable, if ruthless, *realpolitik*, merely a foreign patriotism, with which one should bargain from a position of strength rather than weakness. The officers have a star on their caps so this might be a Bolshevik country or have a Bolshevik strain in it, e.g. be one of those countries which is alternately Fascist or Bolshevik, so that it's often quite hard to tell the difference (and this reading would anticipate some interpretations of the Jancso movies, which do create a not altogether dissimilar tit-for-tat atmosphere even if the reds generally emerge better than the whites). Although by 1938 the threat was certainly Nazi Germany rather than Soviet Russia, the star is a kind of concession to anti-Bolshevik feeling, as well as creating that kind of double-association discussed in reference to the first version of *The Man Who Knew Too Much*. And although the language might evoke somewhere east of Austria, the fictitious country looks more like Austria, thus relating both to (1) Austria as a country in which a noisy minority ushered Hitler's conquest in, and (2) the Austro-Hungarian Empire, which was Germany's ally during World War I. To have made Hartz as obviously Teutonic as his name would have been to court censorship, and the '70s reader may find it hard to grasp just how anxiously both the British and American authorities of the time did Goebbels' job for him, e.g. by banning a film called *I Was A Captive of Nazi Germany* in case it should arouse the ire of Herr Hitler.

The theme of international connections recurs when the young foreign officer states that he himself was educated at Oxford, whereupon Gilbert, standing just behind him, smashes him over the head with a chair, knocking him unconscious, and precipitating general indignation from his compatriots. 'What on earth did you do that for?', to which he petulantly replies, 'Well, I was at Cambridge!' It's just this sort of super-patriotism and parochialism which defies criticism, as well as implying that secret violence which the English sense in themselves, with a kind of guilty joy. Like so many of the best jokes, it produces laughter for reasons so devious as almost to defy description. The foreigner's ingratiating ploy ('I'm British too') is trumped by an assertion of British disunity wildly exceeding that against which Gilbert is fighting. It's thus a parody of the myopic disunity of the appeasers, but unassailably 'holier-than-thou', or rather 'less logical than thou'. It trumps culture by hooliganism. And the unsuspecting foreigner is attacked from behind, implying, 'These cunning foreigners, courteous but ruthless, confused by British subtleties, think we take the fairplay code further than we do, and don't realise that we can spot realpolitik when we see it and retaliate quite smartly.' The thought was to remain a comforting one in British war-films, several of whose themes are anticipated here: the club bore crackshots as Colonel Blimp, their stiff upper lip, Miss Froy as representative of Asquith's *The Demi-Paradise*, etc.

Hitchcock ensures, at least, that the enemy is as diverse an array of stereotypes as possible, and motives are, albeit briefly, implied for the foreigners' co-operation with Hartz. They're not nasty simply because they're foreigners. The gaunt, sinister, black-clad Baroness would be very patriotic anyway, and do what a senior officer asked her to do. An Italian *poppa* is garnished with a complete family, to make him seem as innocent as possible, and shake Iris's confidence in herself, but he is also made sinister by a curious stare (à la Peter Lorre), and a leather overcoat; he is subsequently seen being paid off by Hartz. The nun is another mercenary, and the ersatz Miss Froy, conjured up with remarkable speed to perplex Iris further, is also a common German or Austrian type. Hartz poses as both a brain-surgeon and a psycho-analyst, determined to explain Iris's common sense as hallucinations from the subconscious brought on by a traumatic bump on the head from a flowerpot (meant for Miss Froy, to get her under his 'care'). Thus psychoanalysis, which, with *Spellbound*, Hitchcock was to exploit, and, with *Marnie*, to reassert, here remains part of the cold, sinister, logic which characterises Europeans and to which Britain opposes her own absurd, devious, yet resourceful anti-intellectuality (the evidence of a girl's senses, a testy young musicologist's quickness on the uptake, a 'nun', a whimsical governess). Todhunter follows another intellectual profession, and so, in his way, does the Italian *poppa*, being a magician, in whose trunks of tricks Gilbert and Iris think they may find Miss Froy.

Thus a patriotic polarity interlocks with a theme of mental confusion. Shortly after Iris is hit on the head, Hitchcock interposes a strange, dreamlike shot of three men, shovelling sand or ballast, tiny against a back-projection of huge locomotive wheels. The perspective is wrong, the tonal register is wrong, the size is wrong, and today's sophisticated audiences may see only the least convincing of the film's many unconvincing backgrounds, but, one suspects, this back-projection read as a kind of entry into dream to the less analytical, more rapidly and intensely emotive audiences of forty years ago. (This film, remember, comes nearer to Méliès's time than it does to our own.) These locomotive wheels are certainly being established as a *lietmotif*, for they recur during the heroine's struggle against her semi-concussed state, a struggle reaching a peak of poignancy in the impressionist sequence where Miss Froy's trustfully smiling face fades away behind the slyer smiles of Iris's travelling companions. Its beautifully elegiac evanescence, reminiscent of *Downhill*, albeit in a different idiom, asserts Hitchcock's continued creativity within an idiom in which avant-garde pretension was regularly more conspicuous than the authentic accuracy of impression which he achieves. He returns to the same area of experience in a reverse-angle, spiritually as well as lyrically, substituting a coldly objective close-shot of Todhunter, even after he's been shot dead, trying to explain that all this fighting is nothing to do with him. The Italian paterfamilias-conjurer is subjected to more than a little share of his own mental confusions too, as Gilbert and Iris push him in and out of his own disappearing cabinet and she womanishly indulges in perilous hesitation before plucking up the resolution to return the reviving man to the requisite condition of insensibility. The couple's difficulty in giving him his temporary quietus is all but a dress rehearsal, in the comic mode, of Gromek's death in *Torn Curtain*.

If, as we have implied, the film evinces certain reservations about psychoanalysis and brain surgeons, it is obviously because the villain uses their terms sufficiently convincingly to confuse the heroine who is our identification figure; and only a sense of the spirit of the time can inform us as to whether Hitchcock reckons that this jargon will seem sinister and make Hartz all the more menacing or whether it will seem common sense and all the more plausible, or both. Our feeling that in 1939 an English audience would more easily have had the former reflex than the latter bears up reasonably well to other evidence, while one would also suppose that if analytical language were more generally familiar it would be less unconvincing here, or that some sort of discussion would ensue. So far as a saturnine view of brain surgeons is implied, a poetic connection between brain surgery and sadistic mind control is easily made, given Hartz's role as a threat although no inconsistency would be involved had Hitchcock's subsequent film featured a philanthropic brain surgeon (or analyst, or nun). Our argument is not a solipsistic one, its intention being merely to indicate how easy it is to read into a film meanings which were not intended and which have as little, and as much, place there as a variety of other readings. It is, of course, interesting to discover which readings can be, or tend to be, read into a film, to compare them, and to speculate as to which meanings the director (or the script-writers) preferred, or anticipated, or inserted for their *amis inconnus* (and to discuss which, if any, of these meanings would have a better claim to be in some sense definitive as against others).

Despite the film's, shall we say, unwelcoming, attitude to psycho-analysis, it conforms, in its structure, to the patterns of an approach which was later to loom large in Hitchcock's thought, becoming the overt morality of *Marnie*. As Iris, in the inn, bids her two girl friends goodnight, she places one hand on each of their shoulders, maternally kisses each forehead, and says, 'Goodnight, my children.' The result is a sudden, beautiful and alas brief dilatation within an otherwise conventional characterisation. Miss Froy picks up the theme. Through her window she sees her family, Father Mountain and Mother Moun-tain, with their cloud-caps on, and all their children and relations, with the weather as their different moods. Much later, Gilbert tells Iris, 'You know you remind me of my' (twist) 'father. You're both' (twist) 'rude and——' The train turns out to be full of Iris's (by age) uncle and aunt (i.e. father and mother) figures: Dr. Hartz, the magician, the clubmen, Miss Froy, the false Miss Froy, the 'nun', the Baroness, the magician's wife. Iris and Gilbert are matched by another couple, the Todhunters, who are their spiritual opposites, and yet also are their caricatures, being as similar and dissimilar as the tempta-tions which they might be said to have resisted and which in a pro-founder film they might have been shown as having some difficulty in resisting. Gilbert is quite unconcerned that his father fell in the social scale, and Iris is unconcerned about it too. But Mrs. Todhunter is anxious about rising still further, and facially slightly resembles Iris, who incarnates the social climbing which the spectator who is identifying herself with Iris is likely to be gratifying.

Gilbert, however, has a little of the authoritarian potential which dominates the Todhunters' whole social being. His domineering way with hotel-staff and manager reaches a quick brisk climax when he speaks with quite uncalled-for mockery to a grandfatherly old peasant who was ready to look after Iris when she felt ill (although he later throws him a curt acknowledgement which hovers oddly but pointedly between apology and dismissal). In fact a combination of Gilbert, Todhunter and the clubmen is Gilbert's rival for Iris, her young City gent fiancé, whom she was supposed to meet on Victoria Station platform, but who will find that his lady has vanished too.

Among the foreigners, there is only one married couple—the conjurer with his family. Among the English people, there is only one solitary—Miss Froy, who is at once the saddest, sweetest, and, so far as her, and our, mother-country is concerned, the most important person in the film. She is also profoundly loved, as the final swell-up makes clear. Extending her arms to Iris and Gilbert, across the piano at which she has just finished playing the theme which the amiably megalomanic young musicologist has just forgotten, she recapitulates Iris's gesture to her two young companions. The two gestures are linked when, in the train corridor, Miss Froy holds up Iris's hand, whether just as old ladies will, or through fear, or to create a kind of tactile confirmation of her existence before her disappearance.[1]

Thus the film concludes with the triangle of Iris, Gilbert and Miss Froy, the three English lovers, who contrast with all the foreigners, and the benighted English pairs, on the train. One might schematise some such psychoanalytical pattern as that Iris and Gilbert, to achieve the parent status which they begin by rather emptily parodying, must run the gauntlet of mental confusions, and cling to a simple certainty and concern for a ridiculous old spinster whose whimsies, sentimentalities and even existence it would be perilously easy to dismiss. Conversely, a curious mixture of common sense (Iris), irascibility (Gilbert) and apparent whimsy (Miss Froy) is needed to arouse conservatism from its torpid slumbers and transform, almost too late, unity into strength.

One can hardly say that this parental morality is *in* the film, other than as an unrealised potentiality. And if many of the moral points, like the criticism of appeasers as self-centred liars, are made but lost, it is partly through the competitive effect of immoral delights or mechanical thrills. Thus bullets conveniently kill the engine driver and his fireman, almost anonymous characters, whom we may none the less have time to spot as old-fashioned, obvious victim types— characteristic 'disposables'. But they are also generally similar to familiar British railway workers. So it's up to us whether we feel primarily, a semi-apologetic concern for them, or just a kind of vindictive glee at the fact that enemy bullets have killed only enemy

[1] Hands recur as the guitarist is strangled, as the magician grabs Miss Froy's spectacles from under Iris's and Gilbert's noses, and as we return to the prosaic familiarity of Victoria Station, where Caldicott's bandaged hand is one of those details whose unexpectedness seems to authenticate what has gone before. Otherwise: hands of friendship, hands of pain.

innocents. An exhilaration there certainly is, for their death, emptying
the locomotive cab, gives our Britons their sporting chance of proving
their mettle in a tight spot and living out every schoolboy's dream and
becoming an engine-driver. (The locomen might have been excessively
out of context if we hadn't been reminded of 'base mechanicals' by
the three sand-shovellers in the back projection overture to Iris's
delirium.) I suspect therefore that after a mild and scarcely more than
instantaneous twinge we settle down to cheer our versatile clubmen
on. And there's certainly no sign of their being 'punished' for their,
and our, jubilation.

Purely mechanical and soulless twists abound, e.g. the Britons
disarm the young officer by telling him that the barely conscious nun
wants to tell him something, whereupon he bends low to catch her
words and gets hit with a chair. Later, when their attention is distracted, he revives, unnoticed, to cause trouble again. And later, when
his attention is distracted, the nun revives and creeps out to change
the points. Such simple tableturning briefly reduces the film to the
level of the B Western's succession of 'stick-'em-up' arrivals from one
side of the frame, despite little touches like the young officer feeling
more resolute as he comes to or the nun creeping silently behind the
officer (done largely in a wide two-shot close-up, emphasising prox-
imity), in what is in effect a twist against the positive actions taken
on the two previous occasions. Against competition from such
facilities finer points cannot always compete.

If the plot is hardly convincing, the film is sufficiently cheerful to
carry its absurdities gracefully. The automobiles race alongside the
train in what even then was virtually an allusion to Griffith-era melodramatics (alternatively, the train is the stagecoach and the militia are
the Indians). The occasional, unexpected precision is sufficient to
persuade us that probably the plot *would* make sense. Hartz tells
the dining-car waiter to drug his two English friends, and his phrase,
'I will order three drinks. Mine will be a chartreuse' is a nice piece
of craftsmanship, tersely telling us how Hartz solves the problem of
specifying which drinks must be drugged before he knows what his
victims will order. And although we are provoked to scepticism by
the revival of the apparently drugged Gilbert and Iris, the provocation
is so outrageous that we believe there will have to be an explanation,
for which we wait, mystified (the riddle structure again), rather than
destructively incredulous, until the nun mentions, *en passant*, that she
influenced the barman. And if we then wonder why Iris immediately
passed out, unlike Gilbert, who was only pretending, and brought

her round to work fast before the drug took effect, the answer is that she's yielded to a certain suggestibility caused, or accentuated, or excused, by her knock on the head. Her yielding there although she holds out where Miss Froy's existence is concerned is a humanising touch: no-one hasn't an Achilles' heel, especially the weaker sex, and Hitchcock keeps a happy consistency-in-contradiction going by the humour he derives from her innocently continuing her strenuous anti-sleep physical jerks long after Gilbert and we know there's no need. The bandaged hand at Victoria is a pseudo-authentication of one kind, and another is the smear left on the window after Miss Froy's tell-tale packet of tea has been thrown out with the dining-car refuse. The film has thought of a matter-of-fact detail (garbage disposal) of which we have not, and this surprise is one of those which help to convince us that it all hangs together well enough. Hitchcock can even allow us to, briefly, think out the plot from the villains' point of view, and that would expand into a highly entertaining parallel film. Because a clumsily or unluckily aimed flower-pot hit Iris instead of Miss Froy, Hartz can't rush his victim off for 'treatment' as he wishes. He is improvising desperately as he goes, and none of his actions is anything but the looniest conceivable implausibility.

It seems worth demonstrating, though, just how much structure, finesse and, no doubt, serendipity, has gone into concocting a film which is meant to be taken lightly while also carrying a tactful moral but can't be thought about too deeply without inadvertently turning into a Chico Marx machination. For all that, a film which has nothing about it of a masterpiece may be taken seriously, not because its authors have anything particularly or even faintly original or remarkable to say, but because even an entertainment like this is, on its level, a coherent mode of significant discourse and infinitely more complex than the end-product seems until one analyses it, a process not really much more sophisticated than constructing it in the first place, although the need to analyse and define produces a certain air of incongruity which ought not to be inacceptable. For, in just the same way, the intellectual and emotional process behind a joke is as elusive and complex as intuitive reaction is immediate. Whether or not the best jokes are the product of anonymous, or collective, genius, working in a more or less favourable consensus, is an interesting point. But the complexity behind the simplicity of *The Lady Vanishes* seems of interest as a demonstration that a complexity of detail and an overall simplicity are by no means mutually exclusive. And one may honour the former even while regretting that *The Lady Vanishes*, rather than

Sabotage, with its profounder contradictions, should have remained with *The Thirty-Nine Steps*, the most familiar film of Hitchcock's later English era, for it is one of the most comfortable and least substantial.

Jamaica Inn

Jamaica Inn was Hitchcock's last English film and his first costume piece, and seems, from his point of view, to have been more or less a potboiler made to fill in time while waiting to go to Hollywood.

Spirited young Maureen O'Hara comes to a Cornish village and finds her relatives involved with a gang of wreckers who include Emlyn Williams, Bernard Miles, and Robert Newton. She turns to the local J.P. (Charles Laughton) for help, only to find, *in extremis*, that he is the originator of all these crimes.

Hitchcock complained that his involvement was too obvious too early. This need not necessarily have demolished all suspense, since it is to the master-mind that the heroine increasingly entrusts herself. But maybe Hitchcock would have preferred a situation with the double suspense introduced by a continuing ambiguity, so that, for example, we share the heroine's hesitations as to whether she should entrust herself to him or not. In a more delicately balanced situation, Sir Humphrey Pengallan's every action and gesture would have flicked us, rapidly and briskly, between an ascendancy of hope and terror, but with neither quite free from the other. And in such a climax a hysteria-inducing alternative of terrors might loom large, e.g. as to whether her captor is himself a victim of a miscarriage of justice (the reverse angle, in fact, on *The Thirty-Nine Steps*)?

Because suspense involves a careful balance of intimations and possibilities, it is easy to see why Hitchcock's unusually precise style requires deft and docile actors. And Charles Laughton, who was not only Hitchcock's leading man, but, with Erich Pommer, his producer, had artistic interests of his own which ran clearly athwart Hitchcock's, so that he wouldn't let Hitchcock photograph him until he had hit on the right walk for his character—a detail which, with a director on his own wavelength, he might have mastered much earlier on. Nor was Daphne du Maurier's gallery of full-blooded Long-John-Silver-type Cornish rogues exactly propitious for the development of economical enigmas.

Although it was highly successful in its time, presumably because the suspense, though indelicate by Hitchcock standards, was massive enough to satisfy audiences, the film is no longer viable, on its own terms, debilitated by the awkwardnesses which made it Hitchcock's unhappiest memory since *Waltzes From Vienna*. Laughton's blend of languor and energy, of babyish benignity and strutting self-sufficiency, with its plethora of mannerisms that suggest both country gentry barbarism and a more elegant arrogance, has a current of real artistic inspiration running through it, even though it is stylistically sealed off from everything else in the film, except for Bernard Miles, another 'archaic' and rustic actor. The post-war filmgoer must be rather startled by the young Robert Newton, who six years later would have made no mean Sir Humphrey himself; here he registers only as a Léo Genn-type rather too subdued for the romantic badinage which Robert Donat and Madeleine Carroll handled so much more professionally. The irrealism of the model shots now seems wildly excessive, particularly when a tempest-tossed schooner performs something like a U-turn at Z-car speed.

The film as a whole is keyed to rather Orczian melodramatics which no longer obtain, even if it is clearly an ancestor, along with Thorold Dickinson's *Gaslight*, in the following year, and maybe Lance Comfort's *Hatter's Castle*, of the period melodramas, full of upper-class brutalities, which Gainsborough were soon to make their own, and to which Hitchcock was later to return with a project much closer to his heart, *Under Capricorn*. The artistic awkwardness of both films seems connected not so much with problems of period, as with a certain incompatibility, or rather the difficulty of achieving a successful compromise between the heavy atmospherics with which such films must reauthenticate their barnstormer streak, and Hitchcock's concern with delicately tilting implications. In *Jamaica Inn* Hitchcock seems still to be thinking in terms of suspense continuity as a series of rapid events, flicking the spectator's mind first one way and then the other, as in *The Lady Vanishes*. And to this most of *Jamaica Inn* lends itself none too well, preferring, it would seem, a more brooding and picturesque atmosphere. In *Rebecca*, also by Daphne du Maurier, and virtually a costume piece (as Hitchcock comments), Hitchcock moves towards the terms of suspense as a continuing atmosphere of alternatives; while the sustained ambiguities and the supernatural overtones create a more sophisticated and subtle dramatic continuity.

Uneasily balanced as it is between rapidity of action and intensity of atmosphere, the film can none the less display, apart from Laughton's performance, its dark blossom of lyricism. Pistol to hand, the smug and brutal Squire gags and binds the heroine, compelling her submission, however, with a merely psychological *coup de grâce*. 'Now,' he remarks, 'you have no one to depend upon but me.' And she yields herself to him as a child abandons herself to a father, as if desperately in need of her tyrant, and allows herself to be led, utterly docile, head bowed for her cloak's hood to obscure the gag around her mouth, through a bustling crowd, in a bondage which is more than physical, which is worthy of *The Story of O*, and which is by far the most romantically expressed emotion in the film.

And in some ways not dissimilar submissiveness has become a socially-ingrained second nature among Sir Humphrey's grateful tenants, and dominates, in religious terms, the wrecker who knows himself to be damned but retains just enough bizarrely hypocritical sincerity to offer religious consolation to the man whom he is about to kill. For the Hitchcock universe is dominated, not so much by ambition versus frustration and by desire versus despair and fear (the positives and negatives of an optimistic and progressive creed), as by self-preservation versus a deliciously irresistible fear (a more pessimistic, cautious and English attitude). We cannot but be reminded of lower-class meekness in Hitchcock movies generally, of erotic martyrdom in *Suspicion* and of religious martyrdom in *I Confess* and *The Wrong Man*. A director as individual as Hitchcock is bound to express himself through the overall content of a film, but sometimes one or more of the characters are in a particular sense his representative, within the action, of an emotional pattern particularly close to the source of his inspiration. This may be no less true of light entertainers than of profound artists (for self-expression is not the prerogative of genius), and in *Jamaica Inn* it is tempting to see the religious wrecker, damned in the long term but defiant in the short one, and Sir Humphrey, in his girth as in his quality of director of operations, as incarnations of the black side of the Hitchcock spirit, unleashed.

Rebecca

Rebecca marked Hitchcock's Hollywood début and was his first film under the Selznick banner. It retains a costume atmosphere ('a Brontë thing really') even though it's in modern dress. 'In a sense you could get annoyed with the Joan Fontaine character, because she never stood up for herself, she let Mrs. Danvers' (the housekeeper) 'override her.' Hitchcock defends her on the grounds that she's 'really' a Victorian heroine, and, like *Jamaica Inn*, the movie evokes the British cycle of costume bullying stories (Thorold Dickinson was simultaneously shooting *Gaslight*). It also anticipates, or indeed helps to spark off, an American cycle of films, all very claustrophobic, about the spiritual power of a woman who is believed dead and who appears very late in the film, if at all (Wyler had got in first with *Wuthering Heights*; but the cycle continues through, notably, Siodmak's *Phantom Lady* and Otto Preminger's *Laura*).

Joan Fontaine plays the shy, gauche, plain-looking paid companion to a petulant old lady, until dashing, yet haunted, Laurence Olivier whisks her away and marries her. But, once brought to his dark ancestral home, she must confront the sinister Mrs. Danvers (Judith Anderson). She, quite apart from all the problems which would currently be analysed under the heading of 'territoriality' (that usefully innocuous alternative to bristling words like 'property' and 'power'), may have designs of her own on the widower who is in some Oedipal way like her son-in-law, and who is ominously loyal to the memory of his first wife, who gives the film its name, for she is at once central and invisible.

The level of characterisation is indicated by the name of the Olivier character—Maxim de Winter, *if* you please. No doubt Maxim indicates his aristocratic grandeur, and, Oedipally speaking, male importance, while de Winter suggests his lost youth, his ravaged bleakness. The story isn't without interest. On one level, it does become, albeit tardily, a murder mystery, with Olivier on trial for the murder of his voluptuous, faithless, first wife, many years ago. He is cleared when, eventually, it transpires that she goaded him on to kill her rather than die, slowly, of cancer. It's not quite clear whether he did in fact kill her, in rage, thus being morally and legally guilty of murder as she of suicide, or whether he meant to kill her in rage but she died accidentally (a situation which, as we commented *à propos* the accidental killing in *Blackmail*, was a very convenient one during the Hays Code years, since it allows all sorts of *synthetic* and ambiguous, combinations between moral and legal guilt and innocence).

On another level, the detective story turns inside out to reveal its ancestor, the ghost story (an atavistic but effective alliance later reiterated in *Vertigo*). Rebecca, through her sinister ally, Mrs. Danvers, is like a ghost, reaching from beyond the grave, first to 'haunt' her successor, and then to claim her husband, just as, in *Wuthering Heights*, the dead Cathy summons her Heathcliff. Here, he will come, not so much willingly, as helplessly, even though we intuitively read helplessness as unconscious will, unless his young wife can break the spell. And Rebecca seems to be imposing on him the terrible 'rite de passage' of trial, condemnation and hanging.

Indeed, it's interesting to switch the movie round, to banish the (rather boring) heroine to a peripheral role, and to hinge the film on the passionate and sado-masochistic love-hatred of Maxim and Rebecca—whom I insist on imagining as Ava Gardner in *Pandora and the Flying Dutchman*. Both films have a bitch-heroine who dies in a sunken yacht; one can easily imagine Olivier and James Mason in each other's roles; both are ghost stories, and, most remarkably of all, Ava Gardner's facial bone-structure and general build 'rhymes' perfectly with Judith Anderson's. The story perspective of Albert Lewin's film is in fact analogous to that of *Wuthering Heights*, which isn't insignificant, since the Daphne du Maurier story represents a fascination with, but rejection of, the romantic-erotic perspective which makes Emily Brontë's novel a favourite of Georges Bataille's and of various Surrealist writers. It places romanticism in a perspective which is ambiguously healthy-and-realistic (if one disdains the novel, and romanticism generally, as rather morbid) and prudent-and-pusillanimous (if one prefers a passionate intensity to bourgeois timidity and worldliness). Lewin's film is more fully romantic, albeit at the expense of enclosing itself within a smarty-arty ghetto, although one fears that its rejection by Anglo-Saxon critics was due to its spiritual daring rather than its compromises.

With considerable skill Hitchcock accommodates detective-story realism, intimations of the supernatural, a nostalgia for romanticism even when it is evil, and a reasonably adult drama in which a will to live prevails against the masochisms of hero and heroine. Various interpretations are possible, as usual with Hitchcock, and one of the most interesting is Julian Fox's, whereby 'Maxim relaxes once he is off the hook, even though he knows himself to be guilty', but 'Maxim now has someone to share his guilt with—Joan Fontaine, whom he has told and Aubrey Smith who suspects'. The supernatural and moral aspects in no way preclude a prudently subordinate class theme more typical of Hitchcock (and of English artists) than (at that time) American. For, as Julian Fox observes, 'the Chief Constable of the County (Sir Aubrey Smith) lets Maxim off the hook. None the less, it is made quite clear (by implication) that Colonel Julyan still has his doubts about Maxim, but Maxim is an old friend. This last is the moral point that du Maurier wishes to make—through Hitchcock— friends in the right circles, etc.'

As we have intimated, the film is a diffuse, but effective, version of the Oedipus complex, seen through a daughter's viewpoint rather than from a son's. For the heroine fulfills the archetypal female Oedipal dream of marrying the father-figure, who has rescued her from the tyranny of the domineering old woman (i.e. mother). But in so doing she has to confront the rival from the past, the woman who possessed her father first, who can reach out and possess him once again. And as this aspect would lead one to expect, the cycle of films about absent-but-obsessive women is paralleled by a cycle of movies about mother/daughter tensions (e.g. *Mildred Pierce*; the emphasis is more fully documented by Wolfenstein and Leites. Both cycles are doubtless encouraged by the absence of menfolk at the front, but also, one may suspect, are internal to the evolution of the matriarchal theme in the American cinema). At any rate, *Rebecca*, like so many of Selznick's films, is a rich and ripe example of the woman's film, attuned to a congenial, and by artistic standards somewhat escapist, compromise between the daydreams and dramas of the distaff side.

Critics have long tended to be very dismissive of the woman's film, preferring the equally silly male sentimentalities of the Western, with its never-never-land of virility, violence, individuality and camaraderie. Although *auteur* theory has done much to rediscover Hollywood, it has tended to overstress the extent to which *auteurs* are individualists, and to obscure the older emphasis on genres and on common themes without a sense of which Hollywood is even less fully comprehensible than the Jacobean theatre. Just as the emphasis on Howard Hawks has hindered the rediscovery of the various genres with whose spirit his relatively easy and usually uninteresting films are so thoroughly imbued, so the justified interest in Douglas Sirk has failed to open up the 'woman's film', of which Selznick is a fascinating exponent and a true *auteur*. Indeed, to compare Sirk and Selznick is to remind oneself that only the male chauvinism embedded in film criticism has led to the notion of 'woman's film' being any more simple a genre than 'man's film'. Thus the notion of a woman's film which is a *film noir* may seem paradoxical but in fact there were a great many of them, from *Rebecca* itself to *Mildred Pierce*, and in so far as distinct categories do in effect exist there are many genres and combinations of genres within each.

Selznick certainly influenced many of the directors who worked with him, not only by pervasive and positive interventions in their work, but, it would seem, in their subsequent work also. King Vidor's *Ruby Gentry* resembles those aspects of *Duel in the Sun* for which he has since declared Selznick was entirely responsible, in the face of his own opposition, as closely as any previous Vidor film; and after *Rebecca* Hitchcock's Hollywood career becomes a bifurcation between films which adapt the formulae of his English thrillers (*Foreign Correspondent, Saboteur*), and smooth, sumptuous, female nightmares (*Suspicion, Notorious, Under Capricorn*). The first two, made away from Selznick, have quite as typical a Selznick feel as *Spellbound* and *The Paradine Case*. By and large, Selznick's influence on Hitchcock is artistically unhappier than his influence on King Vidor.

Open to other influences, Hitchcock might conceivably have found his way, helped by the wartime ascendancy of the *film noir*, towards the American equivalent of such films as *Sabotage* rather than of *The Thirty-Nine Steps*, and turned to the 'woman's film' of that profounder kind rather than the glossy hermetism of *Notorious*. Equally, he may not have wished to take risks, nor to work for any public but the largest, and resolved accordingly to take only those minor risks which box-office success demands. The calculation is not in itself prohibitive of major artistic achievement, and Hitchcock becomes, if anything, subtler and more masterly in his manipulative techniques than ever. But not until the mid-'50s can any but the occasional film of his be placed in the same artistic category as comparable *films noirs* by Wilder, Lang, Welles, Dmytryk, Wyler, Renoir and Huston, and one may well prefer relatively minor films like *Gilda* (Charles Vidor), *I Walk Alone* (Byron Haskin), *Dark Passage* (Delmer Daves), *In A Lonely Place* (Nicholas Ray) and *Angel Face* (Otto Preminger).

At any rate, *Rebecca* adds a new string to the Hitchcock bow, contrasting with his rapid, picaresque subjects, and with the distinctly uneasy treatment of such essentially 'enclosed' subjects as *The Skin Game*, *Juno and the Paycock* and *Jamaica Inn*. In so doing, he was, of course, moving with the times. In his last British film, he failed to achieve what Wyler had done with *Wuthering Heights*, namely to interrelate, with a unity of style and a consistency of mood, openness (heaths, seashores) and oppressive enclosure (dark, spacious, claustrophobic rooms). In *Rebecca* he achieves an early success in what was to become a dominant tonality of the period: one thinks of *The Magnificent Ambersons*, *The Little Foxes*, *Les Enfants Terribles*, and even Olivier's *Hamlet*.

Foreign Correspondent

Foreign Correspondent (1940) was produced by Walter Wanger, and set out to give American public opinion a nudge in favour of active intervention in the war against Hitler's Germany. It is even more straightforward, as a propaganda piece, than *The Lady Vanishes*. The isolationists, who were particularly strong in the Republican party, were arguing that whatever was happening in Europe was no concern of the U.S.A.'s, and this film follows Michael Powell and Emeric Pressburger's *49th Parallel* in tracing their infiltration across the Atlantic.

Joel McCrea plays a U.S. newspaperman who finds himself involved in the abduction, disguised as assassination, of an elderly statesman who might have been a powerful force for peace. The film takes him from America to Holland to England and back across the Atlantic towards America, whither the Nazi spy is escaping. The statesman is hidden, by his torturers, amongst a family of terrified German refugees in London, providing, of course, a particularly pertinent appeal to those large German populations in America who during the First World War had proved so influential in opposing America's entry on to the Allied side.

The statesman's faith, even under torture, in 'the little people who feed the birds', is an overt appeal of a kind from which, Wanger and Chaplin and a few others apart, Hollywood shrank, until 1942. And there's a certain asperity in the statesman's promptly succumbing to the tortures being inflicted upon him, an asperity which may well have helped the film to be, as rumour has it, one of Goebbels' favourites. But its spiritual challenge, given its intended audience, shouldn't be exaggerated. For propaganda which sets out to motivate the complacent and apathetic, and sharpen the urgency of the already concerned, must inspire a blend of healthy fear and resolve, an immediate panic combined with long-term confidence, and this is, of course, why so many propaganda films end with the death of our 'hero'. How much further it's possible to go is indicated by Thorold Dickinson's *Next of Kin*, a wartime British movie which is even stranger in its construction than *Psycho* (the principal character doesn't appear until halfway through) and even stronger in its finale (because of careless talk, a British commando raid suffers a terrifying casualty rate). The 'alarmist' purpose fits in well with the long, sprawling plot, as the amiable Nazi wriggles out of one tight corner into another, with calm indestructibility. Since Hitchcock's cultural context is, after all, American optimism, the film avoids the tragic finale of the Dickinson film.

The assassination is a superb text-book example of staging and cutting, developing a spatially complex action at breakneck speed with a force and clarity which, like so many Hitchcock sequences, moves one by sheer aesthetic appeal. For even when a movie is nearer entertainment propaganda than fine art in the profoundest sense (whereby a spiritual challenge or development is involved), its qualities may be equally productive of aesthetic pleasure. This is, no doubt, intense when the material is spiritually profound (even though profound material tends, understandably, to distract attention, sometimes, indeed, in such a way as to perturb and disrupt pure aesthetic pleasure, which often depends on an absence of worry and distraction). By aesthetic pleasure as a spiritually significant experience we mean an appreciation of imaginative craftsmanship not only for its own sake but as evidence of the controlling and surmounting of the disorderliness and instabilities introduced by important experience, and perhaps a vicarious identification with the artist and understanding of his problems and their interaction of practicalities and spiritualities—not a merely passive 'wine-tasting' of merely fashionable or ornamental forms). The assassination in *Foreign Correspondent* oddly evokes Joris Ivens's *Rain*, arousing the perennial question of whether

Hitchcock took inspiration from another film (art inspiring art) or whether similar subjects provoke similar solutions (life inspiring art), or, of course, both, and in which proportions.

Although it harks back to the picaresque English thriller which critics had liked so much, this was critically less popular, perhaps because Hitchcock counterpoints the rapid action and *dèpaysement* of his earlier films with the more deliberate and conversational pace of all his American films. Increasingly, each line of dialogue is established and lingered on for the sake of its 'twist' against the previous line; and this may help to explain why the older critics, who loved speed and thought dialogue had disturbingly anti-cinematic tendencies, began cooling off. Further, the combination of conventional American hero (Joel McCrea), conventionally suavely dapper English friend (George Sanders) and conventionally suavely ruthless villain (Herbert Marshall) is a psychologically deadening one. And though English critics forgave relatively uninteresting characterisation in the context of 'our Hitch', and all older critics forgave it when it was part of fast cinema, here it hasn't those advantages. Hitchcock certainly had a motive in 'doubling' the English hero. Because Americans are, as we have seen, relatively quick to recall 'perfidious Albion', especially if he's upper class, Hitch's fondness for urbane English charmers might have reversed the film's moral for Americans ('Don't trust the English—as Tories, they're Fascists under the skin') if the English villain hadn't been balanced by George Sanders, whom we think may be a spy but who turns out not to be. The Nazi's innocent daughter (Laraine Day) couldn't fill this function because women are conventionally exempt from rigid ideological loyalties. The not-quite-redemptive decency of Hartz has its parallel here, when the Nazi chief sacrifices himself for his daughter's sake, although he sacrifices his cause only once his cover is blown and the situation is all but hopeless. Still, his altruism towards his cause and his daughters can't be overlooked.

None the less, hero, secondary hero and villain are all mechanically characterised, and the heroine isn't much more interesting. The London Hitchcock showed was as stilted, in spirit, as the London offered by Hollywood directors and art directors who'd never been there but found themselves having to make war films for American audiences whose idea of England was *Mrs. Miniver, A Yank at Oxford*, Sirs Aubrey Smith and Cedric Hardwicke, and the old-fashioned, colourless and curiously unreal Cockneys favoured by John Ford in *The Long Voyage Home*. The private 'tec here is of that kind, and, ironically, it's only among the London Germans that the authenticity of Hitchcock's '30s London comes through. It could certainly seem as if Hitchcock had resigned his British birthright in favour of complete assimilation by Hollywood.

And Hitchcock has testified that his journey to Hollywood did require a considerable effort of readaptation, not simply to the 'system', but to all the differences between American and English audiences whose extent he had not, in England, suspected. These are sufficient to explain the alterations which, I should agree with the older critics, are impoverishments, in comparison certainly to *The Thirty-Nine Steps*, and, to a lesser extent, to *The Lady Vanishes* (which retains a rapid pace even though its local colour is quite second-rate compared to the earlier film).

Hitchcock commented on the difficulty that he found in setting up these American equivalents of his English picaresque pursuits. The thriller, in Hollywood, was considered a second-rate genre, and Hitchcock was unable to persuade the actors whom he wanted to participate in the film, perhaps because they feared that the changes of locale and the suspense could eclipse their personality. Behind that fear lay another Hollywood emphasis, on the need for a consistent emphasis with characters and their reactions through situations which, however fast-moving, were continuous and accumulative. This determined, for example, the classic Hollywood emphasis on close-ups and reverse-angles, as compared with the more varied and less emphatic European syntax. Everything in Hollywood was mediated through the reactions of the individual, although the European, and indeed the English cinema, were both more conscious of the group and more tolerant of individuality in the other, and opposite, sense, i.e. all the traits of character which distinguish the screen personalities from the spectator's. This more detached, discursive approach is another facet of the distinction, to which we referred in discussing *The Ring*, between the American 'marker' (which is a non-discursive reference) and the European 'symbol' (which is discursive and tends to loosen rather than tighten the narrative). Hitchcock's picaresque episodes, and his contrasts between drama and background, are, essentially, 'discursive'. And it is interesting that although his gift for 'settings against type' (to coin a phrase on the analogy of 'casting against type') was much admired in Hollywood it was hardly taken up by his fellow-professionals (a notable exception being, of course, the quasi-European outsider, Orson Welles, with *The Lady From Shanghai*). In *Foreign Correspondent* Hitchcock seems to have accepted the conventional

Hollywood wisdom to the effect that the tempo and variety of his British pursuits might have baffled American audiences, so that, if discursiveness of locale and structure was to be maintained, it had to be at a slower pace, with more emphasis on face and dialogue, to facilitate a continuous identification. He also states that he found American audiences much more drearily logical than the British, who shared his own taste for Alice-in-Wonderland logic.[1]

Certainly, some of Hitchcock's English films had been hits in the States; but now he had to work to the main mass of the American public, including the slow, poetically unsophisticated audiences who had scarcely been touched by English importations of any kind. *Young and Innocent*, significantly Hitchcock's least interesting late '30s thriller, was the exception, if we are to accept Leslie Halliwell's statement that, throughout the '30s, 'The few British features which percolated into the territory (i.e. out-of-city cinemas) had no redeeming features whatever. They even did badly in the cities.' And his list of 'What American exhibitors thought of a few of them' begins with a quotation from 'the *Motion Picture Herald*'s *What The Picture Did For Me* column, in which independent exhibitors could and did air their grievances at the highbrow fodder being served up to them'. '*The Man Who Knew Too Much*. About as much entertainment as a funeral. Skip it.' It may well be that this reaction represented a segment only of American response, and that, otherwise, Hitchcock's films made more impact on the American market than any English films other than Korda's or virtually American made-in-England films like *A Yank at Oxford*. But that segment would seem to be a substantial one, in so far as the evidence of the *Motion Picture Herald* is supported by the transformation which took place in Hitchcock's style.

Hence so much in *Foreign Correspondent* smells of the textbook; even the celebrated assassination sequence. It affords great intellectual pleasure at each viewing, what with its cunningly time-telescoped drive from city centre to open country, with its split-second conjunctions of tourist-calendar local colour (trams, umbrellas, windmills), with its brilliant orchestration of time and space (pursuer and pursued moving, not one behind the other, but in parallel, through a crowd); then the rapidly constricting angularity of trams hemming them in, then the rapid transition from all this clutter to flat empty

---

[1] However offensive some critics may find the idea of a calculated adaptation of style, despite an artistically deleterious effect, nothing is gained by a resort to assumptions that what is artistically authentic is universal and self-evident.

fields (emphasised by a lone plane droning in the windy sky), and the transition again from this open expanse into a close labyrinthine windmill interior, and the implicit contrast between all that a windmill implies of the rustic and the idyllic and the torture-chamber associations of its internal gearing. Yet it remains a superb exemplar of style without the spirit of poetry within it.

There are moments and half-tones. The windmill interior, with its maze of spiral staircase and rotating cogs, evokes Piranesi, until melodrama weakens it, and the diversity of settings is given a visual unity by open, yet sombre, visuals, spacious, yet metallic in texture. Westminster Cathedral is a neat setting for an attempted murder, especially since the killer becomes the victim, and begins by pretending that he doesn't want to go in because all that incense and candles makes him feel sick. Whether physically or spiritually isn't precise, but the overtone of a visceral Protestant bigotry (i.e. a narrow but intense religious feeling) contrasts with his own guilty participation (in possible meanings, the contrast is infinitely ambiguous). At any rate, if one substitutes for this bowler-hatted burly male Cockney, Kim Novak, we're not so far from the fall from the Spanish Mission in *Vertigo*—another Catholic 'outpost' in an agnostic or WASP climate.

Mr. and Mrs. Smith

Mr. and Mrs. Smith is Hitchcock's venture into sophisticated comedy, along the lines perfected by innumerable Hollywood professionals: Lubitsch, Cukor, Bolaslewski, La Cava, Hawks, Leisen, Capra, McCarey, and many more. Here, as often, the characteristics of the genre are more conspicuous than the individuality of the *auteur*, and the series owed just as much to a galaxy of stars and writers as to directors. If one speaks of a Garbo film or a Katharine Hepburn film it is precisely because these stars were *auteurs* to the same extent as directors, or even more profoundly and conspicuously. As often in cinema criticism, it is helpful to think in terms of a film as the product of a particular combination of *auteurs*, none of whom is an altogether unique personality (in so far as he shares a great many assumptions and approaches with his collaborators and an entire cultural climate) and none of whom would have done what he did, even within his own sphere of competence, had he not been working in the context of what others were doing within theirs. For example, Cukor remarked that in these films everything was sacrificed to the rhythm of the acting; and this seems to be borne out by the films themselves, even though the concept of rhythm in acting is something to which film aestheticians, preoccupied with the specifically cinematographic, have paid virtually no attention whatsoever, as compared with the rhythm of the cutting, which, in films where the actor is setting the pace, must be subsidiary. It is also evident that the rhythm of the acting will depend on the rhythm which the actors bring with them, and which the director has to accept, even if he modifies it, which is when we become conscious of actor as *auteur* and of the director as an *accoucheur* rather than an *onlie begettor*.

This type of strophe is somewhat alien to Hitchcock's tightly pre-planned style, his tendency to think in terms of storypoints rather than of warm little explosions of the actors' personalities. (Whence the irony that Cary Grant does less acting in a Hitchcock drama like *Suspicion* than in a Hawks comedy like *Bringing Up Baby*; for suspense-ambiguity depends on underplaying where comedy regularly resorts to overplaying, for reasons suggested in the opening chapters of *The Crazy Mirror*.) Hitchcock tends to cut and dry actors' responses, and it's not surprising that Robert Montgomery and Carole Lombard don't bring forth the flow of varied and surprising responses which would add warmth and life to Hitchcock's altogether correct comic cybernetic.

The story has the two leads discovering that their marriage has been annulled and deciding to renew (and test) their love by living apart and repeating their courtship. There are some interesting asides on the American woman's tyrannical insistence on perfect together-ness on every level especially the spiritual one, and the husband's ambiguous feelings when asked whether he'd go through all those complications again. But this degree of barbed mischief is about par for the genre and there's rather more venom in, for example, *The Philadelphia Story*.

Suspicion

It was possible to blame Selznick for the less interesting aspects of *Rebecca*, Hollywood for those of *Foreign Correspondent*, and an unfamiliar and uncongenial genre for those of *Mr. and Mrs. Smith*. But with *Suspicion* there could be little doubt that Hitchcock had chosen to bury himself in a cold, correct, sumptuous, impersonal piece which might have been concocted by a box-office computer—sufficiently sophisticated to insert, at indicated moments in its structure, the Hitchcock touch. It's both a recognisably Hitchcock film, and a spiritually empty one. The light and shadow effects (a light placed inside a glass of milk), the subtly outsize props enabling Hitchcock to anticipate modern wide-angle lens effects, and the bold angling, make for a polished, academic expressionism which has nothing to express that would raise an eyebrow in the illustration to a *Saturday Evening Post* serial.

This isn't to say that Hitchcock hadn't had to fight to go outside the extraordinarily narrow limits which the Hollywood studio system had come to set itself. The novel on which it is based, Francis Iles's *Before the Fact*, concerns a young, plain Englishwoman who realises that her handsome and attentive husband is not only a playboy, gambler and thief, who married her for her money (as even before the marriage she suspected, and accepted) but a murderer, and plans to murder her for money. Something between masochism, weariness and a selfless love inspires her to accept the poisoned glass. She is an accomplice before the fact, and in this sense she's an anti-Rebecca, accepting guilt by turning murder into suicide where Rebecca imposed guilt by turning suicide into murder.

All sorts of fascinating moral and psychological paradoxes are thus involved, ranging from the mysteries of feminine masochism to the morality of suicide and the transference of guilt. One can imagine a Mauriac or a Bunuel exploring the real—or apparent?—watershed between self-destructiveness and a devotion like sanctity. Hitchcock's treatment does retain the necessary framework, in that Joan Fontaine *thinks* Cary Grant is her murderer and *almost* drinks the poisoned milk. And although she doesn't quite and he isn't, this last twist needn't necessarily have invalidated the preceding story, as an internal or interactional psychological study. It certainly allows Hitchcock a favourite, unusual and intriguing motif: the theme of paranoia as self-indulgence, as deliciously destructive as a drug.

And it transposes into a very different key his collateral theme of grateful submission to harshness, whether by men (*Downhill*) or women (*Jamaica Inn*). For Cary Grant's behaviour is charming enough with just a hint of reasonable asperity, and if it seems sinister it is through an apprehension of a much subtler kind of manipulation which, over the last forty years, has gradually replaced the tough and obvious Victorian hierarchies. If Hitchcock's style seems to be a plodding reiteration, it is perhaps because his spectators need a heavy emphasis on apparent informalities and casual details as, in fact, powerful pressures. All the same, the film is in no sense a serious animadversion on the matter; all its says, if it says anything, is that wives shouldn't be exaggeratedly suspicious of husbands who don't match up to every specification of the Protestant ethic, by whose standards they have slothful and sybaritic tendencies. And this would make Hitchcock the very reverse of a severe moralist, but, rather, indulgent to a common-sense epicureanism which was in any case accepted as a norm throughout most of the '30s comedies. As it stands, the film breaks what would seem to be one of Hitchcock's rules, enunciated in discussing *The Lodger*. For if no-one would ever believe that Ivor Novello was a murderer there, how could they ever believe that Cary Grant was a murderer here? Perhaps the answer is that audiences are prepared to take a suspension of disbelief so far, even though one has to work harder to make the point. At any rate, the same point seems to have occurred to the studio, in a completely different way, for during Hitchcock's absence they were so alarmed by the thought of Cary Grant even seeming to be a murderer that they cut out all the scenes which suggested that he was and reduced the film to a completely pointless fifty-five minutes. The present ending is a compromise, for Hitchcock would have preferred to end with Joan Fontaine drinking the poisoned milk and lying back to die while Cary Grant, whistling unsuspectingly, posts the letter in which she has incriminated him. Her motivation would have been that she accepts to die but feels society should be protected from the man without whose love her own life is pointless. This ending differs somewhat from the novel's, whose major point, or so I am informed, is the woman's consent, not only to her own death, but to her wealthy widower's callously happy dissipation. Just this switch turns the story from a study in feminine generosity to a study in a woman's altruistic sadism—towards herself for her lover and towards her lover for society—an altruism which carries evident overtones of direct sado-masochism. At any rate, Hitchcock's original ending would have made her an accomplice in two murders, a victim, and a judge.

Had this original ending been retained, then all the moral points which one can discern in the present conclusion have to be reversed. Instead of warning against paranoia, it becomes a confirmation of it; instead of criticising the conventional Puritan ethic, it tends to reinforce it; and so on. Either way there seems to be no gain or loss in artistic depth, since the more complacent ending is matched by the more unusual temptation. At any rate, the ambiguity created by the suspense is so lively that Raymond Borde and Etienne Chaumeton have no more scruples about seeing the other film within this one than the present writer made about translating half-caste as homosexual in *Murder*. 'We maintain that *Suspicion* should be classified as a murder film.' Sometimes, certainly, a last-minute twist, however crucial, can fail to cancel out implications made heavily over the entire length of the film; which is another reason why no 'objective' procedure tells us what we often want it to tell us, what meaning a film really has for most of the people who really saw it, and not what meaning it would have for the ideal spectator, who is also an extremely anomalous one, if indeed he exists at all.

While this ambiguity makes Hitchcock's film more complex than a literal analysis of its plotline might suggest, it also indicates why *Suspicion* ought to be classed among his entertainments (and our sense is the conventional one, not Graham Greene's) rather than among those of his films which have solid artistic interest. As often, an entertainer achieves two meanings by hesitating between them and examining neither (still less their interaction), whereas an artist would trace the struggle within the characters between different courses of action, and trace it in a way which would shed a new light on human experience. In the case of *Suspicion* the alteration is extremely easy. Cary Grant is hesitating between whether or not he wants to murder Joan Fontaine, and, if not, why not; whether through affection, or inhibition, or fear of being found out. And Joan Fontaine would become aware of his hesitations, but be uncertain as to what her reaction is, whatever his eventual course of action will turn out to be. And if one superimposes the three endings, and puts them in the middle, then psychological complexity follows naturally. That is, Joan Fontaine decides that if she loves him she must trust him, and that if he kills her she wants to die; either way she must drink the glass which she has reason to believe is poisoned. But this decision involves her in a consequent dilemma, as to whether the sort of self-sacrifice which is right for absolute love absolves her from the duty of protecting society or whether that duty merely masks a temptation to unaltruistic revenge. And she might try to sort the matter out, before the poisoning reaches its term, by getting to know all the dissipated friends of her husband and whom she believes may dance on her grave. In the process she might sense that the pleasures of dissipation appeal to her too, and hesitate between wanting to kill herself because of it or to live on because at last she understands her husband. And if she finally realises, not only that her fears are unreal, but that, far from being the innocent lamb turning the other cheek, her view of life ('hedonism is murder') is cynical beyond sanity. So that her final *relief* is paralleled by *horror*—of the murderous guilt within. And it is true that the hypocritically righteous tend to project on to the moderately wicked much more wickedness than they are in fact guilty of, as Jesus Christ never tired of pointing out, with disappointingly little effect.

It's easy to see why Hitchcock couldn't have made that film in Hollywood in the '40s (although Bunuel was making equally complicated films in Mexico in the '50s). But one isn't really doing criticism, or the best in Hitchcock, any good service by suggesting that *Suspicion* is the film it might have been, and in any case Wyler's *Wuthering Heights* and Siodmak's *Phantom Lady* both, in their very different ways, establish the mysteries of masochism and apathy in a principal character.

Saboteur

Hitchcock returned to the picaresque format for *Saboteur*, under the Frank Lloyd–Jack H. Skirball banner. A suspicious-looking character starts a fire in a munitions factory and hands a brave worker an extinguisher filled, evilly, with gasoline. This reverse flame-thrower makes for one of Hitchcock's nastier and crueller disasters. Thereafter, the picaresque machinery efficiency performs its accomplished motions, although Hitchcock feels the film suffers from an insufficiently integrated diversity of ideas. And in a sense the film does sectionalise itself; a munitions factory, fire, a blind man's retreat, a circus freakshow, a rancher's peaceful home, a palatial ballroom, the torch of the Statue of Liberty. But there's nothing in these locations which effectively excludes the emphasis on certain accumulative motifs and markers, preferably props in the plot, just as Hitchcock used to link separate actions in *Blackmail* and even within the confined framework of *The Lady Vanishes*. There are fragments of such a structure here: the fire, the man called *Fry*, the extinguisher in the truck, and finally, although this is lost, the torch in the hand of the Statue of Liberty; indeed the opening conflagration and the final locale suffice to suggest a meditation on the theme of freedom as anarchy and freedom as vision. The hermit and the freak-show nomads would fit in with such a theme, being social outsiders and fringe-groups, while the apparently peaceful and respectable settings turn out to be treacherous or dangerous (the prosperous rancher with his happily gurgling grand-daughter, the ballroom, the Statue of Liberty itself, where the hero can't appeal to the tourists, ordinary people like himself, because they wouldn't believe his story). The slow, deliberate emphasis on the plot mechanics, adopted for reasons suggested in discussing *Foreign Correspondent*, seems to impede the development of a theme, not simply for its own sake, but for the sake of a structure of atmospheres. A theme might be indicated by certain props, and, indeed, Hitchcock develops the use of markers in subsequent films, notably the key in *Notorious*, which, although it picks up overtones as it goes, remains, by and large, more of a marker than a symbol. But a sense of continuity-and-contrast as between atmospheres, determining the visual style of the film, and the selection of certain configurations of details (like hands in *The Lady Vanishes*) is an even more important form of unity. In *Saboteur* each sequence is almost a separate little film with the same characters and one's final mental image is of Robert Cummings drifting in a kind of semi-abstract space.

Only parts of scenes echo the quality of *Sabotage*; notably a mixture of cosiness, grotesquerie, prurience and warmth in the fairground community, which is like an attractive epilogue to Tod Browning's *Freaks* (like which it carries an anti-horror meaning), and the villain's slow, pitiable fall from the Statue of Liberty. Later Hitchcock commented on his 'elementary mistake' in having the villain rather than the hero conclude in peril—presumably in so far as spectators, repudiating the villain instead of identifying with him, don't mind too much if he does fall to his death, whereas the hero's or heroine's danger might be agonising. All the same, one might have expected audiences to identify with the man in his terror, and I certainly remember being vividly wrung, as a child, by a *Boy's own Paper*, or was it *Chums*, serial in which the brutal, crippled, Prussianesque villain, pinned in his wheelchair, sinks slowly to his death in a jungle swamp, with the heroes, unable to save him, horrified rather than gratified by the cruelly slow grindings of the mills of poetic justice. The climax of *Saboteur* affected me similarly, *ætat* 13, in the late '40s, and far from there being any question of an elementary mistake one night well prefer, as morally more sophisticated, and more humane, a sudden suspense of compassion for the bad guy, which is, after all, in the spirit of the final slightly redemptive twists in *The Lady Vanishes* and *Foreign Correspondent*. But it may be that American audiences were more Manichean, punitive and persecutory about enemy spies than Hitchcock had bargained for, and watched his death with a mixture of complacency, exasperation (in case he doesn't die!) and irate bepuzzlement at the hero's attempts to save him ('don't help the guy, stamp on his fingers!').

In *Sabotage*, the woman whose husband has killed her boy and whom she is about to kill has to smile at a Silly Symphony. In *Saboteur* the gunfight on the screen gets mixed up with the gunfight in the auditorium. Between these two cinema sequences there is all the emotional and spiritual difference in the world.

Shadow Of A Doubt

So far Hitchcock had not quite put down roots into American life. *Rebecca* and, as he points out, *Suspicion*, an account of its artistic collaborators, were in a sense English films. In *Foreign Correspondent* only the framing sequences are American and the story itself would have made as much sense if the journalist had been an Englishman. *Saboteur* goes through the moves but the intimacy and poetry don't quite appear. Hitchcock had accommodated America, but had yet to draw from it an inspiration akin to that which nourished his London subjects. His next film might have been intended to bring him into closer contact than before with middle America rather than Holly-wood. *Shadow Of A Doubt* was written with Thornton Wilder, author of *Our Town*, and delves into the intimacies of a small-town, mid-Western, middle-class family. Young Charlie Newton (Teresa Wright) falls in love with her dashing yet courteous Uncle Charlie (Joseph Cotten) from out East—and slowly realises that he has made a prac-tice of murdering rich widows. Torn between horror and something more like sexual love than family love, she doesn't go to the police, but asks him to leave town. While attempting to throw her from the train, he slips and is killed.

In its sketch of leisurely, agreeable family life, the film has a realism and intimacy which in wartime Hollywood was unusual and precious. In so far as the framework allows the film to relish the subtler traits of character, its mixture of the everyday and the nightmarish recalls *Blackmail* or *The Lodger*. It's a story about a lodger who isn't sus-pected enough, and the parallelism extends even to the introduction of a love-affair between the girl who loves the lodger and the detective who loves her.

Certainly Hitchcock's film accommodates a sardonic touch in so far as the young, idealistic American girl is, by her collusion, already, in moral equivalent, keeper of a gigolo and accomplice after the fact. Interesting also is the equivocation, in the girl's heart, between a sexual love (which would be somewhat incestuous if it were more conscious, or if the resemblances between uncle and parent were insisted on) and a family love, which, dramatically, has its own particular interests. After all, sexual love, by convention, explains everything, whereas family love is usually supposed to be good in its moral effects—except, of course, when one is dealing with the Mafia, and even then film gangsters' mothers and brothers usually attempted to be good or moderating influences on them. A connection between family love and something a little incestuous does bring us quite near what Howard Hawks tried to sneak past the censor in *Scarface*. But the wholesome atmosphere of *Shadow Of A Doubt* occludes such undertones, as it might not have done had its happy family shown normal internal tensions of a kind quite common in the woman's film. This isn't to demand that it come into the same harrowing bracket as *The Little Foxes* or *The Magnificent Ambersons*. But it respects Hollywood, and perhaps an authentic American, convention in respecting the generally complete division between normally tensionless families and abnormally tension-wracked ones.

For the peccadilloes of which the decent family folk are guilty are so tiny compared with the crimes of the pleasant uncle, that the continuity between them isn't experienced as is the heroine's guilt in *Blackmail* or the ambivalence of Verloc in *Sabotage*. Theoretically, the niece certainly shares in her uncle's guilt. For she yielded to her fondness sufficiently to ask him to move on—to sweep him, as it were, under the carpet and out of sight. Her weakness boomerangs—his next victim is not a widow in another country, but a virgin, herself. Theoretically therefore there might well be a stern morality of the kind which Chabrol and Rohmer postulate. The girl is both a victim of her own sentimentality (like the widows) and an accomplice after the fact (with her Uncle). And has she not, by her struggle for life, killed the man she loved and tried to save—spared the murderer of others, but loved her own life more than his?

But the film also puts her in something of a tragic predicament, through her opposing loyalties to the young detective, which require her to betray her family to the law, and that's wrong too, at least so far as a vernacular morality is concerned. After all, if an uncle committed a murder, we would find it very strange for even an emotionally unattached niece to promptly rush off to the police about it, and wouldn't find it strange at all if she decided to shield him. Certainly, multiple murder is another matter, but in then deciding whether the niece was right or wrong in giving him the benefit of a shadow of a doubt, about his guilt, and about where her own loyalties ought to lie, we find ourselves in a far from cut-and-dried area which is much more like a tragic dilemma where whatever you do is wrong and nothing is right than a sin-and-punishment situation. This isn't to say that Hitchcock thinks that young Charlie is innocent. He probably thinks that no one is innocent. But the film is interesting precisely because the sin-and-punishment aspect is countered by a disillusion-ment-of-normally-partial-innocence aspect, and I suspect that it is this latter aspect which Hitchcock expects to be uppermost in most spectators' minds.

It is this aspect indeed which he emphasises, by a prologue in which Uncle Charlie seems to be fleeing from two hard-faced criminal types (whom we don't yet know are detectives). So that although he's probably a bit shady in so far as he's mixed up in shady business it might be the kind of morally forgivable crime which would deserve all the support Charlie can give him and all the risks she might have to take for him. All the hints about widow-slaying incline us the other way too, and our uncertainties shift our minds away from the question of what the niece's moral duties would be to what the truth about her uncle is, what effect this will have on her, and what she will do when she finds out.

Young Charlie's guilt is certainly a thread in the pattern, but not the broadest or brightest. It doesn't predominate until very late in the film, and then is tempered by the possibility that he's entrusting him-self to her, and may be in love. The attempted murder on the train rapidly and emphatically makes her a victim, thus re-emphasising the moral polarity between her (relative) innocence and his perfidious cunning. There may be no clear boundary between being someone's dupe and being his accomplice, but if the two are synonymous, all murderers are as innocent as their victims. Thus, although, in outline, the film's transference of guilt looms as strong as in *Strangers On A Train*, its dramatic perspective renders it, if anything, weaker. The earlier film ends on the theme of railroad tracks which the later film soon picks up, and anticipates that intimate way with American families which is completed by *The Birds*.

Moralistic critics noticed Hitchcock's evocative way with two early shots, one showing Uncle Charlie lying on his bed, left to right, the other showing young Charlie lying on hers, left to right also. And they assumed that such similarity could only suggest moral similarity (although it could also emphasise contrast, or merely connection). Similarly, the identity of name was looked on as indication of moral equivalence. Yet the girl's being named after her uncle by her parents might suggest only a family loyalty, while its obliteration of sexual lines might indicate something too effusive, too incautiously affirmative, of family ties. Of that injudicious goodwill, the girl is no more guilty than her parents. She is scapegoat and victim of the cult of the family. Her dilemma makes her a tragic heroine, and, if anything, *less* guilty than they.

At any rate, the family constitutes one area for the battle between an American complacency and Hitchcock's burnt-child fear of reality. With his virtuoso sense of film form as meaning, Hitchcock rapidly develops the theme in terms of social generality. The opening credits feature the Merry Widow waltz and a shot of a 19th-century ball. But this dream of bourgeois splendour, at once exuberant and cosily claustral, is disrupted as the orchestration changes to a discordant, blowsy, '40s swing band style. The camera cuts to a squalid and derelict bridge, with bums lying about. At this time Victorian domesticity was acquiring sinister undertones (Thorold Dickinson's *Gaslight*, 1940, becoming the George Cukor remake in 1944). And Hitchcock equally refuses to equate modern life with a moral falling-off, for, as a series of general civic views bring us to a nicer part of the town, the violins are let back in. Thus Uncle Charlie's city isn't just a city from the (industrial and sophisticated) East. It contains within itself the compromise between two extremes: the snobbery and irresponsibility of 'the gilded age' upper class (now modified, except in dream) and the apathetic poverty of the Depression (which ended only four or five years before this film's date). Hitchcock expresses no opinion as to any link between these antitheses. But both might be contrasted with the intentions of the Quaker founders who gave this city, Philadelphia, its name. And Charlie, with his olde worlde, widow-charming, grace, his lazy fear of poverty, is like an evil sport of 19th-century respectability, while his vulgarly seedy apathy takes its style from the era of the bums under the bridge; between the two extremes, he opposes his insidious intrication of egoism and counterfeit. The Victorian ball represents, not the goodness of the past, but the delusions of nostalgia. It is a memory turned dream, edited into sentimentality by Charlie's widows. Perhaps Victorian respectability is itself a perversion of Quakerism, or, at least, of its best remembered form, which blends unitarianism, social responsibility and faith in the power of good.

A faith which itself is likely to be duped. Its style and smile seem widely spread among the women who, within the film's opening, evoke Charlie's past victims. His landlady maintains her invincible innocence in the face of every indication of his underworld vulgarity (he lies apathetically on his bed, banknotes scattered on the floor). She offers to open his window, falling into the role of indulgent mother-figure. In our first views of young Charlie's town, Santa Rosa, California, a female traffic cop wears the same kind of rimless glasses. Smiling broadly, she seems happily in control of her smalltown neighbours at their wheels. Young Charlie lives in daydreams—of excited passion, of romance—whose sexuality seems not quite specific in her mind. Her precocious little sister (also bespectacled) puts another kind of daydream—storybooks—before telephone calls. Her mother reacts to Charlie's telegram with great joy, and her Victorian hairstyle and cut of dress recalls the opening shot, i.e. the days when Uncle Charlie's victims were young and gay, and which they dreamt of his reviving.

If she has something of a spinster, and therefore unfulfilled, about her, her husband has something sepulchral about him. Calmly he queries young Charlie's youthfully impatient dismissal of the family life which he and his wife have built up. And their disagreement can be moralised in alternative, or, rather, complementary, ways. Young Charlie is partly right; maybe a certain absence of passion leaves both the wife and the daughter part-widows, and exposed to the lure of Charlie's charm. But her father is right too. To expect romance of life is to expect too much, and to lower one's defences to infiltration by the unscrupulous underworld. (Here Hitchcock adumbrates the romance/crime, reality/illusion, past/present antinomies of *Vertigo*.) Uncle Charlie and young Charlie are about to send each other telegrams, and the girl raises the (romantic) issue of telepathy, as if to stress that, even if evil doesn't seek out the innocent, the innocent, being dissatisfied, will call evil to themselves. But if Uncle Charlie looks like bringing excitement (whether romance or murder!), he himself suffers from total apathy (the money lies around unused until fear moves him on).

These complex socio-moral statements depend on Hitchcock's grasp of pure form. And this gave him one of his great advantages over most Hollywood professionals for it permitted him to establish strong connections and to insinuate possibilities very rapidly, and independently of explanation or narrative. Hitchcock remembered Kuleshov, of whom hardly any American directors had ever heard, and whose theories they would have dismissed as precious and airy-fairy if they had, and knew that to juxtapose is enough to create a connection. To cut between two unconnected people is enough to set the riddle, How can these disparate people be connected? Thereafter, of course, the connection must gradually be expounded, in terms of audience philosophy and expectation. But Hitchcock always retained immense freedom to make connections without, or alongside, narrative and verbal constructions. But in *Shadow Of A Doubt*, Hitchcock shows himself a real belt-and-braces man, using a dense verbo-narrative mesh (the synchronous telegrams) to establish connections and affinities with which his aesthetic preferences would incline him to dispense.

More sharply barbed versions of the story might be rather different, and a narrative synopsis is the most convenient way of indicating possible alternatives. Rather than being introduced by association with the big cities of the East, Uncle Charlie would be presented as a local salesman who left home after the death of his first wife, a woman too old for him. His niece's love for him has always been intense, and when her suspicions become near-certainties, she almost destroys the evidence which might give a definite answer one way or the other When she questions her uncle closely, he laughs at her, seduces her, playfully admits the crime, and leaves her. She is tempted to denounce him, partly out of injured pride. Her motives for not doing so are a mixture of selfless love, selfish hope, fear of conviction for suppressing evidence, fear of scandal, and concern for her family's reputation, and illusions. Finding herself pregnant, she rapidly allows the detective to seduce her, and marries him. At intervals she reads of the deaths of rich widows in other cities, from some of which her family receive cheerful postcards signed, 'Love from Uncle Charlie'. She watches her husband playing with 'his' children. Every day the elder son resembles his real father more closely, and has some of his gestures. Her widowed mother-in-law reminds her of the other widows. Uncle Charlie returns, just passing through, and thinks his grandniece is just like her 'father'. She doesn't know if his irony is impenetrable or if he's just too self-centred to see himself in the boy. Her husband is following up the case of yet another murdered widow. Uncle Charlie charms his niece's mother-in-law, but seems to realise, at last, that he should have loved his niece more deeply than he did. Or is he merely out to neutralise a witness? She refuses to leave with him. He proposes to her mother-in-law. Perhaps, young Charlie desperately reasons, his real motive is to settle near her, for their longed-for affair. Perhaps, too, her expressed suspicion is sufficient protection for the mother-in-law. The detective begins to suspect, wrongly, that his wife is having an affair with Charlie, but is as confused and helpless as the detective in *The Lodger*. His mother, scenting her husband's dissatisfaction, hopes that an affair with young Charlie will satisfy him, and keep him near her. And so the film ends. Happy families, *huis clos*.

Some such concentration of the story would have permitted a rather more continuous interplay between the everyday, the nightmarish, and the subversively, yet morally, cynical. As it is, Gavin Millar's criticism of the movie stands. The link between innocence and crime remains as weak, or as carefully camouflaged, as the moral ironies between the slum-mews of *Blackmail* and the loftier treads on the social staircase. Perhaps audiences, or Hollywood's idea of them, were still unripe for much more.

None the less, the film has its claim to a place in the history books. It anticipates *The Best Years of Our Lives* in its mixture of what used to be called 'semi-documentary' freshness, and hometown's subtle moral dangers. As usual Hitchcock was in the van of a Hollywood trend. The film also relates to the dawning interest in family murders (*Arsenic and Old Lace, Home Sweet Homicide, Monsieur Verdoux*). In the Capra film the old ladies commit the murders. The Chaplin sees things from the seducer-murderer's point of view. The domestic murder cycle can also be seen as a transposition, into everyday terms, of the precedent, and concurrent, cycle of 'Gothic family' murders (*Rebecca, Dragonwyck*).

Lifeboat

Hitchcock turned for fresh inspiration to another realistic writer. John Steinbeck is responsible for the original story of *Lifeboat*. Yet it might almost be a development out of the finale of *Foreign Correspondent* (what if the sinking flying-boat had launched a dinghy and Herbert Marshall had stayed coolly in command?). But this lifeboat got clear of a torpedoed ship, only to take on board the skipper of the U-Boat which was sunk in the same engagement. The ship's passengers constitute a cross-section of American democracy: notably a glamorous journalist (Tallulah Bankhead), a Communist worker (John Hodiak), a poker-player business-man (Henry Hull), a jitterbug fan (William Bendix), and a gentle, religious negro steward. The Nazi is the only one with any seamanship, and the fact they need him for their own survival throws an unflattering light on human nature and on the democracies. Eventually they free themselves from the demoralisation that lies over them like a spell and regain their self-respect. They hesitate before allowing another Nazi aboard. But perhaps they have learned their double lesson: to suspect but not to lynch, to balance healthy fear and decent charity, to stand up for themselves yet to prefer mercy to pitiless logic.

On one level the film is a study in human behaviour. It's a—melodramatic—Hollywood equivalent of the 'literature of extreme situations', with a lifeboat instead of a concentration camp, or a shell-hole in No-Man's-Land, or whatever. On another level, it is quite consciously an allegory for the democracies' ignominious and all but suicidal acquiescence in Hitler's expert bullying during the '30s. Lindsay Anderson dismissed such a message as too late (since by 1944 the United Nations was aborning), yet there was surely all the more need for a film to rub salt into the moral wounds and ensure that the scars remained clearly, and reproachfully, prominent.

It's surprising that although the Communist emerges so sympathetically the film was not raked up by the McCarthy witch-hunts, in view of the extent to which, on the third level, it is impregnated with overtones about the ethos of American society after the war. A love-hate polarity exists between the journalist, apparently a spoiled little rich girl, and the Communist, who alone appreciates the Nazi threat—a premature anti-Fascist, without any doubt. Even he cannot solve the democracies' main problem, that of finding leadership which will match the aplomb and cunning of their adversary. But eventually the rich girl confesses that she was born on the wrong side of the tracks and made it, by determination, from the stockyard-side tenements, and her true American-type grit is vindicated when she realises that her slightly pretentious interjection—'Ye Gods and little fishes!'—indicates the solution to their starvation and thirst. So individualism and ambition are, after all, the American way. Even so, she has had to sacrifice her hopes (manuscripts) and gains (jewellery), and a further gesture in the direction of egalitarianism is made when the Communist plays his boss at poker for control of the factories if they get back alive. A timely gust of wind leaves the result in doubt, but it's the boss who shows signs of ratting on the result if it goes against him. One wonders how far the final balance of ideological sympathies expresses Steinbeck himself, or Hitchcock, or Hollywood in its pro-Russian period, balancing, but not suppressing, Steinbeck's left-wing positions.

In its open accusations of a group who is felt to be 'us', it's

Hitchcock's boldest film since *Blackmail*, and it's vastly superior to *The Lady Vanishes*. *Sabotage* apart, it's the first Hitchcock film to arouse critical protests about its 'nastiness', and this furious chorus against its challenge to the propaganda banalities of the documentary film illustrates how the critical so-called intelligensia was even more conformist than the Hollywood studios. For 20th-Century-Fox did, after all, produce the film.

Ironically, the consensus which was so displeased by Hitchcock's 'nastiness' appreciated the tragic pessimism of Wellman's *Strange Incident* (*The Ox-Bow Incident*) made by the same studio at about the same time. *Lifeboat* is also a lynching story, and transposes with only very minor adjustments into a Western covered wagon or stagecoach lost on the salt-flats. The same consensus also appreciated the cynical pessimism of Clouzot's *Le Corbeau*, and it's strange that critics should have condemned in Hollywood movies the very attitudes which they cited as an example to Hollywood when they turned up in French movies! The reason, probably, is that critics didn't expect a Hollywood film to be pessimistic and critical, and although they could recognise that attitude when it turned up in the rather solemnly tragic tone of Wellman's film, the Hitchcock name in particular geared them to expect a 'fun' picture along the line of *The Thirty-Nine Steps* or *The Lady Vanishes*. So they felt that *Lifeboat* must have become pessimistic by mistake, as it were, that it was a symptom rather than a revelation. The idea that John Steinbeck might have been critical didn't occur to them either, since of *The Grapes of Wrath* they only remembered the grit of ordinary people, and that seemed quite unlike the implication that a cross-section of ordinary people could be even temporarily craven. Whether or not *Lifeboat* was artistically successful, to attack it in the way in which it was attacked was to help ensure that Hitchcock would never again try anything that wasn't ultra-conventional. Twenty years later, *Psycho* met the same critical reaction.

A second reason for the film's critical unpopularity in Britain was, doubtless, its daring to deal with wartime hardships in a non-documentary style. Given the assumption that a film is good in so far as it resembles the productions of the Crown Film Unit and Ealing Studios, then *Lifeboat* may well seem an awkward cross between *Western Approaches* (in its actual situation), a covered wagon mini-saga (the emergency operation, the dawning love-affair, a sort of *Reader's Digest* manual of lifeboat problems), and *Thunder Rock* (the moral-philosophical film). Dialogue necessary for the allegorical functions disrupts the extremity of the situation. The real relevance of lifeboat, or *Raft of the Medusa,* or *huis clos* situations, is to the rude basics of human nature (law versus cannibalism, etc) rather than all the other issues which the film introduces—its fourth area of reference being 'How should we treat the Germans after the war?', as per Noel Coward's song 'Don't let's be beastly to the Germans' and Ealing's *Frieda* (1947), whose hero daringly brings a fräulein to the North of England. And her Nazi brother comes too.

Although the film is set in a space stretching from one horizon to the other, it's also the first of Hitchcock's tightly 'enclosed' dramas, like *Rope, Under Capricorn, Dial M for Murder* and *Rear Window.* The shots of the journalist coolly getting the correct focus on struggling survivors through her ciné-camera anticipate the somewhat culpable activities of James Stewart in *Rear Window* (although if his are considered so sinful as to deserve the fright of being nearly murdered, it's difficult to know what sort of punishment this ambitious newsreel-cameraman deserves—hanging, drawing and quartering, no doubt, a thought which should have led the young Jansenist Fathers on a crusade against documentary, cinema-vérité and indeed the cinema in general. But film criticism is a suitably ambiguous and impure position for which they will no doubt be suitably chastised; by becoming film directors, perhaps?). Later, Hitchcock might have been tempted to ten-minute takes, or even, given the technical means, one ninety-minute take, using backs as time-lapse fade-outs and given a solution to the stubble problem. As it is, the visual compositions are resourcefully varied, and far from oppressive. If not emotionally convincing, the film's intellectual intricacy is altogether fascinating. The shifting alliances between the characters, their fluctuations of attitude, bring the paranoid uncertainties of the detective story very near a more orthodox, and mature, attitude to the moral ambiguities of human nature. Thus, the generally kindly and trusting William Bendix character is startlingly eager to throw the Nazi overboard, and isn't afraid to explain why. He changed his own name to Smith from Schmidt and it's these Nazis who make his own ethnic group seem dishonourable. It can indeed be argued that American xenophobia and race-snobbery spring from American uneasiness about non-WASP origins, although here the issue is raised with reference to a group not too low in the American ethnic hierarchy.

Bon Voyage, Aventure Malgache

In 1944 Hitchcock returned to England and directed two short films
for the Crown Film Unit, both using the Molière Players, a troupe of
Free French actors in exile, and played in French. Since the themes
are French also it arouses an interesting question about the nationality
of the films. *Bon Voyage* involves an R.A.F. officer escaping from
Occupied France under the escort of a Polish officer whom he is later
informed is a Gestapo agent; and a long 'flashback' brings out the
significance of a variety of details unnoticed the first time. The idea
of discrepancies emerging during a reinterpretation of an apparently
clearly shown reality is developed in a more sophisticated fashion by
Anthony Asquith in *The Woman in Question* in 1950, the same year
as Kurosawa's *Rashomon*. In the course of discussing the film with a
group of Free French advisers, Hitchcock realised how internally
divided against each other French forces were, and made this the theme
of his next film, *Aventure Malgache*, which centres on a young lawyer
organising the Resistance in Madagascar. Chabrol and Rohmer describe it, briefly and enigmatically, as 'a homage by Hitchcock to
France, the land where one eats well', although they don't say whether
they consider this as gourmandise or gourmetise or whether it constitutes a sin and whether civil disunity is a punishment for tucking-in.
The last film was never released, due, appropriately, to disagreements
about it, and it's not quite clear what propoganda purpose, if any,
these movies served. My recollections of a long extract from the former
run at the National Film Theatre seventeen years ago, are that the
film's images dangled rather listlessly from its commentary, and the
only obvious Hitchcock moment involved a German spy talking over
the telephone while turning out the pockets of a man he's shot.

Spellbound

Returning to Hollywood, Hitchcock lost himself once more in what
was for him, although not for all, that most suffocatingly congenial
of Marienbads, the Selznick Studio. With Angus MacPhail, co-
scenarist of *Bon Voyage*, and Ealing stalwart, Hitchcock prepared a
version of Francis Beeding's *The House of Dr. Edwards*. Hitchcock
describes the novel to Truffaut as the story of the madmen taking
over the lunatic asylum; 'even the orderlies were lunatics and they

The
Master

1

2

3

or film
tles see
st of
lustrations
n page 11

God's Eye Views

6 7

Upstairs and Downstairs

8

Ordeals by Han;

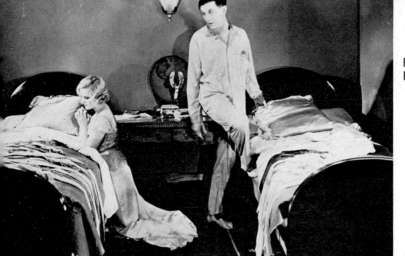

12

13

14

An
Avant-garde
Aesthetic

15
16

17   18

19

The Pa

20

itics

The Paranoia of Politics

Pity our Simplicities

30

31

Goodnight La

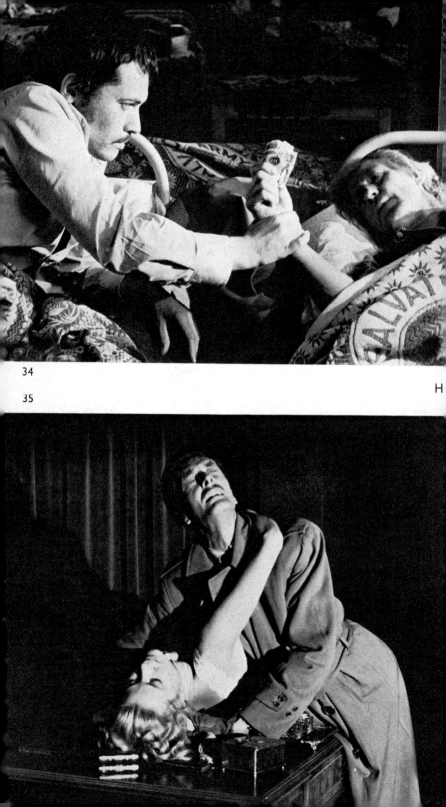

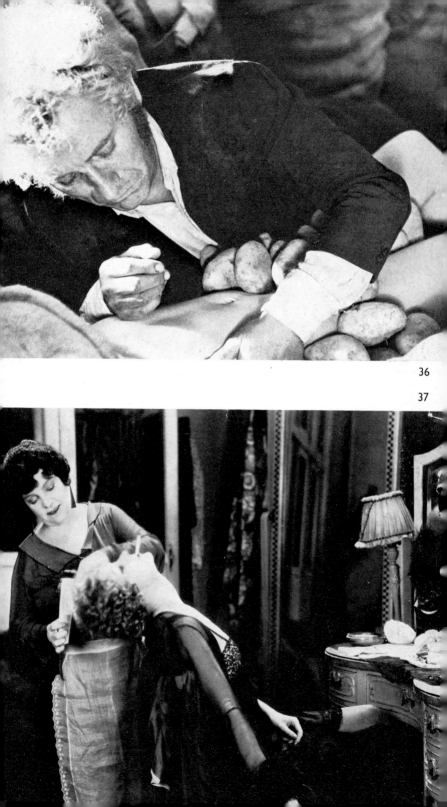

38

39

bours

41

What's your Poison?

44

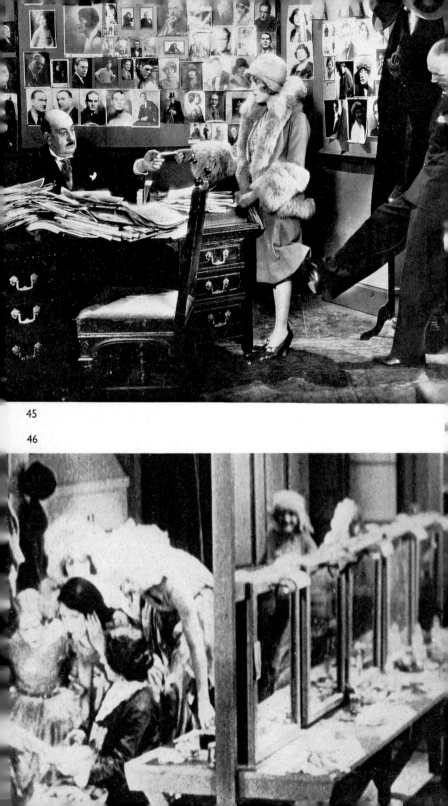

45

46

47

48

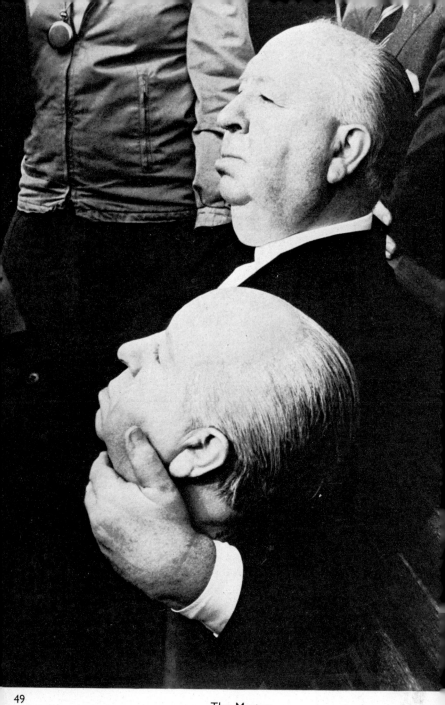

49 The Master

did some very queer things'. Chabrol and Rohmer add that the original project was to switch between colour and black-and-white, depending on whether sanity or madness was involved. Memories of *The Cabinet of Dr. Caligari*, of Lang's *Mabuse* series, of Richard Oswald's *The Living Dead*, held the highest hopes for the deepest, darkest, most Surrealist Hitchcock yet. After all, in England, Michael Powell and Pressburger had used monochrome and Technicolor to distinguish objective from subjective worlds in another tale of rescue from madness, *A Matter of Life and Death*. Although the hour of the horror film had yet to strike, themes of amnesia and shell shock were edging Hollywood and Denham alike towards a tight-lipped, rationalised expressionism. *Spellbound* isn't, as is sometimes said, the first movie about psychoanalysis, since Pabst had made *Secrets of the Soul* about twenty years earlier, back in the silent era, and Hitchcock is agreeably frank about his intellectual ambitions here. 'It's just another manhunt story wrapped up in pseudo-psychoanalysis.' Precisely because of the fantasy elements in the theme, he preferred a 'sensible' approach, 'sensible', that is, within the idiom of romantic wishfulfilments; and though the film was extremely popular, no doubt because of this solid, as it were, three-cornered foundation, the result is a romantic whodunwot, closer in style to *Rebecca* than anything else.

Gregory Peck plays a mentally ill patient who has sufficient air of sanity to masquerade as a psychiatrist, and then to persuade his robustly healthy colleague, Ingrid Bergman, to run off with him. As they go, she analyses his dreams, whose distortions of a childhood accident conceal the criminal past of the mental home's real director—another, even less obvious, madman. It does sound rather like a subject that might be rewritten along the ideological lines of R. D. Laing, David Cooper, Erving Goffman, and others, whose criticisms of institutions as microcosms of society run parallel to the spirit animating the original script of *The Cabinet of Dr. Caligari*. Their hour had not yet struck, however, and Hitchcock, obviously, is content with a more enclosed and private world, with a complex structure of parent-figures, identifications and guilts.

The asylum's current director, Dr. Murchison (Leo G. Carroll), is due for retirement. His replacement is to be one Dr. Edwards, whom John Ballantine (Gregory Peck) impersonates and whom he comes to believe that he has killed. But Constance (Ingrid Bergman) takes him to the analyst who analysed her (Michael Chekov) and he ascertains that Ballantine is suffering from (1) guilt at seeing his younger

brother's accidental death while playing as a child, and (2) its reinforcement by witnessing the death of the man whom he pretends to be,
and whose real murderer turns out to be Dr. Murchison. Obviously,
in analytical terms, Murchison is the evil father-figure, angry at being
supplanted, and Constance's analyst, her father-figure, is the kindly
father-figure, willing to yield the mother-figure to the son. Both the
age-groups and the social positions (psychoanalysts as father-figures)
conform to this pattern. Thus the Carroll-Peck-Chekov triangle
becomes as oppressive as the Rebecca-de Winter-Mrs. Danvers
triangle. The idea of a mad murderer posing as his victim finds its
most conclusive expression in, of course, *Psycho*, although it also
appears less centrally in *Vertigo*. There are some brilliant links; thus
forktrails in the tablecloth recall ski-tracks in the snow which in
turn recall a children's slide near spiked railings. That sort of associa-
tive visual thinking certainly isn't pseudo-psychoanalysis, and would
be looked upon as pretty sophisticated as part of a critical interpretation of a film. Hitchcock's skill at clarification is so great that it's
easy to underestimate the skill and imagination which goes into
making something so devious seem almost self-evident, while im-
buing its demonstration with considerable emotional power.

The recurrent paranoia motif is charmingly turned. Thus Chekov,
when asked by the cops for data about a patient of his, demands 'Vot
is dis persecution?', and it's agreeably ambivalent as to whether he
really has a paranoid streak which doesn't take much stimulation, or
whether he's only using a paranoid turn of phrase so as to confuse the
police and play for time (like 'I was at Cambridge' in *The Lady
Vanishes*), or whether he's really or apparently touchy about his
status and thinks he should be above the law, or whether he has nasty
memories of fleeing Austria and Germany as the Gestapo came in, or
whether he resorts to a paranoid phrase for all these reasons including
the fact that on an unconscious level he *is* paranoid as well as being
a weighty citizen and a benevolent soul. There are also some neat
interchanges between the roles of detective—'In my job you have to
be a bit of a psychologist'—and psychologist—since it's dream-
analysis which reveals the crime. In a general way, the film associates
cops with inappropriately severe, punitive attitudes, and analysts with
appropriately understanding and lenient ones, except that suave
friendly and intellectual father-figures are likely to turn out to be
extremely dangerous—a standard Hollywood pattern. Part of the
shock of *Psycho* lies in the fact that the psychiatrist who explains
Norman Bates to us doesn't say 'To understand all is to forgive all'.

And the idea that the menacing cops are, though wrong, less berserk, in the end, than the apparently friendly older intellectual, recurs in any number of American movies from *Phantom Lady* (that touchstone for Selznick-era Hitchcock) to *Kiss Me Deadly*.

Reminiscent, in its slow, dark, talkative style, and its obsession with past guilts, of *Rebecca*, and let down by a disappointingly mounted dream sequence originating from Dali, the film lacks the dramatic concentration of the earlier film's second half and the awesomeness of its reference to cancer. Ingrid Bergman, at first cold, bespectacled and managing, subsequently passionate, seems, in Hitchcock's iconography, a transition figure between Joan Fontaine and Grace Kelly.

Notorious

Notorious resumes the general visual key of *Suspicion* (both being produced by Hitchcock himself at R.K.O.). Cary Grant is common to both films, like the theme of domestic poisoning, and Ingrid Bergman again substitutes for Joan Fontaine. To that film's single-minded study in undeserved paranoia, this counterpoints an undeserved contempt and trust.

F.B.I. agent Develin (Cary Grant), seduces the depressed and therefore dissipated Alicia, daughter (Ingrid Bergman) of a Nazi sympathiser. He even pretends to be in love with her, so as to drive her on to marry, and incriminate, her father's accomplice Sebastian (Claude Rains). The tables are partly turned when Grant feels guilty about deceiving her and also gets twinges of jealousy which duty demands he repress. The Nazi, on the other hand, is in love, his intentions are honourable, and one has to have an uneasy if venomous respect even for his sinister mother, who counsels him, when she realises the truth, which she suspected all along, to poison the deceitful heroine.

Not only does the hero prostitute the woman he ought instead to love, and on a physical level at least is very involved with, but he mistakes the first symptoms of her poisoning for the result of her heavy drinking, thus, if anything, inspiring her to gratefully accept the antidote to alcohol, coffee, which contains the poison. No clear lines distinguish the hero's sins from the ironies of fate from the way any man might dismiss a wife's complaints of feeling unwell; all of which prevent any unambiguous interpretation while creating an exciting synthesis of tragedy, cynicism, heroic martyrdom, absurdism and the everyday. The cup of poisoned coffee is passed, politely, from hand to hand, until it reaches its intended victim's. And the big close-up, far from being merely a vulgar emphasis, converts the process, quite illogically, into a kind of Russian Roulette (will it not get there?), or daisy-chain. . . .

For Raymond Borde and Etienne Chaumeton, the film's moral tone is keyed by Hitchcock's acceptance of cynicism. 'We cannot resist the pleasure of evoking the final scene, which achieves an extraordinary mastery in suspense. In the great entrance-hall of the villa, three groups interlace and oppose one another. First, Alicia and Devlin, who seek to escape. Then Sebastian and his mother, who have unmasked them, but cannot denounce them without dooming themselves, since the spies permit not the slightest error. And finally the suspicious accomplices. Sometimes the camera takes the place of the couple formed by Alicia and Devlin, and descends the stairs, step by step, deliberately; sometimes it follows them in a lateral movement; sometimes it stops on the enigmatic group of conspirators. . . . They pass the threshold, but Sebastian follows, and begs them to take him with them. Met with their refusal, he turns back into the night, towards the lighted rectangle of the door, as if towards the sacrificial altar. We hear a distant voice: "Sebastian, we have something to say to you," and the door closes once more.

'The denouement is somewhat cynical. Devlin knows that he is sending Sebastian to his death, but he is getting rid of Alicia's husband the easy way. All in all, it is a perfect crime, and all the more perfect for being patriotic.' If it is excused as poetic injustice—the would-be murderer allowed by his victims to be murdered by his friends—its calm application, by the couple, as well as something glacial in Hitchcock's smooth glossy rhythms, put it beyond any particular severity or nihilism or culpability. It is part of the world's cybernetic, as impassive as the divine face in the British Museum, at once just and unjust, humanly fallible (for revenge is sweet) and beyond morality.

French critics generally have rated *Notorious* high in the Hitchcock canon. Truffaut describes it as 'truly my favourite Hitchcock picture' and 'the very quintessence of Hitchcock'. Borde and Chaumeton speak of a 'pitiable novelette' transformed into 'a misunderstood work', comparable to *Gilda* (which perhaps it is), and Chabrol and Rohmer compare the mixture of directorial virtuosity, particularly the camera's smoothly sweeping movements, and a rigorous screenplay, to the mixture of expressionism and simplicity in Carl Mayer (a comparison which is formally if not quite spiritually valid). The cold, glossy surface, with its carefully magnified, bland objects, finds its spiritual counterpoint in the fact that, as Maurice Scherer remarks, its heroine is constantly in a semi-delirious state, either half-drunk, or half-poisoned, or sexually infatuated. And the same tension operates as between the personalities of the actors—the dapper matinée-idol neatness of Cary Grant, the robust warmth of Ingrid Bergman—and the moral queasiness and calculation within their roles.

Although Hitchcock all but transforms Hollywood glossiness into an expressionism which is all the more fascinating for being, paradoxically, cold and calculated, it does not seem to me that a poetic breath animates its sumptuous mechanism. In the end, the surface style smothers the moral and emotional ambiguities. One remembers two beautiful people kissing, and Ingrid Bergman in elegant distress rather than a dipsomaniac prostitute betraying her father's friends for love of a man who manipulates her as Uncle Charlie might have wheedled money out of his widows. The interrelation of an elegant style and an underlying ignominy has its fascination, but its reverberations, here, are dampened by all the superficiality of spy and counter-spy. If it fails to disturb as a film which recalls its elegance, *L'Année Dernière A Marienbad*, disturbs, it is not because Robbe-Grillet's solipsist formalisms are any less evasive a picture of the human, or the bourgeois, condition than spies and counter-spies. If anything, Hitchcock is a regularly profounder artist than the novelist. It is because, to reach the disturbing gratuitousness of the Resnais film (and it is Resnais's film, not Robbe-Grillet's), one has to endeavour to forget the McGuffin and all its ramifications, including the overriding role of patriotic interest versus something like absolute power in the hands of absolute evil—the National Socialist atom bomb.

If in style *Notorious* harks back to *Suspicion*, certain of its relationships prefigure *North-by-North-West*. In both films American security agents persuade the heroine to prostitute herself to, and betray, a man who loves her, and he feels many a qualm before the truth sparks off his megalomanic ruthlessness and he sets coldbloodedly about murdering her. Claude Rains in the earlier film corresponds to James Mason in the latter and Cary Grant appears in both films, once as seducer, once as incidental victim. It's amusing to concoct a Monty Pythonesque parody in which one twin—Cary Grant in *Notorious*—prostitutes the girl who fascinates him, whom he despises and whom he will come to love, without realising that it is the other twin—Cary Grant in *North-by-North-West*—who has become her victim. Their devious relationship might then involve certain coincidences which might well be the product of the legendary telepathy between twins, who, however, are antagonistic to each other, thus opening various doors, ad lib., on to themes of hallucination-or-telepathy, or spiritual takeover as in *Rebecca* and *Vertigo*, and sibling ambivalence. Except that one can't quite imagine Cary Grant succumbing to mental turmoil as Gregory Peck or James Stewart might. To Hitchcock's films Cary Grant brings with him something smooth, minimally but effectively caustic, and sybaritic, exteriorly attentive yet resiliently self-centred, which sets a worldly ideal much like that of Lubitsch and is alertly responsive with no unfunctional complexity. Indeed, in *Suspicion*, *Notorious*, and *North-by-North-West* it is from just such a self-sufficiency that moral dissonance appears, tentatively however, or rather, with a calculated restraint, characteristic of the expert entertainer who seeks to create, as Hitchcock ceaselessly reiterates, 'pure emotion', not reflection. Certainly the less profound purpose must acknowledge emotional and moral dissonances while integrating them into an overall polarity of fear and hope. But the crucial difference remains, between the concessive clause which secures agreement to a statement, and the contradiction which challenges the statement. In this respect Hitchcock cannot be said to be of the Hollywood vanguard. Moreover the '40s were an uneasy betwixt-and-between period, unable quite to forsake an earlier idealism and lyricism, yet too liberal, and/or too cynical, not to sense the shadows lying across it.

The Paradine Case

Hitchcock returned to Selznick for *The Paradine Case*, adapted from a somewhat ponderous and antiquated drama by Robert Hichens. The enigmatic Mrs. Paradine (Alida Valli), who, gracious though she now is, might once have walked the streets of Rome, is accused of murdering her blind husband. Defence lawyer Gregory Peck steadily falls in love with her, and centres his counter-attack on an alternative possible suspect, her groom and lover (Louis Jourdan). After brutal questioning, the groom commits suicide. Thereupon Mrs. Paradine declares her love for him, and her own guilt, adding, for good measure, that her defence lawyer is in love with her, thus ruining his career. Maybe life will hold some sort of saving grace for him in the continued devotion of his wife (Ann Todd). The paradoxes of feminine devotion (Valli's and Ann Todd's) form the background to Peck's infatuation with a woman who punishes him for defending her too well and destroying her reason for killing, and living. His devastatingly frustrated infidelity finds a grim counterpart in the unpleasant judge (Charles Laughton). Frankly callous, to the point of sadism, he is prejudiced against the defence lawyer, whose wife has rejected his lecherous advances, and trembles with vindictive joy at his courtroom discomfiture. The lawyer's infatuation is blind; the judge lucidly exploits fear and self-interest in the service of lust. But are his interventions any more tendentious than the 'innocence'—or unconscious idealisation and jealousy—which led Peck to make his beloved's lover a scapegoat for her crime?

This equation remains a passing tone, a concession, subordinate to the obvious and continuous polarity between the essential generosity of the defence lawyer, the evident perfidy of the judge, the undoubted dissimulation of the groom, and the eventually devastating perfidy of Mrs. Paradine. His is a tragic journey through the maze of passionate involvements which, Hitchcock's style insists, although his story does not, remain no more treacherous than the sternness of the legal system. One may wonder whether Hitchcock wasn't, despite himself, seduced by the fascinating grimness of the judicial scene, and was not the right director for a subject which might have called for a more subversively romantic style.

There are sudden stabs of bleak sensuousness. Mrs. Paradine's hair is caressed by a maid. A wardress uncoils Mrs. Paradine's hair to ensure that no forbidden objects are hidden within. This echo is as eerie as all the verbal evocation of the missing woman's scent in *Laura*. But Preminger's sensuality seems cerebral where Hitchcock's seems more spontaneous, more poetic, part of his being.

Hitchcock complained to both Bogdanovich and Truffaut of miscasting. Peck lacked the ultra-dignity of an Olivier or a Colman, and Louis Jourdan was hardly the 'manure-smelling stable-hand' who would have contrasted with the glacial dignity of Mrs. Paradine. To Bogdanovich he drops a hint of an interestingly ruthless puritanism: 'Any beautiful woman is a compromise for evil'; a puritanism going far beyond Chabrol's and Rohmer's, if it means, as presumably it does, that beauty always appeals to the animal, the base, the nonmoral in man. Alas, the courtroom is less promising a setting for such nuances than the straightforward presentation of a crime in progress. As so often, the whodunit, or didshedunit, keeps us on the periphery of the action, expressing, perhaps, that particularly middle-class combination of a pervasive suspicion of others (a shy keeping oneself to oneself) and veiled distance from the cynical facts of life (which are elucidated only to be condemned), with certain half-logical, half-legal rules replacing, or overriding, all the nuances of involvement. The lower, less-refined class prefers the thriller with its direct and brutal involvements; and from the thriller, closely connected as it was with the underworld *film noir* which accommodated so much that was best in Hollywood before McCarthy, Hitchcock always remained aloof.

The Paradine Case finds impressive advocates in Borde and Chaumeton; who praise it as 'a good documentary on English justice. The preparations for a criminal trial, the meetings of the lawyer and his client in a glass cage under the surveillance of a wardress, the particular role played in England by a solicitor, the lawyer's subtle precautions during his meeting with a prosecution witness, and finally the development of a major trial at the Old Bailey; all this gives the film the quality of a testimony.' One recalls the opening reel of *Blackmail* and anticipates the opening sequences of *The Wrong Man*. So far as visual texture and short sequences are concerned, one can agree that 'As for the images of the trial, they perhaps number among the best trial scenes which the cinema has given us. They are worthy of those of Dreyer's *Joan of Arc*, of Mervyn LeRoy's *They Won't Forget*, and of Orson Welles's *The Lady From Shanghai*.'

Oppressive as is the film in its gloom and emotional constriction, one may prefer, quite apart from its prestigious Hollywood counterparts, its more weird yet livelier British counterpart, Compton Bennett's *Daybreak*, another strange, expressionistic meditation on adultery and the injustices of injustice, also with Ann Todd and very retrospective preoccupations. Eric Portman plays a public hangman who succeeds in hanging his 'manure-smelling' rival (Maxwell Reed) for his own murder. A sensual echo links his two professions—hangman, and barber—and a strange flashback-within-flashback structure corresponds to all those verbose courtroom exhumations. *Daybreak*, vastly more awkward than Hitchcock's film, and seemingly without similarity only because it has chosen a series of opposite options about the same axis, was critically disdained for a bizarrerie which was both strength and weakness, just as Hitchcock's deftness was both strength and weakness. But it is useful to see the connections between apparently dissimilar films, which, after all, share an audience, and a culture. *Auteur* theory has been a useful stepping stone, but it's high time to go beyond it, and trace out, not only the *genre*, as a few critics have already begun to do, but the *cycle*. Just as a consensus of conventions and preoccupations is as much the 'creator' of any given Western, or gangster movie, as a particular director, writer or producer, so the *zeitgeist*, the spirit of the age, seems to be the demiurge behind the predominance of certain themes, settings or moods. Siegfried Kracauer put the case as formidably in his *From Caligari To Hitler* as Wolfenstein and Leites put it in *Movies: A Psychological Study* and Borde and Chaumeton in their *Panorama du Film Noir Americain*, all studiously ignored by devotees of extreme *auteur* theory, which is nothing more than academically-based romanticism hiding from itself some facts of creative process. It is certainly possible to trace, in Hollywood, two contrasted streams, one running towards realism, the other towards a kind of tight-lipped expressionism, borrowing certain lighting techniques from the German cinema and, from the French (*Le Jour Se Lève*), a disruption of time by flashbacks, associated with themes of mental confusion, anguish and suspicion. *The Dark Past*, with its flashbacks in negative, marks the affinity between these films and the atmosphere of amnesia, shellshock and demented crime, in such films as *Blood On My Hands* (*Kiss The Blood Off My Hands*) and *He Ran All The Way*. *The Blue Dahlia* asserts the link between these films and private eye movies like *Farewell My Lovely* and *The Big Sleep*. The incomprehensible plots (here, at least, the Americans ceased to demand plausibility, since even the writers and directors never understood who did it or why—or at least claimed not to), the night rain, the cryptic faces, the guarded words, of these movies express a kind of oppressive bafflement about human intention which extends, of course, to such claustrophobic dramas as *The Little Foxes* and *Laura*. Certain directors, like Hitchcock himself, with *Rebecca* on one hand and *Shadow Of A Doubt* on the other, shuttle between the two approaches. Similarly, Jules Dassin makes *The Naked City* at the 'semi-documentary' end and *Night and the City* at the expressionistic end, while Cavalcanti, erstwhile partisan of documentary, produces at the same time his richly artificial *They Made Me A Fugitive*. Hitchcock can claim some credit for setting the ball rolling, with *Rebecca*.

CHAPTER 7

Rope / Under Capricorn / Stage Fright / Strangers On A Train /
I Confess / Dial M For Murder / Rear Window / To Catch A
Thief / The Trouble With Harry / The Man Who Knew Too
Much / The Wrong Man / Vertigo / North-by-North-West /
Psycho / The Birds / Marnie / Torn Curtain / Topaz / Frenzy

Rope

After his last film for Selznick, Hitchcock formed Transatlantic Pictures with Sidney Bernstein of Granada, thus becoming his own
executive producer (as, at about the same time, were other Hollywood
talents like Frank Capra, Burt Lancaster and the Enterprise Studio),
and resuming a British connection.

The production technique of *Rope*, and possibly even the choice of
subject, was based on the idea of loading Hollywood cameras to their
(then) ten-minute maximum, and arranging careful transitions so that
the action seems to flow continuously, despite the unavoidable break
for reloading. Welles had had one extremely long take in *The Magnificent Ambersons*, but *Rope* acquires a somewhat Murnau-like
quality through the continuous, smooth camera-movements. The
play runs to actual time, and the film more or less preserves its spatiotemporal quality.

Two young men (John Dall, Farley Granger) have just murdered a
third, David, placed his corpse in a wooden chest, covered the chest
with a tablecloth, and invited the victim's fiancée, and parents, and
some mutual friends to a gourmet dinner by candlelight. The guests
include their old philosophy lecturer, James Stewart, of whose teach-
ings they feel this aesthetic crime to be the apotheosis. Their discussion reinforces one's impression that this grisly jest is a late outcrop of
the 19th Century Decadence, with all the *fin de siècle* trimmings.[1]

---

[1] Which have lingered on, in the folklore conception of the devil as an urbane,
narcissistic dandy (inspiring the Hammer Dracula), as pederastic iconography,
from Oscar Wilde down to Kenneth Anger's *Inauguration of the Pleasure Dome*.

Rope, appearing at a time when such attitudes were rather in eclipse, is retrospective in its terms. The elegantly appointed meal evokes Walter Pater's sense of life-style. A phrase like 'a ceremonial altar for the sacrificial feast' evokes the Black Mass craze of Paris in the 1880s and 1890s. The two boys owe a great deal to dear Oscar. Their admiration for their Professor betrays a calf-love-cum-hero-worship, and a vicarious narcissism about his superior intellect ('You need someone else to see how brilliant you are'). They parade the idealisation of aesthetic sensation and style ('You often pick words for sound rather than meaning') and the notion of art as moral licence ('I've always wished for an artistic talent. Murder can be an art too'). They are elitist snobs ('Murder is a crime for most men but a privilege for the few') and their tendencies to a demeritocracy combine with a variety of challenges to philistine complacency ('Perhaps what you call civilisation is hypocrisy?'). This harking back to Decadent aestheticism wasn't to the taste of the critics of the time, and although Albert Lewin had filmed *The Portrait of Dorian Gray* and presented a Decadent version of Gauguin in *The Moon And Sixpence* in the early '40s, the English film industry had forgotten the Decadent Wilde and remembered him only as the darling of the fashionable establishment or the gently ironic poet laureate, as it were, of Edwardian glories (Korda's *Lady Windermere's Fan*, Asquith's *The Importance of Being Earnest*). But, albeit in eclipse, the cultural tradition of amorality and exquisiteness which it arraigns was by no means dead in the late '40s, when the pre-Communist Gide was still a living influence in France, when Anger had yet to make *The Inauguration of the Pleasure Dome*, when Truman Capote had yet to write *In Cold Blood*. Throughout *Rope* there runs a strong undertone of Gide's *The Vatican Cellars*, in which a young man attempts to prove his emancipation from traditional morality, his spiritual freedom, by committing a motiveless murder, an *acte gratuite*, which is something more than a shallow aestheticism, since its search for proof of spiritual freedom is central to any existentialist assumptions.

Yet to say that the film has an undertone of Gide is to point to its limitations. Anglo-Saxon versions of the Decadence were rarely more than imitative importations from the French, just as the Decadence according to Wilde was a likeable, curiously harmless and in an odd way humane, imitation of that French spirit which, in Baudelaire and Huysmans, tackled the issues first, and seriously. Much in Wilde does lend itself to what Asquith and Korda made of him, a kind of upper-class, home-front counterpoise to Kipling, hardly seeing eye to

eye with the old boy's neo-Populist fulminations (often to the effect
that the strength was at the bottom while the froth was at the top),
but offering, at least to the nostalgic '40s, another form of English
glory. Amorality, for Gide, is serious, is a form of spiritual responsibility, attractive, yet agonising, and not to be undertaken lightly.
And it is obviously arguable that the puritanical guilts and the
philistine callousness against which Decandence was a reaction were
far more destructive than the immoralists had any intentions of
being.

Hitchcock's adaptation of Arthur Laurents' adaptation of Patrick
Hamilton's novel sees the issue as, on one hand, a democratic moral
fundamentalism, and, on the other, a too-sophisticated playing with
morality. Even if the Hays Code had allowed the homosexual intimations to be stronger, it would remain true that, in this formulation,
the only reason for Decadence is—decadence. Hitchcock's film is
serious enough, but not profoundly so, because there is no case for
the murderers to put. We're not to be won over, even for a moment,
by any stage in their arguments. We're meant to be chilled by their
charm and their elegant pseudo-justifications. Not that Hitchcock is
building up a simple hatred; one of the aesthetes (Farley Granger) is,
also, sensitive in a sympathetic sense. Our attitude towards the murderers is meant to be rather like that of the Victorian bourgeoisie
towards Wilde. We detest the callous, brilliant insolence of John Dall,
feel a strong moral need to see it humbled, if our world is to be made
safe. For Farley Granger, we feel sorry; but sternly sorry. He must
pay; we cannot feel indignant if he pays with his life for the life which
he chose to help to take. Even if the film went on to show him in the
dock before a Judge as personally corrupt as Charles Laughton in
The Paradine Case, we should feel distinctly worried unless some
definitive sentence were pronounced. Rather a hypocritical and sadistic
judge than all the perplexities and dangers of deciding when the
wicked are really only weak.

True, the film goes on to pin some blame on someone far nearer
our own attitudes. James Stewart, their old mentor, may protest that
'You've given my words meaning I never dreamed of . . . There's
always been something deep inside me that would never have let me
do that.' But he then is made to admit that if that was the case, he
should never, even as a university lecturer, and for the sake of argument, have implied that there wasn't, and been soft on Symbolism.
He is partly responsible for misleading these lads. And behind his irresponsible playing with ideas there is a subtle, but real, megalomania.

'Wonderful Miss Wilson—I may marry her,' he muses, flippantly, but with an easy superiority, a mixture of affectation, arrogance and teasing.

The interaction between teacher and students here is certainly in a serious moral tradition. It undoubtedly has affinities with Dostoievski's *The Brothers Karamazov*, where the atheist's words, meant earnestly, are misinterpreted by the idiot servant—a servant whose idiocy is, however, typical of something subhuman in every human being. Yet, here again, the idea is weakened (although to be weaker than Dostoievski is hardly to be dismissed). James Stewart didn't mean what he said; he was only playing. In other words: 'Even to play with moral ideas is *verboten*,' and although it isn't exactly an attack on free speech it is certainly a fundamentalist stricture. Ideas are so arbitrary that only the ones we have are safe. Nor is the film a study of the very *serious* factors (intellectual, or moral, or social, or psychological) which lead the students to misinterpret the older man's words. Enough is suggested to make for plausibility—a homosexual fixation by the two boys, each in his own, neatly differentiated, way on the intellectually brilliant master-spirit, as he would earlier have been called, or guru, as he would have been called if the two youths had been mid-1960 pop-singers, which, amazingly, edges us a little but appreciable way towards decadence, aestheticism and violence as per *Performance*. But this presentation is fairly schematic, and even if the Hays Office had allowed the homosexual element to unfold its full peacock's fan the temptation would have been considerable to have substituted a pathological explanation for a moral soul-fight or for intimations of the moral issues involved in the adoption of homosexual positions to begin with. This may seem to be expecting much too much, but if we are considering the proposition of whether *Rope* is a masterpiece and whether Hitchcock is a moral master, something of a guru himself, then much too much is what one would expect to find. As it is, what we have instead is a fundamentalist put-down of intellectual activity. 'Only unbalanced people put intellect above moral convention. Only the immature imagine that masterminds seriously question the everyday decencies. People who take unconventional ideas seriously get life wrong.' Ironically, Chabrol puts the same issue the other way round in his *A Double Tour*; it's the conventional who hate the aesthetic beauty they desire (Antonella Lualdi, who has tropical fish swimming through the transparent windows through which she looks out on poppy-fields) and kill it.

The basic weakness of *Rope*, from the higher standards, is that what

is basically a serious issue about serious ideas and their serious consequences is approached from a fundamentalist anti-intellectuality. To
show us three intellectuals, of whom one is over-impressionable, two
have a heavy penumbra of homosexuality, and all three in varying
degrees snobs and megalomaniacs; and then to contrast them with
on the whole ordinarily mixed-up intellectually and emotionally
honest people is to conform to a long, glib, anti-intellectual tradition
which includes, for example, Capra's attack on poets, opera singers
and psychologists in *Mr. Deeds Goes To Town*, the Clifton Webb
character in *Laura*, the sculptor in *Phantom Lady*, and everyone with
any artistic interests in *Kiss Me Deadly*—none of which films deal
with intellectual matters. Intellectuality, snobbery, aestheticism,
amorality, morbidity—the whole syndrome is a too-familiar affair.
After all, WASP culture abounds in schoolmarmy, prissy intellectuals
(that other stereotype!) who incessantly denounce, among other
things, the fleshpots of Hollywood, while Hollywood itself offers
examples of the many forms of amorality which have neither intellectual origins nor intellectual pretensions. As scapegoats the villains
of *Rope* are too convenient, as types they are too alien, for the film
to provide a great deal more than a fascinated shudder and a relieved
repudiation in the way of thought. The film might have come a little
nearer the knuckle if the father-figure had been a well-known Hollywood master of suspense who brings his scriptwriter friends home
and says, 'Wouldn't it be fun to kill her this way?' He's a quiet,
decent, almost pious family man, and neither he nor his son suspect
what may be going on in the mind of the son's friend, an affable
and charming youth who not only pleasantly disturbs the producer's
mother and daughter, but listens carefully, until the crime which is to
be the *pièce de résistance* of the producer's next macabre masterpiece
is found re-enacted, a week *before* its première, on either the producer's own family or their visitor's.

   In a way quite distinct from this merely external tit for tat, a profounder resonance with the audience's own attitudes might have come
from the story of the seduction of the sensitive, ordinary youth
(Farley Granger) by the other. And later this is just the form of
Strangers On A Train. But here too Hitchcock slides deftly around
the crunch. Farley Granger remains an innocent, Robert Walker is a
fruity weirdie, and we are then never drawn into aspects of an amorality which in any case is simple expediency. None the less, it arraigns
a more contemporary form of sybaritism ('Have you ever flown a jetplane at 600 m.p.h.?'), and the relationship between the two men

has the seductive soupçon of the Mephistopheles story. Again, the most serious Hitchcock film is by another director, René Clément's *Plein Soleil* (*Purple Noon*), also after Patricia Highsmith, with its homosexual murder, its invisible but omnipresent corpse, its stress on affluence, its exchange of lives.

This said, *Rope* possesses its own qualities. It most certainly isn't run-of-the-mill or nasty in the pejorative sense in which critics use the word (perhaps murder stories should always be nice?). The elegantly simple yet disturbing situation is developed with such finesse as to allow a little complicity into the picture. It's not that we morally or spiritually identify with the two young men; none the less, throughout the opening sequences of the movie they remain our identification figure in details, even though, as moral monsters, they infuriate us. We are within them as human beings even as we struggle to repudiate them. Our involvement is paradoxical and tension-charged, and the fundamentalism is balanced by a primitive form of that horrified curiosity which develops into a more complex attempt at understanding with Richard Brooks's *In Cold Blood* over twenty years later. Every detail suggesting that we might be, as the lads are, relishing the delicate bouquet of an aesthetic intoxicant, rubs our nose in moral excrement. Whatever Hitchcock's film hasn't, what it possesses in abundance is an extended lyricism, slight, yet haunting and piercing; a quality emphasised by the virtual unities of space and time. The dramatic action seems an aspect of the lyrical, rather than the other way round. The penthouse has an appropriately soft, superior, hot-house atmosphere, not Decadent so much as simply rich (Hitchcock taking care not to allow his heroes to stray too far from spiritual realities which the audience is likely to accept as familiarly monstrous rather than eccentric or apparently implausible). Only exterior light and sounds, carefully spaced, let society in. The crescendo of police sirens under John Dall's calm piano-playing neatly expresses the discordance of emollient art and harsh morality. Although David is never seen, a detail like the initials inside his hat gives him a bodily and mental presence, while the final credits put the invisible victim in the centre of the screen at last and speak of 'David's fiancée, David's rival . . .' They are tombstone credits, elegiac rather than macabre.

John Dall plays the more dominant of the two murderers as a sort of Vincent Price Jnr., his intriguing ambivalence as between the male partner (to Farley Granger) and feminine (to James Stewart) paralleled by his mixture of assurance and a slight, almost elegant stammer. Farley Granger attracts a queasy but real sympathy, feminine in his role to the other only because he has sufficient normality remaining to be hesitant and undecided. This agreeable pre-James Dean, lost within Samuel Goldwyn's suburban and hillbilly families, came nearer in Hitchcock's film than anywhere else outside Robert Wise's *They Live By Night* to finding his discrepancies with the conventions and, therefore, his role. James Stewart slides just the right patina of superman smirk over the homespun (and penitent) moralist whom he eventually turns out to be. It's none the less interesting to follow up the affinities between the aesthetic finesse which gives Hitchcock's films their slightly dandy air, and imagine the murderes as two plump, middle-aged, lugubrious Londoners.[1] Their aestheticism would be hilariously tragic, and the film would have retained the intimate realism of the English Hitchcock as well as advancing further into the increasing indulgence in amorality which this film intimates without accepting.

Warnercolor turns the boy's faces a spongy yellow. André Bazin contrasted Hitchcock's use of the moving camera here with the 'true' track or pan, since here it merely slides from one fairly conventional set-up to another, rather than moving in relation to the primary visual elements. On a storyboard, the film would read as a conventional affair of close-ups, two-shots and deep-focus groupings. None the less the incessant visual glissando creates, in this context, an appropriately creepy, slithery and serpentine mood, an unpleasant as a softly excessive attentiveness; a Uriah Heep camera. The compressions of stage time interact effectively with the shuffled continuity of screen space to produce a tension which, brilliantly, is both theatrical and cinematic. In its bizarre aesthetic way, the film is a curious antecedent of the Warhol aesthetic: precious, morbid, insolent, stagnant, insistent on the relationship between the reality we are shown and the process of showing it. For Warhol, though scarcely an artist, is certainly a fashionable aesthete of inert *ennui*.

Under Capricorn

Filmed in England, Hitchcock's second Transatlantic film was another period piece, set in Australia in 1835. It was a resounding commercial failure and Hitchcock himself commented very frankly on all his

---

[1] Which, oddly enough, would correspond to the original of Anthony Perkins in *Psycho*, where Robert Bloch's Norman Bates is middle-aged and obese and more like a Robert Aldrich grotesque.

mistakes and misfortunes with scriptwriters, actors, producers, and, later, critical misunderstandings.

In a sense, it is a development of the lady-and-the-groom theme from *The Paradine Case*. Lady Henrietta (Ingrid Bergman) becomes fascinated by her lover Sam Flusky (Joseph Cotten); and when he is transported for killing her brother, under extreme provocation, she follows him out to Australia. There he makes good, becomes the colony's richest citizen, and marries her, although scorned by the local establishment, centred around the Governor (Cecil Parker). The film begins with her amiably feckless cousin (Michael Wilding) arriving from England. And through him we are shocked to find her become a dipsomaniac (like the heroine of *Notorious*) and dominated (like the heroine of *Rebecca*) by a shrewish housekeeper (quite a few of Hitchcock's films would bear as subtitle something like Losey's *The Servant*). He sets about restoring her self-respect, and, of course, falls in love with her, as well as persuading himself that Flusky is one of the principal villains of the piece. He nearly goads Flusky into repeating, on his wife's cousin, the crime which he perpetrated on his wife's brother, and eventually Henrietta breaks down and confesses that she, herself, was her brother's murderer, and that Flusky chivalrously bore the blame on her behalf. The cousin bravely swallows his disappointment, and his guilt, and goes on to expose the housekeeper (Margaret Leighton) for slowly poisoning her mistress (the domestic poisoning theme of *Suspicion* and *Notorious*), out of love for both her master and her master's property.

The ricochet of guilt makes a fascinating structure. The guilty woman finds that the fruit of her crime (marriage) is like ashes in her mouth. She is hounded by a woman of her brutal yet chivalrous husband's class. The cousin who thinks he is a St. George and that the rabble-class ex-convict husband is the dragon discovers that the dragon is St. George and that he himself is a particularly sly and dangerous kind of dragon—a snake in fact—since he has set out to break up the marriage, and nearly goaded an innocent martyr into becoming a murderer, thus depriving the woman he loves of the man she loves.

Taken from Lady Henrietta's viewpoint, chronologically rather than retrospectively, the story *before* the film as well as *within* the film might have been as romantically grim as *Rebecca*. Yet it's lightened, and probably weakened, because it's seen through a far less involved character—the cousin, who doesn't make emotionally very heavy, or even interestingly stormy, weather of the realisation that in the life of the woman he loves he is a dear, but supernumerary friend, who all but wrecked everything before he helped her. Undoubtedly this story perspective has various conveniences. The cousin and the governor between them can fill in a great deal of explanation very rapidly, the plot is tighter than a ten-year sprawl, a format enabling the climax of the drama to be spread over ninety minutes instead of being restricted to five or ten. Yet the double detachment (in time and perspective) from most of the main story arouses a suspicion that Hitchcock is rather afraid that it would be too grim, or sordid, or bleak—too much a matter of courts, convicts and cells, like *The Paradine Case*, or requiring extensive reconstructions of Australia's past, if this bleakly claustrophobic element is to be played off against any spatial expansion. And the experience of *Rope* might suggest that, in a climactic situation, every detail of dialogue, atmosphere, symbolic prop and mood would carry a great intensity of meaning.

Essentially, the narrower approach seems to be perfectly feasible, and the film snarls itself on details, not on general strategy. None the less it is worth unwinding the story, in one's mind, and beginning with the original affair, the murder, and the titled lady following her lover out to Australia. The social contrast then becomes central rather than past; indeed, it would evoke the polarity between Miss Havisham and Magwitch in *Great Expectations*. The dramatic foreground would be occupied, not by brooding over guilt in luxurious surroundings, but by a high-born lady's love- and lust-inspired struggles to adapt to the brutal surroundings in which he, chained, protects her as best he can. The housekeeper would be introduced as a fellow-convict of Flusky's, who knows that her rival for this man's love is the real murderess and thinks that class alone must account for Flusky's attachment to her. Thus she sees herself as a 'scourge of God', a tormenter, damned herself, but none the less avenging and protecting the innocent man they both love, without being less egoistic than she seems here. And in those terms the interplay between the 'deserving poor' and the frivolous lady getting her comuppance might become rather more interesting than the film's business with a scary shrunken head (not really a gimmick, but so compressed a symbol, so *unfair* a device to use, as to seem so, and so to deprive the moral polarity of much complexity). Hitchcock had dealt with the problem of a poor little rich girl's necessary adaptation to another social stratum in *Champagne*. But he treated that in a tricksy style which comedy didn't of itself require, and he might well have felt that by 1949 there had been a surfeit of grim and gloomy costume melodramas. Better by far to soften and lighten the story's externals, by sumptuously comfortable colour interiors and by concentrating on the nuances of table manners at grand dinner tables and balls.

By itself, the combination of retrospective allusion and peripheral centre needn't rule out a gripping film. Most stories begin *in medias res*, and films which begin with the fourth or even the fifth act of their story are quite common; one need only cite *Rebecca* or *Johnny Guitar*. And for good reason. The events in the fifth act are a continuation, or anagram, or reversal, of previous issues. Their moods are likely to be in the same or a similar key. It's quicker, terser and stronger to, as it were, superimpose the two series of events. The expressions on the characters' faces as they remember what then they felt need not necessarily be much weaker, dramatically, than their reactions if the script had gone into a flashback of that earlier scene, or begun the story with it. Some distance there is likely to be, but our knowledge of time past may suffice to make even an in itself 'weaker' expression extremely eloquent. After all, to remember what one felt then may impose no more restraint on one's feelings than the mask which one regularly wears in the present. Thus, in dramatic terms, the past can be made just as present as the present, while acquiring all the richness and irony, sadness or triumph, of the present to which it has given way. It is often convenient to use the situation itself as the symbol for the feelings involved in it; but a mixture of words and face is a source of infinite eloquence also. In this sense Bresson's approach, turning a situation into a meditated response to it by stripping it down to bare essentials and a face, is simply another modality of reminiscence, and no more paradoxical or anti-cinematographic than the remembrance of things past which occurs in *Citizen Kane* or *Under Capricorn*. Nor is it surprising, when one remembers the whole range of Hitchcock's styles, that *The Wrong Man* should evoke Bresson as often as it does.

In any event, past-present relationships are a natural part of our thinking about, and reacting to, the present, and stories in which the characters never referred to their past tend to strike us as enigmatic or at least unusual, as Resnais proved in *L'Année Dernière A Marienbad*. At least I don't know of any critic other than Jacques Brunius who found himself speculating about the characters' present relationships without also speculating about something they might have been or done before they got to the hotel or sanatorium or whatever it was. And if that film suppressed the past it certainly didn't suppress the future, because I doubt whether any spectator found himself watching what was happening at a particular moment without wondering what was going to happen next or in the end. And even if Robbe-Grillet reproaches them for doing so, it is hard to see how he can have introduced the game (the game of Nim) without admitting that the concept of game introduces the concept of what will happen next, i.e. winning or losing. Having admitted which there seems no point in denying that the invisibles of past and future are just as present and palpable a part of the film as the images of the present, just as these become a solipsistic incoherence without the operation of invisible realities such as the force of gravity, or mental intention, or emotional preference. And because he admits them it is Hitchcock, not Robbe-Grillet, who achieves the feat of becoming Bishop Berkeley's God, and creating a world which he keeps in being by thinking about it, Robbe-Grillet producing merely a series of images which he increasingly garnishes with pornography in order to conceal the extent to which they're not worth thinking about, opening on an infinity of possibilities, which is to say, none. In any case, the theory that everything in a film ought to be made visible, including the past, would only oblige one to invent yet another past to explain that past, and so on in an infinite recession.

Certainly, from around 1940, the cinema is much preoccupied with the weight of the past in the present. Whence the flashback structures of such films as *Le Jour Se Leve* and *Citizen Kane*, although Welles demonstrated, in *The Magnificent Ambersons*, an alternative way of dealing with the passage of time and the remembrance of things past. Whence also a plethora of films about dead or missing women whose portraits assert their continuing presence. Whence also the cycle of time fantasies which ranged from *It Happened Tomorrow* in Hollywood to *A Matter of Life and Death* in England. Whence, perhaps, the costume and historical movies which flourished in French, English and American films. Hollywood in the '20's lived in an optimistic present, the past was enjoyed for romance and adventure which were sheer exoticism and in no way opposed to the present. The characteristic pace of the '30's was fast, terse, and slick, as if a determined optimism were skimming over uncertainties and stagnation. Possibly the war was felt as the wages of sin, past irresponsibility and disunity, so that the past was felt as having caught up with the present; while simultaneously the past offered a nostalgic haven from the hazards and disruptions of war. Such British movies as *The Man In Grey*, *Caravan* and *The Wicked Lady* view the past with an unusual and, on the face of it, paradoxical, mixture of romanticism and grimness. Subsequently, by the mid-'50's, similar issues are presented in terms, not of past sins looming over the present, but of present problems over which the characters brood (the fatal, dead woman of *Rebecca* is replaced by the living *femme fatale* of *Snows of Kilimanjaro*). Gradually a sullen expressionism is clarified into moral controversies, whose challenges become increasingly sharp, urgent and militant right through into the '70's. Hitchcock compared the lady-and-the-groom theme of *The Paradine Case* to *Lady Chatterley's Lover*, and the 1970 version of *Under Capricorn* might look rather more like a cross between D. H. Lawrence's novel and the B.B.C.-Time Life *British Empire* series.

The filmed theatre which looms so large in '40's style is closely related to the past-present theme. For obvious reasons, the mainstream theatre has always tended to concentrate its action into the story's fifth act, and so to present the past, obliquely, through the present; even contrasts can be obliquely and economically rendered very vivid (e.g. the more bitter the disillusionment we see, the greater must have been the love we don't, and the more sullen and anguished it may still be. Indeed, a classic 'montage' effect is possible, the *tertium quid* being our sense of loss, or of disdainful irony). But these past-present films tended to be claustrophobic, dark, verbose (cf. Welles's *The Magnificent Ambersons*, Wyler's *The Little Foxes*, Cocteau's *Les Parents Terribles*). Although this style may have been encouraged by the lighting problems then associated with deep-focus (itself a great facility in permitting flexible groupings in confined and continuous space), a variety of other solutions were possible, whether one thinks of Milestone's *Rain* back in the early 1930's, or of *All My Sons* or indeed Hitchcock's *Rope*. It is difficult to believe that Hollywood would have accepted a dark grim claustrophobic mood simply on technical grounds and without any sanction in terms of the spirit of the time—particularly when so many fast-moving thrillers were in the same emotional key-signature as well. But the enclosed plays take on a special common quality, whoever their director, as naturally as reticence and landscapes condition the Western genre. With intensive dialogue, and deep-focus echelons of faces talking or listening, usually in spotlit darkness, sound and image seem to merge into each other, superimposing, yet conflicting. As the image shades to black, words take on a hard continuousness. The present (images) seem weighed with the past (words); the latter are like chisels, working away at, shaping the ominous amorphousness of, the former. The climax of 'invisibility' is attained in *Laura*, whose dialogue harps on the honeysuckle perfume of a missing woman's perfume, which becomes a kind of hallucinatory lietmotif. *Rope*, with the body invisible within the chest on which the boys dine, is another variation on the unseen—especially when the conversation veers to the dead boy. One can speak of a Racinian cinema, in the sense that heavy verbal forms take on an almost granite-like chunkiness against settings whose areas of dark space seem to be making them, already, memories.

Under Capricorn loses out as secondary ramifications, in the present, distract from the past. It isn't a matter of colour, which, as in *Rope*, is carefully disciplined. The cousin, being as peripheral to the principal dramatic interaction as he is, calls for an even more centrifugal element, the governor's disapproval of his flippancy. The pattern of sympathies during these long introductory scenes are so obvious that they all but swamp the thoroughly perfidious behaviour of the Governor in one late, key scene. The earliest scenes with Ingrid Bergman drunk and humiliated are appropriately gruelling, indeed, electric, and Hitchcock seems on the brink, for once, of creating a warm, harrowing performance rather than a neat, dry one, while Ingrid Bergman seems, in turn, on the edge of losing that gently exuberant radiance which invariably belied the moods of degradation and depression for which the actress felt a natural curiosity, but which Hollywood so often used her to ennoble, that is to say to sentimentalise, and so to betray.

If Hollywood, over the long haul, wins, it's not by a knock-out. For Sam Flusky, Hitchcock's first choice was Burt Lancaster, and something in Joseph Cotten's screen personality, rather than his perfectly correct playing, lacks the cruder animal energy, the atmosphere of suffering turning to a passionate resentment and therefore a systematic yet essentially erotic cruelty which the film might have shared with Gainsborough-era James Mason. The shrunken head which the housekeeper leaves in her victim's bed, to tip her over the edge into the D.T.s, is a crude paraphrase for the heroine's self-accusations and regrets, particularly since it effectively moves her into the position of innocent victim through most of the film. Margaret Leighton, the film's cruellest character, is also the most moving one, and I found myself wishing that she had thought of a less brutal method for estranging husband and wife, for I sympathised with her in the same way as one sympathises with Margaret Lockwood in *The Wicked Lady* or with Dirk Bogarde in *The Singer Not The Song*. For Hitchcock and Margaret Leighton, in the many scenes which establish her as a person, clinging to, yet bitterly resentful of, her servant status, understand one another perfectly. They seethe with grit, spite and tragedy, and one becomes very interested in the story as seen from the housekeeper's point of view. We are again in the presence of Hitchcock's persistent, half-submerged theme of masters and servants, lords of the earth and deferentials. Ingrid Bergman's attempts to treat her convict-servants humanely, without opening the floodgates of anarchy, establish the double facets of the Hitchcockian morality. And, equally in step with trends in the British, rather than the American, cinema of the time, he seems fascinated by Cecil Parker's Governor, a traditional authority figure, bumbling, amiable, thoroughly perfidious in one key scene, yet not in such a way as to rule out the impression established earlier. For underneath the American Hitchcock the English Hitchcock remains.

Although the ten-minute take is suggested rather than observed, Hitchcock feels now that the flowing camera-movements may have been too smooth for so tense a drama, coupled with the misexpectations aroused by the Hitchcock name. None the less the curious impression of a drama half-lost behind a lyrically queasy mood has a certain slippery power even if the film seems an on the whole intelligent, if pallid, Gainsborough-style period piece.

Stage Fright

Stage Fright was kindly received by English critics, probably because it marked an apparent return to Hitchcock's English style and settings (garden-parties, theatreland), some realistic detail, bold cutting, angling, shadows and movement.

Richard Todd tells Jane Wyman that he's on the run from the police and shielding the woman he loves (Marlene Dietrich) for murdering her husband. Her father (Alastair Sim) also suspects the foreign actress of collusion in the crime, and sends her a doll stained with blood, as her robe was stained. But the flashbacks through which Richard Todd told Jane Wyman his story were lies. The real murderer is eventually crushed under a theatre safety curtain. Thus the apparent dramatic opposition, between Jane Wyman as plain, familiar, innocent righteousness, and Marlene Dietrich as the exotic, alien, sophisticated *femme fatale*, is subverted; instead, the latter is the victim of everyone's easy credulousness.

A minor bone of contention was the opening flashback, which turns out to tell a lie. Hitchcock reckons that he was wrong not to have foreseen critical objections to it, and that he should have accommodated them in some way, while insisting that, in itself, it's not at all misleading, a flashback being simply an anecdote in visual terms. Indeed, the critics ought to have objected to *The Wizard of Oz*, on the grounds that Judy Garland never really went over the rainbow, but only thought she did, and only objective reality ought to be shown in visual terms, and they ought to have objected to *The Cabinet of Dr. Caligari* even more strenuously. Perhaps they felt that subjective realities were allowable, but that lies weren't, in which case it becomes relevant to remark that the flashback may have represented what goes through Jane Wyman's mind as she listens to his story, as well as to observe that if lies aren't eligible for visual form then neither the German nor the Czechoslovakian versions of *The Adventures of Baron Munchausen* ought to have been made, nor could one make a film of *The Thousand and One Nights*, culminating in the absurd situation whereby fiction films must never feature a story-within-a-story. Rohmer and Chabrol remark that there are no misleading visuals anyway; it's only the commentary (voice over) which lies.

It's difficult to say why the film comes over much more weakly than the pre-war English films, since dramatically it is stronger than most of theirs. Perhaps part of the trouble is that the contrast lies between bland upper-middle-class behaviour, and persecution which isn't revealed as such until the end, so that we are left, with, virtually, a classic, decorous, English story, located in some spiritual territory halfway between Ealing Studios and Agatha Christieland, with the surface manners only too effectively setting the dramatic tone. One may play with the idea that the lack of social contrast and diversity induced by the picaresque action of the earlier films weakens the film. Yet *Stage Fright* is no more restricted in this respect than *Sabotage*, of which it is, in a way, a counterpart. There the solitary foreigner menaced the unsuspecting English, and here the unsuspecting English menace the solitary foreigner. Indeed, *Stage Fright* might have been a great deal stronger if it had been seen from the actress's viewpoint. She knows who dun it, and she can't quite bring herself to believe what she feels it disloyal to suspect, that he is framing her. She can hardly defend herself as the net closes in, but is driven slowly towards disloyal confession or suicide. And from her point of view, until she learns the whole truth, the murderer's final sortie against the amateur sleuths would come to seem almost a deliverance by a Judex-like avenger against the confusions of vindictive righteousness, an unholy alliance between ungentlemanly amateurs and professional interest.

At this point we begin to move into the orbit of Joseph Losey's *Blind Date*, where we do see things from the point of view of a German suspect. Even if there were problems in requiring an identification with a solitary foreigner, and this is doubtful, they were no greater than those in the case of *Rope*. Indeed, the German woman's discovery of the crime might have been used to persuade us that she may have been guilty. As it is, the scenario only presents itself with the reverse problem, whereby the English behave, from one point of view, and with all sorts of extenuation, rather badly, and throughout the first part of the film Hitchcock is caught between the difficulty of showing this bad side without menacing our identification (although he might have) and throughout the second part he avoids the spiritual problems of a firmly unflattering reinterpretation of this poison-pen type carry-on. It might have opened more options to have begun in a key with certain misanthropic intimations, like *Poison Pen* in the '30's. Maybe these problems, coupled with those of gentility, of which they are indeed an eventual derivative, explain the general weakness of characterisation and therefore of emotion. Jane Wyman registers as stupid and determined, rather than misled and devoted, the former being a much less interesting combination, and Alastair Sim, whom, of all actors, one would least expect to do so, falls between the two stools of whimsicality and vindictiveness. Perhaps one should describe it as an unusually interesting Ealing film.

Strangers On A Train

Strangers On A Train enjoyed a more favourable critical reception than any of his films since *The Lady Vanishes*, and remains a favourite with older and younger schools of criticism alike. The former like its combination of movement and lively, observant drama; while for Borde and Chaumeton 'from a certain point of view, the film is a satire, implicit no doubt, but not unsparing, of various social levels in Washington'. The moralist critics concentrate on its moral criss-cross.

Tennis champion Guy Haines (Farley Granger) is accosted on a train by playboy Bruno Anthony (Robert Walker), who suggests that they 'exchange crimes'. Guy will kill Bruno's hated father, Bruno will kill Guy's bitchy wife Miriam, whose acrimony and avarice are, Bruno knows, a threat to Guy's hopes of marrying Ann (Ruth Roman), the rich Senator's daughter whom he loves. Bruno will acquire his hated father's money, and no motive will guide the police to the killers.

Guy rejects the offer, although, humouring a madman, he doesn't actually say no, and Bruno interprets a gesture with a drink as agreement, picking up Guy's forgotten lighter as a whimsical afterthought. He follows Miriam through the fairground, lures her away from her companions and strangles her. Angry that Guy has not fulfilled his part of the bargain, he begins to put the pressure on him, showing him a plan of his house and offering detailed instructions on how to find his father's bedroom and kill him. Guy follows the instructions but instead of putting a pistol to his head goes to wake him up and warn him—only to find that the sleeping figure is Bruno. Guy is shadowed everywhere by two detectives, and while he is engaged in a championship match Bruno goes to plant Guy's cigarette lighter on the site of Miriam's murder. The two men have a climactic fight on a fairground roundabout which eventually goes out of control, killing one.

The fact that Guy has a perfectly 'reasonable' motive for murdering Miriam, and that he ought to have gone to the police on learning of her death, certainly does suggest that he is guilty, if in a subordinate way, or on some unconscious level, of acquiescence in a highly convenient crime. Thus Bruno symbolises the repressed evil in Guy who, as an ordinary, decent 'guy' is our screen representative. Indeed, one can sketch out such resemblances rather more closely, as part of the astonishing pattern of symmetries, unusually complete even for Hitchcock, on which the film is based.

1. Guy and Bruno are obviously contrasting characters. One is decent, the other is Mephistophelian. One is of humble origin, athletic, and sensitive, the other is wealthy, sybaritic, and suavely homosexual. Yet these contrasts aren't the whole story. We might take Bruno for a spoiled softie but physically he's at least as strong as the sportsman. And both men are mother's boys. For while Bruno is a mother's darling, has a sickly ambivalent love for and charms old ladies at Washington parties, before something inside him takes him over and sets him strangling one, as he strangled Guy's wife, so Guy seems to 'belong' to two women, Miriam and Anne, by comparison with whom he seems rather boyish, a little weak. Guy is bound by two young women, Bruno strangles two old ones. And of course the good guy is morally weak. After Miriam's death, he should have gone to the police, and what he, and his fiancée's family, seem to fear is not so much a miscarriage of justice as a scandal. So he is legally an accessory after the fact, and maybe his fear of scandal is a mild form of Bruno's wickedness. Both men are somewhat put upon by their families: Guy by his ex-wife and his fiancée's formidable and numerous family, and Bruno by parents who seem to have brought him up extremely badly,

his father remaining a shadowy, preoccupied character, his mother living in her world of sentimental unrealities and paintings turbid with repressed nightmares.

2. Miriam, with her round face and glasses, is the spitting image of Ann's younger sister, Barbara. She's so similar that the resemblance starts even the cool Bruno into choking an old lady at an exclusive reception. But the audience noticed it long before—whenever we saw the sister we thought of Miriam, and she thus performs the functions of a ghost. Her role as 'marker' is emphasised by her morbid fascination with the murder, so that her questions persecute Guy, paradoxically, since she also seems staunchly loyal by nature. And her interest is a second form of spiritual complicity in the murder. Critics interested in connections between on- and off-screen realities won't overlook the fact that she is played by the director's daughter, Patricia Hitchcock, so that the Hitchcock family appears in the film twice.

3. Bruno comes to the party to terrify Guy. Twist: the sister being there, he gets terrified himself. Thus Barbara terrifies both men. Maybe she accuses the audience too, incarnating as she does their ghoulish enjoyment of murder pictures like this one. Nor is Hitchcock himself altogether innocent in pandering to our pleasure. (Maybe he is like the wrecker in *Jamaica Inn*, piously allowing his victim a chance to repent, before finishing him off?)

4. Barbara 'merges' Guy's two wives—the double of Miriam, the sibling of Ann. Moral: you can't escape.

5. Guy, under suspicion, is followed everywhere by two F.B.I. men. The friendly one seems to believe Guy innocent, the harsh one seems to think he's probably guilty. But it is the amiable one who at a key moment warns his colleague to watch Guy especially closely, and it is the tough one who gives Guy a break so that he may lead them to the real murderer. In our sentimental way, we preferred the apparently indulgent person. Wrongly.

6. Just as Barbara brings Miriam to the reception, so the two Washington old ladies bring Bruno's mother to the reception. Looking at the first, he strangles one of the latter (a 'criss-cross' glance). He cajoles them into the idea of murdering their husbands, just as he cajoled Guy into the idea of murdering his wife. Their interest in murder echoes Barbara's (who promptly appears). Hers is the interest in murder which has a benign function rather than Bruno's malign one. Bruno accidentally strangles a substitute for his own, apparently beloved, mother; Miriam is about to become a mother and Guy makes a point of respecting her pregnancy.

7. There are two little boys in the film. As Bruno follows Miriam through the fairground to murder her, a little boy with a balloon in one hand points a toy gun at him and says, 'Bang' (yet another form of innocent-guilty complicity in the idea of murder). Bruno retorts with a neat tit-for-tat—bursting the balloon by gently pointing a cigarette against it—which scares the little boy. The cigarette, of course, picks up on the incriminating cigarette-lighter. Later, on the fairground carousel, Guy saves a little boy from death (and in so doing is very nearly killed by Bruno). This act presumably enables Guy to expiate his legal-moral guilt.

8. Guy is shadowed to the fairground by two F.B.I. men. Miriam, on her way to the fairground earlier, also had her 'guardian angels'— two hefty louts. Foolishly preferring Bruno, perhaps because he is better dressed, i.e. has more money, or perhaps the other two are old friends and she isn't averse to a change, especially with this amusing sophisticate, she throws off the two men (who could have saved her).

9. Before Guy can give his shadows the slip he must defeat his opponent in a tennis match. This opponent thus becomes a vicarious 'agent' of Bruno's—just as Barbara is an 'agent' of Miriam's. (This might have implied something about cut-throat competition in professional sport, e.g. Guy's friendly-faced opponent murmuring to him, sotto voce, 'I'm going to kill you!'—but doesn't.) This 'echo'—the partnership-in-antagonism of two young men—keeps a consistent tone throughout the film. Hitchcock further unifies the two actions—Bruno reaching for the lighter, the tennis-match—by intercutting hard volleys at the tennis-match with big close-ups of Bruno's fingers straining for the lighter, which itself is ornamented with crossed tennis racket handles. Bruno strangling his vicarious mother while looking at his vicarious Miriam is another kind of 'criss-cross', with the high-backed sofa visually like a net.

10. The two detectives wildly shoot at the innocent Guy, not only endangering the life of an innocent man, but endangering the life of a great many innocent men. And they hit, and kill, an altogether innocent old man, the man running the carousel, which is why it goes out of control, thus endangering the lives of everyone on it, including, in particular, the little boy whom Guy risks his life to save. So just as Bruno kills one person and nearly kills two others (his father and the reception lady), and tries to make Guy seem guilty, so the detectives kill one innocent man, and nearly kill a number of others, notably the little boy, Guy, and Bruno, whose guilt at that stage they barely suspect. Nor is it just a matter of bad luck, the devil misguiding the

bullet, because, as the carousel speeds up, one detective turns to the other and suggests he crawl under it to stop it. The other is hardly keen, so they both turn on the partner of the man they have just killed, another old man, and tell him to crawl under the out-of-control machine, at, the sequence makes clear, great danger to his life. In other words, the detectives, after a wanton orgy of shooting, refuse, out of cowardice, to risk their lives, and an old man has to save Guy and the boy. Guy, however, risks his life, under Bruno's attacks, to save the boy from falling off, and he emerges as morally far superior to the detectives who are, one hopes, in line for something of a reprimand.

11. Two young men (Guy—Bruno); two little boys; two pairs of strong 'guardians'; two old ladies (Bruno's mother, his near-victim); two old men. If, as is obviously the case, the reception victim is a surrogate for Bruno's mother, then it becomes logical to see the old man at the carousel as a surrogate for Bruno's father. It is the detectives, therefore, who by wantonly killing one innocent old man, achieve, by ricochet, the crime which Bruno wanted Guy to commit for him. Wheel of fortune is a mild phrase for the operations of law-and-order, which come to resemble nothing so much as Russian roulette.

12. Bruno's modern, rich, frivolity (jetplane speeds), made possible by his father's wealth, is complemented by all the old-fashioned fun of the fair, where the steam-organs play such popular melodies of yesteryear as 'And the band played on'. Victim-type father-figures are the custodians of this declining and less prosperous form of pleasure by speed, and one of them acts in the bravely benevolent way which one would expect from a father-figure. He stops the machine, although, characteristically, its stop is so sudden that it's catastrophic and might have killed Guy and the little boy, although, providentially, it only kills Bruno. But providentially is an odd word, since there was no need for the carousel to have gone out of control in the first place, if the detectives hadn't been so careless, or berserk, or ultra-aggressive ('Better that several innocents should perish than one innocent suspect should escape our surveillance for a minute'). It must be said that we hardly have time to feel sorry for the innocent old man who's killed or admiration for his partner; we're too preoccupied with our Guy; and we forget them as rapidly as we forget the equally innocent locomotive driver and fireman in The Lady Vanishes, whether because they're merely base mechanicals or because we've hardly had time to get to know them yet or because they're rather weak and

boring-looking. Hitchcock shows no more concern for them than he makes any criticism of the detectives, which is not to say that he may not feel indignant or ironic or pessimistic or even amused at the injustice of it all.

13. There are other strangers on Guy's trains. Guy badly needs as witness the university mathematics Professor who spoke to him; and who could be more omniscient, more objective, than such a mind? Alas, if the man seemed pleasantly drunk at the time, he was drunker than he seemed, and can never remember anything whatsoever after one of his binges. And after the carousel has spun amuck and put Guy's life back on its right rails he is affably approached by a kind-looking clergyman, whereupon he panics, a comic finale from which one might draw the conclusion that Guy has learned not to trust even the most apparently innocent strangers, or the opposite conclusion that Guy has been psychologically damaged by his experiences and is now paranoid, reduced to the state of a little girl who's been told she mustn't speak to strange men, or, of course, regressed from a reasonably outgoing American responsiveness to the suspicious English reserve of the clubmen in *The Lady Vanishes*.

14. The strangers on the trains complement a stranger on the stairs, i.e., the ugly-looking big dog which bars Guy's way to his master's, Mr. Anthony's, bedroom. But Guy's moral earnestness proves sufficient to take the risk and the dog proves friendly (one may remember an analogous episode concerning the ferocious lions confronting Christian in *The Pilgrim's Progress*). In one way this guard-type dog is a sad disappointment, letting an intruder go unhindered about his business. In another way man's best friend proves unusually sagacious, recognising a friend, just as the murdered man's dog learned of his master's death by telepathy in *Secret Agent*. And maybe he would have been less indulgent if his master had actually been in the bedroom instead of his master's son. And if he had been both Bruno and Guy would have been in trouble. So all in all this 'guardian beast' doesn't do any worse a job than the 'guardian humans'. And as a creature whom Guy meets and who might testify to his presence he contrasts with the men whom Guy meets on trains, and whose professions are intellectual or spiritual ones. The inclusion of the dog in the film's moral patterns is vindicated by *Secret Agent*, and puts Hitchcock in the stream of English thought, as well as reminding us that America is the land of expensive canine cemeteries, and inclining him to an evangelical-Anglican side of the fence, since popular theologians of these schools are readier than Catholics to allow that animals have

souls or natures whose relationships with man have the same sort
of moral significance that post-Darwinist or Freudian thought might
see. Of course, the diehard partisan of Hitchcock the orthodox Catholic might say that the dog symbolises the inefficacy of pagan deities
like Cerberus, or that Hitchcock means the dog as a contrast with the
intellectual and spiritual 'guardians' on the train even though his
presence is as indecisive. While it would seem to me to be doing
Hitchcock an injustice to see the dog as merely an opportunistic
suspense dodge, unrelated to the rest of the film, the scene has too
many possible associations to have any clear meaning, except as part
of the pattern of surprises which are also ironies. The dog is to *homo
sapiens* as the menacing detective to the kindly one; no worse and no
better; for if he is less fierce than one fears, rather fiercer than
one hopes, that is all part of life's chaotic pattern—the chaos which
rails and carousels and criss-cross ricochets, all superimposed on one
another, constitute.

If one gives priority to a crime-and-punishment pattern, then
Hitchcock's principal point may seem to be that 'Bruno is Guy's Mr.
Hyde, and, like Guy, we're all guilty deep down'. But in fact Guy
never assents in the murder and only appears to do so because he
thinks Bruno's as nutty as a fruitcake, which he is, and hopes to
appease and dismiss him, which is a reasonable though careless mistake.
His is a clean-cut, sportsman's insouciance, and his panic at the
clergyman isn't merely an epilogue-gag but a reversal of his assurance,
even though he's achieved all the worldly things which at the beginning he hadn't, and for which he has Bruno to thank. On the other
hand, by the '50s, a great many American spectators had, as the
content of many Hollywood films makes quite clear, absorbed sufficient vulgarised psychoanalysis to see Guy's mistake, his equivocation,
and his leaving of the lighter, as, together, an unconscious collusion
between social hypocrisy and the unconscious mind abandoning his
virility and willpower and sexual life into the hand of a seducer as
ambiguously sexual and moral as the devil. None the less, the symbol
remains dramatically weak, since no shadow of assent in the murder
enters Guy's consciousness; and of all possible Hitchcocks it is the
orthodox Catholic Hitchcock who, following Thomist philosophy,
ought most strenuously to insist that so long as the rational soul has
not given its assent then the subject is the victim, and not the accomplice, of 'the monster from the id'. In this respect Thomism would
agree with common sense and with the stress in psychoanalysis on the
meaningfulness of repression. It must also be remembered that Guy's

forgetting of the lighter is, psychoanalytically, a masochistic act, so that while one might take his masochism as evidence of a secret but un-committed crime which Bruno is about to commit for him, one might also take it as evidence of the excessive guilt arising from Guy's excessively high standards. The interpretation which stresses Guy's guilt is strengthened by the degree to which Miriam's death is con-venient and to which he unabashedly profits from it; but if you apply to this Guy the morality which allows Devlin and Alicia to condemn Sebastian to death in *Notorious* then Hitchcock seems to think im-penitently taking advantage of situations is a fairly normal human reaction undeserving of punishment (and so do I). On the other hand, the interpretation absolving Guy of guilt is strengthened by his respect for Miriam's motherhood, and by his saving of the boy in circumstances which render this act a clearly masochistic act (giving Bruno the upper hand in their struggle). So that one can't use Guy's masochism as proof of his unconscious guilt without also remember-ing that it is proof of his redemptive innocence!

The fact is that however you twist it and turn it Guy is innocent except in a minor degree and generous, while Bruno is guilty and callous except in a minor degree, and that this creates the moral polarity which not only takes all sorts of concessive clauses in its stride but reduces them to the status of the small print which only the litigiously-inclined are likely to read. And one doesn't really clarify the issues by reading only those small-print clauses which make Hitchcock seem to be accusing the innocent and by omitting all the contrasts and extenuations which, in both large print and small, insist on relative innocence as innocence and as undeserving of punish-ment. Given the moral conventions of the time, it would have been perfectly possible for Hitchcock to make Guy unequivocally guilty of a very real and strong intention of murdering Miriam; and yet still be innocent; and there's an absolutely clear precedent in another film adaptation of a story in which Chandler's name was involved, George Marshall's *The Blue Dahlia* (1946). There returning veteran Alan Ladd finds his wife (Doris Dowling) faithlessly living it up with nightclub owner Howard da Silva. He points a gun at her, and all but pulls the trigger before throwing it down and striding off into the night. Later she is found shot dead, with that very same gun, and the man-hunt is on. Although a crime-and-punishment aspect is obviously present it's most certainly subordinate to our anxiety on behalf of an innocent man who has been framed. It's interesting to imagine *Strangers On A Train* had Guy in fact grabbed Miriam by the throat in the record shop booth, in a murder whose silence would have contrasted with the murder by fairground music. The symmetries follow thick and fast: the 'murder' seen through the glass is completed by the murder glimpsed in Miriam's glasses; one kind of reproduced music is echoed by another; a light, silent place by a dark, noisy one. And the symmetries crowd in because, I suspect, this is in fact a missing scene, not in the sense that it was written but never filmed, but that the film's moral logic requires it, and that nothing rules it out, even by the conventions of the time, although it would have been important to have insisted that Guy came to his senses after nothing more than a gesture, or a brief impulse overcome not because of the certainty of detection but because of an internal horror at the deed.

Alternatively, Hitchcock might have had Guy express, involuntarily, a certain, if only fleeting, pleasure at his first wife's death, or, at the end, of the way fate has worked out. 'It was worth the ordeal' might have indicated, sufficiently quietly not to turn us against him, a soft self-centredness which is just a little like Bruno's. In the most drastic variorum of all both these points might have been combined: the suggestion that Guy half-believed Bruno, and dismissed it from his mind in bad faith. Had that been clear then not only would his guilt have been very guilty but we could sympathise with Bruno as being correct, rather than merely a victim of his own assumptions, when he inveighs against this hypocritical lad who's ready to profit from someone else's crimes but won't lift a finger to return the favour.

Alternatively, or additionally, it wouldn't have been difficult to underscore one's brief suspicion that Miriam's entire family might both have suspected Guy of the murder and resolved to be loyal to him; Barbara on the grounds that it was a provoked and understandable murder; Anne on no grounds at all expect that she's in love with him as Joan Fontaine with Cary Grant in *Suspicion*, and her parents because they don't want a scandal to touch them and they will do nothing, in bad faith, reckoning that their daughter is safe because she's an altogether different kind of a person. At which point we're not too far off from turning Guy's family into Bruno's mother, which, of course, would figure, in so far as Guy was Bruno. And Hitchcock, in interview, agrees with Truffaut that Guy and Bruno are 'a single personality split into two'. But he also agrees that he 'preferred the villain', which, apart from raising certain issues as to whether he's quite such a stern moralist as Chabrol and Rohmer assume, also establishes the oddity that while he has constructed the film around

'the rules of suspense' which presuppose the audience's preference for
Guy, his own sympathies go the other way round, towards an un-
abashed and honest villain. Far from being a gratuitous variation on
Hitchcock's film, our most drastic variorum scenario above is in
accordance with it. The film is a battle between a hypocrite and a
psychopath (and the law isn't much less hypocritical and psychopathic either). No wonder the visual motifs begin with a convergence
(footsteps approaching one another; then the rails of the train on
which both men ride), and move through shallower or steeper criss-
crosses, scissor-diagonals, and ricochets, to the climax in which good
and bad, the little boy and the trampling horses, old man as victim
and old man as saviour, successively take each other's places while
the wheel spins until finally the carousel of ironies reaches a delirium
like vertigo and is unhinged.

As their footsteps approach, it is as if Guy and Bruno are moving
to an encounter, from their separate orbits; the sense of movement
round is made rigidly linear by the railroad track. Convergence completed, divergence remains, Guy and Bruno approaching or receding
from one another in terms of our sympathy, as if the joint line were
opening and closing, like scissors, which, when at 180°, suggest a circle,
so that the diagonals and ricochets of the tennis-match abruptly open
up into the carousel, whose yin and yang of full circles return us to
the opening of the cycle, except that Guy now dreads meetings even
at a tangent.

The limits which, artistically, maintain the film within the limits of
a minor achievement are, precisely, that although Hitchcock sees Guy
as more than a little guilty, neither the audience nor Guy does, and
Rohmer and Chabrol who do can still assume that Guy is being
punished for not being even more innocent than he is. For although
Guy learns not to trust appearances he hasn't yet met the Bruno in
himself, and the film's whole suspense structure depends on Guy and
Bruno being poles apart, in terms not only of moral immaculacy
(which isn't very important) but of basic generosity (which is). Only
in one scene does Hitchcock make us care for a Guy who (we think)
means to kill Mr. Anthony (and the last twist takes the edge off this;
he came not to kill but to warn). But this doesn't take the form of
probing self-criticism, it merely makes us hope that something will
happen to prevent him, or that he'll change his mind. Nor does it
make us vicarious accomplices in murder, as Chabrol and Rohmer
seem to suggest, it only means that we can understand other people's
weaknesses. Hitchcock certainly shows weaknesses in the hero, and

allows us sympathy for the murderer, but in the years after films like *Gilda* and *Duel in the Sun* and *The Woman in the Window* and a hundred more it would be surprising if he didn't.

It is possible, of course, to argue that Hitchcock's severity expresses itself in the extent to which, although Guy is innocent in terms of any morality which can conceivably be applied to human behaviour by anyone below the unique level of omniscience enjoyed by God, he none the less maintains that he is guilty, in much the same spirit as Cardinal Newman's argument to the effect of the minutest venial sin being such an outrageous anomaly in the context of God's goodness that only someone as kindly as God could bring himself to forgive it. And the Jansenists certainly took such arguments to the point of denying any difference, theologically speaking, between degrees of sin, so that Guy and Bruno are on a moral par. The moral tension of the film lies in the extent to which Hitchcock suggests this, without at the same time ceasing to maintain that there are degrees in sin and that it's important that Guy shouldn't descend to Bruno's level by murdering the latter's father. This may be a paradoxical position, but it's also a commonsensical position, i.e., that everybody's guilty at heart, and guiltier than they think, and that there but for the grace of God go we, but that some are guiltier than others, and we shouldn't be the others. Murder mysteries fascinate us because we know that somewhere in us all is the capacity to commit a murder while at the same time finding the idea of murder inadmissible. There is an analogy with the Faust story; we all have it in us to yield to Mephistopheles, and Faust's being persecuted by him makes him a tragic figure, who earns, not our reprobation, but our sympathy, because he was led into temptation instead of being delivered from evil. Even if Guy were as guilty as Bruno, the same polarity would apply here. But the converse would then be true. Bruno would be as innocent as Guy[1] and we would very rapidly find ourselves in the territory of James Hogg's *Confessions of a Justified Sinner*, a book which makes it quite clear how rapidly Calvinist and Jansenist severity can turn moral turtle and become a Machiavellian indulgence—as well as reminding us how Protestantism, by following other options, achieves its extraordinary power of secularising itself without losing its conscience. Chabrol and Rohmer, having lived in a world where the frontiers between clerical and agnostic have ever since the *Encyclopédistes* been more sharply drawn, can do something like justice to the severely theological

---

[1] Thus if Guy is half-guilty for forgetting the lighter, Bruno is half-innocent because he 'accidentally' drops it.

aspects of Hitchcock's vision (in so far as they aren't an expression of pessimistic aspects) but not to the reversibility arising from their compatibility with a rough-and-ready consensus as between the religious and the irreligious. But even if it were true, as there seems no reason to believe, that Hitchcock's films had, as private meanings, just those patterns which Chabrol and Rohmer ascribe to them, it would still be necessary to establish the public Hitchcock, whether one conceives this Hitchcock as being the Hitchcock of 'the tale, not the teller' (as Robin Wood, following F. R. Leavis, puts it), or whether one can bring oneself to be interested in the Hitchcock experienced by the ordinary man-in-the-seat, the man in the Clapham Picture Palace, *l'homme moyen morale*. In any case we have seen how psychoanalytical ideas loom rather larger in Hitchcock's *œuvre* than theological ones, and it would be very remarkable if they didn't have a certain influence on the overall meaning of the films.

If one thinks of Bruno as part of Guy, then the film certainly isn't a psychological study, even in allegory, of temptation and complicity, because Guy never agrees with Bruno, and, objectively or subjectively, is less guilty of murdering Miriam than law and order is of murdering the old man. Guy is all but ground between the upper and nether stones of the subversive son (Bruno) and Superfather (law-and-order as disorder). That crazy carousel resumes the expressionist meaning which Kracaeur ascribes to fairgrounds in *The Cabinet of Dr. Caligari*. Here chaos is braved by Guy and an old man, who take risks for others.

Hitchcock's secret sympathy for the villain is rather carefully sealed off from any attachment of blame to Guy, but indulged via Robert Walker's Bruno—at once so sly and so frank, briefly so tired and yet so insolent, as charmingly amoral as the psychopathic Peter Pan he is, yet as understandably indignant when Guy behaves 'immorally' by not living up to his side of the 'bargain' which didn't exist outside Bruno's own incautious assumptions. When supping with the innocent, the devil needs a long spoon, being too intelligent and effective himself to realise that Guy not only isn't half as subtle but is too unimaginative and unembarrassed and clumsily slick to make his refusal to be involved in a murder clear.

Guy's secret guilt is on the same level as his secret homosexuality. For Bruno's soft, smiling, wheedling style evokes a type of seduction other than the purely moral, and links the film with the intermittent homosexuality motif (the transvestite in *Murder*, Peter Lorre's cloyingly caressive assassin in *Secret Agent*, the aesthetes of *Rope*). But here aestheticism is replaced by a more topical and democratic kind of thrills and fun—getting money and the freedom it brings. Bruno is kicking off from the social level at which Guy is just about to arrive, and the film has moved on from Symbolist-era sybaritism to a more open-air kind of fun morality. The French moved to parallel themes in the decade following. In *Les Cousins* Chabrol makes more or less the film which he felt *Strangers On A Train* implied (and the difference is clear; 'Guy' kills 'Bruno'), while Clément makes *Plein Soleil*. In 1972 Bruno would be a rich hippy who gets Guy high on drugs and wrests from him a soul's outpouring which Guy subsequently doesn't remember very clearly and in so far as he does remember it he doesn't dream that Bruno wouldn't sense it was the product of an abnormal condition and quite indignantly and reasonably repudiates it when Bruno tries to hold him to it. Even in 1951 old-fashioned, ultra-respectable alcohol would have done the job.

In every detail of story-telling technique, the film is a model of its kind, from the symmetries listed above. They are far from being exhaustive. One need only add the theme of staircases: the staircase to Mr. Anthony's bedroom on which the dog stands; the steps by the Capitol on which Bruno stands; the steps which Bruno's and Guy's feet take towards one another; and the hooves of the carousel horses, rearing and stamping above the heads of the fighting men; together with hands—strangling, gripping tennis-rackets, slipping out for or straining lighters. Mrs. Anthony's paintings pick up the theme of resemblances and contrast with something empty in Guy's in-laws' home. The contrast between fingertips straining for a lighter and tennis-champions smashing volleys at one another has a beautifully orchestrated physicality about it, as empathy alternately provokes and represses energy in the spectator. And the irony reappears in the carousel's fate—because it's going too fast it's got to be braked abruptly—which smashes it, which is what would have happened anyway. The opening, with the approaching feet, is one way, although not the only way, of assuring us that characters who haven't met yet certainly will, analogously to the Young Charlie/Old Charlie matching shots of *Shadow Of A Doubt*. And the conveyance of information by the two men's lower halves about their social class and character type has a curious effect. We are able to sum them up reasonably well, yet with the most obvious perceptual centres blocked off; we know but we don't quite know how we know; it's as if fate is written all over everyone and yet, in real life, we never quite manage to read it; so that although this sequence might reassure us that we can easily know more that we usually assume, the predominant sense of its arbitrary refusal to look higher than the men's trousers reminds us, rather, that we choose to know much less than we ought. The film knows everything, but we're stupid. We're caught in the grip of a machine when we needn't be; just like Guy. And as the shoes meet, the train moves off, with the camera almost at rail-level, as if fate, having drawn into itself the combined energies of the two men, were now moving irresistibly towards its predestined goal. Only Calvinism could have invented the railroad; the convergence of parallel paths at infinity; the scissors which complement the wheel of fortune. There's no narrative need for this opening. One might just as well have begun with an angry scene between Guy and Miriam; followed with a scene between Guy and Anne; then had Guy assume that the man following him is a detective paid by his wife to find evidence of apparent adultery; rounded on him indignantly only to be met with a startling counter-suggestion; and so on. Hitchcock's opening is much more bland and ordinary and strange. Montage effects are crucial to it, and Hitchcock remembers the silent film too in the record-shop scenes: how much we can see, through glass, without words![1]

The screenplay is particularly clever in that the two principal characters so rarely confront each other, while remaining obsessively and intimately linked. It's an interesting exercise to substitute for the mental link and the spatial separation some spatial link and mental separation. It might be the story of an innocent man who is unjustly sentenced to life-imprisonment, or even death for murdering his wife, and who finds himself handcuffed to a smooth, amiable professional killer whose escape-plan involves a higher degree of risk—but not a certainty—of killing a guard, but only if the guard struggles. Obviously such a situation is too devoid in itself of everyday associations and half-tones to create the intriguing Hitchcockian mixture of the everyday and the excessive, and the possibilities of developing a handcuffs situation not unreminiscent of *The Defiant Ones* into a handcuffs-situation not unreminiscent of *The Thirty-Nine Steps* will only infuriate those admirers of Hitchcock's subtlety who dismiss Kramer as a mere moralist for saying what he means in a manner sufficiently clear and emphatic to be understood by almost everybody instead of almost nobody.

Which reminds us that Hitchcock's film doesn't belong to the moralistic genre at all, although morality is certainly part of its pattern. To put it another way, if one transposes *Strangers On A Train*

[1] Recalling the glass booth (the screen in *The Paradine Case* and anticipating all the silent screens of *Rear Window*).

into a Western, with the smiling soft-spoken bad guy offering to exchange victims with the good guy, and cast Jack Palance and Henry Fonda, then the plot is as clear an opposition of bad guy and good guy as any admirer of Buck Jones and Rin-Tin-Tin (who turns up on the staircase) could hope for. It's a Tolkien Western. And that the comparison is unfair only reminds us that the film draws its fascination, not from its intrinsic moral pattern, but from something much more complex and allusive and intricate. While *Strangers On A Train* may not be a masterpiece in the usual sense of the word, it's certainly a piece by a master of the medium (for the medium's not the master), with its conjunction of its aesthetic finesse and its suspense, its social observation and a half-infantile, half-adult morality—perhaps adolescent is the right word, so long as it is not misunderstood as a pejorative one. The spectator's enjoyment of aesthetic form can easily seem, or indeed be, irresponsible or minoritarian, just as the suspense can seem childlike. All the more important then for the critic to refrain from reaching for falsely respectable severities or esotericisms, but instead to point out that *Strangers On A Train* is an astonishing example of art's ability to commingle the playful and the earnest, the subtle and the gross, in a way which reduces the most earnest of moralists to infants and produces a rejuvenation of the spirit which is neither serious in a conventional aesthetic sense nor entertainment in the insignificant sense but an extremely interesting hybrid between the two.

I Confess

The Catholic influence on Hollywood being what it was, *I Confess* is all but condemned to a pious solemnity, from the fact that its hero (Montgomery Clift) is a Canadian priest guarding the secrecy of the confessional at the price of his life. A sacristan (O. E. Hasse) commits a murder in the course of theft, and the priest hears his confession. But the murdered man knew of the priest's affair, before his ordination, with a married woman (Anne Baxter), who has recently reappeared in his life. The priest has both opportunity, and motive, for the crime, and is put on trial. Will he break his priestly vows to save his life?

The moral conflict, and the suspense arising from it, is foursquare and basic enough, but a sophisticated concern with moral issues would surely require a complication of the priest's dilemma in such a way as to lead him to query at least one of the codes—or all the codes—to which he subscribes. The possibilities are endless but let us, by way of illustration, modify the scenario along fairly obvious lines. The sacristan and the murdered man are nodding acquaintances. The sacristan's wife confesses to the priest that she is having an affair with the victim. The victim begins to blackmail the priest, as here, who repels him but is worried. The sacristan finds out the truth and, in a distraught state, confesses to the priest that he is undergoing the temptation to kill the man. The priest refuses—wilfully?—to believe that God's grace will not help the sacristan to resist the temptation. He does too little to prevent the crime, or he does what he does perfunctorily, perhaps because of his own distraught condition, perhaps out of a secret complicity. He then succumbs to morbid guilt, and becomes convinced that his ineffective action was, spiritually, homicidal self-indulgence— all the more culpable since he has, in fact, succumbed to his own old, only human love, but succumbed only after the sacristan's confession and before the blackmailer's death (or simultaneously with it, facilitating intercutting between his memories of his happiness and his vivid imagination of the murder). His yielding to temptation helped him to understand others with a new charity and humility. He can now at last understand the murderer, who, far from being a demoniac figure, becomes more than ever, his fellow-human; in Hitchcock's words, 'There are no blacks and whites, only greys.'

As it is, the film goes beyond the usual depths of Hollywood piety only when it hints that the temptation to which the priest eventually yields is something between the lure of martyrdom and masochistic passivity (the latter being the temptation of Mr. Deeds in his trial). Acquitted, he has to endure the threats of a crowd which, like the mob in *The Lodger*, won't believe in his innocence. It's the murderer's wife whose confession restores his reputation and popularity.

A more ruthless treatment of the subject would have concluded with the priest aware that, spiritually, the jeering crowd is right about him. But he has to go about his priestly duties, confronting the complacent, sympathetic, almost patronising murderer every day, thus being confronted, in a sharp, personal form, with affable, suffering, evil whose omnipresence must be more familiar to any priest. The Hitchcock of *Rich and Strange* might have contemplated some such film; and the real heretics are the Hays Office and the Catholic pressure-groups, with their insistence that justice must be seen to be done in this life. But if such compromises complicated Hitchcock's problems, let us imagine one other possibility which is morally less anodyne than his solution. The priest might finally connive in some dishonourable trick which brings the murderer to book, clears his own name, and brings on him the congratulations of his parishioners, of the law, and of his ecclesiastical superiors. But his strategy is despicable to him, and he reaches, through this disillusionment, a more complete dependence on God alone, which the spectator is, of course, at perfect liberty to view as a tragic severance of human contacts. Just this structure brings us very near that English Western, Roy Baker's *The Singer Not The Song*, which develops its thoroughly Hitchcockian pattern with a rather greater theological refinement and ethical challenge.

Hitchcock deploys his usual precision in establishing intimations of crime and sin by purely civic and ecclesiastical images. But the film lacks lustre, possibly because the murderer, the victim and the priest alike are rather isolated in their own psychological worlds, while Hitchcock hasn't solved the problems aroused by the Hays Office's disapproval of a handsome priest committing adultery and the audience's finding celibacy a rather dismal triumph. To Hitchcock's credit, he ignores any sentimentalisation of the priestly vocation, but a kind of emotional doldrums between the priest and his ex-love render this relationship relatively undramatic. Hitchcock deeply regretted that his original choice for the girl, Anita Bjork, arrived with a lover and a child, which aroused problems of scandalous publicity; and it's interesting to feed this point back into the storyline. The priest's ex-love turns up with emancipated ideas and a child, and the priest finds, to his shock, that he still loves her, that worldly happiness is still possible with her, that it would be deep, and that the 'common-sense' morality which is so deeply built into his choice of a vocation is invalid (although his vocation may not be). As it is, the priest has a kind of self-sufficiency which isn't rare in Hitchcock's heroes, but which, because of his priesthood, Hitchcock daren't show as radically threatened, and hasn't time to isolate as an actual or potential source of sin—or even of vocation as sin. In questions of such radical loneliness, of faith in God as remoteness from man, Hitchcock, priest, and *spectateur moyen sensuel* might have found common ground. The issues certainly reappear in the relationship between God, the sacristan and his wife. Apparently simple points of censorship often rule out a great many more dramatic possibilities than at first they may seem—and of course do a great deal to keep religious issues off the screen and out of the consciousness of the spectator, thus confirming, and justifying, them in their general equation of religion with pious tedium. Hitchcock, and the public, found his film too sombre, too serious.

Dial M For Murder

Dial M For Murder is a slight, safe stage-success and murder-mystery, made in 3-D, which added its pleasant clarity of laminated depth to the enclosed interiors.

The opening situation is no less interesting for being honeycombed with echoes. This time an ex-tennis champion (Ray Milland) wants to get rid of his wife (Grace Kelly). He blackmails a burglar into doing it. But the wife's refined exterior conceals cool grit and she kills her would-be killer, sticking scissors in his back. The husband impudently uses a letter to start framing the wife for murder. Eventually an old-fashioned Scotland Yard officer confounds not only the suavely cocksure murderer but a second American—a thriller-writer (Robert Cummings) who is the wife's lover and turns private-eye, taking it for granted that he's sharper than these dim-witted and old-fangled limey fuddy-duddies.

The pleasure of tracing connections between films would be more obvious than ever if the tennis champion were played by Farley Granger and the brilliant writer by Robert Walker; or if the wife underwent, however briefly, the temptation of allowing herself to be murdered by her husband (*Suspicion*); and so on; as it is the scissors in the back recall the knife in *Blackmail*. One must admire the economy of the plot (murderer frames victim for self-defence). The justification of an apparently bumbling establishment Briton possibly mortifies some American assumptions, but Carol Reed and Graham Greene had been there before as Trevor Howard and Bernard Lee enlighten another American writer, Joseph Cotten, in *The Third Man*, whose plot, incidentally, fits every requirement which Chabrol and Rohmer think are specific to Hitchcock (particularly the very obvious 'transference of guilt' between Orson Welles, Joseph Cotten and the suitably chastised spectator, who has identified with the latter).

With *Dial M For Murder* Hitchcock seemed to have attained the state of suspenseful abstraction, of spiritual nullity, towards which, despite the finesse of *Rope*, and the itself somewhat suspicious gesture towards a grand religious issue in *I Confess*, he had gradually been tending. And he himself describes it as a case of drained creative batteries, of running for cover. His next movie suggested that his hesitations might have been concealing a deeper reorientation.

Rear Window

Rear Window brilliantly conjugates the enclosed setting and the social cross-section. The penthouse window of *Rope* showed colours; this apartment window looks into the secrets of the city. Jeff (James Stewart) is a photographer who has suffered a broken leg in the course of photographing an automobile race-crush. His daring seems connected with his perhaps slightly childlike idea of rugged living. He frets on his bed, between visits from his abrasively wise masseuse (Thelma Ritter) and his fiancée, Lisa (Grace Kelly). To pass the time he pries into the comings and goings of the apartment dwellers opposite; idly initially, but then, to clear up some odd points, with a telephoto lens. Gradually he comes to suspect that a crime has been committed; although his detective friend (Wendell Corey) sees little more than an idle fantasy. The murderer finally spots the paralysed peeping tom, and looms over him, kept at bay, briefly, by the dazzle of flashlight bulbs. Help arrives, but not before Jeff's second broken leg fulfils his craving for thrills.

Our uneasiness stems from the curious coldness of the telephoto relationship, a high-powered, one-sided, prying contact/non-contact, a morally ambiguous rebellion against urban solitude. Separate, yet exposed, the denizens of the apartment jungle live their lives emotionally deprived or tragically ill-assorted. A young couple fritter their happiness away in little bickerings. 'Miss Torso' entertains her admirers—and when her husband at last returns, he's a bald little man who clearly won't content her. Miss Lonelyhearts has candlelit suppers with imaginary admirers and her one real guest turns out to be heartbreakingly coarse. A childless couple lavish their love on their dog. The same maladjustment menaces Jeff and Lisa. Just as he craves the escape of the manly life (which rewards him by putting him back here), she loves the mundanities of high society. And the hair in the domestic soup is predicted by her use of his immobilism to titillate him into acceptance of her terms. (Obviously, the conventional glamourisation of our foreground identifications is observed; and Hitchcock's 'subversion' of the conventional happy end, far from being remarkable, is much less pointed than the more substantial tensions explored within the already glamorous key of, say, *The Man in the Grey Flannel Suit*.)

A camera peeping from outside at lighted windows usually has, if not sadness, at least nostalgia, as in passages from René Clair and Max Ophuls. And here the movie style, the social vignettes and the

macabre yet pathetic marital murder, create a thematic unity so open
and so felt that one doesn't have to decode the film. These bright,
translucent, open-plan cells are like a hen-battery for human beings,
a teasing limbo which is the human condition. Our lives are lonely but
not private, painful but without much dignity, at least in the eyes of
others. A balance between emptiness and being overwhelmed is precarious. The photographer concludes with another spell under the
affable domination of his smiling, patient mistress, and her complementary character, the masseuse. The murderer whom he brings to
book has, certainly, the brooding violence of the sacristan and *I Confess* in his type but also the suppressed rage of the henpecked man
who finally turned and slew his tormentrice—his invalid wife (who was
also an invalid, a nice echo of her avenger's broken leg). Jeff may
have helped the cause of abstract justice, of good order and civilian
discipline, but his victim is in a way a less fortunate version of himself,
the tensions between himself and Lisa writ tragically large. Jeff thinks
he's 'just visiting' in this square in the communal board; in fact he's
in another cell of the same social prison whose name is human relationships. The difference between the murderer and the sleuth is a
matter of degree, rather than of radical kind. Moral rules are necessary, as they are also unjust. Visually, at least, in its sense of separate
cells, in which quiet atrocities occur, this film's *complément de programme* is Borowczyk's *Les Jeux des Anges*. And spiritually they have
points in common, although if the films illuminate one another it is
through moral contrast rather than affinity.

Jean Douchet compares Jeff (the photographic viewer) to the cinema
spectator (also immobilised and peeking through a lens). The wall
opposite Jeff is the screen opposite us. What he sees is the action
which we want in the film. We want a murder to have been committed,
so as to get our thrills. And what he gets is what we deserve, a puni-
tively bad fright.

But such a moral is suspiciously schoolmarmish, if only because its
condemnation of voyeurism is also an inhibition of ordinary human
curiosity. It's possibly very naughty of us to look into one another's
windows, but several old ladies down my street are usually to be found
with their elbows on their window sills, and I can't say I hastily avert
my eyes from intriguing vignettes in crowded rooms. What badly
needs privacy isn't usually done before open windows. And would,
one wonders, those morally fastidious film critics, if bedridden, really
turn their backs to the window and refrain from speculating about
their neighbours' comings and goings?

Certainly Jeff's resort to a massive lens acquires an hubristic and ominous edge. But it possesses also a daring zest, an exhilarating ruthlessness, and it is his crossing of this Rubicon which enables him, in the end, to detect a murder. Far from seeing his voyeurism as sin, one may see it as also the beginning of involvement and intervention—divine intervention, if one's tastes run that way. The risks he and Lisa run, far from being a punishment for their involvement, are incurred as a result of the fact that they're *not* coldly detached, but are ready to put their bodies where their glances are, to get involved. Of course one may say that even this degree of involvement with the truth is morbid; and Hitchcock isn't the man to allow such an overtone to go untouched; 'You're a couple of fiendish ghouls! But at the same time the gratuitousness with which the murderer, is their final confrontation, can, justifiably, reproach Jeff, is also a disinterestedness, satisfying whatever spiritual instincts are satisfied by the search for truth. Knowledge, sadism, justice are no doubt closely related; but it would be a curious morality which required absolute purity of motive from human curiosity, or allowed a murderer's distress to inculpate the detective, or condemned Jeff and Lisa for involving the police.

In fact, Jeff is in a dilemma. If he doesn't try to find out where the wife has gone, he is guilty of that notorious New York callousness which just shrugs off murders and muggings as somebody else's business. If he does try to find out, he is guilty of being an interfering busybody. It is because he can't do right that it's difficult to condemn him. And therefore the spiritually hypochondriacal school of criticism condemns him, not for what he does, but the impurity of his motives. But here too a balance is necessary. Hitchcock carefully constructs the situation and maintains the balance of sympathies, so that Jeff's 'persecution' of the murderer remains a passing tone in the audience's possibly unreflective support of him in his quest for truth and justice. First, he asks the detective to investigate a missing person. Second, the murderer turns on Jeff, who has to be saved by the detectives. The accusations of Jeff and Lisa remain, which is one reason why the film becomes, spiritually, one of Hitchcock's more interesting films. It depends on a conformist, perhaps complacent, enthusiasm ('Murderers ought to be caught!') and it maintains it with qualms. It's not a subversive film; but it arouses an honest ambivalence. One says 'arouses', advisedly; it can hardly be described as a challenge, a shock. And there's certainly no suggestion that Jeff is being 'punished' for his curiosity, by God, in any sense of that much-abused name. In so far as the threat to his life comes from the murderer, it would be truer to say that he is being 'punished' for his interest. Or perhaps he's not being punished at all. Perhaps Hitchcock believes, as most of us do, in a multiplicity of cause-and-effect sequences most of which are independent of moral variables.

The idea of a kathartic correction of the audience seems to me as theoretical as it is one-dimensional. The supposition that suspense, or identification with a person in danger, is, in an entertainment situation, *unpleasant*, doesn't bear a moment's reflection. However suspenseful the climax of *Rear Window* may be, it won't deter us from returning to the cinema the following week, or if we're film addicts later the same day, or from looking forward eagerly to the promise of kathartic correction in Hitchcock's next film. Still less will it induce us to heave our television sets into the nearest junkyard in case newsreels or documentaries should trespass on someone's privacy. Of course there are ironies galore; as I write this the B.B.C.2 announcer proclaims 'Next, our prize-winning documentary, *Gale Is Dead*'. Prize-winning! Who isn't, in passing, profiting from someone else's tragedy? And what alternative for human beings is there? All the talk, in connection with *Rear Window*, of the spectator's vicarious punishment for being a spectator derives from the conjunction of a one-dimensional psychology (which knows nothing of such complex yet everyday experiences as pleasurable fear, as at the funfair, or of the pleasures of fear recollected in tranquillity which art shares with nostalgia).

Predal, determined to maintain the guilt-and-punishment pattern, observes that Jeff begins by looking at a dancer's legs. And his own preoccupation with whether or not to marry leads him to notice the unsatisfactory love-lives of his fellow-humans. But the point might equally be that his observations don't remain exclusively anatomical (as an immature male's might), and that the plethora of unsatisfactory situations is not Jeff's but Hitchcock's, or the world's, doing (although rays of hope are by no means absent). One gets nearer Hitchcock's irony, I think, by citing as example Lisa's venture into the murderer's apartment to find the wedding-ring. Her argument is that no wife would leave her wedding-ring behind, and that if it's there, she's dead, and if she's dead, her husband has lied, and if he's lied, he's probably a murderer. In other words, the symbol for marital harmony has become the symbol of murder. Finding the ring, she brandishes it, triumphantly, through the window at her fiancé. It has one meaning: 'Look, a clue! It took a woman's logic to find this clue! Look how indispensable I am to you!' It also has the opposite meaning, because we can see, though she can't, the murderer on his way back to the apartment, and if she stands there waving the ring around, just like a woman, she's going to be the opposite of indispensable, like the old B Western heroine who was always falling into the villain's hands and queering the hero's pitch. As Truffaut observes, the ring is a hint to Jeff; and, one might add, it's an unfortunate one, since it's the ring of a wife who drove her husband to chop her up into small pieces. And the irony produces reversible morals. Maybe Lisa's innocence about the ring signifies her hope and life-instinct triumphing over the death-instinct; or maybe that takes a pathetic meaning, since Death is creeping up the stairs. And one can draw the symmetries another way. The murderer returns to find a would-be wife replacing a posthumous one; Lisa is his wife's 'ghost'; a doubly taunting one, since she is desirable and happy. Hitchcock isn't unaware of such symmetries, commenting on the contrast between the murderer's household and Jeff's; in the former the woman is immobilised, in the latter the man.

My point is the inseparability of the alternative meanings in the case of the ring. For Hitchcock, I suspect, Jeff's sin is like the tails of his decency. You can't have one without the other. To suppose that he is being punished for his sin is like wanting a coin to come down heads every time. In fact his danger is the product of his defects and his qualities conjointly, so that the element of justice in it is balanced by the element of injustice. Hitchcock is a moralist and an immoralist. And, on reflection, most of us are. We readily accept that any line of conduct is likely to have several distinct and morally contradictory motives. We believe that the purity of our motives isn't insignificant in determining our fates, but that it is far from being the only consideration; there are very real amoral factors, like beauty, or cleverness, or the wisdom which comes with experience, or bad luck, or complicated situations, in which tiny errors have exaggerated consequences. And so most of us, if pressed, will elect for, or at least acknowledge the importance of, moral factors independent of connections between our conduct and consequence, and look to the shaping of human character so as to institute purely internal imperatives and rewards, some variant of moral stoicism, some amoral praxiology, a resilient life-force, certain external social sanctions to redress the internal imbalance in favour of egoism. Most vernacular moralities are intrinsically illogical, but culturally coherent, admixtures of all these elements, and anything more logical and less complicated can't do justice to Hitchcock's ambiguities. Everything Jeff does is right and wrong. Maybe he shouldn't allow Lisa to endanger herself while he stays safely in his home. But if he is a man of action, how can he deny her the right to be a woman of action? And maybe she is guilty of dominantly over-riding his scruples on her behalf? Scruples which are absurd precisely because she is dominant? Or does he know better than she how dangerous life is? And so on and so forth.

At any rate, to suppose that Jeff's prying deserves that he be scared stiff and left with a second broken leg seems to me not only arbitrary, but an acceptance of a nonsensical scale of moral values. Supposing he hadn't gone so far as to use a telephoto lens, should he only have broken his ankle? Supposing he hadn't been spurred on by a crime as serious as a murder, should he be considered as less guilty (as being less morbid) or more guilty (the crime being less serious)? What punishment should be suffered by all the people who dismissed his suspicions as unfounded? Such an infinity of perfectly possible moral interpretations opens before us that it's obvious that the film's primary polarity isn't a rigorous morality at all, but a very obvious one. Jeff is naughty but justified and an agent of social order, the murderer is pitiable but unjustified. The pattern which Douchet and Predal observe is certainly present, but as an undertow, and, I would suggest, its spiritual connections are less with moral rigour than with poetic justice, that is to say, a curious mixture of sensitivity about human transactions with superego irrationality and severity, i.e. injustice. Moreover, it may be that Hitchcock sees moral rigour as an aspect of the absurdity of the universe. For, as the murderer protests, if Jeff hadn't pried, he would have gotten away with it, and wouldn't have had to commit the murder which he is now about to commit, i.e. of Jeff. The murderer maintains that Jeff's curiosity killed Jeff, and the parallels in the moralist's logic suggests that it is very hypochondriac indeed, closer to Sade's than Jansen's, and either way quite alien to the audience around whose reactions the film is obviously constructed. I should argue that Jeff's 'voyeuristic' tendencies are unusually developed, and well within the range of psychological normality, but benign in the medical sense, and in no need of apology, or punishment. Moreover, one must beware of the extent to which 'voyeurism' is in this context an insidiously loaded word for what might equally be described as a journalist's, or artist's, or humanly ordinary, interest in other people's lives, whose inhibition produces the spiritual myopia of *Rich and Strange*. But Hitchcock keeps a certain sentimentality about good neighbourliness at bay, and weaves a crime-and-punishment thread into his overall pattern, by the contrast between this globetrotter's supercilious air, as of a successful, self-contained man temporarily stranded among these little people. Eventually the privileged cosmopolitan endures as great a fear here as he could elsewhere; greater, perhaps, for to be pushed through a window into midair in a wheelchair is such a mixture of freedom and helplessness. . . .

This unreflective contempt is reiterated when the couple's obsession with their little dog, conventionally risible, turns out to be a clue to the truth. The dog was a danger to the murderer, and he killed it, and neither the dog nor the couple were as stupid as we thought. In any case, the couple deserve a certain sympathy; as Hitchcock observes, 'the dog was their only child'. And the fussing over the dog, which seems so excessive, reveals another clue. The scene ends with everyone concerned about it, except the murderer, who sits alone, in his darkened window, the tip of his cigarette, well back in the room, glowing. And again one presents the characters with no escape. To care about a dog is too absurd. To look out of the window is wicked. Just to sit in the dark is wicked. There are so few options that I wouldn't even attribute to Hitchcock the outer-directed, conformist moral to the effect that deviants and recluses are sinister—we know how naturally this moral would come to an American audience by the number of films that have denounced just such attitudes, or appealed to them. 'The man who doesn't care about his neighbour's dog is the alien in our midst!' The film avoids this just because we are, simultaneously, finding all this fuss over a duckie-wuckie doggie-woggie, a little comic, a misplacement which can only briefly alleviate the other solitudes. As this community develops, the camera moves outside the apartment, for the only time.

The murderer kills his wife, chops her up to fit his fridge, and disposes of the body in nightly packages. (Meat to meat . . .). Hitchcock is too much the fundamentalist and legalist to allow the murderer more than a limited sympathy, and his burly, surly air deprives him of that consistent sympathy which some domestic murderers might deserve. Yet occasionally we sense the story's possible reverse angle. A passionate man has lived a dog's life and only once has his latent violence got the upper hand. Neither masochist nor sentimentalist, he tries to save himself. He has no regrets and strong nerves. Indeed, the days after the murder were, for all their exterior anxieties, his days of sombre self-respect. But he gradually becomes aware of this gratuitously prying eye across the way, smugly bringing what seems a Big Brother surveillance to bear upon him, and goading him into a second outburst of violence whose only result is to ensure that he loses any chance of mercy.

The story presents a variety of formal problems to which Hitchcock's solutions are all the more exhilarating for their diversity, as opposed to the overall schematism of the ten-minute take. Hitchcock delights in the film's 'pure cinema', i.e. montage. Certainly the abundance of reverse angles between close-ups of Jeff's face and whatever it is that he sees exactly corresponds to Kulyeshov's classic experiment, and it's ironic that, just as Truffaut made the term 'well-constructed script' a pejorative one, without commenting on how exceptionally well-constructed the scripts of his idol Hitchcock were, so none of those critics who admired both Bazin and Hitchcock have ever paused to discuss the contrast between Bazin's dismissals of montage as contrivance or second-rate, as an offence against some sort of phenomenological continuity and unity, and Hitchcock's delight in it, along with Eisenstein's and Grierson's, as being of the cinema's essence. Devotees of impure cinema, like this writer, are in the happy position of being able to share both Hitchcock's delight in discontinuity and Bazin's in its opposite, while disagreeing with the latter only in the aspersions which he casts on montage as the rupture of a real *continuum*. For in any work of art the only significant continuum is a sequence of ideas, or stimuli, or selected perceptions, of which spatiotemporal, intellectual and even perceptual discontinuities are an inevitable concomitant; e.g. things shown on the screen have limits, or change; the screen itself has limits; even if it were a 3-D sphere surrounding the spectator, it would have only limited depth; and so on. One of the purposes of thinking, and, for that matter, seeing, is to rearrange the elements of reality, or symbols for them, in *another* order, i.e. to *cut*.

It is probable that *Rear Window* could, with enormous difficulty, be filmed in long takes and deep focus, but the number of 180° pans, and turnings about by Jeff in his wheelchair, and peculiar conversational positions, would fail to obviate innumerable visual irrelevances (in particular the sides of the courtyard). One might make things easier by having the wall which Jeff is observing placed at 90° to his window instead of 180°, thus decreasing the visual irrelevances which a panning camera might have to traverse, but it's hard to see how disastrous tracts of irrelevance could be avoided. Worse, the movement from Jeff's face to the facing wall would be cumbersome and slow, so that the loss of reaction shots would, in fact, disrupt the connection between action and reaction which, arguably, constitutes the real phenomenological unity of the film. To equate a visual continuity with a phenomenological unity is quite ludicrous. And in any case the fact that a shifting of the wall through 90° goes a long way to solving certain problems reveals them as merely formalistic fetishes and nothing to do with any coherent phenomenology at all.

As it is, the camera's creation of mid-air sight-lines at right-angles to the wall-to-windows, i.e. the screens-within-the-screen-within-the-screen, creates a visual excitement analogous to the counterpoints of dramatic, architectural and compositional features within the Renaissance pictorial tradition, of which the cinema mainstream has been the visual heir, just as, in narrative, it has prolonged the 19th century novel. Reverse-angles, as a 180° relationship, fit this pattern of right-angles well enough. But Hitchcock never allows the facing wall to become an analogue of the proscenium arch. The camera approaches, retreats, pans, tilts, switches between a diversity of details and configurations, with Hitchcock making particularly effective use of an extremely asymmetrical *échappée* to the street beyond, a real ex-art-director's conception, where a narrow, edge-of-screen alley is balanced by its depth, its lights, its narrative intensity, against the façade as a whole. With all the variations of weather, time, day and night, activity, etc., one hardly realises that Jeff's room and the courtyard together form quite as 'enclosed' (i.e. continuous) an area as the rooms of *Rope* and *Dial M For Murder*.

The vignettes may seem merely American equivalents of the threads or episodes in English omnibus movies of the '40s. It would certainly be absurd to praise *It Always Rains On Sunday* for its realism while dismissing *Rear Window* for its superficiality. And the application, to the American scene, which is almost always seen from one man's, or family's, viewpoint, that is to say, individualistically and romantically, of the English awareness of mutually exclusive worlds, of passive imprisonment at separate tables, is something of a step towards thinking of society as a whole, of social relationships. It's a tentative kind of neo-realism, not rendered insignificant by its anomalous crime and its studio set.

It recalls another dream paraphrase of the social cross-section, Jerry Lewis's *The Ladies Man*. It's entertaining to imagine various possible mixtures of the two. There's the Tashlin parody of Hitchcock, with Jerry Lewis in the James Stewart part and Dean Martin in the Thelma Ritter role and Lisa as the girl they're both after. Or there's the Hitchcock variation on the other film's theme, with a misanthropic janitor (Anthony Perkins) in a valley-of-the-dolls theatrical boarding house finally at bay against the real murderer—Miss Cartilage, an acrobatic dancer who comes after him with a cut-throat razor in each sinewy hand.

Rear Window shows Hitchcock moving, in the Hollywood vanguard, certainly, but with the Hollywood current, in the gradual rediscovery of American life as a matter, not merely of individualistic impulses, but as a socio-spiritual network, with built-in dissatisfactions. It's paralleled in *Bachelor Party*; in *The Bells Are Ringing*; in *The Chapman Report*; and, on the level of spiritual banality, by *Peyton Place* and the 'holes-in-the-wall' format of the *Rowan and Martin Laugh-In*. (Most of these films, and in particular the Jerry Lewis one, are, far from being apolitical, of the right, crediting society with an equality, a fluidity, which is denied by films of the left.) Divergent as their attitudes are, Hitchcock's film would make an intriguing triple-feature with Antonioni's *Blow-Up* (another story of a photographer involved with murder) and with John Boorman's beautiful *Leo the Last*—even though Leo looks below the middle-class level (at any rate, its relevance to the American urban situation is sufficiently obvious without needing reference to *The Landlord*). Rewarding such contrasts, yet remaining prudently within the purlieus of the middle-class detective story, Hitchcock's film reveals a greater range than any of his work since *Sabotage*, and moves into those areas where a delirium of interpretation becomes an authentic rather than a mechanically cerebral response.

To Catch A Thief

With *Rear Window* Hitchcock had ventured as far as he wished along the controversy-infested paths of the social jungle. Direct challenges to the ideology of the end of ideology he left to such then critical unfashionables as Richard Brooks, Elia Kazan and Samuel Fuller. His next film, *To Catch A Thief*, is a plush, relaxed affair, connected to the cycle of comedies of spectacular high life which had been sparked off by *High Society* and which M.G.M. and Paramount, remembering their '30s triumphs, tried hardest to revive.

Cary Grant plays John Robie, a brilliant cat-burglar who has purged his crimes by Resistance feats and retired to a Riviera farm, to cultivate grapes and flowers. He has come under suspicion for a renewed cycle of crimes, carbon copies of his unique exploits. Heiress Frances Stevens (Grace Kelly) thinks him all the more exciting for being the thief which he is glad he no longer is. Eventually he tracks down the real culprit, Danielle (Brigitte Auber), the daughter of an old colleague.

Hitchcock's most earnest admirers have agreed in finding *To Catch*

A Thief a plush, relaxed affair finding the Master in a relatively playful, for once indeed almost morally tolerant, mood. The adjective 'Lubit-schian' is allowed, in a way which slides suspiciously lightly over any incompatibilities between the former's worldly cynicism and the latter's supposedly severely apportioned chastisements. With what surprise, therefore, we discover that the structure of *To Catch A Thief*—we do not say moral structure (yet)—is a mechanism every bit as complicated as that of *Strangers On A Train*.

In a key exchange, Robie defends himself against accusations of recidivism. 'Why should I steal? I'm rich.' 'How did you become rich?' 'By stealing.' True, he never stole from anyone who would have gone hungry. And his interlocutor would like to believe that he fulfilled some sort of Robin Hood role. But Robie candidly denies it. What he stole he kept, and 'by stealing' he was enabled to live out that capitalist ideal, and idyll, of enjoying, while still in his prime and fancy free, a rural retirement within financial and geographical reach of exhilarat-ingly fast drive by exhilaratingly fast car to the most opulent hotels and restaurants of Nice.

True, Hitchcock hedges. Robie escaped from prison (i.e. crime does not pay) during the war, and became a war hero (redemption by patriotism). He has paid his debt to society, in another way. None the less, the serene plushness of his social milieu and his personal style leave us in no doubt that crime, in moderation, pays. The wages of successful crime are gracious living.

That society itself lives by moral equivalents of theft is adduced, less to trouble our peace of mind than to justify Robie's. Society as tempter, and, therefore, accomplice, is introduced in the person of H. H. Hughson (John Williams), a London insurance agent whose City Gent garb goes with what, by contrast to Robie's smooth crisp savoir-faire, is an effecting gaucherie, a naivety extending even to the pleasures of the palate. Prematurely convinced of Robie's guilt, he seeks to bait a trap. If Robie eventually persuades him of his inno-cence, it is in a way which, far from abolishing the spectator's identi-fication with guilt, merely alters it, without condemning it. As Robie, irrefutably, observes, the fiddling of expense accounts, or of income tax, are merely another form of theft. The cat-burglars merely prowl the roofs of civilisation, but the mouse-burglars gnaw at its founda-tions, often showing no skill or audacity at all. And Robie seduces Hughson into trusting him with information about his most bejewelled clients. Rather more extended, and emphatic, is Hitchcock's develop-ment of yet another of dishonesty's Protean guises. Mrs. Stevens's late lamented lived a hard and unlucky life and died, with hilarious loser's pathos, just before an oilstrike transformed her into a wealthy, lonely, vulgar widow. So much for the Protestant ethic. Later we learn that the dead man was, in sad truth, a small-time swindler—a reminder that home-town America had its seamy side also. Both Mr. Stevenses are familiar images of loser types. What matters isn't your morality but striking oil.

The widow relishes her wealth with what seems, at first, a malicious ostentation, although gradually we learn that her aggression accommodates a vehement nihilism about mere wealth, a kind of exasperation with its emptiness. At any rate, she finds Robie so gorgeous that she would like to buy him for her daughter. And maybe she means as a husband by dowry, but a kind of transference-cum-sublimation of the gigolo theme is not exactly conspicuous by its absence. Her rapacious way with the almighty dollar may seem like utter cynicism about human relationships; but then again maybe she's only uttering the calculations which common sense does quietly; and such cynicism may be the exasperated product of a deep loneliness. In the event her moral honour is redeemed by her earthy disenchantment. She'd rather be poor with her late lamented, in the backwoods of Oregon, swindler though he was, than have to 'cuddle up with her jewels' Rubies aren't a girl's best friend. . . .

As the film nears its climax, her spiritual probity emerges more clearly. In addition to maintaining her faith in Robie's innocence, she refuses to mourn the theft of her jewels. So unmoved is she by their loss that we believe that even their non-insurance would have left her philosophical. With her, as with Hughson, we see a pattern of reciprocal seduction. As Hughson tempts, she buys. But both come to be persuaded of Robie's honesty, although both these persuasions, as we shall see, involve an overtone of seduction by sensual pleasure.

Frances both parades and hoards her jewels. Her style of flirtation, mingling aggression, assurance and immaculacy, suggests that she is a *demi-vièrge*; and should her poise and her sexuality together prove inadequate, well, 'Money handles most people'. Except, of course, those who steal it. Robie's reputation as a thief so fascinates her that she tries to make him love her, so as to capture him, and become his accomplice. Meanwhile she provokes him to provide her with the illusion that he is doubly despoiling her: (a) by seducing her while (b) stealing her diamond necklace. In reality she is seducing an impressed but slightly diffident man who finds her fetishism slightly sick, masochism being less natural than criminal egoism. Eventually she reveals that this particular necklace is a sham anyway. None the less, her pleasure in the fantasy betrays a certain truth, a mixture of the predatory, the prudent and the masochistic which underlies her cynical pride which underlies her gracious and conventional social *persona*. And here indeed we dip one toe into the shallow end of life à la Jean Genet (winners play loser games, but dupe themselves and others as they do). When she gives her body, without being loved, which, since she loves crime rather than Robie, would be a generous repayment, and loses not the sham necklace but the real one, then she switches to a revengeful brooding and calls the police to hunt Robie down. Hell hath no fury like a masochist wronged. It is the 'aggressive', hard-edge mother who tries to put the police off the track. Finally, Frances is able to believe in his innocence, to love him despite his respectability, and to help him over his temptations to bitterness, just outside the cemetery gates.

Eventually, he returns, happily enough, to resume his contented solitude in the villa. She must pursue him and declare her love, frankly, albeit she is allowed to do so by requesting him to declare his love for her. Amiably he does and his equanimity (be it assurance or diffidence or both) receives a rude shock. She translates that old music hall lament, 'And her mother came too', into a suaver form of bourgeois appropriation (i.e. deceit, i.e. theft), by appreciatively surveying his bachelor castle on its plateau and observing, 'It's a nice property, mother will love it'. Marriage is the biggest theft of all.

Robie, throughout, is self-contained, enviably, admirably, but to a fault. He has, if not his ivory tower, his Riviera retreat, of wine and roses. A scene in which he visits a restaurant whose chefs and kitchen-hands were his accomplices once, but have not enjoyed his subsequent ease, underlines the solitude which success, far from imposing on him, has presupposed of him. He is a nonchalant, passive seducer, his appearance and manners being enough to melt both the hard-edge matriarch and the semi-*demi-vierge*, and it is never quite clear whether this is the result of diffidence or confidence or both. His difficulty in escaping from an elderly flower-seller suggests that either characteristic links with a certain passivity and helplessness where women are concerned. At the burial of his old friend, the wine-waiter (whose murderer the police suspect Robie to be), Danielle, the victim's daughter, hysterically denounces him as a murderer, and he slaps her, effectively. His calm deliberate reaction startles us, even though, for a man on the run for his life, it is a restrained action, and even though we too have suspected that the vehemence of her love for him conceals something

stranger. He stalks away from the midst of her friends, who close in on
him, chivalrously, threateningly. Briefly, he paralyses them by an
authority which, even if at heart it is a moral one, is, exteriorly,
completely amoral. Outside the cemetery gates his old friend's black,
heavy hearse is balanced by Frances, blonde and perfidious in her
high-powered sportscar. Though the film's style is too light for us to
worry, we are certainly wondering whether to worry that his bitterness, now, will lead him to turn his back on a friendship which our
sense of stars reassures us meets both their needs. He hesitates, but
climbs in beside her. As they continue sparring, she accelerates to a
breakneck speed, and we may seem to have the always enjoyable, if
scarcely original, scene in which the spoiled rich girl tests the nerves of
her outlaw lover. Sooner or later, we see, as she has seen, but he has
not, the reason for her 'aggression'; the police car behind them. His
mixture of anxiety and acquiescence is expressed in terms of his
hands tensing and lifting, spread, up from his knees: the gestures, not
of taking, but of letting go.

This scene marks a brief, inconspicuous junction of two themes
which otherwise are separate: the pursuit (with Robie as passenger or
prize), and hands (theft, trust). Near the beginning of the film, he
evades the police in a long automobile chase, taken entirely in long
shot. Later, Danielle, after trying to persuade him to go to South
America with her, sweeps him off in her speedboat. Already he is no
longer in control. Finally, in a joke recap of the opening pursuit, he
is back at the wheel, fleeing Frances who follows in hot pursuit. The
theme of hands, unsurprisingly endemic, is climaxed in two scenes
which also involve *falls* from heights. The first involves a blow with a
monkeywrench and the body's shallow fall into the blue Mediter-
ranean; but we know little more than that someone has murdered someone. The victim might, theoretically, be Robie, although the fact that
the film has so far to run ends our brief startle; and we do not believe
that Robie is a murderer, so that the suspense begins when we realise
that the police think he is. The real suspense is the riddle, of who
killed who and why, and what is meant by this graver modulation,
involving murder, which, diffusely, puts everyone in more danger than
before. The victim is revealed, not without pathos, as a 'little man'
Danielle's father; and eventually the murderer turns out to be Bertan
(Charles Vanel), who is Danielle's father's employer in the restaurant
Danielle's employer in her role as cat-burglar, and Robie's most
trusted, most successful ex-associate. Later, Robie, grappling with the
copy-cat on a palace roof, finds 'him' to be Danielle; she slips and

clutching her by one wrist, he threatens to let her fall unless she yells a full confession to the police below (as later, of course, Frances insists on a full confession from him).

Hitchcock criticises *Saboteur* for the 'elementary mistake' (which in *North-by-North-West* he corrected) of basing his climactic suspense on the hanging of the villain from the hero's hand, rather than vice versa. In *To Catch A Thief* he repeats this 'mistake', excused, no doubt, by the lighter nature of this particular entertainment. But is it a mistake? Those for whom Hitchcock is an impeccable moralist haven't raised the question of Robie's morality in threatening to let Danielle fall to her death unless she confesses, not only to him, but more loudly, all over again, to the police below. One might well object that if Hitchcock were in earnest this touch of mental torture is rather more deserving of punishment even than his prowess as a cat-burglar. If we have retained sufficient detachment from Robie to preserve either some sort of moral objectivity or some sympathy for Danielle, or both, then a criticism of Robie must touch our minds, and I would suggest that most spectators are in this position. But it passes lightly by, for a variety of reasons: the tone of a romantic comedy (with its muting of suspense and its implicit reassurance); poetic justice, with its leniency towards the tit for tat; Robie's self-defence; and the distractions of the context, with the police firing away like madmen at just and unjust alike. The scene pairs with Danielle's behaviour at the graveyard. Both are denunciations, both put someone in fear of his life, this substitutes a grip for a slap. The hand holding the hand, is, as almost unavoidably, a parable of human solidarity; and given human solidarity as our standard, then human fallibility becomes our norm (as, in entertainment, it usually is), so that we can quite understand in Robie a certain persisting egoism, a certain rage, a certain ruthlessness. One may doubt whether he would actually murder her by letting her fall. And maybe only her predicament panics her into believing that he might. But he comes very close to it, and it's just as well.

For fear is a great moral power. Hitchcock's moral psychology would seem closer to that of Loyola, or Wesley, or Freud, than to Kantian moral psychology, with its stress on the disinterestedness of the truly moral, and the same theme underlies Mrs. Stevens' declaration, which will be our subject later, that she should have spanked her spoiled young daughter rather more than she did. Not that Robie's behaviour isn't preferable to that of the police, who, far from symbolising God, as Douchet maintains, act like moral lunatics, blasting away indiscriminately at two people, one of whom is in fact neither a murderer nor even a thief, while they have no idea of the identity of the other. The guns they use are intimated in the opening sequence, where Robie escapes arrest by retiring to change his clothes, locking the door, fixing up a shotgun and firing it off, thus luring the outside policemen inside and clearing his escape route via the window. His absence of trust in the police and in society turns out to be thoroughly justified, and his pitilessness on the roof is merely another permutation of the same necessary, but always uneasy, balance between independence and solidarity. It is *amorally* necessary not to be scrupulously moral. Hitchcock contemplates Robie's easy complicity in corruption in a happy visual opulence, and a sensuous hedonism, whose style is conspicuously nearer that of Lubitsch than that of Bishop Jansen.

Another aspect of the film's morality is indicated by the relationship, or lack of it, between the past cat, Robie, and the present cat, Danielle. A rigorous moralist might have argued that Robie, by proving that the wages of crime is elegant affluence, must bear a great deal of the blame for the audacious criminal enterprise of his old colleague's daughter. We are also introduced to other ex-accomplices of his. Having eluded the police, he calls at the restaurant whose staff seem startled at this return of an old friend. A waiter lets a champagne bottle bubble into mid-air. The open yet alert face of a capable-looking female receptionist introduces a note of soft seriousness and danger for Robie, re-emphasized by her turning to the switchboard. Robie saunters easily through a darker, more devious realm to the kitchens, where, in a slack moment, a scattering of chefs and hands work in a quiet, steady way to which their white clothes give an almost pastoral note of honest toil. Almost immediately we learn that these are Robie's ex-accomplices, who didn't become rich. Fleetingly, we feel, we may be watching a variation on the once favourite Hollywood scene, of democratic fraternity between the rich tourist and all the foreign *petits-gens*, or, if it's an American setting, immigrant-class *restaurateurs*. But one of the kitchen-hands half sees him and whispers to his seniors. As they continue to work, quietly, blank furtive glances from their lowered eyes darken the scene's emotional tone. As Robie stands behind a pane of glass a flung egg spatters, in front of his face, over the pane. A hefty brute advances on him and Robie deems it wise to seize, defensively, a wine bottle. But nonchalantly he tosses at the approaching savage an object which the other, with an employee's reflex, obediently catches, raising a quiet laugh at his own expense, and leaving Robie just enough time to slip away. (Robie's behaviour matches the graveyard scene; here, he is the least violent man, there, he introduces physical violence.) Thereafter he discusses matters, in a civilized way, with Bertani, the restaurant proprietor, another ex-accomplice, but one who has made it, and so, it seems, is free alike of toil and of ignominious spite.

It is not quite clear, at the time, how far the men are reformed criminals who fear that Robie's exploits will bring them under suspicion again, and are warning him to keep out, or how far they hate him because he has reaped the ease which they have not. And much later, we learn that they are all Danielle's accomplices, and that he represents a rival operator; and that their leader is Bertani, who should be sufficiently wealthy to retire, from theft, at least; and all these eventual factors should render any overtones about class envy superfluous to explain their attitudes. None the less, Occam's Razor lacks, in art, or entertainment, or, indeed, in sociology, the cogency which it possesses in philosophy. While we watch the scene, there applies something of that very unJansenist and very unChristian feeling that, other things being equal, it's better to be a successful criminal than an unsuccessful one, and that it's better to be rich than poor, for, among other reasons, moral ones. The poor have to bear, not only all the spiritual evils to which flesh is heir, but, in addition, all the strains of being poor, notably, temptations to servility (like the obedient catching reflex), and violence (given one's anxieties and absence of other resource), and envy, and all the sterile negativities of resentment, which do indeed degrade one's soul. Riches are better than poverty in precisely the same way that intelligence is better than stupidity. Both are matters of amoral endowment. The purpose of riches, Robie makes clear, is selfish pleasure. But the servility and violence of the poor are familiar to us from earlier Hitchcock films, although never, specifically, as that alternative which radical and/or pessimistic thinkers are more likely to want to crystallise than conservative ones. (Hitchcock's skirting it here is worth comparing with the treatment, in certain films by Roy Baker, whom we noticed as an 'anti-Hitchcock' in discussing *I Confess*, of the neglected lower orders turning to wanton violence. One wonders how Hitchcock might have handled the responses of the steerage passengers in his version of the Titanic story which is the basis of *A Night To Remember*.)

Scarcely has this lightly touched note of class friction been allowed to die away before it is struck afresh by Danielle's awareness of being only a wine-waiter's daughter. Whence such admirable lines as Robie's remark to Frances, 'You're a jackpot of admirable character traits'—a line which he means defensively and ironically and which takes its meaning from the financial meanings of 'jackpot'. But behind this sense of wealth lies another, purely personal, sense, in which the kitchen staff, and Danielle, and Bertani, are not in Robie's class. Robie is a winner; they are losers. As often in the cinema, the metaphor for this is a matter of personal appearance and style, most commonly, indeed, degraded into mere 'beauty' or 'glamour', but capable of revivification, as it is here, into notions of *élan vital*, of biological exuberance smoothly controlled, of generosity and pride as opposed to meanness. As Robin Wood notes of *Marnie*, pallor can be Hitchcock's physical metaphor for a lower level of human energy. Something of that pallor is in Danielle, as opposed to the softly glowing colours of Frances Stevens, and in Hughson, as opposed to Robie. Danielle's protestations verge on a superficiality, a subjacent exasperation, such that while we feel sympathy for her, we cannot feel more; her intensity is at an opposite extreme to Robie's relaxed energy. *Le style c'est l'homme.* Far from being superficial detail, such traits determine the basic polarity of a great many films, this included, for it has determined the direction of our hopes long before we suppose Danielle is anything more than a wilful teenager seething to possess a man whom she cannot quite please, let alone satisfy, and who must be, for him, a threat, or a distraction, or, at best, a useful friend, perhaps insufficiently valued by him. Later, of course, we learn that whereas Robie's exploits endangered only his accomplices, she is ready to make of him the victim of her false identity, from the moment he refuses an invitation, which is rather too demanding to be really friendly, to flee with her to South America. Hitchcock, like Lubitsch, is saying that it is the lack of personal class which either condemns one to remain prisoner of one's social class, or lack of it, or renders one free to rise above it, or incapable of becoming free by stooping from it.

Not that the director of *Blackmail* and *The Wrong Man* shows contempt for the lower middle classes or for mediocre contentment. Perhaps, after all, it is better, by far, to be contentedly, but not complacently, what one is, than to envy, to covet, to snatch, and to rage at failure. It is never easy for moralists of this persuasion to distinguish between a valid ambition and pride and an invalid one, other than by the indiscreetly amoral test of success—a success to which American audiences, more than any other, are none the less likely to respond. Yet there are those differences which we can feel between Frances and Danielle, between Robie and Houghton. Certainly, a modest contentment comes more easily to the rich than to the poor, and an assurance which is a moral quality and which is to be desired. But there are those who, whatever may have happened to them (under-privilege, prison, danger) have retained that abundance of smooth energy which enrolls them amongst 'those whom the Gods love', and who, in American optimism, far from dying young, live happily ever after.

Amongst the manifest paradoxes and ironies of a life-force morality is that which the film's early shock-cut asserts and with which Hitch-cock plays in acknowledgement of a third distinction, that between Frances and her mother. In the window of a tourist agency, where a red neon sign suggests its commerciality of intent, a poster proclaims, 'If you love life, you'll love France'. The camera's slow, deliberate track-in abruptly yields the screen to a shot of a middle-aged woman, rendered worse than homely by face-cream, shrieking on discovering the loss of her jewels. People who aren't qualified for 'life'—i.e. adven-ture, romance—are bound to end up losers if they're unrealistic enough to court it—and it isn't merely her appearance and age that are at stake—it's everything that's greedy and querulous in that face and that scream.

Middle-aged or old ladies recur to startle us. An old lady driving an automobile identical to Robie's, upbraids the police for halting her. Later, Robie is almost captured while being belaboured by the elderly flower-seller, from whom he finds it so hard to extricate himself. As Robie's hands tense open at Frances's driving she nearly runs over an old lady, and although our uneasiness at her coolly selfish risking of the helpless and the innocent is kept within bounds by our reflection that she knows what she's doing it isn't resolved until a squeal of brakes from the pursuing police car inculpate the guardians of law and order equally. The three old women are all surrogates, in the *Strangers On A Train* manner, for Mrs. Stevens, whose mixture of qualities and defects qualifies her as a transitional figure between the heroes, the villains and the also-rans.

Like many such figures in entertainment films, she is easily the most colourful and interesting character, and not surprisingly, since she combines, in a relatively realistic way, the tensions which the heroes experience in only an idealistic form, thus creating the derisive or Manichean structure of comic relief and villains. A spiritually pro-founder film might have dwelt on an evolution from, or the tensions within, her nagging about tipping and her philosophical adieu to her jewels—a climax reversing the film's opening shock-cut. The very actions with which she seemed, at first, to epitomise the crass vulgarity

of the nouveau-riche—the cigarette in the face-cream, and in the egg—
are her, and perhaps, Hitchcock's, comment on 'the good life'. And
another permutation of the same underlying attitudes is found in
Frances's celebrated complaint to Robie, just after her seduction, 'Give
me back my mother's jewels,' equating money with virginity in particular, and sexuality in general (cp. the phrase 'family jewels'). This
climaxes the series of quiet equivocations between personal relationships and money, between purity and corruption, ironically, since her
virginity is a prickteaser's, and her resentment makes her virtue as
vulgar as her jewels. Earlier, dialogue coyly equates the warmth of
worn jewellery with Frances's breasts.

But the theme of sexual pleasure is itself only an aspect of a broader
theme, that of sensual pleasure as moral corruption. Everything implied by the background of Riviera wealth is contradicted by sudden,
soft, sensuous shocks: the egg spread on the pane of glass, the cigarette
in the fried eggyolk, the cigarette in the face-cream. What we took for
vulgarity was primarily a response, as exasperated as Danielle's, but
redeemed by an underlying integrity, to the implicit lies of luxurious
living. Robie, contentedly living alone, has renounced jewels and
affairs for grapes and flowers. The winebottle which he grasps in the
kitchens might contain one of his own vintages. Flowers bestrew the
market and the woman's rage is a righteous but mercenary one. The
theme appears also as Robie persuades Hughson to drink wine at
midday (for the first time in his life) and offers him Quiche Lorraine
('I've heard about it but I've never tasted it'). (Hughson accords with
American fantasies about the square and puritanical British, but is
also an exotic scapegoat for the steak-and-ice-cream-bound spectator.)
Simultaneously Robie persuades Hughson to entrust him with details
of his most heavily insured clients. The bon viveur's ascendancy over
the more obvious father-figure's has just that little soupçon of, not
sexuality, exactly, but a mixture of sensuous effect (wine and food)
and the authority of energy. If one recalls that Hughson is playing a
role parallel to Frances's, thoroughly selfish, but required, by the
nature of his purposes, to negotiate and to provoke, and that he, like
her, becomes the seducer seduced, then the overtones of epicurean
refinement as per *Rope* and a very different kind of relationship between two men scheming a quasi-crime indicate a relationship which
is common and benign enough but which is essentially as significant
as that between a man and a woman.

'I've never caught a jewel-thief before. It's so stimulating!' says
Frances, to which Robie replies, displeased, 'You make it sound like

sitting in a hot bath!' And light as the line is it hits its target perfectly;
her selfish romanticism is a petty-mindedness, expressed, characteristically, in terms whose sensuousness abruptly becomes nauseous, not
because Hitchcock is particularly puritan about the pleasures of the
flesh qua flesh (the film is certainly a defence of gastronomy), but
because she is describing a relationship between two people and his
destiny. In which context his coolness ceases to be merely a banality;
it is a little achievement in self-control and counter-attack. In a sense
To Catch A Thief is the reply to the moral Hitchcock originally
intended for *Champagne*. There, a girl, wiser but sadder after her fling
at high-life romance, ends, by thinking, every time she sees a bottle of
champagne, 'There's trouble for someone!' That is the lower-middle-
class English Hitchcock of the '20s. If he doesn't disapprove of champagne being poured over the tired boxers in *The Ring*, it's perhaps
because of the gesture's absolutely fascinating mixture of pain-rather-
than-pleasure, of brute functionalism, and of propitiatory sacrifice, but
perhaps also because of a basic moral ambiguity. But in a maturer logic
of twists and contrasts everything recalls its opposite. Riviera luxury
recalls a hot bath, bringing us back, with the impeccability of mathematics, to the bucket of water in *The Ring*. A similar return to classless
basics occurs when Mrs. Stevens, despoiled of her jewellery, tells her
daughter, despoiled of her virginity, but not yet of the brittle pride
and volatile resentment of youth, that she deserves a spanking for her
petulance and spite. The two women prowl around the room, the
movement creating a kind of identity-cum-alternation of mother and
daughter, conspicuously equals. But the evocation of spanking, undoubtedly rendered sensuous by the daughter's wilful beauty, offers
an answer to the question of how even the rich can be protected
against their superabundance of privilege. Hitchcock's answer is one
which, though rarely put about by moral philosophers, who find it too
illogical, too misanthropic, too religious, too authoritarian, too utilitarian or too disgustingly lower-middle-class, or, especially if they are
linguistic philosophers, everything together, is common enough nearer
ground level: that natural selfishness isn't quite countervailed by
natural benevolence and the social instinct, and has to be conditioned
out of people by aversion therapy, that is, an effective modicum of
bullying, so that a decent humility depends, in the end, on a kind of
initiatory ordeal, and a submission which, at first enforced, gradually
becomes introjected and so, at last, a legitimate matter of modest
pride. He who loseth his pride shall find it.

This is one phase only of the constant association-contradiction

between mother and daughter. If Mrs. Stevens offers to buy Robie for
Frances it's through a fascinating mixture of nostalgia and realism.
She fancies him herself, she knows she could only get him as her
gigolo, she knows that's only another form of cuddling up with her
jewels, but with her daughter there's hope of decently mixed motives;
and the urge to buy is the urge to snatch, that is, it's a wilfulness like
her daughter's, and it's theft. The sudden appearance of older women
is itself as disruptive of the unreflective enjoyment of sensual pleasure
as the cigarette in the eggyolk or ointment, and connects with our
fears, on Robie's behalf, that Frances will come to resemble her
mother in some way, following the well-known rule of thumb that if
you want to know how your possible wife will wear look at her
mother. And the outcome of the mother-daughter conversation,
Frances maturing, twists back away from a conventional happy end
when Frances announces that her mother will be coming too. Robie's
irritation is at once natural, justifiable and ungrateful.

One can demonstrate the film's underlying structure a little further
by imagining a more sentimental conclusion in which Hughson and
Mrs. Stevens find one another, and, perhaps, she makes some caustic
comment to the effect that he's just as much a con-man as her late
lamented rascal but probably won't be any worse for her and anyway
he's all she can expect. And Hughson is aware of her fortune. But
they'll be good friends, and that's all most marriages are, and all they
need be.

Thus Hughson would 'resurrect' the father-figure so conspicuously
absent in the mother-daughter line. A psychoanalytical approach
might interest us in hidden mother-daughter hatreds, and indeed
Frances narrowly swerves round an old woman, and a hen, which
obligingly returns us to the mother's angrily poking a phallic symbol
into an egg. And when Frances is interested in the erotic fantasy of losing her mother's jewels, which are also a masochistic self-punishment,
rather worse than a spanking, and which would bear a more detailed
teasing-out in relationship to Oedipal desires to rob, i.e. murder, i.e.
supplant her mother, even at her own expense, so long as she can
attract the absent father, who, she unconsciously knows, is a con-man.
But if the film is anyone's dream it's Robie's, and his contented
bachelorhood might result from just that balance of appreciation and
revulsion which produces other happy celibates, e.g. the priest of
I Confess. Screeching mother-figures are quite important in his fantasy,
which is symbolically extended into the film itself, and he gets a quite
lovable version of what he fears, with Frances to sugar the pill. A

similar structure obtains between Frances, who wants to be a thief, like Danielle, and Danielle, who wants to give up thieving, but when rejected by Robie becomes his substitute instead of his accomplice. Thus Robie is uneasily suspended between three women who form an overlapping series: Mrs. Stevens, Frances, Danielle, while Hughson and Bertani are complementary father-figures, one apparently treacherous but really friendly, the other apparently friendly but really treacherous, with Danielle's father to form a trio.

The 'substitute identities' between Robie the cat-burglar and Danielle the copy-cat-burglar enables the theme of affinities to cross the sexual lines, and link with other oddities of social role, e.g. the restaurant whose kitchen staff are largely crooks and the fancy-dress ball whose waiters are mostly policemen. The disguise theme doesn't say much more than that things aren't always what they seem (an assumption on which every detective story hinges), and one might well find any such grandiose banality much less interesting than wondering whether Hitchcock means us to ooh and ah and be awed by the plush fancy-dress costumes, as the other guests are, or to survey with Olympian disdain, or petty-bourgeois puritanism, the ceremonies of conspicuous consumption, which are as ridiculous as anything in Kane's Xanadu, or whether we are meant to be split between the two, or whether we are allowed to opt for whichever we choose, so that different spectators will see, in effect, different films, retaining their complacency as they wish.

In sensuous terms, the jewels which Robie once stole contrast with the grapes which he now cultivates, just as they become Frances's virginity. They are also evoked by the bursts of fire comprising the brief nocturnal bouquets which herald Frances's forthcoming defloration. As the firework colours cascade silently, seen through the window of a creamily luminous hotel bedroom, their slow, quiet fall is beautifully dreamlike, especially as counterpointed against caressing yet guarded voices, whose words imply the female's fetishism and the male's reluctance. Not until the more swiftly-cut climax does the scene yield to its cliché possibilities, and then, perhaps, because the general fountaining suggests a vague emotional ecstasy rather than all which the prelude has suggested of the suave and the precise.

One doubts whether Hitchcock structures his film according to the theories of Bachelard; but his sensuousness, coupled with his structure of contrasts, were bound to produce fragments at least, of such structures. Fireworks are balanced by water. Danielle's father falls into water; Danielle helps Robie escape over water; and there is an uneasy waterborne *tête-à-tête* where Frances discountenances Danielle, and the two women's velvety ferocity leaves Robie altogether at a loss. Cats, of course, don't like water. The film begins with a cat prowling over rooftops and the cat-burglar holds the copycat from a rooftop fall preluded by the latter's father's shorter fall into the sea. Both the swimming pool scene and the rooftop climax feature the theme of suspension (floating or hanging), as well as whispered or veiled verbal violence.

The relationship of height, lateral planes, and speed is more conspicuous in *Vertigo*, and will be commented on there, but it is never absent from Hitchcock. Here, certainly, speed ranks among the sensuous pleasures of affluence, none the less exhilarating for being hair-raising, and among the spiritual pleasures also, as the contrast between Frances's sportscar and Danielle's father's hearse makes clear. A sustained helicopter shot of an automobile pursuit beautifully restores to the Riviera coastline its stately yet energetically contoured strength. We have a sense of both topographical integrity and of human change wrought upon it; here is the timeless stone face and the scurrying human, in a generalised, sunny, affable aspect. The shot astonishingly counterpoints the static movement in the landscape; the mountains' slow drift past the camera; the excitingly varying yet continuing visual relationship with the automobiles which we are pacing; and our sense of the camera's flight over the sea. The pursuit is reversed at the end, creating one of those psychological *lacunae* of which it's hard to say whether it demonstrates Hitchcock's radical disregard of psychological plausibility, or a profound psychological revelation all the more astonishing for its witty ellipse, or an agreeable example of teasing the audience for the sake of jokeyness. That Frances has to chase Robie at breakneck speed suggests that the latter is in a terrible state of panic at the prospect of being 'caught', although when they're face to face again he seems cool enough and either indifferent to her or testing her persistence or her honesty or just teasing her, whereupon with splendid aplomb she turns the tables on him. All the answers fit, and although the meaningfulness of all the previous scenes suggests that there may well be a psychologically coherent answer, we can choose whichever we like best, since the scene is a blank, and our guesses about it are all derived from the context in the first place. In other words it's got to fit the structure. And Hitchcock is given more possibilities rather than fewer by the fact that no scene in the film is psychologically analytical, in the sense of attempting to isolate any one motive as 'the' real one. Dramatic structures thrive on multiplicity of motives, which are everyday experiences, and indicated by such homely sayings as 'the last straw broke the camel's back', i.e., 'he did this for as many reasons as there are in a bale of straw, and an entire bale of different reasons didn't break him, but an insignificant extra did'. Our analytical assumptions about 'the' reason might lead us to suppose that the bale of reasons are being ruled out by their being productive of no effect, and that the one little reason is somehow the clue to someone's psychology. Such dramatic structures certainly exist, but there also exist structures which are accumulative rather than analytical, additive as well as subtractive. Even within the same dramatic structure, some scenes exist to rule out motives, while others exist to allow them to pile up, or to indicate shifting balances between shifting combinations. So it would, I think, be wrong to assume that Frances now loves Robie for himself in a purified or mature way virtually devoid of pride, masochism and jewel-thief fetishism, although we probably assume that she's moderated her position somewhat, at least to the point of being prepared to be an ex-jewel-thief fetishist, which is rather different from being an ex jewel-thief-fetishist. Thinking along these lines certainly prompts one to reservations about the extent to which Hitchcock's protagonists need to be 'purged' or 'purified' for their psychological patterns to be optimistic in a non-puritanical but non-nihilistic way, and to this degree we may connect Hitchcock with, *not* the nonconformist or the Jansenist conscience, but with either an orthodox Catholic position, or a man-in-the-street common sense, or a Freudian acknowledgement of ambivalence, or quite probably some combination of all these attitudes. What may come as a surprise is that, in terms of psychological interplay and evolution, *To Catch A Thief* achieves greater complexity and precision than *Strangers On A Train*, and maybe one should not too completely rule out the contribution of John Michael Hayes, nor that of Ernest Lehmann in *North-by-North-West*.

It is surprising that those who adduce the complexities of Hitchcock as a moral psychologist should accept *To Catch A Thief* as an agreeable divertimento; that Hitchcock does so should no more discourage them than his many characteristically modest or disparaging comments about films which they continue to hold in high regard. But to prefer the morality of *Strangers On A Train* to that of *To Catch A Thief* is, I suspect, an earnest-seeming pretext for preferring the thrills of melodrama rather than the finesse of comedy. Admittedly, it's not half as bizarre as preferring the melodramas of Howard Hawks to the comedies of Billy Wilder. But, for a variety of reasons, whose diverse origins are beyond our scope, critics are quick to assume that whatever is not obvious must be profounder in the spiritual sense, or more serious, than whatever is immediately obvious, and that to cast a certain thematic in cryptic structures in the Hitchcock style must be artistically superior to any direct dramatic presentation. Without deprecating the particular contribution of the riddle and *discovery* to aesthetic experience, it may be worth recalling that the succession of expressions across an actor's face (to which criticism currently devotes relatively little attention) is as much a matter of structure as the most recondite permutation of motifs, and that the characters and the situations are not only the most obvious symbols but also the most complex, and the most delicately nuanced.

If we take as our example Robie's descent into the underworld of the restaurant kitchens, we can begin to see how Hitchcock's intricate structures have their origin in purely entertainment terms. The wine waiter's comic discomfiture assures us of Robie's general superiority to the situation. The switchboard operator worries us a little. The kitchens are a climax (many people), although the tone is a relief (a pastorale), albeit rife with possibilities of tension (honest workmen versus a crook), which rapidly modulate via soft violence (the egg) to something harder (the attack) and a quick climax (fighting with bottles); but the brute is servile and violence is no sooner indicated than negated (laughter). Robie's retreat is a deflation appropriate to comedy (possibly needing more preparation in tragedy) and followed by another contrast (from the lowest kitchen hands to the owner). The continuous line of the narrative is analysed down into a sequence of contrasts and surprises. In other words, the narrative continuity is recomposed into 'a series of shocks directed at the spectator', to recapitulate Eisenstein's definition of montage. Hitchcock's fidelity to 'pure cinema' and editing by montage principles reveals the perhaps surprising but none the less profound affinity between Eisenstein's conception of montage as a dialectic, and that Hollywood formula whereby the most effective storytelling is a succession of 'twists'. The word 'twist' is simply a synonym, rooted in the idea of narrative as line, for the 'shock', a term which may owe less to the hazards of translation than to Eisenstein's sense of the 'collision' between strong visual compositions. And certainly Eisenstein's montage, in its maturity, and in practice as well as in theory, depended heavily on the acceptance of montage-within-the-shot, or within the camera-movement, e.g. the sportscar and the hearse. Once one has accepted that, then the cinema of montage and the cinema of *mise en scène* or of camera-movements cease to seem incompatible, even though editing, *mise en scène* and camera-movement all constitute different elements in the montage. And with the acceptance of the continuous presence of contrasted objects (sportscar-hearse) we have all but arrived at the notion of both narrative change and dramatic conflict as a continuing state as forms of montage. Conversely, montage comes to something like contrast-within-continuity.

Although the kitchen surprises which, for the sake of brevity, we have schematised, form a continuous series, it involves a 'discontinuous' structure also. It begins with a champagne bottle and it climaxes on the non-use of a wine-bottle. And it abounds with references to other scenes in the film; in fact without them it wouldn't make sense. If a shot may be related to its neighbours merely by position (although it usually also relates by the implications of its content), it also forms part of a discontinuous series. The splattered egg is one of two maltreated eggs. The receptionist's palish face may remind us of facecream. The wine bottle may have been filled from Robie's own grapes. The kitchens themselves link with the film's interest in gourmetise. Our assumptions about the staff are later revised, and then revised again.

Analogously with the 'doubles' in *Strangers On A Train*, a plethora of (at least) middle-aged ladies serve to introduce Mrs. Stevens, to remind us of her in scenes in which she can't be present, to contrast with her (how boring they are, how interesting she is), but, most important of all, to assert that polarity between Robie and old ladies, as victims and/or threats, of which she represents the fullest development. In opposition to F. H. Bradley's assumption that the action of a story existed to express its characters, Elizabeth Bowen remarked that the characters exist to justify the action, and it might be truer to say that both the characters and the action exist as carriers of, or cues for, experience. A landscape may be a character (like Egdon Heath in Hardy's *The Return of the Native*), and the characters of Dickens or Balzac often take on a topography and a geology. Some types of experience, being introverted, can only exist within the psychology of individual characters, while others, being extroverted, depend on shifting relationships, and others again, being projected, depend, *pace* Robbe-Grillet, on the mood of the place. Sometimes, of course, external actions function as metaphors for intrapsychic process (e.g. *The Pilgrim's Progress*). And an artist may also wish to present internal and external factors of which the characters remain unconscious. It is here that partisans of the theological Hitchcock are on their strongest ground. It might be of the essence of Hitchcock's vision that his characters are always unaware of the eternal import of their actions. Apart from the perhaps unimportant point that any gnosticism thus attained would be distinctly heretical, it remains difficult to account for Hitchcock's abstention from his usual processes of clarification. Normally, the overt dramatic elements might relate to the covert ones (whereas, in *Strangers On A Train*, the overt good-evil polarity is at once vehement, self-sufficient and contradictory to a purely hypothetical affinity of Bruno and Guy). Second, the normal and clear presentation of a character's ignorance is to show his refusal of failure to achieve knowledge. Third, a combination of dramatic irony and reasonably unambiguous symbolism (via props and atmosphere) is normally sufficient to establish another plane of meaning. But as we have seen, in film after film, Hitchcock's use of symbolism is extremely ambiguous and imprecise in its meaning, however precise in its formal structure.

Within the last decade, as the result of a variety of influences, ranging from improved exegetical techniques to derivatives from structuralism, many critics have come to concur with S. I. Hayakawa's earlier observation that the meaning of a narrative is the total of all the associations of all the symbols. This definition in itself poses problems enough. Unfortunately the need for a summarising shorthand has often resulted in the substitution of a once-for-all, unvarying 'meaning' for a symbol, whose nature it may be to include ambiguities, connotations, and alterations. Thus Hamlet in Act V is not the same man as Hamlet in Act I; he has evolved, internally; and to define the axis of his evolution is not at all to describe the (imaginary) man at each stage of his evolution, particularly since dramatic characters frequently evolve from one position into its negation (even in relatively unsophisticated films). Second, the elucidation of structure in terms of 'meaning' frequently omits the final phase, which is a referral back of the structure to the complexities which the structure creates at each point, as of the superficial atmospheres which the structure exists to modulate, to recall, to interconnect. In other words, the structure exists to create complex blendings which exist at one point only and so remain, as a whole, outside the structure as a whole. The analysis of structure becomes a rationalist formalism unless it's remembered that structure must be functional, that it exists to transfer loads and stresses in exactly the same way as an engineering structure exists to diffuse or to concentrate or to reorganise pressures which are exerted at particular points. Far from being continuity without contrast, a mere tautology, structure consists of a pattern of continuities and contrasts, none of which are sealed in on themselves, but unfold again in a way which can only be paraphrased by talking of intangibles, and uniquenesses of overall atmosphere at almost every point in the structure.

Structure and such intangibles as 'atmosphere' are not even sufficiently distinct for one to speak of a symbiosis between them. They are as identical as our old friends 'style' and 'content'. The map is not the territory, being a mental construct, and may reveal far less than the view from some particular vantage-point; it often happens that a still or a clip from a film represents it far more fully than a detailed synopsis. And there is a danger that critical 'structuralism' may become a fixation akin to that of *Sight and Sound* on a film's storyline. Hitchcock's complex structures may be arrived at by nothing more thoughtful than a concern for (1) economy in storytelling, (2) that degree of repetition which is necessary for coherence, (3) evolution (including accumulation by repetition!), and (4) a desire for as many surprises and contrasts as possible. From a narrative point of view, there is no reason why Hitchcock shouldn't avoid middle-aged ladies until Mrs. Stevens appears. In terms of simple causality it wouldn't matter if the first victim of, apparently, Robie, but actually Danielle, were a young woman, or a man; and so on. But the middle-aged ladies provide a series of contrasts with everything with which the plot involves us, and reminds us of the other, sadder, drabber side of Riviera pleasure. The robbed woman introduces a note of cynical pathos. We, and the police, expect a disconsolate Robie to emerge from the car; a spitfire termagant is an even stronger surprise after the hysteric victim. The flower-seller corresponds to the face-cream lady in being a hysteric victim, to the automobile lady in being a redoubtable battleaxe, to Mrs. Stevens in her sense of money, to Frances in that she very nearly catches Robie, and to the kitchenhands in using physical violence and depending on small pay. The first old lady gives the alarm; the second gives Robie a clear getaway; the third almost stops him from getting away; and later on another old lady doesn't slow Frances down but gets the police swerving. Clearly the petulantly screaming face-cream lady is everything which Mrs. Stevens might possibly be but isn't. They are as different from each other as Bruno is from Guy. Far from being morally interchangeable, one has overcome the temptations which the other has not. The old ladies and the unattached ones converge in the final scene.

Why does Mrs. Stevens call for a battery of old ladies, whereas

Houghton has no corresponding repertoire of masculine doubles? The pattern is asymmetrical, because Frances calls for Mrs. Stevens who brings her mother intimately into Robie's life. There is none the less a secondary pattern, of mercenary men, who include Robie, Houghton, Bertani, and Danielle's father. One may include, as honorary members of this series, the police (although they are predatory rather than mercenary), and the young cat (until her unmasking links 'him' with the theme of unwanted women). There is nothing magic about all these affinities-in-contrast; characters can't interact dramatically unless they have both points in common, nor very interestingly unless they differ from one another. Hence, as I suggested in discussions of *Johnny Guitar* and *This Island Earth* in *Films and Feelings*, it's the most natural thing in the world for the hero and the villain to be variations on the same theme, or complementary characters, or anagrams of each other. Polar opposites in one or two respects, they are also different balances of the same characteristics, or similar sins with and without redeeming virtues, excuses and variations of degree. And at the present state of the game one might distinguish a profound film from a shallow one by the extent to which these affinities are developed openly and dramatically so as to revise our more infantile assumptions about human nature. Once one has established the opposites which constitute a conflict, intermediate positions may be derived in the same way. In *To Catch A Thief* a series of old ladies all react in different ways to frustration and disruption. Similar figures, different attitudes. In *Marnie* the heroine, a self-possessed, beautiful young woman, and a little girl, compete for the caresses of Marnie's mother. Different figures, similar attitudes. Although both sorts of pattern may be used together, it is obvious that the need for surprise as well as the asymmetrical aspects of relationships will press strongly towards the avoidance of obvious patterns, even when the narrative dimension is taken into account. Thus it is quite easy to see why Hitchcock avoids a temptation which a less interesting artist might have thought a very clever solution: Mrs. Stevens pairs off with Houghton, and either we end with a double wedding or they both come and bore the pants off Robie. Hitchcock doesn't wish to negate the loneliness theme.

The old ladies in *To Catch A Thief* exemplify the idea of symbol-as-marker discussed earlier in considering *The Ring* and exemplified by the patterns of doubles in *Strangers On A Train*. The human marker is particularly useful, given the variety and intensity of feeling rapidly carried by the human face. It is true that this depends on a categorising process by the spectator (by sex, age, types of face, and so on). But it's a natural process, even when what becomes conscious is not so much the resemblances between the characters as the shock which they create against the context. In any case the altogether un-analytical spectator can catch a film's major meanings well enough from one or two shocks produced by the structure, provided that they are backed up by a general mood or drift, and provided, obviously, that their idiom and experience are not too alien for him. Clearly, different spectators may react to different points in the structure, and usually dramatic continuity and consistency ensure a reasonable variety of types of point (thus the cinematographic rhythm will not be altogether unrelated to the rhythm of body movement and facial expression). But it is certainly possible for spectators to be disorien-tated by unexpected counterpoints and contradictions and find weak and indecisive a film which is merely complex or unusual, laying its stresses in unexpected ways, and criticism presupposes that much art, far from being intuitively self-evident, requires gradual adjustment.

Far from disputing the existence of sophisticated structures in Hitchcock's films, we are merely arguing that a workmanlike word like 'construction' gives a far better idea of their quality and finesse than any search for the meaning of a symbol as extraneous to the atmosphere of which that symbol is part. (As we saw, the function of a symbol may be simply to re-evoke an atmosphere; and it's 'meaning' is the synthe-sis between that atmosphere and the present situation, which is some-thing far more organic and indefinable than those one-for-one abstrac-tions ('key = guilt', etc). Clearly such purposes may be served; but the recall is generally of a situation, and of the emotional tension involved within it, rather than an empty abstraction. The meaning of a symbol includes the associations clustered about it and the shock-waves which it produces.)

Some of the film's motifs are purely quiet, commendable jokes. Thus an early sequence indicates the burglar's presence, and teasingly underlines its concealment of his identity by shots of a cat prowling over the rooftops, on which Danielle is later trapped by Robie. The shots of the cat serve no narrative function (even the apparent dys-function of concealment!) since any number of other ellipses were possible; but the parade of concealment is a teasing and pleasant one, and it introduces the climactic squabble on the tiles. It is a nicely heavy Lubitschian joke and as the film story develops we may sense that Danielle is a bit of a spiteful cat and that therefore she's the other cat. The burglars wear cat-suits and the dialogue helps us along with reference to copycats and cats having kittens and a reference to Robie

losing his ninth life, and from there on it's a matter of taste whether
one decides that Robie's present self-sufficiency is a dramatic translation of cats walking by themselves, whether Danielle's jealousy is the
green-eyed monster, whether she is showing her claws in her confrontation with Frances, and whether the fact that this occurs in a swimming pool is a little joke about cats not liking the water (it's into
water that the film's only corpse later falls). The real effect of all these
references is a neatness like wit, and spectators who aren't too conscious
of the aesthetic reality will admire the style of the conversation and
spectators who are will admire that and the film. The references to
cats are markers, like the middle-aged ladies, but have a rather different function. Clearly one might go astray by looking for meaning
behind the symbol, or trying to find some infrastructure whereby the
image of a cat tells us something about Robie that isn't told us quite
directly in terms of Robie. It's important, obviously, that a cat isn't
unfitting to Robie's character, but the effect of the symbol has no
connection whatsoever with any information which it provides.

Much subtler information is provided by such brief, 'one-shot'
felicities as Robie's crisp, nonchalant yet fastidious style, or Frances's
question to him: 'Do you have time for me now?'—a question so
directly posed that it proclaims more than it veils a perfect self-
confidence experimentally relishing a humility whose purpose is to
disarm by flattery as well as to indulge in the delightfully masochistic
pleasure of presenting the speaker as a little girl shyly begging for
admission to her father's world. Later, she encourages Robie not to
be discouraged by her air of cool self-possession. The goddess has a
weakness such that she can be possessed. 'But if she tells you it spoils it.
You have to find out for yourself.' The diplomacy is admirable, and
is strangely reversed by his real or pretended flight and her pursuit
which, far from being importunity, is her placid spring, and these
smooth solutions to problems of communication (which are also,
alas, problems of negotiation) take a real piquancy from the misunderstandings and fetishisms with which they are interwoven. Such
scenes seem to me far closer to the texture of reality, and more interesting, than various bravura passages in more celebrated Hitchcock films.

It is of course quite arguable that the very ingenuity and intricacy of
the structure of *To Catch A Thief* indicates its fragmentation of the
issues which in more profoundly probing works of art would be more
concentrated and more straightforward. It isn't difficult to imagine
how, for example, Billy Wilder or Blake Edwards, at their best, might
have dwelt on Robie's hesitations as to which woman to exploit, the

mother or the daughter, and combined it with a rougher edge of rivalry between them. Nor, in such a treatment, would other sub-themes necessarily be lost. For just as Robie involuntarily seduced his daughter-figure, Danielle, into imitating his feats, a seduction of a kind more serious than others, and to which she feels impelled pre-cisely because he won't notice her as she wishes to be noticed; there, his sin is that he won't seduce her. For there are interesting moral possibilities in the extent to which each of us treats different people differently, and in morally contradictory ways. In so far as Danielle has learned from Robie, and Frances from her mother, and given the theme of transvestite impersonation, there arises, potentially, the interesting question of how far everything we are is borrowed, or stolen, unconsciously, from others, and how, by making ourselves them, we feel impelled to compete or control those whom we should feel as other selves. A reversal of perspective might have placed, in the foreground, the sadder story of Mrs. Stevens, a story which, as it is, is rather less gracious and rather more interesting than that of *Summer Madness* (*Summertime*). A version along Paddy Chayefsky lines (cf. *The Goddess*) might, beneath a glittering surface, be more realistic still, and morally at least as complex. That more realistic versions might run a correspondingly greater risk of presenting aspects dis-agreeable to the box-office is doubtless sufficient to explain why Alfred Hitchcock preferred to start from the Lubitschian end of the spectrum. And while his lighter-fingered touch fixes the film's artistic qualities within fairly narrow limits, the modulation from the conventional carries several uneasy notations not without authentic artistic effect.

The Trouble With Harry

The Trouble With Harry continues in comic vein, still, perhaps in reac-tion against the solemnities of *I Confess*, and still in partnership with John Michael Hayes, a writer whose smooth finesse was possibly instrumental in easing Hitchcock towards a fuller dramatic register.

The trouble with Harry is that he's a corpse—whom the characters palm off on one another; cold meat is hot potato. In this picaresque story what goes the rounds is not the suspect or the sleuth but the corpse; and he also goes up and down, or in and out, since he's buried and unburied rather like a bone. The absence of the usual thrills pro-vides something of a field day for a series of free-wheeling studies in individual character and neighbourliness. If *To Catch A Thief* is

Hitchcock's equivalent of the Lubitsch comedy of high life, its successor has something of that tolerant yet scathing misanthropy which one finds in earlier populist comedy, from W. C. Fields (whom one can almost imagine in the Edmund Gwenn role, and whose movie stock company caters for the vigorous spinster, the child horror, and so on) down through *On Our Merry Way* and *We're Not Married* (or *I'm Not Buried*).

'It was shot in autumn,' Hitchcock observes, 'for the contrapuntal use of beauty against the sordidness and muddiness of death.' Even in its dialogue, it adheres closely to a novel by Jack Trevor Story, whose gift for mischievously accurate and cynical observation makes him the true *auteur* of *Live Now Pay Later*. The conjunction of Story, Hayes and Hitchcock is an auspicious one. Several of the body's embarrassed custodians have a reason for believing, or pretending to believe, that he is the murderer. Hunter Edmund Gwenn thinks he got him with a careless shot. Shirley MacLaine, his, or its, widow, thinks she clobbered him a little too hard with a bottle. Finally the doctor diagnoses as the cause of death a heart attack which may or may not have been aggravated by the shots or the blow on the head or both. And Hitchcock nicely balances the absurdist possibilities of just one darn thing after another with implications about collective and individual responsibility.

The film acquires a further dimension from the extent to which those of its characters who are less directly implicated have to come to terms with it in other ways. A young painter who only paints abstractions is moved to depict it as, in Simsolo's words, 'a Roualt Christ'. Through this image of human suffering he falls in love with the widow, who is egged on in her turn by the ruthless candour of her young son. Replying to an offer by a millionaire collector, the artist replies that all he wants is a double bed. The corpse is repeatedly buried and exhumed, by a increasing number of people each time; he's quite a social lion; in the midst of life is death, and saying yes to life means treating him as unceremoniously as refuse. If his portrait has eyes as soulful as serene, any Christian overtones (his soul's immune, his humanity accuses this profane utilitarian contempt) are qualified by an eventual acceptance of human egoism. The black irony of that acceptance, at once sharpened and softened by the brashness of a child, is matched by an optimism which in American films is often slickly complacent or Social Darwinist or both but to which Hitchcock gives rather more depth; attention, attention, must be paid to this corpse. . . .

One might risk the following schema: the corpse = A. N. Other = Everyman = a tragically derisory end = *memento mori* = a human condition = a lump of inedible meat = Christ as man (with big Charlie Chaplin feet). He gets a merely physical re-re-re-resurrection, which none the less brings solitary people together, makes a fact of life a little less furtive, so that the film, in its decorous, uneasy way, paraphrases the Classical Greek pattern, of tragedy followed by a fertility play. The tragic movement appears with prudent remoteness, in the manner of the dead man's hard day's dying: slow, gradual, absurd, demented, sinning, he is almost a scapegoat in the original sense. Why Hitchcock hardly hints at, or more probably hardly thinks of, satyr play obscenity is easy to see; it's little more than the line about the double bed and the boy's desire for a father (an anti-Oedipus complex which Leslie Fiedler could no doubt incorporate in his study of male friendships and death in American culture). But the corpse with his comically large feet and disturbing presence has a disconcerting obscenity which if it isn't exactly erotic creates just that disruption of complacency which can lead to nihilism, or religion or a double bed (not twin singles)—alternatives through which the artist himself evolves. Hitchcock, so often putting the corpse in the foreground, creates a balance so equal between that silent, ubiquitous, inverted sphinx, who becomes Here Come Everybody, and life's ongoing, that it becomes almost as uneasy as *Rope*, where the corpse is invisible in another kind of 'beauty', and it seems not to have been popular with the American public, whose taste in black humour is dominated by violence, and has little that is philosophical about it. It delighted the Parisian public, who favoured it with a six months' first run. In England, or so it seemed to me, the publicity laid too much stress on the deadness of Harry and too little on the liveliness of the reactions which he provokes, and the film has become something of a rarity.

The Man Who Knew Too Much

Hitchcock's next film marked a return to the tried and true, being his remake of *The Man Who Knew Too Much*, painstakingly and boringly reworked for the family market. The humour of the British version is played down into milder details, like James Stewart's problem in disposing of his long legs around a low Mohammedan table. The sumptuousness is souped up to indulge the full appeal of local colour, or rather, vicarious tourism. There is a concession to picturesque seediness in a visit to a Camden Town taxidermist. Instead of the Sidney Street siege the child is incarcerated in a foreign embassy. But mother (Doris Day) is a famous singer and, at a reception there, sings the family's favourite song, *Che Sera Sera*. The sound drifts up to his room; he responds, and a captor allows him a chance to escape. Father (James Stewart) is exploring the corridors too, and gets the better of the other, malevolent, guard.

The newer version clarifies the theme of the family's divided togetherness, and a neat irony obtains between the finales of the two versions. In the first, the famously unarmed London bobbies settle down with rifles; the climax of the second occurs in a foreign embassy, where the police may not enter, and where a mother and a father find their more pacific paths. One wonders whether Hitchcock, casting about for a more topical conclusion, immediately thought of the opposite to the original version. Such patterns and ironies seem inseparable from his thought, for they exist between different films as impeccably as within them. None of which can be taken as evidence of a dialectic or of depth. The thesis of complacency is challenged by the antithesis of crime, or sin, or danger, or Communist spies, or other obviously unpleasant things, and the synthesis is that the world isn't as safe as we might have thought it was, which of course we never did. At the same time, one can't appeal to the text for meaning. The song *Che Sera Sera* might, theoretically, have been inspired by Mohammedan fatalism borrowed from the earlier scenes, even though it's in Italian, as being, no doubt, less alien, less pagan, more aristocratic. But it's being sung as part of a resourceful effort by homespun Middle America private enterprise. It's difficult to find any attitude in the film corresponding to the words of the song. They certainly influence the atmosphere, with their overtones of motherly consolation for the quirks of fate, and it mightn't be absurd to link the film with an Orphic myth (a mother's song revives her child, lost in the land of the dead). But it would be absurd to take such an overtone as a theme.

Were Hitchcock's intention to disturb and chasten us by moral paradox, then, of course, *The Man Who Knew Too Much* needed a much more intimate concentration on the family than either version allows. Its basic conflict is defined in the scene where Doris Day goes to the Albert Hall to hear a concert at whose climactic cymbal clash *either* a noble statesman will be assassinated—or her own child, held hostage, will be slain; and the choice is hers. One can imagine, for example, the wife keeping the child's disappearance a secret from her husband, for a few hours, until after she has met, socially, the man whom her silence would condemn to death. In her horrified search for grounds on which to make, as she must, her decision, she might spend an afternoon getting to know him, having to half-seduce him from more pressing affairs, and finding him a complex mixture of idealist and philanderer—so much so, indeed, that she can't decide whether she loves him or hates him, whether indeed an infatuation which might be either hysteric or a true love come too late might not checkmate her mother-love. As it is, the film ventures very briefly only into the nervous friction which a kidnapping might well unleash between husband and wife. Middle America behaves very, very well.

Ian Cameron observes that Middle America is none the less not perfect; the husband has made his wife give up her career as a singer (giving a second meaning to her song); they found their holidays monotonous and their desire for excitement is over-fulfilled. And while innumerable details (especially narrow-eyed Arabs and an accident with a woman's veil) seem ominous but turn out to be anodyne, others seem innocent but turn out to be merely the public face of evil. Hitchcock 'has raised the red herring to the level of metaphysics'.

As indeed he has. Critics accustomed, as all Hitchcock's critical admirers are, to the canons of high culture still enjoy relatively little middle-brow art, whose complexity touches off high-brow expectations, and, by frustrating them, exasperates. But the simplicities of low-brow art have great nostalgic and infantile appeal, and are consequently preferred. Hitchcock incorporates the simpler low-brow starting-points (e.g. melodrama), and then takes them as far as characteristic middle-brow reflections. One need only imagine the novel from which Hitchcock's American version of the story might have been taken to realise that those who find the film profound because metaphysical would have rejected precisely the same points, in their verbal form, as platitudinous. It is always, of course, possible for 'style' to transcend 'content'; but I have yet to find any description of the content of Hitchcock's style which doesn't *either* settle for Ian Cameron's entirely appropriate title, 'the mechanics of suspense', i.e. assertions of efficacy in creating atmosphere, whether within the characters' experience or arising out of it, *or* require a kind of symbolic coding which would invest with profundity any film-maker or novelist.

It is tempting, of course, to argue that if Hitchcock *has* attracted particular intensity of exegesis, it must be because of the exceptional artistic qualities of his work. But our suggestion that Hitchcock fascinates high-culture critics because of his escalation from low-culture simplicities to middle-brow ones offers an alternative possibility. And it seems to be sufficiently well borne out by cultural trends to be beyond dismissal. Thus one finds, for example, that the extremely boring Marilyn of the Fox publicity machine is taken into the high-culture sphere via Andy Warhol images and the ethos of Pop art, while the relatively complex charge of certain Marilyn movies—from Roy Baker's *Don't Bother To Knock* through to *Some Like It Hot* and *The Misfits*—goes unnoticed or forgotten. Similarly, the face and figure of Elizabeth Taylor are abstracted from her screen roles, the most interesting of which come well into the middle-brow category (e.g. Richard Brooks's *Cat on a Hot Tin Roof*, Joseph L. Mankiewicz's *Suddenly Last Summer*, Mike Nichols's *Who's Afraid of Virginia Woolf*). The comic strip is adopted into high-culture favour; the middle-brow novel is not. Not all the reasons for these preferences are unreasonable. None the less, their interaction produces an unfamiliarity with the content of 'midcult' such that when, as with Hitchcock, it is clearly grasped, it is hailed as an exceptional achievement. Thus the mechanics of suspense are confused, in Hitchcock's case, with spiritual exercises, or consensus morality is simplified and presumed to be unique, or the films are endowed with an esoteric metaphysics rather than consensus metaphysics (which certainly exist), or possibilities which are provoked only to be negated are taken as cathartic affirmations.

Undoubtedly *The Man Who Knew Too Much* reveals the same finesse and paradox as *To Catch A Thief*. In both cases the essence of Hitchcock's skill lies, not in profundity, but in a structure of twists. The deeper films are distinguished from the shallower ones by a choice of terrain; whether the twists take one around a superficial story or whether they require the moral and psychological conflicts to be experienced, dramatically. It is relatively rarely necessary to distinguish between inspiration or its absence within these impeccable Hitchcockian machines; the purposes of art, in the usual sense, as assumed by the exegetical procedure, are transversal to, although they intersect with, those of entertainment; and it is to the latter category that I should assign such matters as effective suspense.

This is not to deny that there is a Hitchcockian vision of the world, or that it possesses some poetic or moral truth. So does a great deal of minor and middle-brow art and entertainment. This vision of his is revealed with some force and subtlety in his major films, and, although touched on, also soft-pedalled, watered-down, and bowd-lerised in his minor films, which certainly reveal deeper meanings if related by complex deductions and decodings based on the important ones. Since the minor films add little or nothing to the major ones, the decoding is a fairly academic exercise, with the disadvantage of dis-missing or reversing the presented meaning. The film which Hitchcock went to some trouble to make is represented as a mere façade, as, indeed, a lie.

And it is, in so far as they are lies that they fail to fulfil themselves, to embody themselves, in the way in which the early films of Clouzot, or the novels of Graham Greene or Gerald Kersh or Georges Simenon, fulfil and embody themselves. No doubt one reason why Hitchcock has so much less to say than these artists is that until very recently the Anglo-Saxon cinema was allowed less freedom, had more fundamentalist-minded an audience. Hitchcock could probably have spoken more clearly had he been willing to run more risks, had he less jealously guarded his reputation as a maker of outstanding commercial successes. In this worldliness one may see a kind of prudence, akin to the wise fear which emerges as a fundamental attitude. Hence the peculiar dichotomy of this intimate Vistavision drama, as of a Simenon working to the functional requirements of Cecil B. de Mille.

The Wrong Man

It would be untrue to say that Hitchcock never incurred risks. We have suggested, earlier, that public response to *Secret Agent* and *Sabotage* taught him caution; that strong dramatic effects might enrage or alienate an audience rather than enthral it. We would date earlier than most critics the beginning of a decline. Yet, by the late '50s, it was becoming apparent that Hollywood was losing the battle against television, and must increasingly rely on a certain audacity. Not that Hollywood had ever been totally lacking in that quality; and Hitch-cock, while treating various shibboleths with respect (e.g. the tabu on a reluctant hero), remained aware that any individual factor may be transformed by its context, and not infrequently breaks such rules, or experiments with cross-breedings between genres which are, in their way, adventurous and creative.

When, in England, Hitchcock erred, it was on the side of the un-heroic and the atrocious. When, in the '50s, he erred, it was on the side of the bleakly serious. At any rate, *The Wrong Man* is the antithesis of its predecessor. Both are studies of man and wife under strain. But from Middle America's sumptuous tourism and an ordinary but heroic couple valiantly involved in extraordinary events, he turns to the nerve-racking city, and a passive, bewildered hero who is scarcely adequate to events depicted in a bleakly realistic style. *The Wrong Man* differs so much from usual notions of box-office ingredients that it is easily assumed to be in some way a highly personal film. Its religious overtones immediately commended it as such to Hitchcock's French Catholic admirers, and it has been described as a present for them in acknowledgement of their *hommage*. Certainly, from this viewpoint, the structure of melodramatic coincidence, of miraculous possibility, of facial resemblances suggesting *alter egos*, and the explicitly Catholic frame of reference, could seem confirmation of all their theories. But it may also have been Hitchcock's present to himself, and he seems to have been, if not more concerned, at least more satisfied, with the first section, which is almost a documentary on the effect of induction into prison routine. We remember his digressions in this direction in *Blackmail* and *The Paradine Case*, and his remarks about his long-standing fear of the police. We may also remember that J. Lee-Thompson's extremely bleak study of a woman in the condemned cell, *Yield to the Night*, had been an unexpected success in Britain the year before.

Indeed, *The Wrong Man* analyses fairly readily into an amalgam of two box-office genres which had recently emerged. On the one hand, it derives from the Paddy Chayefsky films, which met with varied success, but produced a string of imitations, several being as commercially unsuccessful and artistically interesting as Hitchcock's film. Given the reminder by Lee-Thompson's film of the perennial popularity of bleak prison dramas, the prison theme might act as insurance for a middle-class urban hero who possesses no particular heroic qualities and is ravaged by worries. On the other hand, it borrows from the religious themes to which Hollywood was also turning (e.g. *A Man Called Peter*, *The Left Hand of God*), albeit arguably in default of more genuinely popular novelties during those shifts in public taste which, not yet clarified, produced the *crise de sujet* of Hollywood and Pinewood alike in the mid-'50s. At any rate, it can equally be described as Hitchcock's present to his older critics, who looked back nostalgically to the location everyday of *Shadow Of A Doubt* and longed for him to be more realistic and dramatic (rather than melodramatic). At any rate, its intersection of the realistic, and the apparently or really miraculous, is an extremely intriguing one.

Henry Fonda, double-bassist at The Stork Club, turns out to be the exact double of a hold-up man. He can't raise bail and goes through the depersonalising horrors of jail procedure. When at last he is freed, he embarks on a search for witnesses, with repeated failure. The strain tells on his wife (Vera Miles) who has at last to be consigned to an asylum. Alone and desperate, he sinks into apathy, but accepts his mother's advice to pray. His face dissolves into that of the Sacred Heart and that into that of his 'double'—recognised, and caught at last. But this still isn't the end, for Hitchcock rarely makes an assertion without a reservation, whether chastening or equivocal; nor would he commit himself to anything as open to Protestant and agnostic criticism as a vulgarly pious *deus ex machina*. The musician very logically and naturally hopes that another prayer will induce another miracle and cure his wife. It doesn't, although, as a nurse counsels him, human patience can accomplish miracles.

The intersection of a melodramatic structure (coincidence), the spiritual (providence) and the harshly everyday is a promising one. The film makes a serious social comment, indicting the cattletruck judicial system for which New York is notorious, and with its big, grey close-ups of Henry Fonda's subdued, anxious countenance, it is curiously evocative of a Bresson film.

Alas, it is almost as dull as it is abundant in qualities, perhaps because of the conjunction of the hero's passivity with Hitchcock's dramatic dryness. John Frankenheimer, Delbert Mann, Lee-Thompson (in his *Woman in a Dressing Gown* mood, which is a better comparison, lacking the special excitement of an attractive woman in a death-cell), might have imbued it with the energy from which Hitchcock abstains, with a rigour and a discipline which he must have known entailed a box-office risk and which it is impossible not to admire. One suspects that they would have had less hesitation in introducing the elements of revolt against, and criticism of, the system which Hitchcock leaves so implicit that it is not easy to tell whether he believes it to be self-evident, or whether he is more concerned with the personal, internal suspense of internal struggle between hope and despair. It is almost as if Hitchcock were exorcising a personal nightmare about arrest and a helplessness. He comes, briefly, close to Sternberg's *The Salvation Hunters*, *Underworld* and *Crime and Punishment*, whose theme is the problem of retaining one's morale in a cruel and bewildering world. But Hitchcock refuses their partial release in insolence, triumph and efficacity. His little man becomes almost the prisoner of, not one system, but two. The coincidental resemblance typifies this unjust, unredeemed world, and providence another, higher, intervening force. Society's judicial processes are another system, as blind and unseeing as the British Museum sphinx. At the bottom of this Kafkaian hierarchy of powers and orders, man and wife can do little more than worry, endure, weaken to apathy or take up the burden of effort, to which, and here is the release of energy and of hope, providence will respond. The innocent man can depend also on the moral strength of his mother. Weak as one is, passive as one feels, powerful forces can be unleashed on one's behalf. But—and again the end doesn't negate the opening tension—one's relationship towards them is also one of passivity. They are not to be controlled.

Phrased in so many words, the film's comment on the relationship of man and the powers whose pawn, yet partner, he is, is banal enough. 'If you follow your mother's advice and pray, God, or destiny, or accident, may, or may not, give you what you seek, and if he, or it, does, it will set limits to itself and chasten you as well as oblige you.' And yet the film's mood gives that message a bleakness which is dignity; impeccably Catholic, its sense of inexorable machinations evokes a grim Calvinistic reproof to some 20th-century views of Instant Happiness through Salvation, and it works its paradoxes of helplessness and the need for self-help more thought-provokingly than its predecessor, to which it is by way of a sombre but not nihilistic rejoinder. One would like to think of it as Hitchcock's confession of faith—although there is no real reason to give it more authority than the far more activist emphasis of *The Birds*.

One might have expected the shift from the worldly to the providential level to impede the film's emotional accumulation, but, firmly controlled by Hitchcock, the style and tone remain consistent throughout. Hitchcock told Truffaut that he felt that the study of the wife's strains interrupted the trial; and one can put it the other way also; the trial interrupted the study of the family tensions. Hitchcock, concentrating as he does on the husband's predicament, his being tightly locked in a situation, has, with the wife's madness, to switch into something psychologically more personal, more, not eccentric, but distinct from a kind of generalised tension. As it is the film achieves a sense of the wife's evolving condition—her breaking up—but it seems an idea, an arbitrary imposition, rather than an evolution of a state of mind. A story not based on fact might have allowed Hitchcock more freedom. One wonders, indeed, if the idea of nervous strain such that the wife has to be hospitalised isn't a dilution of the domestic tension, and whether that might have been more particularised had the husband sensed that something passive in his personality, rather than his actions, was partly responsible for her strain, and that only after his prayers for her does her breakdown become complete. The sequence then allows more time for rising tensions, for their particularisation in terms of interaction between husband and wife, and for a stronger double twist at the conclusion (a slap in the face by God, and a humbled determination which is the middle way between ignoring and exploiting Him). As it is, the sense of time passing, whether in the cell or in the home, seems to cut across the possibilities of establishing a connection by simultaneous, contrasted rhythms of behaviour and action, a kind of tearing apart of the family as each lacks the rhythm and presence of the other.

It seems to me that while it is the prison and the trial which most interest Hitchcock, it is the family, not the trial, which is the natural junction of this story's tensions, for it is here that the destiny-systems affect the husband one way, the wife the other, making each the other's victim, and executioner, rather than his succour. Schematically, too, something might be said for characterising the guilty man as something more than simply *mean*—as (however restrained his personal style) the incarnation of all that is missing in the wrong man's passivity—a demonic life, an instinctive rage. Both 'tragic flaws' would express the bewilderment and demoralisation of man without community, in the big city. One longs, in fact, for a spiritual, rather than a facial relationship.

Douchet, thinking along similar lines, sees the two men as alter egos—the criminal's facial resemblance suggesting that he is the same soul that has made the other choices, been subject to a different destiny. It is just as possible that the physiognomic resemblance is absurdist and that the differences of expression correspond to differences of soul. The use of split screen in Hitchcock's film, as in Robert Wise's *Two For The Seesaw*, another exploration of metropolitan solitudes, indicates the extent to which the film can be taken socially rather than metaphysically, as a meditation on the city and its sustained assault on individual pride. The roar of the subway past the victim's apartment evokes the crushing and carriage of bodies, and souls, of which the prison system is no more than an intensification; while the hazards of ill-luck are part of the city's nature, its brutal mixture of movement and confinement, of junctures and solitudes, of crowds and cells. *The Wrong Man*, with its climatically split screen, rejoins the wall-of-cells in *Rear Window*. And it may well be that the '70s, pondering questions of alienation, bureaucracy, imposed routines and citizen's initiatives, will find this study in near-defeat and stumbling salvation at once relevant and poignant, not simply on the strength of its first half, but for its metaphysical affirmation, whether or not it is taken as merely one of the figments of the modest hope which sustains Balastrero as it sustains, in a diversity of masks, the heroes of *The Crowd*, of *Lonesome*, of *The Rat Race*, of *The Bells Are Ringing*, of *The Apartment*, of *Midnight Cowboy*, of *Shock Corridor*, of so many other anguished lyrics, tragic, comic, or derisive, of New York, New York.

Vertigo

Across Los Angeles rooftops a criminal flees, pursued by a policeman and a detective, Scottie (James Stewart). The first two jump a space successfully but Scottie, making a clumsily determined leap, stumbles and hangs helplessly over an alley sixty feet below. The policeman turns back to give him his hand, slips and is killed.

Scottie, surviving, resigns from the force but resolves to conquer his vertigo with the help of Midge (Barbara Bel Geddes), his long-time girl-friend and one-time fiancée His careful first exercise takes an ominous turn when a step-up stool leads him to stand on her design-bench and a window overlooking the street below.

A long-lost schoolfriend, Gavin Elster, asks him to keep his wife Madeleine under surveillance. Scottie's misgivings about taking on a psychiatric job give way to curiosity when he learns of Madeleine's belief that she is the reincarnation of her great great grandmother, Carlotta Valdes, a kept woman of the gracious Spanish days. On seeing Madeleine (Kim Novak) he falls in love with her, stalking her along her mysterious journeys between the department store, a portrait of her ancestress in the museum, a boarding house from which she vanishes (if she ever was there), and, eventually, a suicide attempt under the Golden Gate Bridge, soon after she begins to return his love.

Midge, feeling that she is losing Scottie to a half-insane woman and a romantic tale, tries to bring him down to earth. She introduces him to a bookseller who tells him Carlotta's tragic story, and later parodies the museum's painting of Carlotta, substituting her own face. She succeeds only in losing Scottie's trust, and he resolves to intervene effectively in Madeleine's delusions. When she dreams of a Spanish Mission in Carlotta's day, he takes her to it to prove that it still exists, almost unchanged, and that her 'forgotten memory' has nothing supernatural to it. In the livery stables they exchange their first kiss. But she hurries away from him to climb the mission tower. Struggling weakly through his vertigo, he mounts its staircase at a crawl, only to see her plunge to her death.

A coroner accuses him of moral, if not legal, negligence, and he slumps into a catatonic silence from which he gradually emerges, only to suffer from hallucinations provoked by women with the vaguest resemblance to his lost love. In the street outside 'Madeleine's' department store he meets a shopgirl, Judy (Kim Novak), who under the vulgarity and bitterness is her double. Her initial response is a scathing rejection of a corny pick-up, but sensing the force of his attachment she relents, and, like her predecessor, begins to return his love. But his love is for the original, and he has no sexual desire for her until she has perfected the resemblance; and as they kiss in her apartment, he hallucinates himself back into the livery stable, with the other.

Hitchcock has already explained the mystery. Judy was Elster's mistress, chosen by him for his resemblance to his wife, who was absent in a sanatorium. She impersonated Madeleine, until Elster hurled his wife from the top of the tower, Judy's function being to ensure Scottie's presence as witness to suicide, or suspect. Assured of his wife's family fortune, Elster jilted his accomplice. She should break with Scottie but can't because her dawning love was unfeigned. None the less she has lived in dread of the achieved resemblance, and all it might reveal, as she has lived in helpless jealousy of his love for her false self.

It is uncertain, indeed, how far Scottie sees Judy as Madeleine returned or another Madeleine. Casually, carelessly, she dons the jewel which, completing the circle, breaks the spell. He drives her to the Spanish Mission, forcing her up the stairs, his rage overcoming his vertigo, describing her crime to her as they go, while she desperately tries to persuade him that, if she hurried up the stairs leaving him to crawl, it was to prevent the crime which her love of Scottie had made pointless and repugnant to her. But as he cries, reproachfully, 'I loved you, Madeleine,' so a shadowy form appears at the top of the staircase, Judy starts guiltily, and steps back, falling to her death, while the intruder is revealed as a nun and Scottie is left looking down where Judy fell.

One may see the film as a study of a man's attempts to withdraw from the guilt occasioned by each of three falls. Too guilty at a policeman's death he quits the force. Madeleine's fall generates an obsession. If the third fall frees him from his giddiness, and his illusions, it may be at a terrible price. This triple escalation of guilt intersects with a meditation on the beauty and danger of romantic love, notably, the sterility of an all-exclusive love, after the beloved's death, and the violence thus done to the identity of the living. Within these three divisions, other moral factors appear, notably an interchangeability of violence and masochism (Judy makes Scottie her fall-guy, Elster drops her, Scottie turns her into a ghost of her victim). Perhaps Scottie's premature retirement (he's fancy free with free time) betrays him to Madeleine's confusion of fantasy and time. At any rate one can take Scottie quite straightforwardly as a hero of a type long familiar to filmgoers. We esteem him for his qualities, we sympathise with his moral flaws, feeling them as normal human vulnerabilities. He takes guilt too much to heart and loves 'not wisely but too well'. His problems and errors earn him our sympathy as, tragically, rather than culpably, paraphrases, by extreme, of ours. One might subtitle the film: 'Everyman In Search Of His Love-Image'. And when she's found she seems to be the negation of detective common sense only, finally, to confirm it by, cruelly, a criminality to whose suppression his conscious, social self has found its vocation. Conversely, Judy falls in love with the man whose victim she doubly becomes; to please him she must masquerade as her victim, and when she becomes herself it is to be denounced, convulse in guilt, and die.

But Hitchcock's exegetes have seen him as an earnest, hortatory moralist rather than an absurdist, equivocal or casual one, for whom the moral error is merely the occasion for the tragic vision. For them the film's crux must be some sin of Scottie's, and all its unpleasant consequences must be punishment or purgation. And since he isn't a saint it isn't difficult to elevate any moral aspect of his errors to the status of 'cause' of the subsequent narrative. Thus Douchet defines his sin as a will to power, first betrayed by his attempt to conquer his vertigo. And his resignation from the force would be a complementary inability to accept any situation in which any weakness might upset his pride. Equally, his sudden interest, when Elster 'confesses' his inability to dismiss the possibility that Madeleine really is being haunted by Carlotta, is another form of *hubris*. Scottie's detective scepticism is a wish to destroy, or to master, all which in the universe passes man's understanding. He is Faust, Elster his Mephistopheles, Madeleine his Helen. Having lost his Helen, Scottie tries to reconstruct her from sinfully base materials; here is a myth of creation in which it is Adam, who, deprived of Eve, conjured up Lilith from clay. His domination of Judy is another form of Satanic pride, and provokes the lashback of its ironic gratification. Both Elster, the mastermind, and

Scottie, are two poles of the impious Creator, that is, wilful human fantasy. Hitchcock too is a creator, and, between the contemptuously grand assurance of Elster, and the terrible vulnerability of Scottie, he finds the balance; the film denounces the dream.

Robin Wood, less given to occultism and more to a secularised puritanism which insists on responsibility in interpersonal relationships, suggests that Scottie's sin is not so much a hubristic self-imposition, as his ready retreat from full commitment, whether to detection as a vocation or to human relationships. In his '40s, he has never been married, and Midge wisely terminated their engagement of three weeks, although still longing for him to turn to her more fully than he did then.

An existentialist criticism might censure Scottie's 'Bovaryism', his rejection of prosaic reality for a self-indulgent self-submergence in a romantic dream which can be but a half-truth at best. Sartre, no doubt, would adopt towards Scottie, the bourgeois detective, the same severity as towards Baudelaire, rather than the hagiographic thesis of a 'Saint' Genet—although a Sartrean 'Saint' Judy might just conceivably exist. Robin Wood is gentle with Scottie, rather than censorious; and I would agree with him in seeing the film's theme as a tragic one, the 'inherent incapability' of the 'perfect realisation' of human relationships. Equally, one can see the film as a case-history, of a man unfortunate enough to find his unconscious fantasies fulfilled. Douchet, rightly, compares the masklike face in the opening credits to the obdurate maternal glance, and the insistence on women's faces and subjacent violence brings us towards Bergman's *Persona*.

Useful as these thematic axes undoubtedly are, one can too readily assume that the Aristotelian theory of the 'tragic flaw', which was so congenial to a declining individualistic moralism, and which derived considerable reinforcement by annexing the Freudian unconscious, is adequate to account for any drama. But it reveals the narrowness of its psycho-philosophical basis when one compares it with, say, the Promethean myth, or a Saint's martyrdom, or the theatre of the absurd, or the literature of extreme situations, or any morality sufficiently complex to allow for the fact that, far from being adequate to reality in all respects save one (and that's our tragic flaw), we're all in a state of original sin, in the sense of original inadequacy, most of the time. In so far as we survive it's because we're adept at dodging tragic dilemmas, which is why comedy is as true as tragedy, and also why we always feel that the tragic hero is in some strange way a finer being. What distinguishes him is not the flaw that betrays his virtues;

it's the virtues that reveal the flaw. And so it is quite possible to argue that Scottie's perfectionism, or subjacent romanticism, or will to power, are, far from being a sin, an error, or a tragic flaw, one of his qualifying factors, his, in the Socratic sense, 'daimon' which grants him access to a sphere in which human existence reveals itself and in the light of which life must be judged. *Vertigo* may be a Promethean tragedy; it may be right to steal fire from heaven; and the equation of Satan with evil and fire with hell may be a Christian deprecation of man. The orthodoxy of Hitchcock's Christianity, in his art, cannot be assumed; not merely because artists, and indeed Christians, are often quietly, or unconsciously, heretical, but also because the cinema is no more Christian than its spectators, and ours, as is often said, is a post-Christian society. The ambiguity is evident; Hitchcock observes that 'a beautiful woman is a power for evil', but Hitchcock's heroines are as glamorously groomed as anyone else's, and 'glamour' is a word borrowed from witchcraft and faery, meaning 'magic spell'.

Even if we grant that some moral flaw of Scottie's is significant in a way in which his qualities are not, the film must lose a great deal of its richness if one overlooks, or forgets, the possibility that Scottie's flaw is not his intransigent preference of an image, or Madeleine, or Judy, to Midge, but his difficulty in overcoming the mixture of moralistic rage and offended pride which fills him when he learns the complexity of the truth. There is also the possibility that the film is not a moral demonstration at all, but a reflection on the destructibility of human happiness.

That Scottie loves a woman who does not exist, rather than a particular woman with a particular nature and history, can hardly be taken as an index of maladjustment or immaturity. For a woman's appearance, expression, gesture and rhythm may reveal a great deal of her mental and emotional make-up. Love at first sight, which is clearly involved here, is quite compatible with a reasonably experienced man's recognition, in another person, of, to borrow a useful Jungian concept, his *anima*—his sister-soul, incarnation of, schematically, both a maternal part-image and of a possibly obscured or repudiated but none the less powerful part of himself. That Scottie is willing to accept, and to love, 'his' Judy as Madeleine does not necessarily impugn his love of something which is both profound and real in Judy, however disguised. More open to criticism is his inability to love her unless she looks like Madeleine; but a fixation on a certain type of woman is normal enough, and by this stage of the story he is already half-shattered in a way for which he cannot be held responsible (unless

one is going to insist that detectives should spot criminals at sight).
The links between the notion of an *anima*, Goethe's dictum 'There but
for the grace of God go I', and the detective story genre, are obvious
enough, and it is relevant enough that the detective should fall in love
with a criminal. One also has to allow that Madeleine, sane, is Judy's
creation, and an aspect at least of herself; so that the sensibility
which Scottie loved in Madeleine was not quite alien to her, whatever
guidance and grooming she enjoyed from Elster. Indeed, it's arguable
that Judy, as a co-murderer, only lives out the guilts which have
debilitated her victim's mind from within. Given her remorse before
the crime, and her response to Scottie after it, one might well wish
to see them live as happily together ever after as Hitchcock's sense of
flies in ointments allows. Certainly the climax derives its strength not
so much from our fear that Scottie will *not* free himself from Judy as
from a fear that his rage and her guilt will conspire to a conclusion as
tragic as that which I read into the final images. Simsolo sees Scottie's
fate as 'remorseful tears'; Wood sees him as 'cured' of illusion but
'desolate'; and one can equally see him as trembling on the brink of a
traumatic realisation of his tripled guilt. Rage, replacing weakness,
has made him part-responsible for this third accident, thus destroying
the only woman he will ever love. Equally he will be stripped of every
spiritual value represented by his legalistic detective morality. Not
that he'll jump after Judy, or return into a catatonic state once more.
His pain and apathy will be more prolonged, more conscious, more
terrible, more permanent.

It is possible, of course, to see no more than a banally wilful Scottie
who falls for Madeleine-Judy precisely because she's a nonentity
whose mask is the ideal Rohrschach test for his projections. Even his
attempts to help her can be interpreted in some pejorative way; he
must be neurotic to fall in love with a neurotic, and so on. All of which
seems to me a dogmatic mechanism, or a hypochondria neurotic
enough in its own right. Hitchcock seems to me to be playing a more
interesting game, whereby, as so often, the hero's traits are an anagram
of the villain's, but within the sphere of what is morally and emotionally forgivable or benign. For, despite the assertion by two French
critics that Elster is an incomprehensible abstraction, his motives are
quite clear. He appears as a shipyard manager, and tells Scottie that
he married into the business which he manages, because his wife's
relatives are dead, except for those who own the other yard at Baltimore (i.e. far away on the Atlantic coast). After Madeleine's death he
remarks that he will be relinquishing active involvement in the business

to go to Europe, and although the unsuspecting interlocutor might assume a great grief another possibility is evident. He married Madeleine for her property, and murders her so that he can enjoy it in 'gay Paree'. In his conversation he stresses the phrase, 'freedom and power', which Scottie, later, angrily re-echoes. Scottie, too, retires on, it would seem, a generous pension or private income, and devotes himself to the pursuit of love. And to that extent the film accommodates a Calvinistic moral about self-indulgent idle ease as the mother of psychological morbidities and work as a self-curbing, and therefore self-preserving, routine. Scottie's rage on learning of his victimisation by Judy and Elster is natural enough, but it might be said to have something of Elster's proud egoism about it. None the less, these affinities are countered by even more obvious contrasts, and it remains important to distinguish between the hero's and the villain's versions of the same sin. In ethics as in other matters a quantitative difference may amount to a qualitative one; and what could one say, morally, in extenuation of a Scottie who made no attempt to overcome his vertigo? Sin-and-punishment, tragic flaw arguments reveal their weak point when one realises that they allow Scottie no positive human characteristics or course of action at all, unless it leads to a happy end; and, indeed, he later seeks refuge in just that self-negation which our moralistic critics would require of him: catatonia, which isn't a better answer either. One may chide him for resigning from the police force, as Midge does, or for accepting Elster's assignment, as the Coroner does, but, in principle, no alternative to action or inaction exists, except in so far as a little, unofficial, unathletic assignment like keeping an eye on a man's wife is, if not a golden mean, at least a sensible venture between ambitious over-activity and pusillanimous inactivity. To say that Scottie should have been more suspicious of Elster and his 'wife' amounts to no more than a wish for a detective at least as omniscient, and inhuman, as Sherlock Holmes (and even he took a certain period of time to solve his mysteries).

Ironically, the tragic flaw argument derives from expectations of omniscience and impartiality which would fit a computer rather than a man. But to say that Scottie is culpable because he is both vulnerable and fallible is to say that man is culpable because he is mortal. Scottie's decisions, on the evidence available to him, seem to me well within the compass of normal, sensible, human error. The consequences which accrue to him are so grossly disproportionate as to rule out any coherent moral connection. They are a mockery of morality.

Scottie is fallible, and courageous, in two contradictory fashions.

His amiable conformism seems well adapted to the comfortable, bourgeois existence which Midge has in mind for them. She loves him, but, being what she is, she can arouse in him feelings no stronger than a deep friendship and goodwill. Nor is her world free from the taint of illusion-making and glamour. She devotes her technical skills to the design of brassières which make bosoms appear to be what they are not. If we are to see Scottie's attempt to cure himself of vertigo as *hubris*, why should we not see Midge's connivance in a system of deception as, equally, *hubris*—an excess of mediocrity? We can reverse the interpretation which would see Scottie's romanticism as his error. His error is, rather, his tolerance of the mediocre lie, and his championship, as a detective, of the system of which it is part. It is this mediocre quest for pleasure which traps him, from another direction also—Elster's motivations being, in certain respects, similar to the values connected with Robie in to *To Catch A Thief*—one retires from business to live in France. And the criticism of the norm recurs throughout the film. If we are to blame Scottie for falling, we must blame also the policeman who falls in trying to save him. We must certainly condemn the Coroner for his sly and brutal character-assassination by innuendo (which is unjust because it imputes to mere negligence what is in fact due to attempts at a sensible self-cure, to a genuine and recognised illness, and to Robie's agonised love). We must blame Midge no less severely than she blames herself. And most certainly we must blame, as inadequate, and therefore as a fosterer of illusions no less serious than Scottie's, the psychologist who thinks Mozart and, no doubt, a little superficial discussion, can touch the soul.

It is, perhaps, Scottie's dignity, rather than his weakness, that he relates to two other words: the underworld of crime, and the over-world of the supernatural. He is dedicated to the negation of the first and, initially, to the normalisation of the second. And, eventually, he succeeds. Only for one bout of a few moments does Judy deceive him. Far from believing in the supernatural, he remains agnostic; and one wonders what even the most Catholic of critics would make of a Scottie who, on learning of Elster's wife's ideas of reincarnation, declines even to shadow her on the grounds that an exorcist is better qualified to deal with such a case? We would be back in the Middle Ages. None the less it may be significant that the supernatural over-world reveals itself as an illusion rooted in the underworld, and that the love with which Scottie, intuitively, responds to Madeleine-Judy, springs from the possibility of a reconciliation between the three planes of the soul—(1) reincarnation, immortality, romantic love; (2) crime; and (3) the common-sense scepticism which is the normal detective attitude and which Judy, while attempting to rebuff Scottie, expresses in a form which is more embittered yet more vulnerable (she loves him for himself, and at risk), more scathing yet less complacent. The distinction does not lie between the 'real' world of a brassière-designer and the 'unreal' world of fantasy. Nor does it lie between a prudent, well-moderated, existence, in which friendship without love usurps the place of passionate friendship, and romantic excess. It lies between a complacent world which denies all which lies beneath it and above, and a psychological world in which they, too, have been admitted, and accepted, a world in which, to borrow Rollo May's approach, human rationality has accepted the daimonic—a 'daimon' which is both 'demon' in the Christian sense, and 'daimon' in the Socratic sense. Scottie is unable to achieve that reconciliation. But how few people even attempt it!

A more prudent Scottie might have accepted his friendship with Midge as the functional equivalent of love. No doubt the nun's 'God have mercy on her soul!' posits a supernatural realm, or at least a moral code, whose norms are quite different from those of romantic love or from everything implied by the idea of a relationship, outside time, between Madeleine and Carlotta. If the latter's motives can't be precised, it may be because she may not exist. But Hitchcock might have hinted that such motives, if they existed, were egoistic or altruistic or instinctive. In fact he leaves it quite open whether the putative Carlotta is moved by sheer will to live, or by a continuing pursuit of her child. Thus she parallels the moral ambiguities of Judy, who is selfish with Elster but self-sacrificing with Scottie. But Scottie's world is no less excessive, with its mediocre excess of moderation; with its accident-prone policemen, its malicious Coroner, its superficial psychiatrist, with the—poignant—*hubris* inducing Midge to substitute herself, in the portrait, for Madeleine-Judy, and so to try to laugh away the difference between one person and another—to repeat, that is, *both* the confusion between Madeleine-Judy and Carlotta, *and* Scottie's acceptance of Madeleine as Judy, *and* Judy's confusion of the nun with Madeleine. It is quite absurd to list all the errors which arise as a result of the daimonic world, and simultaneously to overlook all the errors which arise within the common-sense, or bourgeois, or sceptical, world. The Coroner does Scottie as much harm as Elster. Midge understands brassières, but not a total love. The nun may be seen as an agent of divine justice, but she may equally be seen as a counterfeit of it.

Poetic justice is not divine justice—or if it is, Christian theology has a great deal of self-criticism to do. Nor is poetic injustice. If we are to blame Scottie for errors which result in his losing Judy, we must also blame Midge for errors which result in her losing Scottie. If we are to blame Scottie for causing the policeman's death, we must also blame the nun for causing Judy's. The pattern of guilts in the film is altogether ambiguous, simply because it is circular. It need not have been. Hitchcock might quite easily have inserted subtle yet effective pointers towards certain aspects or moments and not others. He does not.

Maybe Hitchcock is implying that the romantic world—the world where a woman's will which is also a mother's love survives the grave, where egos merge across time and in love, where Carlotta craves to live in Madeleine and Madeleine craves to admit Carlotta, where all that is sinister in the ghost-story (maybe Carlotta is another Rebecca) shades into all that is idyllic in hopes of ancestor-worship and reincarnation, where the passion for the fetish miraculously conjures up the beloved—does not, cannot, exist, and that its appearance must have some origin which is both prosaic and criminal. One is left with friendships, which must be accepted in lieu of love, and moderate illusions (brassières), and all the ambivalent associations with the nuns (charitable, severe; loving, frustrated; devoted, killjoy; representative of Christ, deluded human). This world has its injustices also; and is criminal in its turn. Apart from the ironic cruelty displayed by the Coroner, and even by Midge, albeit in effect rather than intention, we notice the policeman shooting at a fleeing suspect (which he may be legally entitled to do, although the suspect isn't yet legally guilty) and Scottie's own rage with Judy (which belongs to the prosaic sphere). This world is ordered; but it is empty; and its emptiness is summarised by the image of Scottie standing on the edge of a tower, whose dome is like a grave, and its impression of an indefinite duration before he follows his anima into the grave—whether twenty seconds or twenty years hardly matters any more. None the less: better Scottie dissatisfied than Midge satisfied.

Impeccably, the film's structure preserves its ambiguity. So dramatically strong is the final appearance of the nun that we are left with a feeling that some definite meaning or moral must be implied, some spiritual Q.E.D. But what? Maybe she was sent by a Christian providence to stop Scottie killing Judy; or to prevent their reconciliation; or maybe her appearance was engineered by occult forces—perhaps incorruptible, perhaps malevolent; or maybe Madeleine-Judy's belief in reincarnation is ironically true, and the real Madeleine returned under the appearance of a nun to punish her joint murderess (although, not, apparently, Elster, since Scottie now has no witnesses nor will his word carry much credence if the Coroner's treatment of him is any guide). Or maybe the nun's appearance is absurdist rather than meaningful, and maybe Judy's tragic flaw is the guilt-feelings which are the excess of her ability to love Scottie despite everything, or maybe the nun symbolises the destructive guilt built into the conformist moral system to which Judy has been abandoned by Scottie's mixture of offended pride and moral over-severity, overwhelming his love, temporarily at least, although, thanks to the nun's appearance, he may now repent at leisure.

From another angle, the film conjoins the myths of Pygmalion (Scottie) and Lilith (Judy). Although not without sympathy for Scottie's compulsive bid to re-create an image, Hitchcock doesn't allow us to forget Judy's predicament, whereby to please and hold the man she loves is both to live a lie and provoke discovery. And Scottie's love is at this point highly fetishised, for even after he has forced his way into Judy's life he still hallucinates Madeleine over her shoulder, and his interest, until she has become the other, is platonic in the double sense of reaching ever nearer an ideal and of indifference to sexual contact. One may see it as either a perversion of Platonism (which comes near Douchet's interpretation) or as an exposure of the perversion implicit in Platonism, or as, simply, the debility of an injured man. Scottie's way with her is in contrast to his way with Madeleine-Judy, whom he treats with understanding and whom he bullies constructively. One's natural impulse is to treat the change as the result of his second shock, which accumulates his vertigo, his inability to overcome it, Madeleine's death, and the savagery of the Coroner. His attitude to Midge changes equally, and there is no more reason to accept than there is to reject Douchet's suggestion that Scottie nurtured from the beginning this secret wish to dominate, to create, to rival, God.

As Judy's outbursts remind us, Scottie's relationship with her is one of Hitchcock's astute studies in, not male, but masculine, bullying of the female; for what he masks is not only the truth of Judy's guilt but her whole life experience, including the bitterness which, in her hotel bedroom, she expresses with a hardness which, while possibly exaggerated (to seem as unlike Madeleine as possible), surely has an autobiographical direction, recalling Judy before Elster groomed her. And there's much to be said, after all, for the proposition that Judy

is a good deal more interesting than Madeleine-Judy, and shows a great
deal more calibre. One might even, perversely, argue that Judy's part
in Madeleine's murder is the stronger, more courageous counterpart
of the real Madeleine's self-destructive, genteel neurosis (for the argument that Scottie's fate is the product of Scottie's sins must call forth
the argument that Madeleine's fate is the product of Madeleine's sins).
And Judy's, shopgirl's, desire to replace Madeleine, socially, is the
analogue of Madeleine-Judy's longing to become Carlotta, a child of
the gutter who appealed to a rich man, became a rich courtesan, and
was abandoned. Each clause corresponds to Judy's fate—a shopgirl
who appeals to Elster, paraphrases the courtesan in her exploitation
of Scottie, relents, and is abandoned. Whether or not the real Madeleine had a fixation about Carlotta, or whether it was Elster's inven-
tion, it stands for a kind of sentimentality which is common enough, a
discontent which, remaining less honest than Judy's bitterness, under-
goes a false sublimation into a romantic nostalgia for a time and a
style which, as Carlotta's fate reminds us, was not preferable to our
own.

From one aspect, therefore, Judy aspires to become Madeleine as
Madeleine aspires to become Judy, in the romanticised form of
Carlotta. And my argument is that if Scottie can tolerate Madeleine-
Judy's fixation, he could tolerate Judy's mixture of involvement in,
and withdrawal from, the murder. And if he should pick on the only
girl in the city who *is* Madeleine-Judy it's because, despite his trauma,
a sound instinct has spotted the *real*, the unique, person, all but
emancipated from the hazards of superficial life-style. He is reincar-
nating Madeleine-Judy in a profound and a true way, not at all a
superstitious one. True, he doesn't know Judy as a near-murderess.
But is the near-murderess the real Judy? or is she only what Elster
made of Judy, as unreal as Scottie's Madeleine-image? One might
argue that moral, or poetic, justice required Judy to be killed for
having planned to kill Madeleine. But it is worth remembering that
such justice is rather severer than legal justice; and it would equally be
moral and poetic justice were Judy's moment of terror as Scottie
seems to be about to kill her (as Elster, despite her attempts to prevent
the crime, killed Madeleine) considered to have expiated her guilt.
From this angle the film's tragedy is not that Scottie and Judy fall in
love, but that their *amour fou* proves vulnerable to some contagion in
the ambient social air—or to limitations from which human nature
can never be free.

For if Scottie's love precipitates him, briefly or permanently, into

the privileged supersensitivity of insanity, Midge lacks just that
sensitivity. She loves wisely rather than too well. She is a thoroughly
nice girl, motherly, friendly, loving, worldlywise. One seeks in vain for
a lack in her common-sense perfections, but she can no more protect
herself from romantic unhappiness than Scottie can. During their
brief engagements years ago she rapidly sensed his absence of profound involvement and ended the affair. But she remains, it would
seem, as devoted to him as Scottie to Madeleine. She's by no means
unaware of fetishism as a fact of life, since she's indulgently aware of
both the aesthetics and the iconography of bra design and of the
number of men who wear corsets—which is 'more than you think',
although she doesn't precise whether it be out of fetishism, or vanity,
or by way of private joke about Hitchcock's girth; and all the possibilities are equally relevant to the theme of seeming, by dress, to be
what one isn't. When Midge suspects a rival, she fights in a positive
rather than a negative way, helping Scottie's researches, hoping only
to deflect them in a realistic rather than a negative sense, a process
revealing its unconscious destructiveness and incomprehension in the
parodic portrait which, at a stroke, denies both passion and individuality, losing her, appropriately enough, an individual's friendship.
As for the Coroner, it is surprising that any critic should have accepted
his words uncritically; for the allowance he makes for human frailty
is purely ironic. Between the patient girl friend and the savage man
of law there comes, with perfect symmetry, the intimate doctor, the
psychologist, whose idea of the soul is as shallow as his use of Mozart.
Midge denounces him, as she denounces herself in the ritualistically
threefold denunciation: 'Stupid! stupid! stupid!'

Scottie, as a detective in love, links the common-sense and romantic
worlds with a variety of attachments: love, intellectual curiosity, fascination, fetishism, anger. Elster links them in coldly manipulative
detachment. Like a Dr. Coppelius, he animates his Judy-Madeleine
doll. Knowing everything, he appeals to Scottie's desire to know
everything, including the explanation of Carlotta's apparent 'reincarnation'—for it is Elster's (pretended) inability to disbelieve in that
possibility which persuades Scottie that something more than a purely
subjective hallucination may be involved. His playboy trip to Europe
doesn't quieten the megalomanic undertones of his reference to 'power
and freedom'. He foresees most of his victims' responses and at the
end of the film it's hard to believe that he hasn't, after all, committed
the perfect crime.

If, throughout the film, Scottie is our identification figure, it is because he comes nearest to our norm, our hopes of life, being located at an intersection of four apparent norms each of which is in fact a spiritual extreme: Elster's egoism, the Coroner's mixture of legality and moralism, Midge's common-sense loyalty, Madeleine-Judy's belief in a transcendental realm (reincarnation), and the criminal cynicism which is presumably incarnated by the criminal whom Scottie begins by pursuing and by which Judy is tainted. Scottie's apparent innocence of the world (from male corsets to female doubles) may surprise in a detective, but is of a piece with his gangling, middle-American style, and shouldn't be too readily written off as an implausibility arising from a Hitchcockian concession to the conventional spectator (although no doubt it is that also). It certainly opposes Scottie to, say, Bogart's Chandler's Marlowe, who roamed the same city. Scottie, no doubt, knows more or less the same facts about the world—but he leaves them where he feels they belong, in some underworld from which his own existence, too like Midge's, seems sealed off. But all the crimes which he has pursued across rooftops come, at last, home to roost. Such pillars of society as shipyard magnates and their gracious wives, museums and bookshops, lead him back through a department store and the romantic old quarter of San Francisco to a garishly lit hotel bedroom. If Judy is the prisoner of her masquerade, Scottie is the prisoner of his emptily comfortable world. Its bias accommodates the superficially romantic—the idea of Carlotta—but not the vulgarity and violence of which Judy is capable. He must transform her before he can accept her. Judy seeks escape from a cheapness which is, perhaps, no worse than Scottie's emptiness, and, helped by Elster, she learns to move through the underworld (crime) and the overworld (elegance and spiritual illusion). Her creation of 'Madeleine' is an artistic achievement (like Marlene's 'Marlene'—with Scottie as her Sternberg?), and her sensitivity is attested by her response to Scottie's love. Of her masochism there can be no doubt; but she faces an impossible situation with generosity and courage.

Ironically, it is another world of 'unreality', which gives Scottie his first glimpse of the truth. For his dream locates Elster, correctly, at the top of the Mission tower. Later, when kissing Judy, he hallucinates that he is back in the livery stable kissing Madeleine-Judy. Both dreams are confused and incomplete, but hold a little more of the truth than his consciousness knows. With Hitchcock's imperturbable ambiguity between the miraculous, the stoic, the ironic and the moralistic, both the detective and the murderess, the man who should know all and the woman who does, attain a state of hallucination about

'Carlotta'. In madness one attains a self-destructive truth: and if a
new reality takes its revenge on the dream, the dream takes its revenge
on the old, and the new reality is a desert of the spirit. It is in the
nature of man to be half-mad, and only a prudent mediocrity can
protect one from torture by hope.

Visually the film is structured on the sensations of vertigo—broad
horizontals disrupted by sudden falls, and the spiral, for a giddiness
which becomes an introverted obsession. Siegfried Kracauer's comments on the significance of the spiral in the German Golden Age
are no less relevant than the comparisons with Murnau's smooth,
gliding, mesmeric camera. Historically, too, German expressionism
can be seen as a romanticism which, divorced alike from religion and
nature, found itself trapped within a bourgeois materialism and an
industrial system. Before 1914, in an expressionist play, the detective of
Vertigo might have been a young poet, and the megalomaniac industrialist his father, passionately contributing to Bismarck's battleship-
building programme, and Judy the girl-of-the-people turned woman-
of-the-streets whom both men martyr. For the wider cinema audience
after 1918, the shudder of protest and guilt might have informed the
style, albeit balanced by a common-sense ambivalence closer to
Hitchcock. And the latter's expressionism inaugurates the 'cool
expressionism', the air of glaciated emotion, the sense of searching
and of beautiful self-grooming, simultaneously being evolved from
Antonioni, who takes, after all, as much from Chirico as from Marx.

The film opens on a shot of a hand grasping a horizontal bar. The
criminal hauls himself up and runs away across an expanse of rooftops
which seem as continuous as a landscape—a false landscape, as
Scottie abruptly discovers. Madeleine falls, not to the ground as we
expect, but onto a lower roof, creating a marked visual disorientation.
This laterality is reiterated in the final shot when Scottie, standing at
the top of the tower, looks down; the ledge below him and the open
space in the space behind him suddenly form a grave and a headstone,
an effect particularly emphatic after his dream of steeping down into
Madeleine's grave and finding, instead of earth, an endless fall. The
converse of this layered space—but in ascension—structures Scottie's
'step by step' ascent to normality (stool, steps, workbench), and its
disastrous climax (the chasm-like street glimpsed through the window).
Between the two death falls two shallow falls occur—Madeleine's
first suicide attempt, into water, and Scottie's first descent into the
dream-grave. The two-level floor of Elster's office contrasts with his
palisade of tower-cranes beyond. Over the water into which Madeleine

leaps stretches the Golden Gate bridge, a horizontal as bold as the
steel bar which the criminal grasps, as oppressive as Elster's reach is
invisible, and related, verbally, to the brassières which Midge designs,
on, she says, the principle of the cantilever bridge. The bra, invented
by an aeronautical engineer, must evoke another aerial tycoon's work
on behalf of Jane Russell, and transposes the theme of mid-air landscapes into that of flying and falling. As the chasm-street is glimpsed,
diagonally, so the Bridge is set diagonally. Scottie's house lies on a
slope, lending certain scenes, in the context of laterality, a half-
ominous, half-elegiac quality of decline. The vertical plane of Midge's
window is reiterated in the presentation of her painting another
squarish shape set in a stiff vertical; and as Midge reproaches herself
that image is reflected in the dark window against the night. We can
hardly help but notice that Madeleine, all but drowned in the water,
never loses her precarious high-heeled shoes, and the camera emphasises
them once more as Scottie begins her transformation, by clothing,
into Madeleine. For those shoes are artifice and deception (as compared to being down-to-earth); they are the little lies on which civilisation stalks but which are magnified into heights from which one
can fall. Scottie, in Midge's room, brandishes a walking stick which
is a little too thick, too obstinate, too dominant, emblem of his will.

The vertigo-vortex appears in the spirals and computer drawings
behind the credits; Scottie's automobile following Madeleine-Judy's as
she negotiates a roundabout or turns off; the camera tracking into a
whorl of her hair, like a whirlpool drawing Scottie's eye in; and the
turns of the mission tower's wooden staircase. To these turning forms
one can add the rings in the sequoia trunk which turn past time into
present space, and the circular lampshades so prominent as Madeleine-
Judy confesses her dream to Scottie, and as Judy writes her letter of
confession. But, with Hitchcock's impeccable aestheticism, the themes
of laterality and verticality are linked with the circle to create an
ambiguous double figure. The opening credits (by Saul Bass, but no
doubt in consultation with Hitchcock), feature a woman's face, a
beautiful, almost unblinking two-dimensional mask, and the camera
moves, as if being racked on a rostrum over a photograph, from its
lips to the eyes, then laterally across to one eye, from which the
vortex-like computer-figures and the main titles emerge. To these
images of nervousness, cold scrutiny and iconic perfection Warhol's
screen prints have nothing whatsoever to add; they come limping in
their rear. The mission tower staircase is rectangular in plan, although
the only unspecialised description for it is 'spiral staircase'. The tell-tale

jewel is another double figure, an oval within a polygonal frame. Under the Golden Gate Bridge, Madeleine-Judy destroys another circular form, a posy, contrasting with the computer figures. But circularity without rectangularity is a lie, just as the window and canvas of Midge's set-square common sense are an empty illusion.

Hitchcock has commented on the virtual non-existence of depth in the cinematic image and his restriction to more or less two-dimensional effects. Yet *Vertigo* plays implications of depth off against its devious, spiral inroads—in Scottie s sense of height, in the re-created Madeleine's walking towards him down a long corridor, and in the astonishing combination of approach and retreat whose complex confusions of perspective briefly induce all the sensations of nausea in the spectator. Hitchcock is talking as an artist, not as a technician nor as a showman, when he tells Truffaut how he tried to capture, for *Rebecca*, his own drunken sensation during a Chelsea Arts Ball. '. . . they couldn't do it. . . . I thought about the problem for fifteen years. By the time we got to *Vertigo*, we solved it,' and the combination of a track-back and a forward zoom 'only cost us nineteen thousand dollars'. (One often wishes the French impressionists of the '20's had seen the importance of brooding over details within an effect rather than merely piling one upon another.) In *Vertigo*, dreams possess depth; reality is merely a recession of laminations.

Thus the film's labyrinthine geometry establishes Judy as the loveliest of minotaurs, and her mask-face as the map across which the camera moves—a countenance which, though nervous, defies the camera's scrutiny, to remain as aloof as *Blackmail*'s British Museum God. The confusion of faces matches a confusion of places—Judy's hotel room becomes a livery stable—and the confusion of times, whose prominence in the overt narrative is mirrored by a quieter iconography: the petals cast on the water (the Heraclitean present, as suicide), the sequoia tree (more slow), and the jewel (a 'mineral love', a dead, changeless, touchstone—and eye). The film's sense of time-strata, capsized into one another, is counterpointed by the slow, mesmeric, metronomic pacing of its own visual and dramatic rhythms.

Green looms large in the film's colour schemes, and is traditionally the colour in which stage ghosts are bathed, presumably through association with green as the colour of the fairies and therefore of the non-Christian supernatural in general. Historically the detective story evolved out of the ghost tale, and the association remains in the film versions of two other Boileau-Narcejac novels: Clouzot's *Les Diaboliques* and Franju's *Pleins Feux Sur L'Assassin* (it's an interesting exercise to play musical chairs with the three directors and the three subjects). While following the twists and turns of 'that boundary where the familiar becomes the unknown', where premonition and coincidence evoke the disruption of time, *Vertigo* matches *The Wrong Man* with another play on facial resemblances, involving this time an anti-miracle, a miracle which is man-made, romantic, pagan, occult and materialistic, and which grafts supernatural experiments with time onto the processes of the beauty parlour, thus endowing the latter with the spiritual intimations of the former. Scottie and Judy haunt one another in an exchange as uneasy, as glassily deathlike as the limbo-locked shades of Marienbad.

Apart from relating to Murnau and the German expressionists on one hand, and Antonioni and Robbe-Grillet on the other, the film is also a throwback to the cycle of films about missing women and their portraits which Hitchcock had inaugurated with *Rebecca* and which continued throughout such films as Preminger's *Laura*, Tourneur's *Experiment Perilous*, Siodmak's *Phantom Lady*, Lewin's *Pandora and the Flying Dutchman* and Dieterle's *Portrait of Jennie*. Thus the film is a *film noir*, tardy, and Technicolored, but related to a category notoriously pregnant with expressionism. Yet the sense of quest predominates over that of flight; a sense of yearning in a chromium world ousts the heavy blacks; and here is an authentic '60's modulation of the *film noir* mood, itself a harsher evolution from the older, warmer romanticism of Henry King's *Peter Ibbetsen* and Frank Borzage's *Moonrise*. It isn't difficult to see *Vertigo* as a permutation of *Rebecca*. It's easy to imagine, for example, de Winter, gradually, quite without realising it, asking his young wife to make herself the living image of her predecessor. But her very success in becoming the living mummy of his lost love brings her dead rival back to his mind, and then from the grave, with the governess helping to suppress the living soul whose body now seems a fit bridal-chamber for her. Hitchcock has made no secret of his dissatisfaction with Kim Novak's playing, and one need only recall Ava Gardner in Albert Lewin's film to see a Carlotta Valdes who is at once more Spanish, more vulgar earth-mother, more aristocratic, more warmly lyrical. Many other actresses might have offered a rather less interesting view of pre-Yankee airs and graces. None the less, the story might have remained within reach of an ethnic, cultural and spiritual polarity. For the hardheaded detective named 'Scottie' tracks his quarry to a boarding-house whose manageress has a Scottish name, to a Spanish mission where two superstitions—Catholicism, occultism—intertwine. The contrast of Scots and Spaniards evokes something of America's formative history, in terms of a tussle between Anglo-Saxon and Latin cultures for the possession of her soul. In a characteristically romantic and stylised way we are approaching the immigrant theme which, precisely because its tensions are so ubiquitous a part of American life, was so long all but absent from the Hollywood screen.

And by a curious irony, Kim Novak, with Marlon Brando, was one of the first Hollywood stars to emerge, since the early '30's, with a non-WASP surname, and to bring from her Czechoslovakian immigrant background in Chicago that screen quality which a psychoanalyst quoted by Ezra Goodman described as 'a loss of identity'. The analyst attributes this to 'diffusion of identity', to 'the complexity of society, atomic scares, imminent wars', but it only requires an extension of by now familiar notions of anomie and alienation along the lines indicated by Margaret Mead and Geoffrey Gorer in their studies of America's ethno-cultural diversity to suggest the real meaning behind such sociologically anaesthetised phrases as 'their undistinguished background appeals to most people. These girls have no father or mother, figuratively speaking, and sometimes literally. They seem to come from nowhere.' If the cultural diversity which contributes so much to the specifically American type of anomie goes unregistered, Kim Novak, the orchidaceous icon, before Antonioni, of a modern solitude, brings with her a more contemporary relevance. As one or two French critics observed, Scottie's superimposition of Madeleine's romantic mask on Judy is akin to the depersonalization of Kim Novak's soul-sister, Marilyn Monroe, also embittered by a squalid social reality. The mixture of archaic and contemporary elements makes the beauty of this necrophiliac tale which, with its sugar-coating of glamour, remains a poignant lyric about what David Reisman in *The Lonely Crowd* called 'false personalization' and the alienations of modern life—including that deodorisation, depilation and depersonalisation of womanhood, the secret meaning of whose apparently optimistic perfectionism is a terror of the vulnerabilities which distinguish a woman from a pin-up or a high-heeled machine. No doubt the film's own surface expresses an acquiescence in it. But the same may be said of most of the subsequent European arthouse exercises in the alienated mode, with all the metaphysical space-time warps to which their characters are consigned (two Robbe-Grillet titles, *The Immortal One* and *In the Labyrinth*, suit *Vertigo* tolerably well). Hitchcock must take the credit at least for prefiguring the '60's sextet of blonde heroines whose smoothly perfidious responses to their victimisation or confusion catch a more generalised mood of disjuncted psyche: Tippi Hedren in *Marnie*, Catherine Deneuve in *Repulsion*, *Belle de Jour* and *Tristana*, and the two heroines of Ingmar Bergman's *Persona*. *Vertigo*, like *L'Avventura*, is built round winding journeyings after a missing person.

Somewhat in advance of intellectual culture as a whole, Hitchcock's film paraphrases certain themes adumbrated in Sartrian psycho-analysis. Judy is a *pour-soi* who consents, for greed or for love, to become an *en-soi*; and 'Madeleine's' and Scottie's experiments in transcendence conclude in a disastrous facticity. For Sartre, sexuality depends on consciousness acquiesing in its carnal desire, so as to persuade itself that by compelling the other's bodily desires it can possess her consciousness also; thus sexual desire is a kind of swoon-ing: 'The *pour-soi* experiences its own body's vertigo.' In Judy Scottie can possess his Madeleine, and Judy's assent is half-inspired by the masochistic acceptance of self-abnegation as the price of love. A Dostoievskian Hitchcock might have extended Judy's impersonation into atonement by surrogate existence—opening onto another gallery of paradoxes: for to become Madeleine would be to conjure the redoubtable Carlotta into existence. Thus this *ronde* of facticities becomes a carousel of torments as inexorable as *Huis Clos*. But such interpretations would depend on assent in Sartre's proposition that spiritual integrity requires a full experience, or possession, of experi-ence in consciousness—a possibility which Hitchcock as Stoic, as fundamentalist, as Catholic and as Freudian and as a poet of obsession would be unlikely to allow.

After a first viewing, I felt 'not at all sure that, in the end, *Marienbad* won't prove itself a sterile, frosty masterpiece, while *Vertigo* will testify to the continuing subtlety and flexibility of "conventional" cinema'. Certainly it marks an advance on *Strangers On A Train*, in so far as that basically uncomplicated story uses its echoes as a means towards surprise and suspense, while *Vertigo* catches a deeper psycho-logical structure. If, at a second viewing, its lyricism seemed less mesmeric, it seemed less a matter of miscasting than of the morally antiseptic world which *Vertigo* shares with *Shadow Of A Doubt*, from which it begins and to which it must return, and which deprives the final denunciation of Judy by Scottie of everything which is so terrible and so true in the denunciation of Mary Astor by Bogart in *The Maltese Falcon*. But a second viewing, as often, compensates for what it removes, for, as the wisdom of hindsight predominates over the in-volvements of uncertainty, the style and the pattern seem to crystallise the frosty tragedy of existences separated by time, by fate, by life-history, by split-second circumstance, by irrational disaffinities of temperament. It is normal enough that second viewings should intensify the ironies of premonitory remarks, but the dramatic context of *Vertigo* gives a special quality to any intimations of predestination and tragic confusion. Judy, relieved that Scottie has not, as yet, recognised her as Madeleine, says of Ernie's Bar, 'Well, after all, it's our place,' forgetting that it became their place because it had been Madeleine-Judy's place, hardly realising, in her happiness, that Scottie may still hear 'ours' as 'mine and Madeleine's', and maintaining the theme of occult or fetishistic attachment to place as a constituent of normal relationships. The nun's final appearance gives a new meaning to Madeleine-Judy's remark, earlier, that the nuns prevented them playing round the tower; and doubtless that remark was inspired by experiences of Judy's own. Thus, at a second viewing, the dramatic pattern shifts perceptibly. At a first viewing, the remark is essentially a 'plant' for the final appearance of the nun—not simply in making it plausible, since the mere sight of nuns in the mission grounds would have done that, but in making of it a permutation of the consequences of the nun's eventual appearance (the protective killjoy becomes the destructive innocent). And it endows on the nun's resurgence that quality of ratification by reminiscence which the spectator is apt to recognise as realism (like the bandaged hand at the end of *The Lady Vanishes*). At a second viewing, of course, the first mention of the nuns becomes a reminiscence of the climax, whose mood is thus diffused throughout the film; and it is this diffusion which helps one become aware of a structure most of which, at a first viewing, is likely to pass one by, at least unless one adopts an essentially exegetical mode of attention which is relatively inhospitable to the full dramatic experience—and may be an obsessional participation rather than a hysteric one. A second viewing also renders certain implausibilities more conspicuous, notably Elster's quite extraordinary degree of omniscience concerning the reactions of a man whom he's hardly seen for twenty years. None the less it achieves its strange presumption of occult reality, within an idiom which it isn't too much to qualify as Symbolism (for Symbolism is romanticism beaten back to its ivory tower, to the purely cerebral conclave and to certain atmospheres and patterns of thoughts which recur in *fin-de-siècle* Symbolism as in its psychedelic revival: occultism, esoterism, hallucinationism, all the evidence of imagination aspiring to become a reality in default of a religion).

North-by-North-West

If reports that *Vertigo* was little more to the taste of the American public than *The Wrong Man* are correct, it becomes easy to see why Hitchcock, after his two 'supernatural' films, reverted, for his next film, to a familiar, lighter and regularly successful, format, that of the picaresque pursuit. But *North-by-North-West* incorporates that more sophisticated development of personal relationships which had steadily been developing from *Rebecca* to *Vertigo*.

New York streets: a morass of automobiles and pedestrians. In contrast with this turgid anonymity, advertising executive Roger Thornhill (Cary Grant) moves neatly along the corridors, dictating to his secretary as he goes, and sliding her smoothly into someone else's taxi on the pretext that she's been taken ill. Arriving at his business lunch almost on time, he briefly leaves his table to send a telegram to his mother, having forgotten that it's her afternoon for bridge. A moment before he rises from his seat the bellboy pages a Mr. Kaplan, and two hoods, taking him for Kaplan, stick a gun in his back and whisk him off to a Glen Cove mansion whose front entrance bears the name 'Townsend'. Its occupant (James Mason) refuses to believe that he isn't an F.B.I. agent named Kaplan, and has him force-fed with Bourbon and put at the wheel of a Mercedes on a winding cliff-edge road at night.

Thornhill survives his nightmare ride, and is saved from the surveilling hoods by an abrupt encounter with a police-car. He's taken into custody for dangerous driving, and bailed out by his mother, who, in the courtroom, loudly snorts with disbelief as his lawyer tells his improbable story. The judge is less sceptical, and two detectives call with him at the Townsend mansion where 'Mrs Townsend' tenderly enquires after his hangover and scolds him for his drunken drive in another guest's car. Thornhill finds Kaplan's hotel, and is mistaken by every member of its staff for Kaplan, on the strength, he realises, of his room-number. He tracks Townsend to the United Nations building, where he was due to address the U.N. Assembly—but the real Townsend is another man altogether, and before he can identify the man in the photograph Thornhill shows him, a thrown knife deals him a fatal wound in the back. Flashing cameras show Thornhill knife in hand, standing over the corpse; a babble of voices presumes him guilty, and he runs.

A scene in a government agency clears up for us, though not for

Thornhill, the Kaplan mystery. Kaplan is their fictitious agent, invented to distract the attention of their quarry, the false Townsend, real name, Van Damm, from their real agent, who is under his nose. Their chief, 'The Professor' (Leo G. Carroll), states firmly that for security reasons there may be no intervention with the police on Thornhill's behalf. He seems rather less worried than his middle-aged secretary who muses, 'Goodbye, Mr. Thornhill—whoever you are'. Thornhill boards a train, and meets Eve Kendall (Eva-Marie Saint), evading the police, when they board it, with her help, and spending the night in her sleeping-berth—and perhaps bunk. Eve has an accomplice on the train, but we don't know, yet, with whom she is working. She helps him evade the station police by disguising him as her porter and offers to find Kaplan for him. On her instructions, he takes a 'bus to a country cross-roads, where a crop-spraying biplane suddenly machine-guns him. He takes refuge in a patch of corn. Driven out by the 'plane's pesticide, he manages to stop a gasoline truck into which the 'plane crashes.

Thornhill returns to Eve's hotel, and demands explanations, but she prevaricates, and he follows her to an art auction, where he finds her with Van Damm's hand lying lightly, possessively, upon her neck. With them is Eve's accomplice on the train, Leonard, and the hoods. Thornhill, really, or apparently, preoccupied with Eve's perfidy, briefly arouses Van Damm's jealousy over his encounter with Eve on the train. The latter's thugs block every exit, and Thornhill escapes by insane and obstreperous bidding which upsets the auction and gets him safely arrested by the police. The Professor, quietly present, makes a phone-call.

The police-car doesn't take Thornhill to the station, and his fears of another abduction aren't relieved until he is taken to an airport and meets The Professor, who explains Eve's role as their agent and asks him to help quell the suspicions which his little scene has aroused in Van Damm's mind. In a cafeteria near Mount Rushmore, with the gigantic heads of four American Presidents carved in stone, Thornhill offers Van Damm a deal. He will keep silent about Van Damm's activities, if Van Damm abandons Eve, whom Thornhill passionately hates, to punishment as a traitor. Before Van Damm can reply, Eve shoots Thornhill dead at point-blank range.

The Professor has the corpse whisked off in an ambulance, where it revives, and, meeting Eve in a pine forest, under the Professor's paternal eye, forgives her for sending him off to his death, and understands her patriotic prostitution. But their confession of love turns sour as he realises that she has agreed to the Professor's request that she return, with Van Damm, to the country for which he has been working. Attempting to restrain her, Thornhill is knocked out by a burly Ranger, and wakes to find himself locked in a hospital ward.

Escaping, via a window and a lonely woman's room, he goes to Van Damm's mountain eyrie in a rusticised International style penthouse Through its glass walls he watches Leonard warn Van Damm against Eve and finally prove his point by shooting him with Eve's revolver—loaded with blanks. Thornhill, scribbling a warning on his personalised matchbook for Eve to find, flees with her, and finds himself climbing down the countenances of the American Presidents. He clings to the rockface with one hand, holding Eve, who has slipped, with the other. As Leonard stands over them, he asks, 'Help me'. Leonard's shoe presses on his hand, until he is shot by a police marksman summoned by the Professor. Thornhill hauls Eve into the upper bunk of the berth on which they are now returning to New York, married and without fear.

The film's main pattern is clear enough. Thornhill the slick city manipulator finds himself on the run in a series of predicaments in which he is the manipulated and which are nightmarish exaggerations of all that is predatory in his own cynicism. The melodramatic terms are transcended by a poetic sense whose theme is suggested by settings each of which, in comparison with the Madison Avenue spirit which informs him, might seem idealistic or idyllic—the U.N. Building; the Glen Cove mansions; the farmlands of the Middle West; the world of art; the faces of the noblest American Presidents; a lady's sleeping berth; and a penthouse-type mountain residence. Their *real* moral value is rather different, of course. The farmlands are bleak, spacious, and uncomfortable, because money-making is their object. The Glen Cove mansions and the penthouse-type mountain 'cottage' are merely the luxuries of ambition fulfilled. The art auction indicates the capture of the muses by Mammon. And the shrines of idealism (the U.N. Building, the Mount Rushmore Presidents) are also the locales of extreme violence. At any rate, the apparent contrast is part of one's experience of the film, looming, indeed, rather larger than the underlying affinity.

Roger's profession, his 'theft' of a taxi, a few cynical asides about the insignificance of prestige as against money, are all that's needed to establish shallowness, which is gradually confirmed by his treatment of a not unfriendly policeman, by the mention of several convictions for drunken driving, by his bantering cynicism about his mother, and by the personalised matchbook from which he lights Eve's cigarette at her first meeting. It is a white blank, save for the initials, R.O.T., in a pretentious typography whose central initial looms largest. 'What does the "O" stand for?' Eve asks, and he replies, almost as if bewildered by such a question, 'Nothing. Nothing at all.' Having freely chosen to emphasise the zero in himself, he is spiritually as anonymous as the New York crowd from which he seems socially distinct. And the injustices he endures are poetic. He is mistaken for a man who doesn't exist, and the only people who have any reason to doubt that he isn't Kaplan is his mother who can't believe that her boy can be in any serious danger from anyone, be it the judge or the hoodlums sent after him. It isn't only Eve who betrays him. For everyone else, Thornhill is Kaplan, or Townsend's murderer, or anyone whose social moves he happens to make. His attempt to produce a social consensus as to his identity is frustrated because the real Townsends are away— accident? destiny? a comment on the fluidity of American society? The false Townsend is uninterested in his proofs of identity: 'They forge them so well nowadays.'

Thornhill's initials correspond to, not Joyce's H.C.E., Here Comes Everybody, but H. C. A., for Here Comes Anybody, just as Kaplan's are H. C. N., for Here Comes Nobody. Thornhill has chosen to emphasise the O in himself, for it sounds good, and Kaplan is like the soul that he's lost, the un-man ghost that hounds him, created, not by God, or providence, but by inter-bureaucratic antagonisms and secrecies. Thornhill can't be rescued from the miscarriages of justice. It's another Story of O.

Thornhill's dictating on the run, and improvising, from a conversational hint, the lie that gets him his taxi, starts the film's two kinds of communication, mental (words and images) and physical (taxi, automobile, train, bus, plane). Thornhill manipulates all the communications media, and not just the mass ones. Even under arrest he treats the police officer as a secretary, inducing him to dial the number and then replace the receiver on the hook for him. In the same scene, the substitution of name for identity is the only possible reason for an otherwise irrelevant aside. Thornhill asks the police officer's name, and the officer, after briefly stiffening at being thus rendered personal and vulnerable, replies, 'Emil Klinger', fuming as Thornhill rolls his eyes in exasperated contempt at a name whose absurdity is at once patent and hard to explain. The un-smart pronunciation, 'Ay-mil', fortifies the surname's *klang*-effect, 'clinker-clanger', thus underlining an ethnic reference. The common American confusion between names of Germanic extraction and Jewish names produces the surprise of a Jewish cop instead of the conventional Irish Catholic one. If Emil Klinger is a Jewish cop he's very much an odd man out in his profession (at least by reference to stereotypes about New York Irish cops), and maybe that's why he's slightly vulnerable and slightly patient. It may not escape our notice that Kaplan is a Jewish name also.

To Thornhill's slickness Van Damm opposes a very formidable combination; the high prestige rating of a Dutch name, the suave phraseology of extreme affluence, and the gun in the small of the back, the latter representing, of course, the nitty-gritty. Although he is only pretending to be the Townsend who will shortly address the U.N. Assembly, he would clearly be capable of so doing. He is beyond manipulation, and almost beyond communication. Even when Thornhill is right about Eve's feelings for him, and, either calculatingly or recklessly or both, tries to split Eve from Van Damm, Van Damm interprets the truth as a trick, and so, in fact, frustrates Thornhill's game. The two men swop several cutting remarks about theatrical unreality or over-dramatic behaviour, thus making of informal everyday contacts another medium of fiction, which of course they partly are. And Leonard can persuade Van Damm of Eve's perfidy only by the ultra-theatrical trick of pretending to shoot him, provoking an, as it were, direct, subjective, experience of physical death. This reversibility in the relationship between theatre and reality matches the reversibility of the photographic image, a medium more characteristic of Thornhill. His photograph of the false Townsend is a clue which the real Townsend recognises, but leads only to the half-truth of the newspaper photographs which make Thornhill look like Townsend's murderer. Perhaps it is Thornhill's sense of the power of mendacity which provokes his flight. Eventually he is reduced to a scribble on his match-box, flicked on to a rug, lying white and 'naked' close by the shoe which Leonard will shortly be pressing on his knuckles. In extremes he can utter only two primitive words: 'Help me . . .' and the 'me' isn't selfish, for it means, also, 'help me to hold her'. The phrase assumes that the hand which will let go is not the hand holding her, but the hand holding them both, and that's communication. His plea is the antithesis, also, of the smart, wry remarks which have been sometimes indicative of his resilience, and sometimes, especially in his encounter with Eve on the train, irritatingly redolent of an indefinitely prolonged adolescence. Van Damm's way with words develops in the other direction. After so many little 'happenings' with blanks, a shot rings out and Leonard's shoe ceases pressing on Thornhill's hand, twists sideways, and prompts Van Damm's 'That's not fair, you're using real bullets'. The irony is unfeeling, but appeals to a code which is not so much adolescent as childlike, and quite unreal. The wise-crack, as mask, i.e. as a useful, albeit abusable kind of inauthenticity, contrasts with the humourless forms of high art: the auction whose values and procedures Thornhill disrupts, the primitive African sculp-ture which Van Damm purchases to hide the microfilm, and the faces of Mount Rushmore.

The theme of communication interlocks with that of mysterious functional systems. The spies and the counter-espionage network exist beyond, yet eerily aloof from, the more familiar agencies which attract rather more hostility (and so threaten Thornhill) but have a more human face. Just as Klinger helps Thornhill phone his mother, so the judge is prepared to investigate his unconvincing story of abduction.

The complacency of 'rot' masks not so much familiar dissatisfac-tions and self-disgusts as hidden systems which, more abstruse and dangerous, correspond to a Machiavellianism of power. Adopting the protective colouration of everyday reality, they reduce it to absurdity. The counter-espionage network creates Kaplan even to the dandruff on the suit. Van Damm reduces Thornhill's story to absurdity by calling on his sister, a smooth worldly hostess. She it so happens, re-sembles Thornhill's mother even to the colour of her hair. Mrs. Thornhill, meeting her son's pursuers in the lift, asks, with just that hint of serious concern which endows her incredulity with absurd feminine credulousness asks, 'You men aren't trying to kill my son, are you?'

After a little hesitation they laugh, she laughs, everyone in the lift laughs, and the absurdity is briefly just a little like the musical execu-tion in *Goto, Ile de l'Amour*. Thornhill sinks miserably into himself, crushed not so much by fear as by a shame which links with the theme of communication (this little group being halfway between a 'mass' and something more intimate) and which might conceivably paralyse any attempt at escape. But he has enough *nous* to keep his head and cut and run. The theme of public scandal recurs in the embarrassingly absurd story he has to tell in court, in his behaviour in the art auction, in the public shooting at the cafeteria. And it is arguable that in braving public ridicule and scandal Thornhill is braving the most con-strictive and debilitating fears of modern man. All his vulgarities are the converse of Van Damm's secrecy and suavity.

Thornhill, trying to convince Van Damm of his true identity, adopts a light, prim, irresponsible, slightly feminine posture, faintly reminiscent of Leonard, whose soft easy style goes with cold tense eyes to respond to a familiar stereotype of homosexuality (maybe his name evokes the Leopold and Loeb case which inspired *Rope*). Thornhill, certainly, has his problems with women. He is a ladies' man, a charmer of older women especially, but, in the train, his response to Eve's forwardness has an 'Oh boy, have I hit the sexpot jackpot here!' adolescent glee later exacerbated by his continuing wisecracks. As Eve remarks, his divorces indicate not, as he thinks, that he likes women, but quite the reverse. The climax includes an oddly-placed digression: Thornhill, cliffhanging, alleges that his wives divorced him because he led too dull a life. But if the irony makes an immediately effective gag, it hardly develops our knowledge of Thornhill's past, or taste in women. Yet it's worth embarking on a process which is not so much an exegesis of the remark as concocting another film corresponding to certain clues in this one. Thus one may take our first cue from Thornhill's sensitivity to his own bruises and the extent to which his first response to danger is a realistic yet in a sense feminine confidence in words, in tact, in subtleties like the low snob-value of a name like 'Emil Klinger'. We might suppose that, by affinity of opposites, the women by whom he allowed himself to be married were tougher than he, and either disdained that game or played it more honestly. One might imagine his first two wives as Grace Kelly and Ava Gardner in *Mogambo*, craving a man 'manlier' than he. Better still, we can imagine how the Grace Kelly of *To Catch A Thief* might have reproached him for not being that film's Cary Grant rather than this one's. His previous married wives are like a converse of the situation in *Rear Window*. That image-maker, a man of rugged action, chafes in New York's two-by-four apartments, while his fiancée wants him to lead a comfortable social life in society. This image-maker has to be driven away from his comforts. But if at some time his wives had hoped he might prove less dull than he did, they weren't hopelessly wrong, for, here, at bay, he reveals sufficient resources for survival. Certainly he never ceases trying to manipulate others, but he is independent, forceful and self-reliant, and what he learns is difficult to define, for although the resilience which brought Thornhill his worldly success has to adapt to a more basic menace it's doubtful whether the film is a story of purgation by adventure so much as of revelation through adventure.

Certainly he progresses, we may assume, from a petulant easy-come-easy-go where marital difficulties are concerned, to braving, in his relationship with Eve, a variety of disillusionments and obstacles. And one might leap to the conclusion that this represents a change from irresponsibility to responsibility in the normal moral sense. But the matter as a whole is not so simple.

The melodrama exists, indeed, primarily for Thornhill to liberate himself from an irresponsibility which is not so much an active cynicism as an absence of idealism. It offers him the threat of death, and the possibility of love, and a confusion which makes it necessary for him to clarify just that choice between easy self-concern and affirmation which reality has yet to clarify, thus holding him in thrall. Eve Kendall has already escaped these equivocations. She 'decided to fall in love' with Van Damm, being disillusioned by men like Thornhill who 'don't believe in marriage'. And one may well prefer to read this as a belief in commitment, rather than as the very much more shallow belief in bourgeois forms to which the phrase undoubtedly lends itself. (Here, as in Thornhill's remark about a dull life, Hitchcock, rather anxiously, blunts the edge of criticism of anything except Madison Avenue, about which his audience will be sufficiently cynical already.) But the Professor enlightened her as to Van Damm's nastier activities, and 'It was the first time anyone had ever offered me a chance to do anything worthwhile'. (Thus, diffusely, a note of radical criticism is sounded, although there are various escape clauses, e.g. Eve comes from the class of the idle rich to which Melanie in *The Birds* will also belong, and the dampers of distractive excitement are immediately applied.) If her life has ceased to be dull, it is because it has ceased to be equivocal (and here *North-by-North-West* links with the puritan tradition). It isn't accidental that Eve's idealism is cast in a negative form, i.e. it's a defensive action against a threat to America's power, rather than an attempt to improve America in some way, a hope which might be felt to be subversively reformist or naïvely do-gooder.

Thornhill's difficulties with women aren't a gratuitous sin on his part. His mother is a disconcerting and formidable creature. It's not in the least surprising if, as he confesses (and even if he's only pretending to confess, at least it did occur to him as a thing to confess), he doesn't like undressing in front of women. The critic who saw this as a by implication reprehensible Oedipal immaturity may have overlooked the fact that he's every bit as justified in his defensive suspicion of Eve as he is in the distinctly sardonic nature of his affection for his mother. Mrs. Thornhill snorts loudly and derisively at his story in the courtroom, thus expressing both her disrespect for the law and a perfect readiness to prejudice the judge against her son on what even given the film's comic tone hereabouts we don't altogether forget could be a very serious charge. She's an expert manipulator and can't resist using her skills to accept a bet in a way which suggests the combination of a disinterested dare and an interest in small sums. It's not surprising if Thornhill has just a streak of the sexual diffidence which in Leonard looks like homosexuality, nor that while Thornhill, like his mother, is a manipulator, only Leonard is feminine and misogynist enough to see through Eve. Through most of the film Van Damm is more completely Eve's victim than Thornhill, who is thus situated between the two villains, of whom one possesses a paternal authority and the other is a repudiation of heterosexual concern. It is quite true that Van Damm's paternalism reveals itself as egoist, megalomaniac, and maleficent, in the drearily stereotyped tradition of American melodrama, despite the redemptive conviction of James Mason's playing. But at least Hitchcock arrives at that stereotype via an unusual route, whereby, until the last scene, Van Damm seemed Eve's victim just because he's sufficiently passionate to be paternal and sufficiently heterosexual to be trusting. This sympathy for the devil is achieved without sacrificing our feeling that Thornhill loves Eve sufficiently to brave his jealousy of her other priorities, as the megalomanic cannot bear.

Hardly has Thornhill been liberated, by Eve's confession, from his jealousy of Van Damm before he is plunged into his second experience of rejection by her. Hitherto Eve served her country as an alternative to boredom. In the pine forest Thornhill realises that she also puts her patriotism, or the idealism which it represents, before her love for him. His relief leads immediately to disappointment, observing the traditional rule that every resolution of a dramatic tension must lead to a further tension. On one level the film asserts the paradox: 'I could not love thee, dear, so much, loved I not honour more.' On another level, the preceding variant of the paranoid Oedipal situation, in which the villainous rival possesses status, power and the beloved woman, is replaced by another, morally rather more complex, form. Here the mother-figure's own decision is clear and the father-figure represents a smoothly callous bureaucracy, like a paler Van Damm, but also America *vis-à-vis* Communism, which makes criticism far more difficult and which, whether or not it attracts love, certainly demands respect and sacrifices like love. In case we're tempted, in our sympathies for Thornhill, and our dislike of bureaucracies, or of American intelligence agencies, to query this respect and these sacrifices, we are reminded that America is near to losing the cold war against

Communism. And lastly the Professor recommends to Thornhill the philosophy of Teddy Roosevelt: 'Talk soft and carry a big stick'—a technique which is, of course, Van Damm's as well as his own. For Van Damm is to the Professor as Thornhill is to Leonard and as Bruno is to Guy in *Strangers On A Train*.

Thus America opposes her mixture of idealism and indifference to the unconsidered irresponsibility which has, no doubt, been Thornhill's creed so far. It emanates also from the aloof stone figure of Mount Rushmore, and from Eve's flesh-and-blood, with its crueller mixture of selflessness and perfidy, patriotism and prostitution, as if she were avenging her sister Alicia in *Notorious*. On a third level, therefore, Thornhill acquiesces in her acquiescence in what may be defined either as anti-Communist patriotism, or as responsibility towards ideals. But his acquiescence is not at all complete. Felled though he is by a Ranger's fist, locked though he is in a hospital's private ward, philosophically resigned to Eve's loss although he pretends to be, he sneaks off to the Van Damm house, altogether in defiance of the Professor's patriotic and idealistic plans. Thornhill certainly shows a sense of responsibility to Eve which contrasts to his glee in the train, but the word 'responsibility' can easily conceal the extent to which he is frustrating her responsibilities and her idealisms, and is prepared to wreck everything for which she and the Professor care, on behalf of his own purely personal devotion, which is in every way compatible with American individualism of an irresponsible kind. All in all the film offers no challenge to the social meaning of that relatively self-seeking philosophy whereby, to coin a phrase, 'What's best for Roger Thornhill is best for the U.S.A'. Personal responsibility is accepted, in contradiction to responsibility to others in the abstract. Conversely, Thornhill, asking for help, gets it, from the Professor, whose indifference has no malevolence whatsoever. In a way characteristic of Hitchcock's ambiguity, the film both denies and affirms the link between Thornhill and the government. And the synthesis, or compromise, between the contradictions is one of those valid truisms with which we began; freedom is a compromise between governmental power and individual freedom which allows a mixture of collaboration and an in some sense equal contest between the two. In the same way, there is no need to wonder whether Thornhill will renounce the lies of Madison Avenue as he returns to New York with Eve, or whether he's just a cock returning to his own dunghill. Thornhill and Eve together represent a combination, a compromise, between irresponsibility, and a responsibility which, like Eve's had a tendency to become a little chilling, and suicidal, and match the bleak coldness of the Russia towards which she was prepared to go.

These ambiguities are paralleled by carefully balanced tensions about Thornhill's involvement of the innocent in his attempts to save his own skin. Suspense as to whether, in his drunken state, he'll drive off the cliffs of Glen Cove, is balanced by suspense as to whether he'll crash into innocent drivers. And although it wouldn't be his fault if he did, his simpering slaphappy smile reinforces all the conventional associations of drunkenness with culpable irresponsibility, sufficiently for a little moral concern to appear. This particular drunkenness is only a repeat of the sort of sin a man of his kind might well have perpetrated, and it is likely that if he had killed a carload of innocent people the film's moral tone might have had to become a little more gruelling. Later, an accomplice of Van Damm's gets it, when he crashes into the gasoline tanker and bursts into flame. Hitchcock is careful to show the latter's crew get clear, and it's just as well, since Thornhill, by appealing to them for help, has involved them, and, dramatically, is partly responsible for putting their lives at risk. Less sensitive truck drivers, like those of *Easy Rider*, might have driven straight over him, and it would have been a poor reward for their neighbourly concern had the 'plane turned their bodies into human torches, as per the reverse fire-extinguisher of *Saboteur*. Spatially, this crash is the fulfilment of the Glen Cove cliff-edge drive, where in fact subjective shots compare the Mercedes trademark to a gunsight, just as the pilot's fall preludes that which Leonard gets instead of Thornhill.

Thornhill, by enlisting his mother's help, and Eve's, comes near endangering them, just as Eve, and the Professor, conscript him. His action is more natural, however, for he explains the situation to them, whereas they do not explain the situation to him. None the less, help is a social and human norm, and Thornhill's appeal to Leonard carries overtones which Hitchcock prefers not to develop. If Leonard had helped Thornhill and Eve to climb to safety, could they, fairly, have turned him in? Would they have had to let Leonard get to his destination, microfilm and all? And would the Professor not then have had to say, as Hartz in *The Lady Vanishes* says of the departing British, 'And jolly good luck to them'? As so often, Hitchcock slips neatly past any real moral crux, and those who see him as a challenging moralist only demonstrate how effectively his melodramatic and conformist preassumptions and his absurdist poetry conceal the real moral issues. Another resolution was perfectly possible. Leonard treads on

Thornhill's hand. Van Damm, having arrived by now, and passion-ately concerned, after all, for Eve, pushes Leonard off. The shot aimed at Leonard hits Van Damm, just as he is hauling his rival and Eve to safety. We have to acknowledge the personal decency of one dead spy. Or again: Leonard, realising he is cornered, tries to bargain with the Professor; Thornhill's and Eve's life against his freedom. They agree, and then double-cross him. And so on and so forth. An infinity of highly nuanced moral variants on that last scene are possible, and Hitchcock opts for the simplest, the most stereotyped, the morally slackest and the most banal. All the baddies are worse than you thought they were. And the Professor who at first was so callous turns out to be providential, as beyond criticism as the stern father of *Downhill*.

If the theme of responsibility is, in the end, betrayed, it's not that Hitchcock's passing tones are devoid of subtlety. Thornhill's odyssey includes a brief stint as a porter, and this writer, at least, isn't at all clear how he got his uniform. His escape is followed by a shot of a lean man in undervest and long johns emerging from a wagon and finding five one-dollar bills tucked in amongst them. An easy assump-tion is that Eve bribed him, but the tiny sum and his stunned expres-sion suggests rather that she beckoned to him and that Thornhill, or maybe even Leonard, knocked him out, pushed him in a toilet, undres-sed him and left him with a mean five dollars for all the strain and bother he's had and will have. Was it all the change she had on her, or is it a *mean* five dollars, like Mrs. Thornhill winning fifteen dollars from her son?

Thornhill's encounter with the gasoline truck has the sense of an-other such appeal to others. He 'steals' it as he 'steals' somebody else's taxi. One can imagine how a hard-core right-wing individualism would have handled that cornfield predicament. Pressing himself down amidst the roots and earth, Thornhill remembers his matchbook, and, setting fire to the crops, protecting the flame from the wind by dimly-remembered boy-scout techniques, makes a smokescreen which gives him a chance to run for the road and confuses the pilot into hitting the tanker. Thus the self-help of rugged individualism would replace an appeal to strangers—an appeal which Ayn Rand might well diag-nose as halfway to Socialism. There's an analogy in Ray Milland's *Panic In Year Zero*, where a stream of automobiles, fleeing from the doomed cities of World War III America, stop Ray Milland getting his family in their saloon on to the highway. He throws gasoline across it, and then a match into the gasoline, burning one innocent unfortunate alive (only one—not a family) but creating a flame barrier which gets him into the traffic stream. The contrast between the big city and the farmlands invited just some such test of primitivist survival, to which Hitchcock prefers his far more complex and interesting conjugation of solitude and social interdependence. Thornhill had had an early warning. A lean figure across the road could have been Kaplan, but turned out to be only a local farmer waiting for a 'bus going the other way. 'That's funny,' he remarks, as the 'bus distantly heaves into sight, 'that plane's spraying crops where there ain't no crops'. Thornhill, who in other ways is very quick on the uptake, might have got the point, and found safety in a lower-cost, collective form of transport. But he lets it go. And the lean cautious figure and Thornhill's query as to his name, and his reluctance to give it ('Cain't say it is, 'cos it ain't'), are evocative. As Van Damm's sister resembles Thornhill's mother, so this Nordic Middle West farmer resembles Emil Klinger, and Thornhill's major *dépaysement* here is tit for tat for his callow assurance there.

A theme of fists and hands might have lent itself to the common Social Darwinist emphasis on physical toughness as a moral duty to oneself. Will Thornhill's animal instinct or willpower enable him to overcome the debilitating effect of pampered living on Madison Avenue? Although, on one occasion, he can make a brief running fight of it, he's clearly not a man for physical showdowns, scandal and aggressive questioning being his main weapons. A handful of scenes receive heavy emphasis which establish violence and understanding as heads and tails of the same coin. As Thornhill shows Townsend a photograph of Van Damm, Townsend's eyes open wide in an astonishment which is abruptly overtaken by agony as the fatal knife plunges deep into his back (it is the knife which suggests that astonishment was not merely the beginning of agony; if Van Damm had to have him killed in public he must have known who Van Damm was). Later, the reversibility of physical and emotional pain is reasserted when Van Damm, angered by Leonard's proof of Eve's treachery, punches him, and what seems a valetudinarian wince at his jarred and torn knuckles becomes a spasm of emotional pain as he faces the truth about Eve. Violence is asserted as a brutal truth when Thornhill gets the Ranger's knockout punch, and we get it too, via a first-person camera recalling the photographic flash-bulbs which turn Thornhill's terrified, angry, active knife-in-hand crouch into an optical illusion of guilt. Leonard's shoe on Thornhill's knuckles is only the finishing touch, whereby the series 'violence is truth, truth violence' intersects with a theme which we might describe as the disappearance of the natural.

Madison Avenue is clearly the centre of big city moral corruption. Reality is as overgrown with its images, which are partly, or largely, or by omission, lies, as surely as the earth is encumbered with skyscrapers. There follows a general move towards the rural, the organic, the earthy. As Eve and Thornhill talk in the train, factories and sawmills flash by. Thornhill has a brief stint as a manual labourer (porter) before finding himself among the wheatfields of the Middle West. In the pine forest he hears the spiritually healing truth of Eve's idealism, and Mount Rushmore finds him at bay on the wild mountainside. But this development is contained within, and counterpointed by, a counter-movement. The Middle West is infested with the biplane, which is brilliantly ambiguous, being, as an aircraft, the latest and fastest form of locomotion, but also an obsolete type. At first merely the quiet snore of the drowsing landscape, it suddenly swells into an overwhelming danger. The healing scent of the pine forest is followed by the brutal knock-out punch of the Ranger's fist. And Mount Rushmore, the primal rock, has itself been carved into the faces of 19th and 20th century Presidents. Van Damm's eyrie is another such combination of the idyllic, in so far as it lets Nature in, like a log cabin, and of the egoistic, in so far as its penthouse-like structure is beyond even Thornhill's financial ambitions. It combines nature and culture much as does the African statuette with the microfilm within. And Eve and Thornhill, fleeing from Van Damm's house, find themselves standing just behind the back of the carved heads. The topographical propinquity of idealistic symbol and the spies' *pied-à-terre* invites a paranoid interpretation along Dalinian lines. The mountain becomes a head, and Van Damm's house, not so much repressed libido, as an alien, malign, disaffected intelligence. Eve loses her shoes in the scramble, but it is Leonard's shoe which answers Thornhill's cry for help, in its soft civilised armour. The implication isn't of a pollution of all nature by civilisation; the Presidents haven't desecrated the mountains. But everything is a mixture of the two. And if the white, moonlit carved stone implies an identity of wild nature and social ideal, those faces are sheer, impassive and cold as Thornhill and Eve hang from them. The episode becomes poetic partly because of all the moral which it can bear. Is it that our moral ideals have, by definition, every right to our sacrifices, and to extract them with no acknowledgement whatsoever? Is it that in an absurd world unblinking Providence is as stonily blind as the flashbulbs? Are those archaic stone faces a somewhat perilous haven, as the modern transparent house is a trap? Are those Presidential faces merely African statuettes demanding human sacrifice, one way or another, as of right? Is it essential that the private individual defy them, as Thornhill does?

Although some spectators may enjoy such ambiguities, the narrative's avoidance of genuine moral issues all but obliterates them altogether. The general theme has no great originality, the antagonism between patriotic duty and American individualism having been the matter of a thousand American movies, and one need hardly cite the far less sentimental outcomes of Samuel Fuller's *Pick Up On South Street*, *China Gate* and *Underworld U.S.A.* The second film opposes the essential decency of the American prostitute to Communist idealism, which, of course, it describes as fanaticism. The woman recalling the man to civic duty is another hardy American perennial, vide *On The Waterfront* and *Deadline U.S.A.*, Hitchcock avoiding even the problems of justifying the schoolmarm, do-gooder ethos by aligning the woman with the Cold War hawks.

I should find the film hard to justify as a *bildungsroman*, simply because Thornhill seems finally on his way back to Madison Avenue. And even if Eve will be there to influence him, to act as, in a way, his *anima* and his conscience, her presence reminds us just how little evidence of a profound spiritual experience the film provides. Briefly, his situations changed, and revealed what basically he always was. Perhaps he will backslide from saying 'Help me' sincerely, to stealing taxis on behalf of a damsel who isn't in distress at all. Perhaps saying 'Help me' sincerely is quite compatible with stealing taxis. Perhaps the film is a vindication of Madison Avenue as all right at heart. Perhaps the only reason for believing that some moral change has taken place in him as a result of his adventures is simply that there's some general impression to that effect. The film has to be sensed superficially, because on close examination its meaning turns out to be a variety of possibilities, some mutually exclusive.

But even if the melodramatic world helps Thornhill to go some way towards solving everyone's problem, of exactly how 'to distinguish those parts of our personality which belong to our ability as persons and those which are mere things which happen to us'[1], its conclusion isn't really something we hadn't thought of ('Be very attractive to a good, sexy and beautiful woman and once you've found her brave all sorts of difficulties to win her so that she can be a good influence on

[1] Alasdair MacIntyre, *Chairman's Opening Remarks*, in Wolfe Mays and S. C. Brown, eds., *Linguistic Analysis and Phenomenonology*, Macmillan, 1970.

you'). Its means are so grossly simplistic that neither he nor we waste very much time wondering how we ought to respond to the moral problems that come along. In this sense, indeed, it is very much simpler than, say, *Shadow Of A Doubt* nearly thirty years before, and the extent to which Thornhill's adventures are extraneous to moral or dramatic choices—are *machina ex deum*, as it were—may be illustrated by pondering the moral, psychological and philosophic opportunities which would have been offered by a straightforward *Executive Suite*-style story. One can imagine Thornhill, Eve, Van Damm, Leonard and the Professor as advertising executives and rivals warily circling, liking, confusing and destroying one another and themselves.[1]

It is true that the U.N. Building has a moral significance such that the notion of Van Damm addressing it, and the knife in Townsend's back, give us a shudder. But equally they might provoke the reflection that idealistic organisations are prone to infestation or infiltration by double-edged words and knives in backs, so that the U.N. stands for nothing more than gullibility. And both positions are asserted in different American pictures, e.g. the former in George Seaton's *The Rat Race* and the latter in Tay Garnett's *One Minute To Zero*. By and large the idealism in *North-by-North-West* is hawkish, in anticipation of Hitchcock's revival of the Russo-American Cold War in *Torn Curtain* and *Topaz*. Van Damm's association with the arts is conventional enough in Hollywood villains and spies, and to this extent the film accommodates a preference for the honest venality of Madison Avenue as against the sinister intellectuals, although, equally, the *aficionados* of the arts may object that Van Damm is misusing the arts. Perhaps Hitchcock feels about African statuettes the way D. H. Lawrence feels about them in *Women in Love*, or feels they evince a sinister, spiky fleshiness contrasting unfavourably with America's idealistic stone carvings. Or maybe the primitive fetish, concealing the ultramodern microfilm, is in only apparent contrast to the lofty heads behind which nestles the penthouse of treachery, and which remain impassive as individuals cling desperately to their unseeing features. All these contrasts are as piquant, and as equivocal, as the nun's dress sported by the patriotic criminal of *The Lady Vanishes*. Hitchcock rarely annoyeth for he rarely affirmeth. It is as vain to seek in such contrasts a moral statement as to seek in the contrast of quiet farmland and pesticidal biplane a moral about pesticidal biplanes.

[1] It is possible to see it as primarily a moral story only by taking the moral tensions which are part of the dramatic tensions and assigning to them a central importance, quite arbitrarily, since the film's outcome depends on a great many non-moral factors and amoral or immoral decisions.

These contrasts are synthetic not analytic. One might call them poetic rather than philosophical, in so far as they constitute a montage of symbols whose connotations are of all kinds, social, ideological, sensual, etc., and which by being brought into juxtaposition, create conflicts which aren't quite specific enough to be called dramatic. There is no more radical difference between a dramatic symbol and a poetic one than between a prosaic sentence and a poetic one, except the extent to which the former selects for emphasis one or two facets of its total range of meanings, while the latter, possibly for reasons of context rather than internal complexity, allows a softer, freer, fuller response which is felt as a lyrical atmosphere rather than a sense of alternatives or of utilitarian or exclusivist priorities. Certainly poetry requires a thematic armature. But the moral reading of a poem is not usually its full meaning (and to extend the word moral to cover every aspect of human activity is to deprive the word of any meaning). The question remains how far the moral aspects of this film constitute one of the strands of its poetic aspect, or vice versa, or how far meaning and absurdity religiously practised are positive and negative poles of an inalienable contradiction in man's predicament. Equally, the dramatic logic of *North-by-North-West* is only one of the aspects which make up the whole film, although, I would suggest, it is here, rather than in morality, that we can locate its thickest strands.

If it is here that its limitations are most evident, it none the less achieves (thanks, perhaps, to certain vibrations in the personalities of James Mason and Eva-Marie Saint, whose presence brings out unusually strong undertones in Cary Grant's brisk and efficient style), several sharp and sudden transitions between familiar realities, a particular attention to psychological and social innuendo, and extreme consequence. Within this general interaction, its middle-range limitations record, with fidelity, the only way in which to get to know the very little we know about almost everyone we say we know—through cryptic hints, asides, overtones—cracks in masks; and in this respect the film anticipates *Marnie, The Birds* and *Topaz*. Not that this, psychologically or morally, is in their class. But the strength and delicacy of Hitchcock's poetico-narrative tactics precipitate us into a strange mixture of a persiflage which is opportunistic and predatory rather than amiable, of interpersonal manipulation and erosion of identity, of Freudian structures which at moments are shared, almost as a joke, with the audience yet which, at others, take on an authentic uneasiness, together with bellypunch melodrama whose serial structure and real sense is of mixed nightmare and absurdity. Of the earlier picaresque thrillers, only *The Man Who Knew Too Much* is consistently in its class (and seems to me to surpass it, for its fuller possession of the dramatic middle-range).

Finally Thornhill's attempt to heave Eve back to safety becomes his hauling her back to the upper bunk in their sleeping compartment. It has to be the upper berth because it was there that, earlier, she protected him from the police, at some risk of smothering him. This shared, open berth is the middle term between that *womb*, that maternal constriction, and the cliff-edge suspension. The transition probably disappoints as it amuses us, because of our sense of all the unworked-out tensions in Thornhill's progress, for which it substitutes a neat visual pun on the touching of hands. It may be that this disappointment is part of the film's meaning, is Hitchcock's comment on the sort of spiritual insight that appears during extraordinary situations and disappears as soon as complacency and banal social reality return. If *North-by-North-West* isn't as obviously pessimistic as *Rich and Strange*, there's still some reason to suppose that Thornhill has captured Eve and converted her to his values, and to suppose that the train entering the tunnel on the way to New York is re-entering that spiritually closed world.

If *Vertigo* precedes, develops and surpasses the glint in fashion's eye that was Andy Warhol, *North-by-North-West* continues its paraphrase of Antonioni. Both *Vertigo* and *L'Avventurà* feature labyrinthine windings in search of a missing person. *North-by-North-West*, which dates from the same year, dwells on long train journeys, inexplicable disappearances. Thornhill becomes a non-man as the climax of *L'Eclisse* is a human absence. In the glassy edifice of idealism, Thornhill sees a man stabbed in the back. An idealist lies dying behind a clinic's glassy façade in *La Notte*. A woman who may be nymphomaniac through solitude and imminent death offers and withdraws herself; Hitchcock's romantic lighting suggests that Eve is abandoning herself to sensuality with the man whom tomorrow she will send to his death, and later he briskly dismisses the lonely offer of a woman in a sanatorium's private ward. A man alone at a peaceful crossroads with its aerial danger balances the deserted crossroads, suddenly ominous, with its impalpable atomic bomb. The murder in the park in *Blow-Up* is all but Hitchcock, even down to the elderly woman in tweeds.

In the entertainment melodrama, death-by-cancer becomes death-by-murder; despair becomes distrust, uneasiness becomes terror. Yet the ambiguities are not completely stultified by the either-or of sus-

pense. Certain scenes in Antonioni evoke feelings mimed without the
tennis-ball of vital passion, while Hitchcock, like a fairy godfather,
waves melodrama's magic wand, which transforms the ball into a
grenade timed to explode at the hundredth impact and kill either Guy
or Bruno facing each other across the moral net. Hitchcock's universe is Antonioni's, with atavisms to simple loyalties and unconscious
fantasies. Alongside this modernity, lightness and ellipse transform a
drama into what Robin Wood seeks to defend as 'a light comedy',
but maybe it's more than that. For all the complacency of the conventions which Hitchcock has never, since *Sabotage*, and even including
Psycho, quite been able to bring himself to query, he achieves his un-
canny dislocation of tone.

Eve, being disenchanted with men like Thornhill, sends this Thornhill to his death, and the film's idiom, thereabouts, is of a sad, cool,
clear, conscious apathy. Comparisons with Kafka can come too
easily; her apathy goes with lucidity, with energy. If life were only a
little different, its options a little less veiled. . . . And the best melodrama can play the role of a science-fiction society, indicating not so
much what is unconscious, as what is quite conscious, but can, or has
to, be dismissed because it is in the nature of our society to spare us
those extreme situations in which certain choices might become possible, or even mandatory. One may, of course, prefer, in this respect,
for all its last-reel collapse and its lack of Hitchcock's unique finesse,
Elio Petri's *The Tenth Victim*. None the less, the theme of espionage all
but transcends Manichean melodrama by becoming the basis of what,
in structure, is a comic heroic epic which is rarely denuded of poetry.
The dissonant atmospheres of the settings sap the limitations of the
narrative, compounding its conventionality by an atmospheric morality which is no more Jansenist than it is Methodist or humanist, and
glitters with a magical coldness because of its very ambiguity. A moralist critic has implied that Thornhill's ordeals are the consequence of
his rushing for a business lunch and stealing a taxi. Yet such ominous
consequences reduce the very notion of morality to absurdity. For
stealing a taxi and writing dishonest copy and being unreasonable
with women and preferring cash to prestige are everyday sins best
punished in everyday terms. Such enormous consequences as Thornhill suffers here suggest, poetically, Dante's Inferno, and perhaps
melodrama is Hitchcock's sceptical paraphrase of sermons analogous
to those inflicted on another pupil of the Jesuits in James Joyce's
Portrait Of The Artist As A Young Man. Fritz Lang said something
similar when he observed that if violence fascinates modern movie

audiences it is because they have lost their fear of Hellfire (i.e. violence in perpetuity). But one's objection to notions of Hellfire parallels one's objections to melodrama. Such enormous punishments reduce the notion of morality to absurdity, for even the Old Testament law of talion requires only 'an eye for an eye'. Those who rush around New York will have chronic dyspepsia and taxi thieves will have taxis stolen from them. One may, of course, shift ground, and argue that in Thornhill's case his venial sins are only apparently minor symptoms of a fatal moral disease, that they are, so to speak, the inoffensive little sores of moral syphilis, an attitude certainly compatible with Cardinal Newman's reflections to the effect that, given the remarkable goodness of God, the least of sins is worse than the non-existence of man. And even though this may in turn remind us of the Stoics', and Jansen's, insistence that the least of sins can damn as thoroughly as the greatest, the fact that Newman was a converted Anglican reminds us that Jansenism is hardly appropriate, and that there is no reason to suppose that in any but the exceptional Hitchcock film, e.g. *The Wrong Man*, a specifically or exclusively Christian frame of reference is to be applied. It is, as usual, unclear whether Thornhill is particularly wicked, or whether he deserves his trials because he is particularly redeemable ('The Lord chastiseth whom he loveth'), or whether he is undergoing a trial for reasons as enigmatic as Job, or whether the disproportion between fault and ordeal expresses that precariousness of consequence to which civilised man is as prone as primitive man (one moment's inattention as you cross a busy road and you've passed a death sentence on yourself; or do so many victims of a road accident deserve to die?). A sense of ironically inappropriate injustice accounts rather better for Hitchcock's dramatic structures, whether one refers to the boy blown up by a terrorist bomb in *Sabotage* or the 'punishment' of theft by a particularly vicious murder in *Psycho*. Strangely enough, all the imputations of Catholic orthodoxy, or heretical Jansenism (Calvinism), or Freudianism, respect the impossibility of a 'moralistic calculus' rather better than a secularised fundamentalism borrowed from F. R. Leavis; even though that has the merit of clearing away inappropriate metaphysic and introducing us to a Hitchcock whose audiences are largely secularised. Of these alternatives, a Freudian interpretation seems the most appropriate, not only because of its currency among American audiences, but because of the multiplicity of overt references in Hitchcock's work, and because the equation of Hitchcock melodrama with the super-ego's relationship to libidinal menace, severe reaction-formation, and ego-ideal accounts very wel

for the mixture of rigour, injustice, and absurdity, laxness and humanity in the cause-and-consequence pattern.

This is far from saying that morality has no presence in Hitchcock
at all. Clearly it has, and one might well argue that Hitchcock's preference for melodrama derives from his very reluctance to examine the
divergences between the various kinds of morality summarised by
Maria Ossowska; axiology (what ought, in terms of moral value, to
be done), praxiology (what leads to the achievement of one's aims),
characterology (what sort of character it is best to have) and felicitology (what leads to happiness). It is plain that an axiom like 'Honesty
is the best policy' derives its appeal from its assurance that there is no
conflict between axiology and praxiology, an assurance also underlining the Hays Office Code. And 'Hays Office morality' is perhaps a
suitably opprobious term for a moral complacency in which Hitchcock
too often and too extensively indulges to be described as a 'profound'
moralist. 'Serious' he may be, but only in the sense in which the earnest
and the superficial are combined, as they may be by a Sunday School
teacher. Even less is Hitchcock concerned to delve very deeply into the
divergences between the ordinary man's vague humanism, his vague
conventionalism, his vague Christianity, and his vague Machiavellianism. Films like *North-by-North-West* accommodate rather than query
the man-in-the-seat's sense of balance between (on the one hand) a
consensus conflation of the moral positions most widespread within
the Western world and (on the other) a sense of the effective and even
spiritual limits of that moralism (as marked by, notably, Social Darwinism in America, as *The Birds* makes plain). Hitchcock's, moral
'absurdity' derives from the incoherences, divergences and contradictions between these positions. He seems rather to work to one of
the less unintelligent of the Hollywood rules of thumb, whereby a
certain degree of moral ambivalence can heighten tension, while too
much induces instead confusion, apathy or protest against the film.
This psychological structure shouldn't seem strange, after Freud, but
quite apart from Freud we all know how suspense, to be pleasurable,
depends on a certain relationship between fear and reassurance. Too
little fear, and we are bored, too little reassurance, and our pleasurable
screams become a cold sweat. The very multiplicity of moral positions
which *North-by-North-West* can accommodate is evidence that although it isn't an amoral film it's moral structure isn't its 'moral', its
meaning being dramatic, or melodramatic, and poetic.

The skill with which Hitchcock weaves moral strands into a dramatic, that is to say, a non-moral, web, is evidenced by Thornhill's

drunken drive along the Glen Cove road. He gets away from his assassins (who carefully follow him) by hurtling towards a police-car, a collision with which any motorist dreads above all others, although, here, it scares his assassins off. There's nothing more or less moral about hitting a police-car than any other automobile; but Hitchcock's solution, precipitating Thornhill from one peril to another, which saves him, shows a neat flair for economy and contradiction. Although the threat of imminent death is chilling, the drive is also hilarious, by identification with Thornhill's happy drunkenness, as well as offering a familiar exhilaration (fast and carefree night driving) and three different kinds of fear (1, fear of crashing off the cliff edge, 2, the only partly ethical fear of hitting and killing other road-users, 3, fear of the following hoods). Any melodramatist could derive one fear from the situation. Only Hitchcock's inventive mind and quick bold style could concoct and counterpoint three, and climax them in a manner which simultaneously introduces another.

The same neatness recurs even in little asides whose overtones, far from being moral, are caviare for the connoisseurs of the absurd. As Hitchcock informed Bogdanovitch, 'The whole film is epitomized in the title—there is no such thing as north-by-north-west on the compass'. But the title is also, as a tailfin reminds us, something of an advertising slogan, because there is a North West Airlines, by which the Professor takes Thornhill from Chicago to Dakota. And Van Damm's departure with Eve to Russia would prolong that straight line, which is roughly north-west. The geographically continuous line is a dramatic contradiction, and both the internal structure of Hitchcock's films and their rapport with popular audiences, who may not share his moral seriousness, or his sense of the absurd, depend on this mixture of like and unlike, exactly as does metaphor, not on the simple block-meanings beloved of narrowly rationalist exegesis.

A fondness for simple *lexical* symbols (based on only a signifier-signified relationship), as opposed to what one might baptise the *dramatic* symbol, being based on internal contradiction, might lead one to all sorts of falsely profound interpretations. Thus 'Thornhill' might suggest some sort of moral crown of thorns, with Mount Rushmore as Golgotha, the Place of the Skulls, and thorns linking with rushes to suggest a vegetation myth somehow related to Christian salvation theory, with Van Damm as an obvious snake in the grass and Eve the prize with the Professor relating to the tree of knowledge. It is quite possible that some of these associations crossed Hitchcock's mind; but even in so far as it fits, the allegory adds nothing of great value to the dramatic experience, since it is borrowed from the dramatic experience. It is true that to generalise from part of the content of the film to another sphere, i.e. that of religious thought, and then to feed that back into the experience of the film, may enrich the total complex of ideas involved in the film, but this is simply to say that to arrange interactions between conventionally delimited areas of thought, enriches thought, and it should not be confused with an account of the normative dramatic experience of the film. The objection to these kinds of theological allegorisation is the implication that intellectual generalisation is closer to some real profundity than the dramatic experience. Thus they not only substitute extrapolation into ideology for a full account of the film, but tend to diminish the diversity of thematic within the experience. Thus the theological interpretation can make nothing of the name 'Emil Klinger', which is emphasised within the narrative, whereas the personal (dramatic) experience composes a structure capable of accommodating both the social and the theological meanings. Our argument is not that the latter are *prima facie* absurd, merely that their reinforcement within the dramatic content is so thin that that meaning and the drama throw too little light on each other for the former to be of much worth. One might accept them as an overtone but not as a thematic armature. In contrast, the aside about Emil Klinger's name is all the more interesting for provoking a definite response (a laugh in the audience, a sneer in Thornhill) without being a logical tautology. The theological theme is so thin that it can *only* be developed along conventional lines. As an exegesis it is merely an intellectual drill.

Even when this drill has been performed, it fails to explain the film, because its relation to the ostensible action is one of contrast. It is paradoxical that so brisk, bland and dapper a character as Cary Grant's Thornhill should be considered as walking through the stations of the cross; and this 'meaning' can only exist in contrast, in, so to speak, a 'montage' relationship to the film. Nor is it expressed as a 'sign'; it is a product of a logical process; it is closer to the product of a montage, the tertium quid or synthesis which is itself a term in, not particularly a 'higher' dialectic, but simply *another* one.

It is probably true that the commoner forms of semiological theory, montage theory, and dramatic theory, tend to exclude one another; the first stressing the richness of implication within units of meaning, the second stressing the subordination and transformation of those meanings, the third stressing the importance of psychological experiences and responses. The theoretical reconciliation shouldn't be too difficult, being itself little more than a drill, and anticipated, however imperfectly, by uneducated intuition and traditional critical practice.

Psycho

Hitchcock claims *Psycho* is primarily a fun picture—'you see it's rather like taking them through the haunted house at the fairground'. Most of Hitchcock's work answers to this description, and *Psycho* is a *pot-pourri* of *Charley's Aunt*, *Bluebeard*, *Sweeney Todd*, *Oedipus Rex* with additional dialogue by Sigmund Freud, and *The Laurel and Hardy Murder Case*. All of which doubtless precipitated the initial critical reaction of distaste and revulsion, although second thoughts, by a younger generation of critics, reasserted Hitchcock as an earnest moralist and a film-maker of some finesse.

The camera climbs towards a window like any other window. Documentary-style, a subtitle states time and date; but it really means: Here and Now, at this moment, without warning, imperceptibly, destiny entered these lives. On a hot day, during their lunch-break, in an impersonal hotel bedroom, Marion Crane (Janet Leigh) and Sam Loomis (John Gavin) are half-naked and necking. The nightmare begins at noon. The heat, the bleached feel of the visuals, the half-naked-ness, the time, evoke an atmosphere of unsatiated sensuality (indeed, the heavy petting of so many of Hitchcock's American films, from *Notorious* to *North-by-North-West*, suggests a frustrating coldness, even, intercourse with neither orgasm nor emotional relief). In a very matter-of-fact way the lovers are discussing the man's divorce and the money they need if they are to marry. The general situation—half-stripping at lunchtime and then talking about cash—is vaguely offensive; yet they seem decent people, we accept and care about them. This ambiguity pervades their whole relationship. In some way Sam seems petulant, weak, unworthy; in others, Marion seems prim, tough, less concerned with unconditional love than with—respectability? Are they in love or only convinced they are? At any rate, we're not especially anxious for them to get married. In default of the money, she is tempted to break off the affair, and we are sufficiently disquietened to watch with something between curiosity and concern, rather with an eagerness for them to get married and live 'happily ever after'.

Marion returns to the sane, shallow, superficial people of the office where she works. It's not long before sex and cash are intertwined again. A fat client makes a rather coarse and vulgar attempt to flirt with her, brandishing a fat bankroll in her face. The other office-girl, a plain and silly creature, is naïvely jealous of these gross attentions. 'I expect he saw my wedding ring.' Her self-consoling remarks rubs salt in Marion's wound. We agree with her feeling that she is too pretty, efficient, sincere in love, to deserve to be worse off than this other girl. The fat customer brags that he wouldn't miss the money if it were stolen, and Marion's boss absolutely insists on entrusting it to her. Such smug, imperceptive responses all round reinforce our feeling that Marion has as much right to this excess money as its actual owner. These pinpricks accumulate into a kind of obsession and reinforce the confusion between her respectability (or pride) and her love (or sensuality). The money seems to offer a solution to all these 'raw edges' of feeling. Her theft is (so to speak) an impulse born of converging obsessions, which suddenly click into place forming an irresistible urge. It is also a tribute to her daring, her strength of passion; ~~there is an element of moral *hubris vis-à-vis*~~. There is also an element of *hubris vis-à-vis* her lover, as if in acting so boldly where he has been so weak she is taking over the initiative—and is not going to be thanked for her devotion. Soon she is driving hard away from town, tormented not so much by conscience as by fear. We can't believe she'll get away with it, especially as criminals never do in American films. We hope she will, and there is still a get-out: the theft won't be noticed until Monday morning, she can always return the money. Will she go on to decide to return it, but lose it? will someone else steal it from her? will Sam betray her, by his weakness, somehow?

A big, brutal-looking motor-bike cop with dark glasses trails her, suspiciously. His menacing figure recalls the law-breakers of *The Wild One* and the motor-cyclists of *Orphée* who ran men down in the name, not of justice, but of a law above the law, the brutal Will of destiny. He is 'the law', but he has a special, *personal* brutality of his own. Is he really following her, or is she only imagining he is? The psychological pressures complicate and intensify. To shake him off, she exchanges her car at a garage run by a very obliging character, apparently the very antithesis of the cop. The cop is saying, 'I remind you of punishment: turn back!' the garagehand, 'I make crime pleasant and easy, go on'. She acquires a white car—the colour of her underwear in the necking scene, the colour of innocence and dissatisfied sensuality; but all her precautions are of no avail. The cop still tails her, a terrifying dark angel sent to give her a last chance. Or sent simply to torture her, to diminish her chances: for without him she has a week-end in which to repent. There is danger of, as it were, rape-by-justice. We sigh with relief when at last she shakes him off.

She is beyond the reach of the law—or fear—now. But—where is she? The rain pours down across the windscreen, blurring lights and creating a wavering landscape. She is in what in *Orphée* is called *la Zone*, the no-man's-land between reality and the nightmare. The cop was both danger and safety. It is almost as if he were sent, after all, not to turn her back, but to make her drive on. The theological notion of double predestination provides a clue, 'God sends sinners a chance to repent *in order that* by rejecting it, as he knows they will, they will damn themselves more thoroughly than ever.' But as she reasons with herself, she is beginning to realise the futility of her theft—Sam is too sensible to accept the money. . . .

The rain forces her into a motel, managed by Norman Bates (Anthony Perkins). Norman is an engagingly naïve country youth, very honest, unconcerned with making money, almost a symbol of rustic virtue and country contentment. The whole film hinges on his sensitivity and charm—we tend to like him whatever his faults. His friendliness is all the more reassuring in contrast with the sinister atmosphere (the stuffed birds of prey, the Victorian house just behind the motel, where his petulant, tyrannical old mother lives). He seems tainted by the atmosphere, but the over-obvious horror clichés shift our suspicions from Norman to the atmosphere; they camouflage the inevitably stilted presentation of his relationships with Mrs. Bates; they contrast with the slick, modern, informal style of the film as a whole. Mrs. Bates comes from Norman's childhood and it's fitting that she should exist in an aesthetic idiom now considered childish— she would feel quite at home in James Whale's *The Old Dark House*.

Marion calls Norman's bird-stuffing a rather morbid hobby and says Norman resembles the dead birds of prey. Hitchcock plays fair with his audience, even while misleading us. True, he lets us believe in Mrs. Bates—but so do Marion, and Norman. Maybe, as the psychiatrist says later, Norman was never entirely Norman, he faintly knew the truth about Mrs. Bates—but then again Mrs. Bates is very stilted, we only half-believe in her.

Norman cheerfully admits to his faults of character; he is a very reasonable, modest guy. Gradually Marion realises that she is his superior, that, if unhappy, she is self-possessed, whereas his 'contented' acquiescence in looking after his domineering mother has something weak and helpless. His wisdom about money and the example of his servitude help to free her from the power of her impulse. She realises that what she stole was not love but only money, an attempt to avoid her problems. Norman is almost a sacrificial victim whose tragic example frees her.

But he is not a hopeless case. We feel that she owes it to him to return the favour. We want him to be freed from his horrible mother for he is a decent fellow. There is something dissatisfying in Marion's decision simply to return, alone, to the everyday, with its little degradations, its mutually exclusive choices—while leaving Norman here, unhelped. A sort of bewilderment percolates through the audience at this weird, premature 'happy ending'. We are, so to speak, in another 'zone'.

The film elaborately establishes Marion's search for a hiding-place for her cash. The search seems to turn her indifference to Norman into an entrenched cynicism for he isn't the sort of lad to steal it. As she undresses, Norman watches through the peephole. We laugh very uneasily at his avid voyeurism, but it does not quite put him in our bad books. For he has been lonely and dominated by his puritanical mother; and his spying on Marion represents a movement towards normality and freedom, which we want for his sake. This is almost a dissatisfying love-scene (like necking for lunch). The erotic overtones are juicy, and please us. And we are pleased to feel the story moving again.

The 'movement towards' Marion is intensified—with a vengeance—when Mrs. Bates with a knife upraised charges in and stabs her to death in the shower. The murder is too erotic not to enjoy, but too grisly to enjoy. Its ferocity and pornography are opposed, we are shocked into violent protest and horror, yet they force on the average spectator a rapid, hysteric, moral oscillation between protest and enjoyment. There is a Hays Code sort of moral in the air: 'Look what thieving necking girls get,' but her fate is also ironically unjust: for she had just resolved to return the money.

If the Peeping Tom episode is a 'weak' yet eerie version of the hotel scene, the murder is a sarcastic exaggeration of it—her sensuality's satisfied now, all right. We feel guilty about enjoying this film, but we have to admit we're having our money's worth of fun and fear.

Mom would be a convenient scapegoat; but we are headed away from complacent hatred back into something subtler and far more uncomfortable by Norman's distress at her crime and his concern for her. In the next sequence, he begins mopping-up operations in the bathroom, the action of an exceptionally dutiful son. The presence of Marion's naked corpse is both erotic and extremely uncomfortable.

The film offers us a 'first-person' experience answering the question which so often occurs to crime fans, 'Would I be able to get down to the practical details of clearing up the corpse and the blood'—a thought which appals many people more than that of the actual killing. The answer the film gives is, 'A sensitive and dutiful son like Norman can—therefore, so could you, if you really had to'. We watch Norman doing it, and the feeling that we could too is gratifying to the worse side of our nature, but upsets the other.

Although there is a quietly disturbing contrast between Norman's usual sensibility and his matter-of-fact practicality on this particular chore, we feel that in this way he was on the edge of being 'liberated' by his interest in Marion, that she slew Marion so as to keep him, and that in covering up for Mom, Norman is turning the other cheek, manifesting the equanimity and charity of a saint. The spectator's moral purity is being outflanked at both ends—by morbid, pornographic interest, and by a sympathetic pity for charming Norman.

Not that indignation and disgust are lulled asleep. On the contrary. For example, there is a very precise mix between a C.U. of the plughole down which our saintly voyeur is swabbing the blood, and a C.U. of Marion's open eye staring at us as if to say, 'What about my feelings? Why don't you interview the dead?' She's peeping back at us from beyond the grave, from down the drain, with protest and indignation, eternal and colossal—or surprise and fear—or just nothing. This visual rhyme is not just a piece of sadistic wit but a little essay in metaphor; it never does to interpret visual effects too definitely, but, e.g. the plughole is like an eye-socket, the eye ('Window of the soul' as they say) is just a mushroom out of a black hole. There is a sense of total nothingness and if the 'joke' provides a little hysteria which relieves the horror faintly it insinuates a subtler unease: we must be mad to be laughing at a joke like this.

Norman chews candy as he watches the white car sink beneath the very black surface of the swamp behind the house. As the film uses psychoanalytical ideas it's appropriate to use them on the film—the bathroom scene, very glossy and white, and devoted to the theme of cleanliness, is followed by a scene in which everything disappears into a black sticky cesspool. Norman has pulled the chain.

When the car sticks instead of sinking, we are alarmed, but when at last it disappears we heave a sigh of relief. Thank goodness! Norman is a good boy (despite the candy), it would be wrong to punish him, Marion's a corpse, it's no use crying over spilt blood, bury her quick, tidy up, get her out of the way! But when Norman tosses in the thick wad of cash, which he thinks is just an old newspaper, a cry of shock and regret is wrested from the audience. That valuable money, what a waste! Norman's saintly indifference to Mammon hurts us. We want to forget Marion probably because her murder shook us up so much. But the money had become 'what she died for, what she hid', that is, virtually a substitute identity. Its derisive disappearance creates hysteria as again the narrative seems to 'end'.

Sam Loomis discusses Marion's disappearance with her sister Lila (Vera Miles). The visuals are grey and scruffy. The setting is Sam's wife's ironmongery store where callous chit-chat about insecticides is overheard and pitchfork prongs are visually prominent. The drab everyday is full of trivial or latent cruelty. The meeting of lover and sister is hostile, but their disputes are ironically complacent compared with the terrible truth. Lila seems more sensible, more adult than Marion, and perhaps more righteous—but also worried, subdued. A private detective, Arbogast (Martin Balsam) insists on introducing himself, and tells them that Marion has absconded with the money. They refuse to believe him. They detest his coarse, obnoxious approach —so do we, and, like Sam and Lila, feel he must be up to some dirty game. His cynicism doesn't fit Marion's case—although, in a sense, it is justified.

As he tracks Marion down to Norman's mansion we half-want him to fail—for Norman's sake, and because he may be up to some cynical scheme of his own. . . . Just before he confronts Norman we realise that he is completely, admirably honest. In the battle of wits between Norman and Arbogast we sympathise with them both—Marion *must* be avenged, Arbogast is tough enough to uncover the truth; and yet Norman's motives are selfless, and perhaps Mrs. Bates will be more than even Arbogast bargains for. As he climbs the stairs towards the old lady's room, we realise clearly that his pushful cynicism, hitherto his strength, is now his weakness. He is formidable, and physically is probably Mom's match, but he is too naïve to be looking for whatever he'll find—and Mrs Bates comes tearing out of her room with the superspeed of the superstrong insane and with repeated jabs of her knife sends him tumbling backwards down the stairs, dead, just like that. Is Mom invincible?

Another car sinks into the swamp, the narrative 'ends' at another nihilistic moment.

The whole plot, which has twice ended so disastrously, starts again, as Sam and Lila come to investigate the disappearance of the investigator who came to investigate the disappearance of . . . Probably by now most spectators have guessed that Mom = Norman. But we can't be sure, in such a film. The only thing we can be certain of is the imminence of violent death—again. What matters is not whether we know, but whether Sam and Lila find out—or get killed. They might. Heroes and heroines do, in this film. And if they do find out, what will happen to Norman—saintly accomplice of two—at least—crimes. . . ?

The determined, but prosaic and therefore perilously naïve, couple call on the local sheriff (John McIntire) who explains that Norman is eccentric but harmless, that Mom has been dead and buried these ten years past, and so on. But we heard Norman persuade Mom to hide in the cellar and we saw Mom come tearing out of her room to kill Arbogast. The sheriff's clue is so wrapped up in complacency and ignorance that instead of clarifying our suspicions it confounds them further. The sheriff's suggestion opens up astounding new avenues of depravity: 'If Norman's mother is still alive, then who's the woman buried up there in Green Lawns Cemetery?'[1] If they believe what the sheriff says, they will never go to the old house, and then how can Marion and Arbogast be avenged? But *if* they go there. . . .

Sam keeps Norman talking while Lila sneaks into the house to explore; clearly the most dangerous game to play, especially with a possible Mom waiting for her. As we can't make up our mind whether the danger is coming from in front of her (Mom) or from behind her (Norman), we're no longer thinking very coherently, and as we can't make up our mind what we want to happen to Norman, we yield to a helpless hysteria.

Norman grows more anxious and angry as Sam brutally presses him; he struggles to keep his temper, to quieten his tormentors' suspicions, while keeping Mom from breaking out in himself (if you know) or (if you don't) bravely protecting his Mom or (if you're not sure) both or neither or which? The scene almost shifts our sympathies round—such is Norman's sincerity—to: 'brutal smug adulterer bullies sensitive kid into despair.' After all, whether Norman is weak or maniac or both, he probably believes in Mom, he is only trying to obviate another climax, another killing, he is frantically on the side of peace.

Lila explores the house. Amidst the tension there is an unexpected intellectual interest, and pathos. Norman's rooms are a picture of his mind and everyday life. There is the record-player with the classical L.P. (so out of place in this Gothicy house), there are the fluffy childhood toys which are presumably still played with. Norman is weaker-minded, more sensitive, than we thought, which makes him more

[1] Well might he ask.

pathetic (and more surprising—menacing?). Norman, mad with suspicion, rushes from the motel into the house as Lila takes refuge in
the cellar—where, we know, Norman puts Mom in times of stress.
And Mom does exist, there she is, horribly old, evil and withered, at
a closer look she's dead and withered, but still grinning malevolently,
she's a ghost, and when Lila turns, there's *another* Mom, grinning
malevolently, very much alive, knife upraised. There aren't no Moms,
there are two Moms, then the second disintegrates, the wig slides off,
it's Norman. It's not simply the surprise that shocks; it's the intensity
of terror and the obscenity of the disintegration. In rather the same
way, when Mom came tearing out of her room at Arbogast, she had the
notoriously terrible strength of the insane, and a visible virility quite
obscene in an old lady; the explanation doesn't explain *that* away; it
intensifies its impact because illusion and explanation co-exist.

We are relieved to hear that everything is going to be comfortably
explained for us by the police psychologist (Simon Oakland). As soon
as we see him we begin to dislike his brash, callous, know-all manner,
he puts our backs up as Arbogast did. We expect the clichés: poor
mixed-up kid, it was all the fault of stern, possessive, puritanical Mom.
But gradually we realise he's not saying this at all. It was Norman who
was jealous, who imagined that his (for all we know) normal Mom was
a promiscuous Mom and murdered and embalmed her and then imagined she was a jealous puritanical Mom and then lived out two false
characters—nice normal Norman and nasty Mom. So much for rustic
contentment. Norman was never, we gather, entirely Norman, i.e.
even when he was being charming and we felt sorry for him, he knew
deep down what he was doing. The psychologist's explanation takes
away our explanation: what we thought was 'deep', the 'solution', is
merely the topmost level of nastiness. He restores terror, guilt, injustice. Up till now Mom's gruesome appearance has been in accord with
her character: 'Well, if she's dead, she asked for it, look at how she
messed up her tender and devoted son.' Now all this is reversed, the
cocoanut-faced corpse was once a sunny, apple-cheeked mother. The
boy has literally turned her into his fantasy of her.

But if the psychologist, brutal and cynical, is the most intimate of
private eyes, the joker is still to come. All we've had has been an intellectual, rational explanation. Now we see Norman sitting against a
blank, white, hygienic wall. He is in full-face close-up, his madness is
rammed into the cinema. Briefly our entire world is his face, the
thoughts behind it, *his* world. We have little else with which to identify.
An utter flatness, whiteness, simplicity, in short, eternity. He is cackling

to himself, in Mummy's voice. She is jubilant because she is outwitting them all, pretending to be a sweet old lady who won't even hurt a fly. Mom has just killed Norman and disguised herself as him.

The Chinese sage wrote: 'Now I do not know whether I was then a man dreaming I was a butterfly or whether I am now a butterfly dreaming I am a man.' With Norman it's flies. His ricocheting self-punishment is so total that—well, we can hardly pity him, for there's no one left there to pity. And he or she or it seems to think it is escaping punishment, which is very immoral of him or her or it; but a nausea *like* compassion makes itself felt. We are too thoroughly satisfied to hate.

The appearance of Mom's face under the madman's, and then of a skull under Mom's, has a climactic brutality, but also simplifies, liberates us from the baffling maze of malevolent Nothings which our sensitive boy has become. Needless to say, it is a simplification on the most nihilistic level: are any of us realler than our skulls? There follows a shot of the police lifting Marion's car, wrapped in chains, from the swamp. There is no 'decent obscurity'. And Nothing to the nth degree has killed real people whom we sympathised with. But we too hoped the car would sink (just as we hoped Marion would get away with the cash). We too have been accomplices after the acts—futile acts.

People leave the cinema, chuckling incredulously, groggy, exhilarated yet hysterical, half-ready to believe that everybody in the world is as mad as Norman. A kathartic indulgence in pornographic murder is succeeded by an embarrassed humility, an unsentimental compassion towards insanity. The entire film is a prolonged practical joke in the worst of taste. If it weren't in bad taste, it would not be kathartic, embarrassing or compassionate.

It is not just a sick joke, it is also a very sad joke. Because it is outrageous, it exhilarates, but it is a very depressed film as well. The byplay with the money is strange and disturbing. It is produced as a weapon of seduction by a repulsive but normal male. Its victim resents the implied insult but yields to the money. The money, she felt, would enable her to find, all at once, respectability, sensuality, love. It becomes the last clue, a substitute-identity, an anti-soul. Marion who hoped to avoid choice, and sacrifice (the *hubris* of American optimism), is reduced to a nude body, a car, bankroll.

Everything piles up in the swamp—and is dredged up again. The film is not just a sick joke and a very sad joke, but a lavatory joke. It is a derisive misuse of the key-images of 'the American way of life': Momism (but it blames son), cash (and rural virtue), necking (and respectability), plumbing and smart cars. The reality to which Sam and Lila return is not a joyous one, but a drab shop of insecticides, pitch-forks and—in addition—a vision of horror. The plot inevitably arouses in the spectator a feeling that Lila and Sam could eventually, possibly, consolingly, fall in love. But there is no hint of it in the final image. Each is still alone. This is the sanity that balances the diabolical noth-ing which is the human soul. Marion, striving for everything, lost everything. Only Norman has defied society and superficiality and found 'rest'. Only Norman has found himself, and lost himself.

Like many films, *Psycho*'s aesthetic method is not that of providing enlightening information about its characters; it provides just enough to confuse us; it works by luring the audience into becoming the char-acters, sharing and living out their experiences within them in care-fully determined patterns. The characters tend to be alone on the screen. Even the conversations are filmed mainly in alternating close-ups. The close up both enlarges (intensifies) and isolates (blots out the rest of the world). While each character is speaking the spectator sees, feels, becomes him and only him. The next shot wrenches him into be-coming the *antagonistic* character. Our sympathies alternate rapidly—our feelings are poured into so many moulds which are distended or smashed by contradictions, revelations, twists. Simple as the characters are, in principle, they are, because well acted, convincingly real. The atmosphere is hypnotic, the events so outrageous and managed with such brinkmanship of taste, the hints, allusions and subversive shifts of sympathy are managed with such sly tact, its constant emotional collisions are so quick, subtle and drastic, that the 'sketchiness' of the characters no more invalidates them than it invalidates the plays of Racine.

In its powerful vagueness, it works on the spectator not unlike music. It is planned, felt out, in terms of varied motifs, of emotional chords and dissonances, of patterns. Hitchcock has a very refined sense of sly or brash emotional discords, of how to modulate and combine them. The coarse customer, the cop, Arbogast and the psychologist are in-carnations of the same force—unpleasant common sense. The trusting boss, the garageist, the local sheriff, Norman himself all agreeably fur-ther evil. The woman in the iron-monger's who is determined to kill insects painlessly is mirrored in Norman's final crone-voiced cackle that he won't even hurt a fly (is absurd squeamishness the hypocritical form of homicidal mania?). Norman in conversation, unwittingly frees Marion of the compulsive theft which Sam inspired in her. But Sam bullies Norman like the cop bullied Marion.

Lila is a more reasonable, but 'joyless' double of Marion. Sam loses Marion to Norman but Norman is destroyed by Sam and Lila. Lila, in a sense, is Marion 'come back'—a parallel to the 'second Mom' in the basement. As Lila roams through Norman's rooms, she is almost the substitute mother, the young woman who is kind and normal will therefore destroy him. Norman and Sam are both dark-haired, faintly resemble each other. Norman killed his mother because he thought she had a lover; and is destroyed by a young adulterer and his mistress's sister. The three penetrations to 'the truth about Norman'— Marion's, Arbogast's, the young couple's—are like three movements in music—the first two themes are contrasted (a sensual theme involving a girl, an unromantic theme involving Arbogast, the third combines them—a young couple who aren't quite romantically connected).

All these patterns, like inversions of certain emotional chords, result from the film's simplicity of form, but they are like haunting harmonies placed on a simple, yet eerie melodic line. The cutting has a quick, ragged, Stravinskyian rhythm.

The minor quirks and sins (adultery, a 'thing' about insecticides) of the normal world are the tips of the horns of the real reality, concealed beyond, or below, the 'zone'. In *Psycho* nothing that isn't disturbing or tainted ever happens, and to enjoy it (as most people do) is to stand convicted, and consciously convicted, of a lurking nostalgia for evil (i.e. of thoroughly enjoying it in fantasy). Norman's big mistake is that he let his fantasies enjoy him. The film is a practical joke: it convicts all the spectators of Original Sin. One does not so much watch, as participate in, it, as one might in a religious ritual involving the confession and a—well, one cannot say that absolution is granted. On the contrary, we have to take what comfort, or discomfort, we can from the implied complicity.

Hitchcock may have had a Jesuit education, but surely *Psycho* isn't a Christian film; it has a Dionysiac force and ruthlessness, one might call it a Greek tragi-comedy.

It comes very close to a certain existentialist preoccupation, in so far as it portrays the ravages of emotional inauthenticity which reduce a human soul to a total, complex facticity in depth which it feels is pure freedom but which is merely *le néant*. One postulates the comparison with the same reserves as in the case of *Vertigo*. Hitchcock approaches the same themes from several opposite directions (fundamentalist and Freudian). The disintegration of personality represents an intensification of the themes of *Vertigo* and *North-by-North-West*.

The perfection of the film's mechanism is illustrated by the unusual degree of unanimity and mutual complementarity, displayed by various exegeses (the above, reprinted from *Films and Feelings*; Jean Douchet's initial article in *Cahiers du Cinema*; Robin Wood's in *Hitchcock's Films*, David Thompson's in *Movie Man* and Leo Braudy's in *Film Quarterly*). While the usual variety of moral, metaphysical and psychological systems can be read into it, the full experience of the film is clearly a matter of our involvement with highly specific experiences and attitudes whose interpretation normally involves a variety of conventionally separate disciplines (ethics, sociology, cultural anthropology, depth psychology, etc). Hence the difficulty of 'interpreting' the experiences within films in intellectually coherent terms, although fortunately a considerable diversity of ideological interpretation may coexist with a considerable unanimity of dramatic involvement. And this agrees with Hitchcock's taking great care over the variety of disparate cultural backgrounds to be found within the U.S. market. Hence it isn't too difficult for Hitchcock's films, like many others, to be ideologically equivocal yet adequately intersubjective as between the artist and a variety of spectators.

The Birds

After *Psycho*, three years passed before Hitchcock's next film. The longest interval yet in his career was presumably a result of the complications inherent in the technical conception and execution of *The Birds*. Based on Daphne du Maurier's short story, it can also be seen as a development of the image of the stuffed birds on Norman Bates's wall.

Previous literary treatments of the theme of a birds' revolt include Arthur Machen's *The Terror* and Phillip MacDonald's *Our Feathered Friends*, both of which feature, according to Peter Penzoldt, 'organised revolts of nature against man's tyranny,' the latter story being 'particularly revolting' because it 'describes the common little birds attacking men and picking out their eyes'. Concurrently with Hitchcock's film, Terence Fisher at Hammer was preparing his adaptation of *The Devil Rides Out*, which includes a flock of bats murderously disrupting a vampires' ball. Its British premiere was delayed until after Hitchcock's film had gone its rounds, so, it was rumoured, as not to damage the chances of the more expensive film, from whose precedence it was itself relatively immune, the bats' episode being merely one among several horrific sequences, rather than the climaxes of a subtler story.

Maybe the success of *Psycho* encouraged Hitchcock to venture even further from the safer area of common sense and convention. If *Psycho* is Grand Guignol, *The Birds* is fantasy, albeit nearer the traditionally supernatural than science-fiction. Yet Hitchcock was at pains to stress the documentary instances of which it was an extrapolation. Similar attacks had occurred, occasioned by a disease analogous to rabies in dogs; and at Bodega Bay, the film's location, crows had attacked sheep by first pecking out their eyes, while, in California, thousands of swallows aggressively insisted on nesting all over a house.

If explanation has only a marginal role in the film itself, it is partly because Hitchcock has to allow for the fact that publicity, word of mouth, and failing those, the very title, will have alerted many spectators to what is to come. The credits sequence is sufficient to confirm that expectation and thereafter Hitchcock has only to dwell on a detail concerning birds, or show Melanie Daniels (Tippi Hedren) and Mitch Brenner (Rod Taylor) flirting in a petshop, using the birds' situation as an image for their own, for the spectator to notice every hint of potential tension in the relationship between *homo sapiens* and a species whose life in cages or familiarity in cities enables them to evoke at once domesticity and the wild.

Thus Hitchcock spares us all those scenes with which Hammer's teratologists crushed several otherwise excellent ideas to death, e.g. the characters in a film called *The Gorgon* spending most of their time discussing whether a gorgon could exist. By 1963, the cinemagoers' plot sophistication had been so vastly increased by education and television that, as Howard Hawks told Peter Bogdanovitch, 'They're a little too inclined, if you lay a plot down, to say, "Oh, I've seen this before". But if you can keep them from knowing what the plot is you have a chance of holding their interest.' Thus the long prologue, in which, as various critics objected, 'nothing much happens', constitutes a very definite structure, a movement away from the expected structure. It creates a series of frustrations and surprises analogous to the movement away from reassurance and towards disaster which characterises suspense and precedes the more-or-less happy end.

Thus Hitchcock can explore that only apparently paradoxical area, in which every spectator recognises some of the plot, and, in order that he shouldn't know it all, is offered another, obliquely related, plot. The unexpected and inexplicable feeling of the birds' attack is a quality which any less devious structure would minimise or abolish. A contrast of tone follows (naturally rather than necessarily), resulting in the paradox of a light, playful, Lubitsch-like plot, which has to be scrutin-

ised for signs of a coming apocalypse as relentlessly as any early Calvinist scrutinised the least details of his life. It says something for the
illogicality of the dramatic arts that Hitchcock can combine that sort
of scrutiny, which depends on expectation, with a feeling of unexpectedness, and that, in its turn, with the build-up of suspense required if
the birds' attack is going to create suspense (fear) instead of happening
suddenly and arbitrarily. But the spectators' consciousness faced with
the arts is no less complex and devious than when faced with anything
else.

The similarity, already summarised, between the Hitchcock touch
and the Lubitsch touch is evident enough. The playgirl poses as a pet-
shop sales assistant until the lawyer disconcertingly applies her name
to a bird: 'Shall we put Melanie Daniels back in her gilded cage?' But
the banter and space has a stiffness which is the antithesis of Lubit-
schian grace. A certain acerbity between the two is prefigured by
something nervous, birdlike, it seems, in Melanie's walk. She yields
to an impulse to embarrass him by dumping two lovebirds on him,
but her joke recoils when he isn't at home and she's landed with them
herself. Because she accepts the responsibility of looking after them,
we feel she has a good chance of being one of the saved. But some
cruel and unusual punishments are in store, not only for her, but for all
the women in the film, whose company, as they all hover round Mitch,
she joins. Annie Heyworth (Suzanne Pleshette) loves him in vain, and
has no other ties, and has become the local schoolmarm, to be, at
least, near him. She blames her defeat in love on Mitch's widowed,
possessive mother, Lydia (Jessica Tandy). As Lydia recognises in
Melanie her younger self, and her match, her stare, her gesture of the
head is like a bird of prey with beak drawn back to strike. The fourth
'woman', Cathy, Mitch's younger sister, a young adolescent, begs
Melanie to stay with them and so to bring the world into the somewhat oppressive home—or nest, or cage—where she is almost the
child to the lovingly domestic couple formed by her mother and her
elder brother.

The Mitch-Melanie-Lydia triangle develops alongside, and independently of, the very gradual awakening of the birds. Melanie, drawn
by Mitch, ventures outside her city cage; the director stresses her
gawky unfamiliarity with the boat she hires to silently approach
Mitch's house. He photographs her golden head against the black
metallic bulk of its outboard motor, to persuade us that it will fail,
that she will be stranded in mid-lake, to be exposed, maybe only to
gibes from Mitch which will perhaps be crueller than she deserves,

maybe to the aerial attack we have so long been expecting. But though both these scenes tentatively fade into the spectator's mind, neither appears on the screen. A solitary, swift, bloody swoop from a gull occurs only when she reaches shore. Mitch cares for her wounds, albeit only as a gentleman, not yet as a lover, his kindness retaining its capacity for impersonal dismissal.

Of the three women, all lonely and in some sense unfulfilled, Lydia, the most brittle, dominant and successful, seems the most tempted to a ladylike henpecking of her sisters, and fellow-creatures. She experiences the first of the film's shocks, towards, albeit ambivalently, sanity. She is responsibly concerned with the poultry which shows her to be nearer simple, productive living than, perhaps, we expected. Driving out to Fawcett, a local farmer, for help, she finds him sprawled messily across his bedroom, in his pyjamas, dead, in his skull two wet red rings. Staggering back to her home, she confesses her weaknesses to Melanie, who, warned, can go to the schoolroom and help Lydia help the children to safety.

The birds' second massed attack provokes a variety of responses from a group of townsfolk. Representatives of small-town, middle America, rather than the city, they include a brisk, tweedy ornithologist; an Irish drunk who anticipates the apocalypse with something like relish; and a thoughtlessly bellicose individual who, equally thoughtlessly, drops a match into the gasoline puddle he's standing in. But we soon return to the female-maternal theme, via the brisk, tweedy, lady ornithologist, and a mother whose reaction seemed at first one of vehement concern, as compared to the vague incomprehension of the male authorities. As the crisis mounts she turns on the gilt-haired play-girl, and accuses her of responsibility for the attacks, by introducing 'evil' to this simple and innocent community. Melanie slaps her to her senses.

The birds' attack traps Melanie in a phone-booth. Thus the birds cage the people. But with Mitch she braves a lull in the birds' onslaught to make their way to the schoolhouse. Annie lies where she died, having saved Cathy and the children. Mitch, conscious of the imminence of the birds' attack, merely covers the body with a coat. Melanie orders him to 'take her away from there', a decently 'futile' gesture, but an emotional imperative.

The Brenner family, with the girl who is to be Mitch's wife, batten down the windows and the doors of their home, and await the assault. Lydia hysterically accuses Mitch of failing to be the equal of his father. Melanie finds the attic occupied by the birds. She is pecked into a bloody, catatonic mass by thousands of little beaks before Mitch can rescue her; she shudders in fear from her fellow-humans.

The family take advantage of another lull to creep into their automobile and drive away. Cathy insists on taking the lovebirds, whom she loves, despite their affinity with their attackers. Thus, ironically, tenderness survives terror; but where does cageing begin and tenderness end? The same question is asked of the Brenner house, within which Cathy is kept, from which Annie is excluded, and where Lydia reigns, only to abdicate in favour of Melanie. Is it the cage in which Lydia keeps, not only Cathy, but Mitch? Is it the castle which Annie could not storm but Melanie can?

The lulls are as unexplained as the attacks. But, rather than increasing disbelief, as an arbitrary device, they serve to ratify the situation, giving it a biological rhythm, a complexity appropriate to a natural upheaval. In terms of the Brenners' relationship to the birds' attack, it seems to be the respect, born of fear, that propitiates them. Because birds are everywhere, we take them for granted. And, for that same reason, they might become an obsessive terror, a constant humiliation. Not that propitiation lets us off any hook. The temptation to masochism must be resisted. Nature spares only those who, while respecting her, brave her and fight for their own survival, not so much *against* her, as with her because they are part of her. Nature readmitted into consciousness, complacency is impossible. As the family automobile drives away, the night sky is thick with the menace of the feathered tribe.

A certain wilfulness (which can become courage), family solidarity, and secondarily, a general human responsibility, and the lucid resignation which Lydia must endure; these are the qualities with which the human animal can oppose nature, and take his place in nature. Annie is not quite of their race. Her gratuitous futile devotion is of a piece with all her cultural consolations. Lucid as she is about Lydia and Melanie, she cannot quite see the love and realism which accompanies their wilfulness. A little paranoia balances her idealism. As usually in American films, the intellectual spinster is a pillar of society, but is a little too soulful, too lacking in resilience, to be of the instinctual elect. In this case, it is the rich who inherit the earth, possibly for the same reasons that they became rich in the first place, either because they have inherited a natural superiority from those ancestors who became rich (a possibility indicated by Lydia's comparison of Mitch to his father), and/or because riches confer advantageous personality characteristics on those who have not lost their roots in the practical, the down-to-earth, and a natural discipline. Awkward as she is, Melanie rows well enough; Mitch hammers wood across the windows. The canoe and log-cabin mentality endures, just as Frances, in *To Catch A Thief*, survives the debilitating effect of privilege because her mother was unsentimental enough to give her a few spankings. The primitive is always with us.

General cohesiveness is more distant. The authorities are slow to believe the truth about the birds. Lydia, without turning to the official by the Fawcett gate, hurries home. The lonely folk in the bar are too disparate to rally effectively. As Melanie shelters in the phone booth, a stranger, under attack, hammers to be allowed in. Maybe it's as well that he disappears before she has time to decide whether or not to risk herself by opening the door to give him shelter. The radio speaks of the intervention of the military. And this evocation of the old blood-and-fire Cold War-era horror film, seems to offer the only real hope of effective social action, cumbersome and negative although the film may feel it to be (in contrast to the destructive exuberance of the Korean War Period films). The family, in its home, and its automobile, are the natural social unit (although respect must be paid to the spinster teacher who, like the good shepherd, gives her life for her sheep). Thus a natural biological bond—a lonely woman and her vicarious children—may paraphrase and even extend a family relationship (Annie saves the sister of the man she loves). Within the family Lydia has made a similar sacrifice, giving Mitch to Melanie, and accepting the extent to which even a family is, by its structure, not altogether secure for any of the individuals within it. A movement away from personal relationships to a more generalised responsibility is evident when Mitch, unlike Lydia, tries to warn the town. Unlike hers, his loyalty is not inturned. He is spared of any conflict of loyalties only because the town does not listen. Again Hitchcock's point is equivocal. Does he intend a comment on the futility of trying to put society before one's family? or does he intimate a criticism of American society in particular? Certainly the family is linked with society by a radio and, by the automobile in which it speeds away from its isolation. But the radio in the home keeps society at a distance, and the automobile is a home between homes. At any rate, whether Hitchock asserts it or regrets it, the town centre is the locale of panic and disintegration, and the private home is a castle so long as it is not a cage. It is as a family group that the Brenners rediscover their humanity.

This resignation, or ambivalence, about society recurs in a minor theme, that of the public information media. Melanie's father is a newspaper proprietor, which gives her special privileges. But her tarnished reputation results from scandalmongering by a rival rag. Privilege removes with one hand what it gives with the other. The radio misreports the details of the birds' attack on the schoolroom—but understandably, for the schoolmistress, in her turn, has lied to the children, to avoid panic. The theme implies criticism less than a sense of helplessness. But any pessimism is not nihilistic. The news is sometimes cruelly wrong, sometimes no more wrong than it is in the nature of communication to be, communication being, at best, a functional equivalent of the truth.

An emphasis on Hitchcock's moral severity might suggest that the birds are a metaphor for something evil in man, or an incarnation of his latent cruelty. But in the event, his own comments confirm what the plot suggests. The birds, like the blitz, force people back on to their bedrock qualities, and, although shocking and humiliating them, bring out the extent to which humanity, in a tight corner, is 'all right'. The film chastens the most sentimental varieties of Thoreauism (i.e. the identification of nature with good), preferring a 'herbivorous' Social Darwinism which equally is conveniently American. In *Psycho*, Norman Bates stuffed the maternal principle with its own hatred and came swooping down with knife upraised, manic as a hawk trapped in the home's libidinal cellars. *The Birds* can hardly be held morally responsible for their sudden recourse to aggression. In their attack on the town they act mainly as catalysts. Human disunity, hatred and panic do most of the actual damage. One could speak of a masochistic psychosis rather than a sadistic one. But the birds have already pecked Fawcett's eyes out, and maybe that's an appropriate punishment for a poultry farmer, although this in turn would imply either that *The Birds* is a vegetarian film or that Hitchcock accepts an amoral injustice as part of the way things are. More probably Hitchcock, like most spectators, doesn't see the relationships between birds and men as one in which moral values have much force or precision. But this natural, or supernatural, biological crisis dissolves some excessive and unnecessary moral divisions (e.g. Mitch's hatred of the playgirl whom he thinks Melanie is). The birds are just the Red Indians and like the Red Indians have a certain justification, but must none the less be slain by the thousand. At the same time they are not Red Indians, and one can't, except by hunch or guess, which may well be wrong, extrapolate from *The Birds* how far Hitchcock accepts *realpolitik* as a *de facto* or even *de jure* relationship between races or national groupings. My own feeling would be that it is a great deal further than the moralistic critics like to think, and that he accepts as both valid and natural a great many amoral loyalties; an acceptance which for obvious reasons often goes with a belief in severity as a moralising force. But one cannot overlook the extent to which the Brenners' rich home becomes a log cabin, battened down, as the beak-tomahawks break in through the roof or peck away at the heavy mahogany-backed mirror stand, until, eventually, some biological bugle blows, and the God of Nature cries, 'enough—they have held out—I recognise them as mine—they deserve to survive.' One writes the God of Nature, in the vulgarised Darwinian sense, whereby intelligence is a form of ferocity and effective ferocity a major survival-value.

This may be to exaggerate the film's complacency. For a successful engagement against birds hardly absolves humanity, or the Brenners, of the unnecessary divisions which without this sudden external menace they might never have resolved; and while the Red Indians lost once and for all, this revolt of the birds suggests all the environmental crises opened up by man's mastery of the planet. It's significant that birds aren't mammals, for, familiar as they are, being warm-blooded, cuddly and domestic, they also relate, as egg-laying animals, to reptiles, insects and creatures exhibiting only the blindness of natural forces. All, as a menace, they lack, is the power of organisation, of concerted action, which ants notoriously possess, and which comes less easily to these pampered individualist Americans than to any other of the races which together make up the lords of creation. It is important that Melanie should have connections with a university, and should be working to put a Korean orphan through college. For her loyalties are not narrow. But yet these activities are evoked amidst a dry space of grass and sand dunes. The overall impression of wistful aridity suggests not that this wider social allegiance is a moral defect of Melanie's, but that so far-flung a charity is bound to be spiritually peripheral. Perhaps the Korean child is her equivalent of Annie's schoolchildren. (If so, it remains ambiguous whether it reinforces the point that wide allegiances cannot substitute for family ones, and constitute a clutching at straws, or whether they are a mandatory supplement to them.)

One suspects that any specifically internationalist overtones about Korean children are balanced by anti-Communist overtones; a Zambian or Indian child might well be resented as do-gooder liberalism. At any rate, wider loyalties are forgotten as the family closes itself into its automobile, accompanied by the radio's promise of military action.

Several lines of dialogue mention that the different races of bird

normally remain segregated, and perhaps Hitchcock is playing the
favourite entertainment game, discussed with reference to *The Lady
Vanishes*, of non-committal references to topical affairs, whereby a
chord is touched, lightly and briefly enough to interest, but immediately dampened. A grace note, a passing tone, it contributes to the
general excitement, but says nothing in itself and imparts no symbolic
value to the general theme. It might or might not be significant that
the principal characters are all WASPS, that the birds are agents of
mere chaos, and that the Brenner home under siege anticipates recent
news items about the heavy security precautions felt necessary by the
affluent denizens of blocks of luxury apartments, said to be becoming
ghettos in the original sense of districts whose inhabitants retire to
them for safety. To describe any resultant conclusions about the 'secret meaning' of *The Birds* would be to confuse an overtone with a
theme. What Hitchcock has paraphrased, in his characteristically
emollient way, is not the confrontation of WASP and negro, but the
atmosphere of incipient social breakdown, exemplified by, among
other films, *Panic In Year Zero*, *Lady in a Cage* and *The Chase*.

Hence, perhaps, the insistence, and air of well-disciplined pathos,
with which the film emphasises the negation of social conflict; isolation
in space. Often enough Hitchcockian spatial tensions are vertical, the
villain dying by a fall from a high point, in a poetically appropriate
punishment for megalomania. *Vertigo* counterpointed horizontal
and vertical space, and here, although the birds swoop, it is rarely
vertically, and much more along slanting lines closely related to the
lateral space which weave the film's spatial web. A conspicuous example is Melanie's journey across the lake. Its deceptions as to suspense enhance rather than coarsen our sensuous response to its variations of rhythm and tempo, building up to the 'double-tempo' race between Mitch's automobile, which goes bucking and curving along
every topographical event on the shore, and the boat in which Melanie
dawdles timelessly, as happily intrigued to be caught as to escape.
Hitchcock's gift for classic choreography is intoxicatingly exerted
throughout the gulls' attack on the gas station, with the long trail of
petrol, the criss-cross of warning glances, the sudden blaze, the whirl-
ing hoses. Here Hitchcock disrupts our complacent belief that technological hardware must render animal flesh derisory. Man, in thought-
lessness or hysteria, wrecks the system which he controls, being, despite
everything, imagination, and therefore flesh. The seagulls caw derisively
as they fly over the town whose centre seems to writhe as it burns.

Yet the quieter sequence is as enthralling. *The Birds* is never more beautiful than when nothing important is happening. Even when one has allowed for sheer gloss, it succeeds in taking the *temps-mort* and giving it, not only the Calvinistic severity alluded to earlier, but a sense of dignity, of repose, of time out from chaos. It enjoys idle grace, coquetry, a certain civilised malice; but without illusions.

This sense of space, this disengaged tempo, links with Melanie's social isolation. She telephones a newspaper editor in pursuit of her personal aims, and we assume him to be another victim of her predatory manipulations before we realise he's her father. And maybe a father should indulge his daughter, but should a daughter thus command her father? Her charming of the local storekeeper is also observed with a certain wryness. All the same, her ability to manipulate seems to qualify her as a match for Lydia, and therefore as the 'counterpoison' who will save Mitch from Lydia's domestic and maternal 'spell'. It is important that Melanie in turn allow herself to be manipulated by the frank and helpless appeal of Cathy, incarnating the childlike needs which are at least as basic to humanity as the evil which fascinates us because, although omnipresent, it is also repressed, and therefore a potentiality rather than an actuality. Cathy balances all which the birds represent in the Hitchcock cosmology, for she has none of the masks and pretentions in which all the other characters indulge. It is for her sake that Melanie and Lydia overcome their own falseness. And just as Lydia consents to become as helpless as Cathy, so Melanie, venturing into the attic, confronts, and is rescued from, the helpless terror which is the other half of childlikeness. Sleepily complacent, she proves unable to manipulate the birds, and is manipulated forcibly by Mitch, and thus she, too, becomes a child again, *belonging* to the family.

Despite everything, we must still, like Cathy, love the lovebirds, recalling the old statesman's prophecy, in *Foreign Correspondent*, that the forces of evil will be defeated by the little men who feed the birds. Neither love nor evil are rational forces. We love or hate as it is in our nature to love or hate, not because the birds 'deserve' our love. The birds paraphrase self-sacrifice in their furious attack on Fawcett. His pecked-out sockets are matched by the bird caught and 'crucified' in a splintered window. Birds, like man, are normally ambivalent, splendid as well as malevolent. Thus, quietly, the amorality of Social Darwinism returns. But a tragic acceptance of *realpolitik* is not the same as a complacent one.

A sense of space and of temporal suspension is induced by the deviousness of the opening movement, and enhanced by the lulls between the attacks. It is re-echoed in the peculiar thematic fissure, between the human relationships, on one hand, and the relationships of men and birds, on the other. Two half-stories seem so intertwined as to keep each other partial, or trivial, and yet to create, overall, an incompleteness, an openness, which expresses rejection of psychologism or moralism as explanations of the human condition. It may be that the bird's incarnate repressed aspects of human nature: e.g. Melanie's stiffness, the blind panic with which she fights off Mitch, Lydia's nest-cage-castle. But the Brenners, probably as emblems of mankind, contrive to control these natural aberrations. Conversely, the birds learn from man the ability to combine, and the policy of inter-species war. The interaction of moral and Darwinian issues is more directly and obviously treated in films as diverse as *Island Of Lost Souls*, *The Hounds of Zaroff*, and *Planet of the Apes*, and, of them all, *The Birds* is the most conventional in assenting to the existing hierarchy of species and its amoralism. It queries a little, but conforms.

One can imagine an English film (or Hitchcock in his English period) centring the action in the café, or some public place in which a social cross-section would form a loose group throughout (a 'bus or train would do as well). English films generally would be more likely to emphasise the improvisation of a rough-and-ready social solidarity, or the township as a functional organism, or society as a network of responsibilities, as in *80,000 Suspects* (Hitchcockian title!) by Hitchcock's one-time collaborator, Val Guest. We have seen how something of that film remains in Hitchcock's, although communal unity is seen as inadequate or secondary. And the strength of the film's family scenes is precisely their sense of highly individualised characters together, combining community and separateness in a way which the English 'omnibus film' so regularly denied. But *The Birds* harks back to the family breakfast in *Blackmail*, whose sense of individuals together creates another form of space. Psychologically, certainly, it is reflected in the later films groupings and compositions. And all these forms of spaciousness create its poetico-philosophical quality, whereby every human feeling is half-irrelevant, half-gratuitous, to any other, and half-justified, half-absurd in itself. The looseness of narrative articulation reinforces the spatial looseness, creating to a social and psychological space which, exceptionally, isn't merely a superficiality, but corresponds to an emptiness in man's relationship with the universe—the emptiness left behind by religion, left unfilled by rationalist humanism, and abandoned to *realpolitik* by utilitarianism. To seek something specifically human of which the birds are a metaphor is to miss the point of the film. For it is just as much about whatever is manlike in birds as whatever is birdlike in man. It is our more efficient brutality which is the basis for our 'kindly' complacency. It is true that Hitchcock avoids all those questions of moral relationships between species which one might call 'religious' (although in fact humanists tend to be more sensitive to the life-force and the pain which man shares with the rest of the animal kingdom). Instead, we feel very kindly towards them, and often use them as images of freedom and ecstasy, except when we cage them, kill them, eat them, and so on and and so forth, activities of which Hitchcock gives us admirably sparing reminders. Our relationship is an incoherence. On the one hand Roman Catholic orthodoxy has it that animals have no souls, and that therefore any cruelty, up to and including speciocide, is perfectly permissible. On the other hand, WASP sensibility has it that cuddly animals are almost people and often show finer moral qualities. For many people uncuddly animals (e.g. snakes, sharks, crocodiles) incarnate absolute evil. Hitchcock, evading the controversial crunch, with his impeccable dexterity, substitutes a silent yet palpable uneasiness for a debate which relatively few of us take very far. The emptiness and openness of the film echoes our internal silence, our separation from the universe. St. Francis preached to the birds; here the birds preach to us; either way the religious song falls on deaf ears. The emptiness of *The Birds* is a positive emptiness, like the blank heads of Chirico's mannequins, like Magritte windows. It is an unquiet enigma, an altar to an unknown God, a vacant chair, an outcrop of the absurd. It is a mirror held up to our internal emptiness. And that emptiness is accepted, as natural rather than culpable.

Science-fiction explanations are easy to find. Perhaps some sudden mutation produced a new instinct, or deflected an old one, such as the migratory or nesting instinct, in such a way as to fuse it with co-ordinated violence against any living obstacle. Sparrows turn on hawks in just such ways, and a combination against men would be no more mysterious than the rapid adaptability of butterflies to industrial colour schemes, or of viruses to antibodies. Or a new pesticide might alter the chromosomes or the bio-chemical triggering of birds, as simply as other chemical compounds influence the minds of men. Such explanations would have narrowed the film's appeal to our imagination, and diluted our religious awe before a Nature which is terrible enough in itself to need no tampering. Nature being as arbitrary in everything as is man in his treatment of birds, there is no real reason why our feathered friends should be so kind as to leave us alone. After all, the snake has sufficient wisdom to strike first. Thus if the film has something of the quality of Judgement Day, of sins coming home to roost, of birds as avenging angels, it is quite without temporal finality, or even call to repentance, or humanity towards birds. The film's absurdity is a compound of sentimentality and the fear bred by guilt; but the emptiness is the product of an absence of positive feelings, or even guilts. It is almost as if Hitchcock were exorcising himself of, and extending to the entire universe, the misanthropy implied in *Psycho*. This universe is no less absurd, than man. All this is the product of no crime, no sin, no perversion, everything is as it is. (Alternatively: somehow, all of creation fell with man.) And humanity in the end is morally and socially viable, for all its tensions. The antithesis to complacency is not, after all, guilt, but, simply, a sense of danger, which may strike from a clear blue sky. The film's lyricism is as intense as, but quite different in import from, that of Franju's films about the moral relationships between men and beasts (e.g. *Le Sang des Bêtes*, the bird motif in *Notre Dame Cathédrale de Paris*, *Judex*, and the extraordinary images, in *Les Yeux Sans Visage*, of Edith Scob, Madonna-like behind her mask, liberating the doves which flutter around her head like the free, pure, terrible joy of her insanity). Hitchcock's film has no sense of mercy, Fawcett's is *Le Visage Sans Yeux*, and his heroine is driven insane by the attacks of birds.

For the seeker after symmetries the film is quite as rich as *Strangers On A Train*. Melanie has too little family, Mitch too much. Lydia recognises Melanie as her younger self and as her rival. If the overprotective, paranoid mother in the café links Lydia and Annie, Melanie eventually shares their hysteria and has to be slapped. Lydia redeems herself and gains a daughter-in-law when her love for her daughter—and all Annie's 'daughters'—proves stronger than her love for the son who is a substitute father. Mitch saves Melanie from the attic as Melanie, pursuing Mitch, saves him from remaining a mother's boy; Mitch, Lydia and Melanie are all spoiled, and Annie's masochism is both a self-cossetting which is a converse of being spoiled, and a masochism like Melanie's weakness in the attic, to which she ventures gratuitously. But 'masochism' is a complacent label, and another word for masochism is self-sacrifice, and we cannot dismiss it as gratuitous or sick, since it is the condition of society and parenthood. Mitch has to become a protective father and lover, rather than spoiled son, indifferent beloved (to Annie) and sadistic moral censor (to Melanie). His spiritual, not so much change, as development, is prepared by the three men to whom his mother instinctively turns and of whom we see something only if they're dead: Mitch's father, Fawcett, and the birdseed man. A fourth 'parental' figure, the sherriff, proves sceptical and, on the whole, inadequate. The film's two solitaries are Fawcett, caught alone in his double bed, and Annie, whose home is an oasis of intellectuality in a self-imposed rustic exile. Both are killed. Melanie's spiritual evolution, from spoiled child to parent, parallels Mitch's. It includes two crucial stages; her yielding to Cathy's plea, and her observation of a response of Lydia's. That response could seem very sinister, but she refuses to see it in a sinister light. Lydia seems preoccupied with her broken china, and it would be tempting to condemn her for her preoccupation with delicate property. But Melanie's gaze remains open, rather than censorious, and she understands that Lydia's reaction is a hysteric, self-protective reaction against horror. Melanie's eyes are sharp but her understanding is not glib. Mitch saves her from her own form of hysteric paralysis, as she has saved him from his mixture of complacency and moral censoriousness. He hates Melanie on the strength of newspaper reports about an episode, reminiscent of *La Dolce Vita*, of disorderly behaviour in a *fountain*; Annie exhorts her children to show orderly obedience in a *fire*drill. Both situations are part-lies. There is no fire and there isn't a drill. Melanie's laxity, exaggerated in itself, isn't all there is to her. But Mitch has to forsake his gratuitous moral sadism and use his aggression in a constructive and kindly way: fighting the birds, and slapping Melanie when she succumbs to a masochism linked with her weariness, her fatigue. The dunes by the sea are part-water, part-desert (fire), and her care for the Korean boy is a gesture towards responsibility, but distant and arid. As often in Hitchcock, woman's temptation is to succumb to masochism through guilt, man's to deny guilt by brutality. But the two strategies may make a viable, if hardly idyllic, combination. The sense of combination, of the small society, inspires family scenes, with their distinct yet pleasantly united egos, with solitudes of which some are perpetually anxious and others easily warmed into a pleasant mindlessness.

In so far as the film dwells on issues of moral responsibility and society, it links with *North-by-North-West* (and with the attack by the biplane, another archaic bird, on a solitary man who asks strangers for help). In so far as it derives from *Psycho*, in complementarity, and contradiction, it hints at a covert psychoanalytic structure. The two dead father-figures (Mitch's father, Fawcett) balance the three females clustering around one ideally strong male, whose task it is to protect both his past and future families. As in *Psycho* the threat springs from a savage bisexuality, the birds being soft, feathery and warm in the hand (the female breast) but winged, beaked and thrusting (the phallus). It is felt as hysteria (flocks of birds 'exploding') and the response to it is male firmness (to which all the women succumb). It isn't too difficult to see the birds as an image for childish anger, and sullen brooding. Whence, perhaps, the boyishness, the sudden collapses, of several Hitchcock villains before bullying or authoritative young men, as in *Psycho*; often the victim of the confrontation is an older man, as in *Blackmail, Notorious, Torn Curtain* and *Topaz*. One would expect the same complex situation to have other aspects; like the 'bullying' of Van Damm by the younger, homosexual Leonard in *North-by-North-West*; and the impeccably smooth, older, socially superior villains who secure the hero's, and our, confidence in *The Thirty-Nine Steps* and *Foreign Correspondent*.

Stylistically, too, the film complements *Psycho*, with colour for black-and-white. A woman's automobile journey in sunlight towards her purgation replaces an automobile journey through rain towards her death. Ominous police are replaced by ineffective police. Outdoor birds by day replace indoor birds by night—until the final climax. The house represents safety instead of danger (although the Brenner home is something of a lure for Annie and Melanie). The attic instead of the basement is danger. Dead fathers, and a hero replace a dead mother and a killer. A 'broad' structure replaces a 'linear' narrative. Straight lines and lateral space contrast with windings, stairs and indoors. An absence of morality and explanation replaces their gradual intensification. As 'pure cinema' it is at least as great a *tour de force*, not only for such *pièces de résistance* as Melanie's double crossing of the bay and the attack on the gas station, but for an unfailing visual eloquence: the white fence past which the fleeing children run; a schoolhouse flanked by a church at a sharp angle which invests a regional painting with the anguished emptiness of a Chirico; the vacuity of visual planes in public places. The decor has a loving variety: hot red neonsigns by daylight, the cluttered general store, the dominance, in the more spacious scenes, of blue, gold and grey.

Given his story, Hitchcock picks his ground carefully. Not only does he restrict Hammer-style carnage to one short sequence, of jabbed-in tracks on Fawcett's mutilated countenance (when he might have given the fastidious Lydia a nightmare ride with the living, blinded, mutilated Fawcett jolted on the truck seat beside her—and kept him with the family until the end), but the birds, in too many of the 371 trick shots, are clearly fluttering about, and not going for the

eyes at all. We may surmise technical difficulties, but it seems more
likely that Hitchcock is carefully pulling his punches, so as not to
shock, too unpleasantly, the family audiences of the Middle West,
audiences less saturnine, or resilient, than he. One wonders whether
he didn't, in the event, overestimate the extent to which even this
audience would be rendered, by hysteria, imperceptive as to the details of the physical details of the scene, and had become more realistic, or sarcastic, concerning violence, even when its victims included
innocent children. This restraint is surprising, after *Psycho*, and perhaps it is, in part, a concession to criticism of the savagery in the
earlier film, whose budget Hitchcock had carefully kept low, perhaps
because he was aiming at what he reckoned to be a limited audience,
centring on the youngsters with their taste for *grand guignol*.

Compromise appears again in his reaction to the distributors' objection to his original ending. The family would have arrived at its
'safe' destination, San Francisco, only to find the Golden Gate bridge
thickly clustered with birds. Yet it is hard to believe that Hitchcock,
after *Psycho*, couldn't have talked Universal into whatever ending he
chose; and perhaps he, too, as a Hollywood showman of the older
generation, respected, and all but shared, their feeling that an unusually
expensive film must not take too many risks. It's not necessarily true
that an intensification of horror at certain climaxes would have unbalanced the film, or desensitised audiences to its intervening subtleties.
On the other hand, the existing end shot does the job of the initial
ending well enough. One may indeed prefer, to a merely geographical
extension, the sombre chiaroscuro which contrasts with the preceding
gloss and cool planes, with its compressed, sullen, menacing economy.
One almost suspects that the Golden Gate ending was an idea which
Hitchcock, after some thought, rejected, as too neat a joke for the
film, although well worth proposing in an anecdotal form.

Hitchcock compared the climactic family scenes to the behaviour of
a family during the blitz. It is not through any documentary-style or
neo-realist prejudice in favour of realism as against fantasy that *The
Birds* (more than any Hitchcock film since *Sabotage* and the English
version of *The Man Who Knew Too Much*, and even including *Shadow
Of A Doubt*) provokes the wish that Hitchcock had dealt with just that:
the behaviour of a family during the blitz; bringing to the themes of
domestic and social responsibility all his stylistic virtuosity, combining
a stream-of-consciousness exactness with the strength and trenchancy of
Hollywood narrative at its best. At any rate, *The Birds* completes, rather
than negating, the intimate impressionism of *Murder*. For whether

or not the camera becomes Melanie's eye (and it often does, if only through Hitchcock's deft use of the conventional Hollywood alternation of reaction shots and virtual point-of-view shots), the spiritual eye is more often Melanie's than anyone else's, and the frequency with which the point-of-view becomes Mitch's rather than hers, physically, shouldn't distract from the extent to which what we are watching is her suffering during his attacks which we feel, with her, are unjustified.

The alternation of stressed, significant detail, and a sense of individuals remaining themselves within a group, has a rare, and quite unsentimental, beauty. Melanie's eye for Lydia's reaction to the broken porcelain is the exact spiritual correspondence of Hitchcock's eye for everyone's behaviour in this sharp yet not misanthropic film. The combination of critical acuity and brisk, silent compassion springs from the same stylistic and psychological exactness which achieved so many successful experiments with stream of consciousness, from *Downhill* through *Murder* to *Vertigo*, so many quietly expressionistic idioms, from *Rope* to *Vertigo*, and so many almost aloofly impeccable correspondences of style and content—from the tightness of the ten-minute take to the double narrative of *The Birds*.

It would have been one thing to have incorporated all the controversial issues which intimate realism would quite naturally have raised within an on the whole affirmative film. But Hitchcock achieves the effect of seraphic absurdity by discreetly omitting or dampening them. And for this reason the film seems to me a metaphysical lyric, rather than an epic. Yet much in it has a poetry so authentic and unique as to endow the film with an artistic validity which, whatever qualifications as to the film's overall stature may be made, remains precious and absolute. One would still have liked, in addition, an absolutely uncompromising Hitchcock film about mankind's response to disaster; whether the blitz, or the sinking of the *Titanic*, or, of course, certain novels of J. G. Ballard's.

Marnie

Marnie, a long-cherished project, marks the culmination of Hitchcock's cautious return to the primacy of intimate drama. More uninterruptedly than any film since *Under Capricorn*, it concentrates on a relationship between two people, with no detective-cum-onlooker so placed as to obstruct our vision by seeing too little and too late.

Compared with *Vertigo*, with which it has certain parallels (fetishistic inquirer loves a deceptive woman) its dramatic interplay is relatively devoid of merely external enigma and ellipse. It is more nuanced than *Psycho* (in so far as its heroine is a thief like Marion and fixated like Norman), but her past is brought into the present and reintegrated as part of her redemption. With *The Birds* it shares the screen *persona* of Tippi Hedren, at once bland and brittle, cool and predatory, offering a plausible complexity difficult to imagine from Hitchcock's first choice for the title-role, Princess Grace of Monaco. With the preceding film, the narrative of *Marnie* shares a double movement. In this case the present relationship is moving forwards in time and unwinding Marnie's past in an anticlockwise direction as it goes. The visual style retains the poetic sense of space, articulated with a narrative structure which, while accommodating crimes and traumas of melodramatic strength, is sufficiently human to subsume them (rather than depend on them), along with other elements which, strictly speaking, are extraneous to the drama; a psychoanalytical framework allowing a conceptualisation, and encapsulation, of experience; crime, vice and blackmail; and wish-fulfilment high life, with impeccably groomed personal styles.

Whenever Marnie (Tippi Hedren) applies for a secretarial job, she can produce impressive references, a touching story, a winning personality, delectable legs, a ladylike style, and an authentic efficiency. Rapidly rendering herself indispensable to her employers, she awaits the moment to disappear with the contents of the office safe. Before changing her name, her appearance and her false references, to repeat the seduction in another city, she relaxes by riding her beloved horse Florio, and returns to shower presents on her widowed mother, Mrs. Edgar, who lives in a Baltimore tenement and ekes out a living with Marnie's gifts and by minding little girls like Jessie, on whom she lavishes a physical tenderness of which her grown-up daughter is uneasily jealous. Although Mrs. Edgar seems to accept Marnie's story of undemanding presents from a disinterested admirer, Marnie is unable to win from her mother the warm expression of affection she craves. She sallies forth to become secretary to one Strutt, a busy, harassed publisher's manager. In his office she attracts the attention of the publisher's son, Mark Rutland (Sean Connery). Mark's smooth affability conceals a sharp business brain and a serious interest in zoology. Marnie, responding to him despite herself, becomes hysteric at the sight of a red stain on her blouse, and, while taking dictation in Mark's office, at thunder.

MARNIE   351

After Marnie has repaid Mark's quickening interest in her by robbing Strutt's safe, Mark hunts her down, and bullies her into a marriage. He accepts her plea that it remain chaste, but promises to come to understand her, and win, if not her love, at least a trust that will make marriage meaningful. He takes her on a honeymoon cruise, reading psychological textbooks with forbidding titles like *Sexual Aberrations of the Criminal Female*, and trying to psychoanalyse her, only arousing her mocking resistance. He finally forces his embraces on her, after which he has to rescue her from the yacht's swimming pool in which she has attempted to drown herself.

On their return to the Rutland home, his ex-fiancée, Lil Mainwaring (Diane Baker), whose feminine insight has been sharpened by jealousy, suspects something strange in Marnie's past, tries to warn Mark and invites Strutt to a reception. Strutt, recognising Marnie, furiously demands revenge, but is narrowly fobbed off by Mark's threats of retaliation. Marnie's plight reaches a new crisis when she is unnerved by the red of the huntsmen's jackets, and she fails to take Florio over a jump, so that he breaks his leg and has to be shot. She hysterically attempts, but is unable to complete, another robbery, and Mark forces her to take him back to her mother. They arrive during a thunderstorm, which helps the hysterical girl to re-live her terrors during a thunderstorm as a child. Mrs. Edgar was then a prostitute, and, assuming that a friendly sailor was assaulting her daughter, furiously attacked him. Defending her mother, the child killed the sailor with blows from a poker. Marnie and her mother at last share their past, and Marnie is set free from the worst of her compulsions and inhibitions.

The synopsis reveals, clearly enough, certain favourite Hitchcock motifs, notably that of the woman attached to a harsh or sinister mother-figure. Any outline must immediately expose the scenario's dubieties, e.g. the bridegroom's mini-analysis of his bride, whose compound of success and failure plunges us into pat trauma and instant catharsis. Nor is the characterisation without such elements of soap-opera perfectionism as Mark's immaculate versatility, the perfect manners of both romantic leads, their dignified loss of dignity, and so on. These criticisms may establish the lyrical limitations of a satisfyingly complex work, but they in no way rule out its fascination, which derives not from mere technique, but a complex spiritual vision presented, if brittly, in some depth. Robin Wood quotes from Edmund Spenser in the course of defending Hitchcock's films, and, if we can forget the too automatic comparison of the Elizabethan popular drama and the modern popular cinema, and remember that the post-war cinema's popular audience is at least as well-educated as the Elizabethans who read the more 'courtly' literature, one can see the extent to which a middle-class woman's film like this corresponds to the Renaissance elements rather than the popular ones. It has their expansive pleasure in sensuous riches and in good manners, their adherence to a carefully shaped intellectual convention, their mixture of controlled form, their fascination with minglings of decorum and excess. This line of defence can be applied too undiscriminatingly to too many Hollywood movies, but *Marnie* possesses a spiritual edginess which renders its bourgeois kind of vulgar opulence well worth defending. After all, it is only too easy to fall into the familiar assumption that upper-class Elizabethan literature is less vitiated by very narrow conventions and idealisations of a dubiously moral sort than it is.

For all the traits of matinée idol intellectual, Sean Connery's Mark Rutland shouldn't be confused with his chores as the movies' first James Bond. Here, with a manner as incisive as jaunty, with his saturnine, scimitar mouth, he exists somewhere between two earlier Hitchcock heroes, Cary Grant (particularly as the disingenuous seducer of *Notorious*) and the harder, bleaker, more passive Laurence Olivier in *Rebecca*. Admittedly one itches to deprive him, from the beginning, of his invincible smugness, to have him uneasily conscious of certain failures. One's first thought might be to render him more sombre, almost, indeed, a little masochistic, over his dead wife, even at the expense of reviving the *Rebecca* theme, whose glamorously doomy air now seems somewhat archaic, in this age of amnesic cool and fun morality. None the less to do so would be to cut across any potential theme of almost culpable self-sufficiency, which in the event is hardly explored. Mark's freedom from his past is briefly asserted and it gives us at least a brief jolt.

Just as in *The Birds*, Hitchcock is unexpectedly tentative in asserting the moral weakness and effective vulnerability of the strongly protective male on which a brittle woman depends. It may be an inheritance from such earlier films as *The Thirty-Nine Steps* and *North-by-North West*, where the situation does more to create a sense of urgency than the irrepressibly cocky hero. Hitchcock's females are regularly more interesting, more deeply victimised. By and large even his heroes tend to get off relatively lightly, notable exceptions being associated with particular actors: James Stewart (in *Rear Window* and *Vertigo*) Laurence Olivier in *Rebecca* (Olivier being that rarity, a champion tragedian with a brisk and biting pace), and *The Wrong Man*. Otherwise Hitchcock's most interesting males are his bullies and his victims, and those villains who, like Norman Bates, are both at once.

Hitchcock observes that his intended theme of Mark's own morbidity was intended but somehow got lost. The narrative certainly bristles with hooks on which such dramatic weighting might have been hung. Marnie tartly points out to her bridegroom-analyst-protector that if he's hung up on her, he's in no little psychological trouble himself. One might have related this vulnerability to his own rejection of grief; Marnie's faults are his secret sins, his own temptations, whose victim he is destined to be in her if he can't overcome his own defence-mechanisms (smugness, aggression) against them and both love her despite them and overcome them in her. By marrying her he makes himself as thoroughly hostage to her fortunes as the victim of any Italian *diva* could have done, although his weakness is balanced, or even transformed, by the strength which enables him to bully her, to understand her, and, of course, to succumb to his natural male appetites and rape her. If, in the film, Mark seems to impose himself on Marnie rather than Marnie to impose herself on Mark, it may be through some failed *rapport* with Sean Connery, or through the influence on Hitchcock of his earlier heroes, or through Hitchcock's assent to the obvious story movement, whereby Mark must get a grip on her and she open herself to him. Mark's infatuation is *given*, like conventional Hollywood love at first sight; he states it like a declaration of war. It must not change and it does not change. There is less to be said about it, and it is eclipsed. At any rate, Mark remains a woman's dream saviour rather than an accomplice and fellow-victim. We don't feel that this physician is fighting for his own sanity and sexuality as well as hers, and that in his heart of hearts he knows it even though he's fighter enough to present her with those facts in the only way that fits the case, i.e., confessing his vulnerability but only as a parent might *warn* a fractious child he cares. The film underplays his secret dread of her suicide threat, his temptation of being infected in some way by Lil's well-meant suspicions, his fear of a cure which will liberate her from him, his temptation to abandon her as hopelessly complicated compared with the more comforting, less satisfying Lil (let alone Marnie's half-inclination to steal *him*). Such narrative pointing would probably overcomplicate an already complicated film, and in the event Hitchcock makes the point even though it remains relatively abstracted from the action, as compared with another story of a detective-seducer-bully who becomes his victim in *Vertigo*.

SCAH—M

The position is complicated for Hitchcock in that he is using Mark to vindicate an unusually, for Hollywood, guarded and modest attitude towards human relationships. He boasts to Marnie that he persuaded a South American jaguarundi to trust him, to which she replies disdainfully, 'Is that all?' From one angle, indeed, this modest achievement might hint at a secret defeatism, whether born of masochism or misanthropy or some combination of the two. But Hitchcock is interested also in the other angle, whereby we're wrong to take trust for granted as we do, let alone love between human animals, and that in trust there is a great deal more of real love than our conventionally optimistic assumptions about love, fear and human society suggest.

At any rate, Mark's character is made emblem of an intriguing collection of ideas, keyed by the scene in which the lightning strikes, terrifying Marnie and transforming his office into a disorderly jungle. A fallen column lies crookedly like a tree-trunk, the pre-Columbian vase which his wife had collected evokes the ruins of a civilisation overgrown by jungle vegetation. Mark is drawn to Marnie because she, too, is a predator, in the jungle into which human society is always in danger of disintegrating (and from many of those characteristics it cannot free itself, but must use, if only under the pressure of some severity). In Marnie Mark finds the wild beast who responds to both his fetish-infatuations and his husbandly responsibility. If he has forgotten his grief for his first wife as completely as a wild animal forgets the past, there is a doglike humility about his quite unconcealed mugging up on psychology. He deploys the climactic form of specifically human intelligence (scientific rationality, applied to subjectivity) like a hunting animal following every twist and turn of its quarry's flight. It may seem incongruous that a zoologist, a believer in instinct, should bring to his wife's bedside so old-fashioned a medium as a book. But learning is natural to man, whose nature it is to reorganise his instincts. Mark accepts that the woman he loves may be described by a book with so cruelly objective a title, and that her unique and precious subjectivity can be objectively described. Yet it is just that critical objectivity which binds us all together, quite as importantly and constructively as an uncritical sympathy. Mark groups rationality and objectivity with the animal instincts against the anomie and inhibition of which Marnie is an incarnation. He has to resist her mockery, which has an edge of fashionability, of common sense, and of justification, to it. 'You Freud, me Jane?' But he is right to insist that there is nothing derogatory in being a textbook case, and that man uses books as naturally as he uses tools.

His jungle instincts aid him also in shielding Marnie from the moral order, when Strutt demands justice, and punishment. Mark, to silence him, resorts to immoral pressures, i.e. jungle law, or at least, his position well above Strutt in the professional and financial pecking-order. Some of our sympathy goes to Strutt as he protests that Mark wouldn't be taking so magnanimous a line if he'd been the victim of the wrong—a line whose full irony is minimised by Mark's air of invulnerability. But it's also clear that Strutt is motivated, not by any positive purpose (the money has been returned), and certainly not by an abstract love of justice, but by a vindictiveness stemming partly from his own character, partly from the anger of a frustrated, or repressed, seducer. Not only are both emotions ungenerous, but neither has any animal function. Revenge relates to the past, like Mark's grief for his wife, and must not envenom the present. Perhaps it is as well for Hitchcock's reputation as a moralist that Strutt's meanness saves Mark from having to choose between his animal's concern for his mate and his social concern for equity as between her and Strutt.

Himself a big cat, he stalks Marnie and finally springs. But his chase has her freedom to love him also in view. The privileges of his financial caste may well have helped him preserve his animal vigour. But they carry their own temptations and debilitations (as so often in, notably, *To Catch A Thief* in particular, but also *The Birds, Downhill, Champagne, Murder*, and the theme of deference in *The Lodger* and *Waltzes from Vienna*). Mark's ventures from his natural habitat into the jungle spring from, and enrichen, an innate energy and realism. He has revived the fortunes of the family publishing firm, neglected, apparently, by his father, who prefers an existence which, apparently ultra-traditional and conventional, is curiously isolated, misplaced, and functionless. He observes all the paraphernalia of riding to hounds and four o'clock tea, like a kind of stockbroker belt pseudo-country gentleman. Mark runs his finger ironically about the Rutland car, as if to ensure that we notice its sarcophagus-like shape. A transition zone between this pseudo-English 'idyll' and business offices is constituted by the race-track, where sport meets money. There Marnie is nearly recognised by an unsavoury character, a double for Strutt, whom Mark routs, in accordance with the definition of a gentleman as a man who never gives offence except deliberately. Marnie is upset also by the jockey, whose red-and-white shirt recalls stains of blood, and whose crabbed body is like something from the slums. Mark's father makes a verbal parade of healthy animality and direct action, and it seems sadly fitting that Marnie's horse should suffer its fatal fall in Mark's father's anachronistic Nowhere Land. Maybe the sequence is more sardonic than it seems, in so far as popular American audiences may react more derisively to these 'effete' English manners than the English, or cultured Americans, suspect. Maybe Hitchcock is reminding *them* that just such an upbringing protected both Mark's animality, and his flexibility as between a defensive alertness and an assurance of trust, a great deal better than the 'normal' worlds of Marnie's various employers—and sailors. Its snobbery has two sides. Mr. Rutland complacently assumes that Marnie's all right, and that Mark's animal instincts are uncomplicated, while Lil Mainwaring, immediately spotting her as a sinister outsider, begins her skin game. Marnie's own penchant for keeping a horse may well have overtones of snobbery and social climbing. But, what matters is her love for it, a love as masochistic as Mark's for his jaguarundi is modest: 'If you must bite someone, Florio, bite me.' Her horse is the one male animal which she can unconditionally love, whereas her neurosis drives her on to cheat one father-figure (employer) after another.

Lil has something of Mark's sensible clarity, as of his qualities as a fighter. But her assumptions are bound by her social set, and by jealousy, so that she misunderstands the nature of Marnie's hold on Mark. She reverses the truth by assuming that the outsider must be blackmailing the man of her own kind. The cat in her is still ready to lash out, her claws sharpened by a lover's honest disappointment. But, in the end, she helps Mark out, in a modest, useful, perhaps insufficiently appreciated way. Although, as a loser, she recalls Annie in *The Birds*, she never succumbs to forlorn passivity, keeping her life force intact, so that her final relationship with Mark is a strong, casual, unpossessive trust, altogether different from the perfidious blend of respectability and titillation which Marnie maintains towards human males, until her loss of her horse leaves her only Mark to turn to.

Essentially, however, Marnie has no more snobbery than Mark. He is her natural mate, for, like him, she is one of the best human animals —in intelligence, in audacity, in impulse, in calculation, in grooming. The affinities between them are those of an instinctual meritocracy. Any barriers of class are to be jumped as naturally as the barrier which Marnie, because she is still guilty, fails. But only after she has been cruelly deprived of her surrogate animal, and her guilt has been critically doubled, and she, herself, been reduced to a condition of dependence on a human male who controls her sufficiently to refuse to allow her to surrender to the perverse reflexes which are her last temptation. On one hand, she feels a gratuitous sadism (a renewed theft of the safe), on the other hand, a moral masochism (yielding herself up to the police). Eventually she decides to entrust herself to Mark's judgement, and accept the embarrassments of natural gratitude and responsibility, rather than prison, with its gloomy freedom from fear, from guilt, from gratitude, from love.

The narrative movement might have encouraged an increasingly vindictive attitude towards Marnie's mother. Mrs. Edgar seems satisfied with accounts of an employer-admirer whose gifts might well arouse a certain suspicion that Marnie is either his mistress or is in some way exploiting his weakness. So Mrs. Edgar is presumably guilty of a disingenuous innocence, and even of vindictiveness towards the male sex. Her apparent assumption of her daughter's virtue is quite as hypocritically complacent as old Mr. Rutland's belief that Mark and Marnie are a pair of healthy animals. She refuses Marnie the physical contact she craves, while lavishing it on a neighbour's child, Jessie, a golden-haired creature who 'is' the younger Marnie, and who banishes Marnie now, just as, in *The Birds*, Melanie 'is' Lydia as was and banishes the older woman now. One might take a very bleak view of Mrs. Edgar, and feel that her 'unconscious' hypocrisy and rejection now compound her unsavoury profession then, and that by this combination of emotional incompatibles she, above all, is guilty for Marnie's neurosis. Conversely one might feel that her circumstances made it impossible for her to be other than what she was, and that what matters now, for Marnie, is to correct her own attitudes. As Robin Wood observes, Marnie's craving for affection is a regressive craving to be a child; from another angle, Marnie, seeking to buy her mother's love with presents, has unconsciously become a client.

But, as Hitchcock's quiet, elegiac tone reminds us, the truth is more complex. Both women may be blamed, and must be forgiven. Marnie *was* the real murderess. Mrs. Edgar suffered much for a child on whose behalf she first became a prostitute, and then stood trial. It is impossible to tell how far her reluctance to caress Marnie springs from her own harsh upbringing (which one suspects knew little of such tenderness), or from Marnie as both cause and reminder of a profession of which she has become ashamed, or whether it existed in the past, but not the present, when she is normally enough unconscious of Marnie's craving, or from a half-conscious repudiation of an anomalous craving which it would be wrong to indulge. Her hypocrisy is not malign; when the child lost all memory of that terrible event, Mrs. Edgar saw the Lord's giving her a chance to 'start over'. For her, that renewed innocence is truer than the truth.

Nor can one find a scapegoat in Mrs. Edgar's fundamentalist sense of right and wrong. A certain hatred of sex, or men, is evident in her assumption that the merely friendly sailor was interfering with her daughter, and in her angry attack on him. And if Marnie's only too efficacious intervention might be said to echo her mother's rage, it is also in accordance with the film's Freudian slant to attribute it to universal childhood projections, motivated by jealousy and hatred, about the 'primal scene', i.e., the mother's sexual relations. Fundamentalism, as opposed to an enlightened liberalism, has no more to do with it than the opposite of fundamentalism, prostitution. Similarly, Marnie's amnesia was an equal, and spontaneous, hypocrisy.

The connections can be read another way. Both Mrs. Edgar's tenement exile, her need for money, and the fundamentalism, to which, after her 'accident', she reverted, belong to another culture, that of the poor white Bible Belt, whose harsher morality was as imperfectly appropriate to a harsher society as a liberal morality to ours. It is a world as archaic as Norman Bates's rustic mansion. But it bequeathed to Strutt's world, and to Mark's, both good and evil. We are clearly to assume that Mrs. Edgar did right by Marnie in renouncing prostitution, even if she could not do all for the child that, theoretically, she might. Is liberal culture much less obscurantist about the brutality of life? Mrs. Edgar's life is the most broken, the most tragic, of all, and her wan happiness at the end has the most poignant meaning.

There is also something incipiently Faulknerian about the continuous, circuitous, ravages of a long-concealed crime, and about the long, pitiless chains of causation and chaos which arise from the mother's rural Southern world and extend, in its more genteel, diffuse and evasive forms, into Marnie's slickly well-groomed world, and which lure the sophisticated, upper-class animal into its toils. It traps him as Norman's mansion traps Marion Crane. But Mark achieves the blend of responsible possessiveness, of frivolity, animality and intellectual search, which are scattered between the characters of *The Birds*. There is a quiet bitterness, after all, in Hitchcock's constatation of two now inadequate cultures. One still comfortably plays the genteel yet bloody charade of English country squire. The other is uncomfortably split, by its financial and cultural indigence, between prostitution and puritanism. None the less, something in Mark drove him to find new roots in the jungle, and in Marnie, and something in Marnie drove her to the true gentility of her love for Florio. Neither could be free until they had crossed class and moral lines.

For if Marnie has to shed her frigidity, thus abandoning puritanism, Mark, too, accepts a voluntary sexual abstinence, i.e., the vital human principle of the puritan ethos, only too easily corrupted, whether into dogma or permissiveness. Nor can we forget the Puritans' God, with his mysterious ways. The storm which rings in the child Marnie's ears as the sailor dies is re-echoed as lightning reveals her fauve terrors to Mark, and recurs as he rushes her home for her kathartic ordeal. Without it, could she have relived her past so intensely, so effectively, and spoken with her child's voice, like Norman at his maddest in *Psycho*? Doubtless God's presence is not certain (the weather might be what remains of nature, when the asphalt jungles make the green one dead). Perhaps they remind us how much even our deepest selves and drives depend on chance, on fate, on the Uncontrollable. But Hitchcock, so sophisticated in weaving menace out of empty fields, didn't need storms for merely atmospheric purpose. The moralists might also bear in mind that Marnie's path to salvation, liberation, happiness, respectability and prosperity depends on her having been a thief. Perhaps, in Hitchcock, amoral energy and responsible morality ought to be yin and yang.

Marnie constitutes an explicit integration of problems which remained implicit in *The Birds*: morality, animal energy, spiritual judgement. Both are philosophical articulations as well as psychological ones, or rather the psychology exists as an expression of the philosophy. This is nothing new in Hitchcock, nor indeed in the cinema. Popular philosophy has a continuous history of expression through fable, parable, anecdote and tale. If confusion over this function has arisen, so that for forty years or so critics often assumed that if a film wasn't 'poetically' lyrical or heavily symbolical then its action existed to express the characters (to paraphrase Elizabeth Bowen), rather than the characters the action, it is in part, at least, a reflection of the extent to which, in English-speaking culture particularly, philosophy has retreated into a ghetto of technicalities, abandoning most of its other cultural functions to a few 'human sciences' of which only individual psychology has loomed very large in general culture. More recently, however, anthropology, social psychology and, with particular relevance to *The Birds* and *Marnie*, what one might call human zoology have been filling out the picture. In any case the writings of Jung and Freud illustrate how easily and naturally the individual case history (or story) becomes philosophy. Conversely, the writings of such philosophers as Nietzsche and Sartre make any clear distinction impossible. The dismissal of *Marnie* as merely a psychological case-history implausibly melodramatised overlooks the extent to which what the film loses by its recourse to shorthand for much of its psychological structure it gains by that structure's expansion into a larger framework.

Most of Hitchcock's earlier films presented a conspicuously stylised view of happiness, depending on two attitudes. One was a dread of human and natural possibilities, linked, it seemed, with a fascination sometimes wavering on the brink of a Sadeian approval, or at least a masochistic-paranoid acquiescence in the tragic. On the other hand, a repudiation of the ravages of these evils seemed associated less with hope of anything more positive than a distaste for discomfort, a stoic *apatheia*, a sense of duty and a cultural conditioning whose language happened to be a partly and diffusely Christian one. All of which would produce both the lordly, sphingine countenance, so like the gods of the British Museum or Mount Rushmore, and the wryly comic face of rueful discomfiture. The masks of happiness are assumed in a deference to prevalent optimisms which is, no doubt, genuinely respectful as well as prudently commercial. Often the effect is of two worlds—the foreground world, frequently verging on the vapid, and the background world, realistic and melancholy. The mandatory not-too-unhappy end could seem, according to the spectator's temperament, either just another case of the evil which wins a limited victory before being defeated, and is, therefore, essentially temporary and anomalous, or as, more ominously the 'tip of the iceberg', or, more frighteningly still, an outcrop from a bedrock underlining our seeming decency.

Our contention has been that Hitchcock's position was equivocal as between these three possibilities—and that his films often had, for audiences, a curiously double sense. The happy end provided a temporary reassurance although the intensity of the uneasiness sapped that reassurance more than a little. Thus he restored to the spectator a little, although not more than a little, of the equivocation which comes very easily to popular audiences outside the cinema. But since many films do this it can't be evidenced as an indication of Hitchcock's special status (which, given the importance of an essentially precarious balance, we would accord to some films only). But as Hollywood, trailing well behind European audiences, gradually became more thoughtful, so Hitchcock was increasingly able to explore the articulation of his vision. With *Psycho* he looked more deeply into the abyss (maintaining, of course, that it was a 'fun picture', as of course it also was). *The Birds* posits an *external* abyss. *Marnie* marks a change. More convincingly, because more intricately than almost any other Hitchcock film, it explores the structure of possible happiness, and offers, rather than a flight from evil, or a chastening by a realisation of its eruptions, a positive seeking-out of the nightmare, seeking not to obliterate it, in that old-fashioned puritanical way, but to understand it and to untangle the energies locked within it. It may be linked in some way with Hitchcock's spiritual biography, although one must bear in mind that it had been a project of his for many years, and records, rather than synchronising with, an experience which one would expect to have been gradual rather than sudden, and complementary to, rather than exclusive of, its saturnine antithesis, *Psycho*.

'You Freud, me Jane' expresses the overlap between two approaches by instinct theory; the psychoanalytical, and, given the reference to Tarzan, who, we remember, was King of the Apes, the biological approach lately revived by Konrad Lorenz, Desmond Morris, Robert Ardrey and others. Marnie's might seem a journey from a passion-inhibiting puritanism to a man-as-animal philosophy and a liberation of passionate love. But Hitchcock refuses any simple equations of instinct, love and sex; his human animals remain human, whose values entail a mixture of discipline and spontaneity, force and understanding. It's arguable how far Mark's fascination with danger (the jaguarundi, Marnie) is a natural expression of the life-force (like mountaineering), how far it is a fetishism, and how far it is a *natural* fetishism, and whether its import is predominantly narcissistic (ego-enhancement), or sexual, or ambivalent. At any rate Mark's fascination with danger is an intriguing sublimation of aggression, for he seeks, not to kill, but to *tame*, and not merely to tame, but to marry. He is neither a big-game hunter nor a Don Juan. We easily equate a 'civilized' man with a tamed one, as if man were naturally a solitary animal. But he's more probably a social animal of some sort, and Mark, though civilised, isn't tamed. Marnie is anti-social but, erotically, tamed, in the pejorative sense (inhibited). Mark is sociable, civilised, but certainly isn't philanthropic. Towards others he has a curt politeness which isn't mean or ignoble or ungenerous but certainly has an animal indifference. And so a certain uneasiness returns. On the one hand, Mark's love for Marnie has its masochistic possibilities, reminding us that love without trust is masochism, from which Mark is spared by his intuition that Marnie is *basically* and *potentially* trustworthy. But on the other hand trust without love is a non-relationship revealing its negative side in the vindictiveness of Strutt and Mark's recourse to naked power. Like Freud, Hitchcock sees love as the end-result of complex psychic processes each of which is not love and therefore rather less ethical, but a mixture of animal need, of family imprinting and of humanity as a herd—with all that herd's internal tensions.

We have suggested that Mark's interest in Marnie's consciousness can be seen as a variation on Scottie's interest in Judy's appearance in *Vertigo*. But one shouldn't too hastily conclude that appearance has little to do with consciousness, or that Mark's liberation of Marnie isn't also an imposition of a certain existence upon her. And one can fairly easily develop a Sartrean criticism of Mark as a luckier Scottie. Mark is resolved to alter Marnie's consciousness so as to justify his appropriation (by the 'true love' of bourgeois monogamy) of the frigid reserve which he craves fetishistically, as the 'icy water of bour-geois calculation'. That he has to reform a thief (the anti-bourgeois) only renders his project more odiously hypocritical (Scottie, at least, is attempting to liberate himself from a complacent world). The equa-tion of full instinct with the efficient management of wealth, and of theft with psychological disorder, is strenuously conformist, and what the film asserts is not animal generosity, but the assurance of success. It takes Marnie from one tragic plight to another, as one would more easily see without the mystique of domestic bliss—if, for example, Marnie were replaced by a youth played, perhaps, by Alain Delon, for whom Mark hoped to find a respectable employment. *Marnie* is the anti-Genet.

It's equally plausible to see the film as repudiating the hypochon-driac scrupulousness typical of liberal, and sometimes radical, thought, e.g. the notion of psychological violence as unnatural or harmful. Just because Mark respects Marnie's ego, he dares invade it and dismantle it; force is an essential ingredient, although obviously balanced by restraint and consideration, as in Mark's abstinence. Although the film doesn't make much sense if considered as a 'crime and punish-ment' affair, Hitchcock gives Marnie a brief soliloquy on 'decency' during which she looks straight at the camera, and what begins as an ironic accusation of the hypocrisy of respectable folk becomes an expression of her disgust with herself, so suggesting that an underlying intuition about right and wrong is second nature to most of us, that Marnie always had some sort of conscience, that man is naturally immoral but not naturally amoral.

The film certainly refuses the argument, often relevant, easily abused, that the hypocrisy of the merely 'decent' justifies the most odious crimes of the outsider. The argument is often also self-defeating, because it is so easily reversible; and because odious crimes often exist in complicit combination with the aims of respectability. Given Hitchcock's Hobbesian tendencies, an imperfect order, indeed, one verging on the tyrannical, might seem to him a lesser evil than chaos, on hedonistic grounds, i.e. even if tyranny is no more 'moral' than the chaos, and less spontaneous. Certainly, Hitchcock admires Mark's generously anarchistic obstruction of police justice. But Mark's decisive strength is needed for the anomic Marnie to be forced to be free from her own freedom, i.e. from her past ties, so as to feel that she belongs, not *to* Mark, but *with* him. Apart from blackmailing her into marriage, Mark's taking her to her childhood home to relive her trauma is an abduction, an emotional rape, just as much as his earlier, seduction-rape of his bride. In the influence of any human over another, for good as for evil, power is as necessary as freedom, yin to its yang.

As in *The Birds*, the elaboration of details lifts them altogether out of the category of plot mechanics into that of corollaries. Alongside the familiar category of symbol one may adduce that of symptom, and that of mask, whose function is not to express something but to conceal it while permitting a covert (and deviated) discharge of its energy. In many of Hitchcock's earlier films, the astonishingly regular structure of detail is a by-product of conventional constructional techniques. From *Rear Window* on, however, Hitchcock returns to an elaboration of narrative detail which matches that of his livelier English films. There the structure is discursive and picaresque, but in the American films it is reconciled with tight narrative unities. Hitchcock's expertise in the matter derives not merely from ingenious and aesthetic craftsmanship, but from the extent to which his art is essentially a matter of obsession. Impatient as he claims to have been with American audiences' concern for logical plausibility, he dutifully respected it, until the increasing sophistication of the '60's made more allusive, intricate and poetical structures commercially viable. *Psycho* is freer in form than *Sabotage*; *Marnie*, while as tightly structured as *Spellbound*, is infinitely richer, not only in external incident, but in what aren't so much *temps-mort*, as moments of normal social tension linked to climaxes of which the melodrama is merely a symbol, a symptom, and a mask. If we imagine a version of *Marnie* in which Mark discovers that the childhood episode was not a repressed memory, but a repressed fantasy, the whole film would have held

together just as well. It might have provoked the queries suggested by
the final family photograph of *Repulsion*: what distinguishes the
development of normality and abnormality? But it would still be
interesting to observe Marnie's blends and oscillations of compromise
and hysteria, nostalgia and rejection, provocation and solitude. As it
is the traumatic memory is eminently reversible. In showing the
childhood killing, Hitchcock's kaleidoscopic close-ups of straining and
intertwined limbs imply the primal sexual scene. Marnie is misconstruing this struggle as sexual intercourse, mirroring, and recalling,
Freud's theory of children misconstruing sexual intercourse as struggle.
Marnie's unconscious guilt would then be due to her having accidentally-on-purpose murdered the 'father' for not being permanently
lured away from her mother. Earlier (in the film), but later (in chronological time), the image is anticipated when, as they grapple, Marnie's
riding-boot is shown, in close-up, braced against Mark's leg. Her
mother's client was a sailor, and the dead end street abuts on docks
in which an ocean-going ship blocks out much of the sky. Her honeymoon is spent on Mark's ocean-going yacht, and the desolation of the
honeymoon rape is expressed by a close-up of a porthole framing a
waste of ocean, a shot fascinating for its ambivalence as between a
desolation of emptiness (the vagina numbed, the contrasting textures
of steel and water) and a treacherously romantic beauty (the theme is
visually opened up as Mark pursues his missing wife on deck, with its
steel superstructure and the swimming pool within the steel surrounded
by sea). The whiteness of the sailor's uniform reappears in one bunch
of flowers. Another bunch is as red as the bloodstains which distress
her. That Marnie doesn't faint at every red patch isn't in the least
inconsistent; what is required is a conjunction of red and sexual
crisis; other kinds of crisis leave her unaffected. She hardly notices one
conspicuous red chair because the compulsive gratification of having
robbed the safe represents a triumphant defence-mechanism against it,
and the bright red magazine on which she places the revolver doesn't
upset her because she's just shot Florio—a repetition of the experience
against which she has attempted to defend herself (so that now the
substitute terror is drained of its emotional energy). When Marnie
'sees red', and the screen is suffused with that colour, Hitchcock
doesn't merely tinge the emulsion. The red seems to be sprayed down,
its liquid pulsation recalls the bloodstains; and the colour seems to
burst, against pressure, just as an emotion does.

Red and white are subsidiary themes in a colour structure stressing
yellow, blue and green. The opening shot centres on a blatantly

yellow bag nonchalantly held by a grey-suited girl on a starkly empty blue-grey platform. The converging perspectives appear as the camera which has the bag in close-up falls behind it. The bright excitement of loot contrasts with the tedious desolation of—flight? or society? or both? The dominant colour of the business world—another desert—and Strutt's suit is blue. The ship blocking the end of Mrs. Edgar's street is a steely blue. Blue is conspicuous in the Edgars' home. Yellow is the colour of false freedom, the colour of the bag triumphantly reappearing as Marnie euphorically lifts her bright blonde hair from the basin in which she was washing off the black dye of her disguise. Her corn-coloured hair tosses conspicuously as she follows the hunt, just before Florio falls, and the ambivalence of gold is asserted by Marnie's jealousy as her mother brushes the rival child's blonde hair. The multiplicity of pale yellows and dull ochres in the Rutland home is that of *its* false freedom, less extreme, and therefore paler; and from this pseudo-haven she is rescued by the crisis precipitated by Strutt (forcing her to choose assent to prison, or love and hope) and by the brutal side of gentility (hunting pinks).

The empty perspectives of the station mark Marnie's nadir, in so far as her transient triumph and freedom can only affirm her bondage. The irruptions of the jungle are like the smashing of her shell, as in Mark's office and when, in his car, he bullies her into marriage, through its wet windows the roadside trees become softened and blurred by speed and rain, evoking a damp steaming jungle. The film's hottest colours are reserved for Mark's transformed office and for Marnie's reliving of her childhood terrors. The serried red brick of Mrs. Edgar's waterfront street is a kind of stiffly paraded heat, contrasting with the Rutlands' pallid yellows.

Here, too, a curious spatial correspondence occurs. The optical effects which the unfriendlier critics found most ludicrously implausible were (1) this street and (2) Marnie's hunting ride. Both scenes struck me as artificial, certainly, but with an expressionistic concentration, in the tradition which crept into English studios from Europe and there lingered on. One thinks of Hitchcock's debts to German expressionism in *Murder*, of Cavalcanti's nocturnal streetscapes in *For Them That Trespass*. The sailor and the horse are pseudo-fathers; the wall and the ship prefigure the fence over which Marnie cannot ride Florio. The ship, visually dominating her childhood street, masks her memory of the sailor within her home. Visually, the empty station is a converse of the ship. Florio on which she rides and which she owns matches Mark's automobile, in which he owns her, and which is a family sarcophagus. The theme of intimate movement is continued through into the ocean honeymoon with its delusive sexuality. It is at sea, on board the yacht, that consummation is parodied by rape and Marnie suffers her relapse towards suicide (although, as Robin Wood observes, her choice of swimming pool signifies her wish to be rescued). At Mrs. Edgar's, Marnie's pillow is embroidered with the world 'Aloha', and all which that implies of ships leaving ports, of false escape. Thus her mother, and social myths, collude, with Marnie, to see that her dreams reverse the truth (the *happy* sailor leaves the dusky *maidens* of a *foreign* port). Living in a dead-end street, like riding to hounds, is a way of getting nowhere, of not having to face the fact of killing. Marnie's free associations include a reference to Jack and Jill who went up the hill; Marnie's trauma occurs on the stairs, as per the phrase 'up the wooden hill to Bedfordshire'. The children playing in the street sing, 'Mother, mother, I am ill, send for the doctor over the hill.' The ship and the fence are two other hills, both leading away from the truth. Her only escape is through theft—the perspective of emptiness in the opening scene. Spatially, the film confronts Marnie with four ways out: the station emptiness, the ship, the fence, and the staircase up to the truth. A film of climbs rather than falls, it is the converse of *Vertigo*.

As in the reports of the schoolroom attack in *The Birds*, *Marnie* has its careful discrepancies. Marnie wails, 'I hit him—I hit him with a stick!' when in fact she hit him with a poker. As a result of the 'accident' her mother limps with the aid of a stick, returning us to the theme of legs. The colour of deceptive freedom is near enough the colour of Marnie's hair; and Marnie hit the sailor over the head. No wonder she's jealous as Jessie's golden hair is brushed at her mother's knee (a very gentle hitting), and she proffers her own, only to be pushed away from her mother's 'aching leg'. She has to shoot Florio in the head because of a broken leg. When Lil volunteers to do it for her, Marnie cries, 'You like killing things!', making a paranoid projection into her rival of her own sexualised anger. All the same, human nature being what it is, paranoia isn't altogether wrong; Lil *is* out to persecute Marnie, unjustly, albeit in a different way, with paranoia on her side too. The link between the stick and the poker (which kills the sailor) and the pistol (which kills Florio) is established by the finger which the otherwise flabby Strutt points with startling rigidity at Rutland. 'Just you wait till you've been victimised!' he cries. And in Hitchcock's original version, of course, Mark was more Marnie's victim than Strutt will ever be.

Thus, in innumerable ways, the discursiveness of *Marnie* is more apparent than real. Even more than that of *The Birds*, it offers an unusually acute intrication of the melodramatic, the oniristic, the overt nuance and the cryptic notation. We can inspect almost every detail to find correspondence with the elaborations of unconscious obsession, in a manner exactly analogous to the brief free association 'rally' into which Marnie, with would-be irony, taunts Mark, and which provides clues that neither ever gets to understand. (Mark, far more directly animal than classical analysts, breaks all the rules of treatment. He offers a committed love, he sexually assaults his patient, he quits the consulting room to force her by the scruff of the neck into a direct confrontation with the past, so short-circuiting the transference.)

While some of these details and connections have at least an atmospheric effect, none add anything to the cruder aspects of the melodrama, and must wait for a second, third or fourth viewing for their connections to appear. One might explain it in terms of that unconscious appropriateness which is part of Hitchcock's, as of many artist's, 'dreamwork'; or his vein of exceptionally sly private joke; or his calmly hermetic aesthetic satisfaction; or his hope that details register in the spectator in some subliminal or preconscious way; or his feeling that while some audiences still require an obvious story unencumbered by puzzles, others enjoy puzzling over half-apparent connections. At any rate, there they are, sufficiently numerous and conspicuous to set up, with their opposite pole, of melodrama/unconscious fantasy, an alternating current. Everyday insignificances have the tension of significance. The *temps-mort* is accommodated, but only to be deprived of its innocence. The film's osmosis of symbol and detail paraphrases the only way in which we can get to know the very little we know about so many of those we airily say, 'Yes, I know him well,' or indeed ourselves, opaque and devious as we are.

The effect is accentuated by the strong conjunction of loose images, as in *The Birds*. Apart from its function as highlife gloss, the vividness of decor and atmosphere becomes part of the film's (apparent) discursiveness. The narrative is preoccupied with secrets, with emotional refusals, with the past, with invisibles. The decor is the present, a surface, an emptied dimension, accepted, socially and sensuously, yet, in its living, emotional aspects, refused. As in *Vertigo* and *The Birds*, gloss becomes necrophilia, it is the mummy case behind which people's vital organs lie scattered and embalmed. It exists, in itself, in a curious correspondence of the sphinx-like face in *Blackmail*, of the exterior landscapes of *North-by-North-West*, and of the bland composure which Hitchcock himself, before the publicity cameras, loves to affect. The diverse perspectives of the waterfront and the hunt are diversified by the open-plan labyrinth of the scene in which Marnie cleans out the safe while a deaf woman cleans out the office.

To explore the film's qualities is not to elevate it to the level of, say, *Wild Strawberries* (another study in recollection and absolution), or *Pickpocket*. But it matches, if it does not surpass, their intellectual intricacy. And even if its way with the texture of experience is relatively dry, glamourised, and light, that quality has a dandy glaciality which isn't merely negative. Its relationship to experience is that of the detective-story, rather than the soul-fight. Yet its stylisation, even more than that of the less uninteresting of Douglas Sirk's dilatations of the soap-opera formula, opens out on to, rather than glossing over, its own antitheses. Its substance isn't accounted for by the Bergmans or the Bresson. Even in Bunuel's *Belle de Jour*, where another cool blonde leads a perfidious existence, the separation between glossy surface and secret mechanisms produces a dislocation which may be experienced as artistic weakness before its unity is revealed. Hitchcock's film has its place along these (rather than Sirk's) on their own terms, and in its own right. *Psycho* revealed a quasi-hero as a villain, only to dismiss him. Marnie is both heroine and villain, and only a cure maintains what may, depending on one's perspective, seem either Hitchcock's Manicheanism, or his prudent conventionality, or his obstinate, old-fashioned preference for health over illness. Perhaps all sentiments apply.

The film marks a movement by Hitchcock towards a more affirmative position. Earlier he had combined the glossiest Hollywood settings and formulae with overtones of a darker world. *Psycho* is black as a blacker era gets under way. Thereafter, in an epoch particularly propitious to a darker vision, he postulates, but refuses, pessimism, whether in the cosmic form of *The Birds* or in the introverted form of *Marnie*. The three films thus form a group, moving from bleakness to a positive faith in a humiliated moral decency. As the animal symbols recurring in all three suggest, they are not so much moral, as philosophical, enquiries into man.

Torn Curtain

North-by-North-West invested Hitchcock's picaresque chase with an emotional complexity developed from his Selznick period, and with sensuous luminosity of the Technicolor '50's. One might have expected *Torn Curtain* to add the intricate psychological and moral balance developed during *Marnie*.

Instead, *Torn Curtain*, is the first of two films to take as its framework the Cold War (albeit at a time when, despite the Cuban crisis, its urgency in most minds was diminishing). During the previous two decades, Hollywood's overall experience had been that Cold War themes were box-office liabilities. This presumably arose only when the too-obvious moral polarity was allowed to rule out interesting emotional conflicts. Thus the films were reduced to melodrama, except that the continuing reality of the Communist menace, rather more profound and incomprehensible than Nazism, undermined any merely filmic happy end. The exceptions arose either from concentrating on personal conflicts within what was in effect merely a backdrop, or from finding areas of ambivalence within the simpler polarity, even at the cost of hysteric belligerence. Hitchcock's discussion of his earlier Cold War projects with Truffaut suggests that he saw things in this way, and had no intention of querying the prevalent American identification of Communism with evil.

From a box-office point of view, the two Cold War films represent a compromise between the spy themes popular in forms as diverse as the Bond films, but with more real a framework and with identification figures who, while more familiar than the Bond-type hero, were also more positive and prosperous than the heroes of Len Deighton—although the latter were better attuned than Hollywood tradition supposed to the public's increasing acceptance of moral seediness as part of espionage and, indeed, life. Other talents were responding to America's sharpening domestic tensions with a revival of the *film noir*. And although Hitchcock had always held aloof from their concentration on criminal milieux (or indeed, anything below the middle-class level), *Psycho* and, certain of the films of Robert Aldrich, indicate how the changed climate of the '60's might have given the subversive side of Hitchcock fuller expression than anything since *Sabotage*. But Hitchcock turns aside from the complications of the domestic scene, perhaps because he belongs, after all, to the older Hollywood, perhaps because the lean and anxious man within is no longer struggling to

get out, perhaps because his increasing interest in balanced affirmation veered into moral complacency. It is interesting to apply the
paranoid logic of spy films to Hitchcock's films and wonder if he had
been asked by the C.I.A. to make films which would keep the Cold
War image alive in everyone's mind.

While other delegates to an international scientific congress shiver
in a clammy fog, Professor Michael Armstrong (Paul Newman)
snuggles cosily under grey blankets with his fiancée, assistant and
mistress, Sarah Sherman (Julie Andrews). After a mysterious telegram, he callously breaks with her. Doggedly she follows him, even
on his flight to East Berlin, where, to her astonishment, he declares
that he has defected to the Communist bloc. The East Germans are
gratified, but still suspicious, and Sarah remains with him, more,
perhaps out of personal devotion to Michael than a firm conviction
that he couldn't really be up to anything immoral or unpatriotic.
Eventually, in their hotel suite, he reasures her of his real intention,
which is to contact one Professor Lindt from whom he hopes to
learn key scientific secrets; but further than this he won't take her into
his confidence. They have been given a 'guide', Herman Gromek, an
ugly, burly man who reminisces affably about his New York days.
Michael gives him the slip long enough to reach a farmhouse connected
with a resistance group called 'Pi', but Gromek follows him there, and,
Michael helped by the farmer's wife, contrives to kill him, slowly and
messily, by recourse to a pudding bowl, a spade, a carving knife, and a
gas stove.

The East Germans send Sarah and Michael to Leipzig to be inter-
rogated by scientists there. Lindt sits remotely in the lecture room's
upper tiers, testily refusing to speak privately to Armstrong, from
whom he maintains he can have nothing to learn. But he softens to
Sarah, on whose co-operation Michael is now forced to rely. With the
secret police hunting through the academic buildings, Armstrong
goads Lindt into revealing the vital information—out of contemptuous pride, and with nothing given in return.

They are able to catch Pi's freedom bus, which, running a few
minutes before the regular service, gets them to East Berlin. Michael
misses his contact, but is recognised by a rather gruesomely colourful
Polish Countess (Lila Kedrova). The Communists are willing to allow
her to go to the U.S.A., but the U.S.A. requires a sponsor, and she
blackmails Michael into promising to act as hers, and passes him
on to his next contact, before his pursuers oblige him to abandon her.
He finds Sarah, and they are surrounded in a theatre, from which he

escapes by shouting 'Fire!', even though, in the confusion, he and Sarah are all but separated. A bribe to a venial stagehand gets them into the ballet company's baskets, and, although they are nearly betrayed by an imperious ballerina, they swim to Sweden and safety. There they have to take refuge from press photographers under a grey blanket.

The film begins and ends with the couple under a grey blanket. At first, an apparently idyllic couple, they alone aren't lost and shivering in a grey blanket of fog. But the telegram reveals the profound solitude which we, like Sarah, have yet to suspect. Personal treachery opens into a political one. Michael is a loner. Although he will accept help, in a purely impersonal, businesslike way, he offers nothing in return. One of those who take great risks on his behalf, is the East German farmer's wife, Sarah's older, harder, sadder 'double'. She helps him kill Gromek. Her similarities to his fiancée not only maintain the latter's presence from scenes from which she is absent, but complicates the sense of the close and strenuous physical struggles in which her older double and the two men engage. Then only Sarah has nothing to offer, and Michael mistrusts her, strikes her off, until he finds that only her personal aura can get Michael into conversation with Lindt, whose intellectual megalomania doesn't rule out a relaxation into the pleasures of the flesh. Indeed Lindt's excitability proves his undoing, as opposed to Michael's subtle, steely playing on his vanity. Pi's entire organisation risks itself to get their *passengers* back to safety, on that conspicuously gregarious form of transport, an (omni)bus. Michael meets another variation on his own, by now rather shaken, aloofness: the supplicant Countess, whom he betrays. The confusion of the theatre offers both freedom and loneliness, enables them to escape their pursuers, although also threatening to separate them. Michael reaches the right door only through Sarah's help. Like the suburban couple of *Rich and Strange*, the pair return to the symbol of their intimacy; the grey blanket for the semi-detached fireside. But maybe Michael has learned something; that though a forceful will is a *sine qua non*, it must be mellowed, balanced, chastened by some such humilities as gratitude and guilt. The moral is, in the end, merely a conventional mixture of private purpose and mutual dependance. Sarah apart, all the people from whom Michael accepts help, only to fail to reciprocate it, are aliens or exotics with whom it is difficult to identify and with whom one's social bonds are in any case problematic. This general balance may well reflect Hitchcock's sense of other than intimate social bonds as being decidedly peripheral—

returning us to *The Birds*, and to *North-by-North-West* which offers only one alternative loyalty, patriotism, which Thornhill rightly relegates to second place.

Michael, 'going it alone', exemplifies Western individualism. Its temptation, a ruthless individualism, might lead him to defect, but, fortunately, is only apparent. None the less the motivation for his apparent defection is mixed indeed. He has narrowly failed in his attempt to develop an anti-missile-missile, and this not only irritates his intellectual pride, but threatens his career as a government-sponsored scientist (and, one might add, bureaucrat). He seems reasonably patriotic. And perhaps some sort of apprehension that, to quote Nurse Cavell, 'patriotism is not enough' underlies his feeling that the missile is an ultimate weapon which will make war impossible. That it will do so only, it seems, if the U.S.A. has it too, makes for an extremely suspect reconciliation of international sentiment and patriotic power-politics. Hitchcock is altogether equivocal as to the balance between Michael's ambition, his patriotism, his internationalism, and his presumably quite strong feelings for Sarah. If this very equivocation precludes any profound analysis of morality, whether personal or public, it represents the film's common-sense morality, whereby the only viable solution to the problem of man's egoism is to make it possible for him to reconcile selfish and altruistic activities and to select activities which will satisfy both his needs. This is extremely un-Jansenist and un-Calvinist and would reiterate the tolerant, cynical, but not misanthropic wordliness of *To Catch A Thief*. Michael is just as much a thief as Robie and Marnie.

Our sympathies lie with him because he is in the centre of the action and our most continuous identification; because he is trying to do something at high risk; because he offers us an agreeable balance of superiority and worry; because he combines force and generosity, in a way which is sufficiently obvious as reinforced by Paul Newman's hero *persona*, to re-assure us that his disloyalty, meanness or ideological confusion are merely theoretical possibilities, and because the real moral tension is between an enterprising individualism and an enterprising if ill-disciplined patriotism. We would feel the former to be a sin and a temptation only if it were strong enough to operate without the countervailing power of patriotism (to prevent him defecting) and its reinforcement of inspiration (to inspire him to his private enterprise espionage).

Our fears of his defection are shifted to Sarah, and in a weaker form. Her first test comes when she must decide whether or not to stay in East Germany with him. *Either* she has faith in his goodness, *or* she is prepared to betray her country for a reason which is both selfish and altruistic. And we may believe that, on the spur of the moment, with her mind upset by his betrayal, what moves her is her personal devotion to him rather than her belief in his patriotism. This order of priorities is normally felt to be excusable in woman, although her intuitive faith in Michael is omnipresent, as a kind of moral safety-net—rather like our intuitive faith in the intuitive judgement of anyone played by Julie Andrews. But the moment of truth is held back until she is invited by the East Germans to reveal scientific information as a proof of her sincerity. Her resourceful refusal to do so wins Michael's respect, and trust in her Machiavellianism, which hitherto he had underestimated. It is still possible to hold that Sarah's refusal to divulge America's secrets is motivated less by patriotism than by her sense that Michael is, after all, patriotic, and that to divulge those secrets would lose her his love; but the most apparent sense is, that for her, as for Michael, 'I could not love thee, dear, so much, loved I not honour more.'

Although the success of Michael's enterprise would seem intended as a vindication of his basic morality, he sinned in not taking Sarah into his confidence. Not that the director of Marnie would axiomatically condemn interpersonal deception any more than, in *Marnie*, he condemns interpersonal violence. But Armstrong prolongs his callousness and distrust needlessly, albeit excusably, and so expresses his essential solitariness, which is also egoism. But perhaps he will be chastened, or simply revise his attitudes, as a result of his experience of dependence—on Sarah, on a farmer's wife, on the good brave busload of Pi, and, of course, on the venality of a stagehand. Neither Michael, the individualist, nor Sarah, the personal altruist, can ever be sure where personal freedom ends and obligations to strangers, groups and collectives end (although Hitchcock, following American lines, would see the more widespread obligations as weaker than is usual in English films). At any rate, the couple's togetherness under its blanket is less different than at first it seemed from the dully grey shivering of scientific internationalism, which is even more suspect in American than in English films of disdaining close personal and patriotic relationships while proving naïvely gullible about the apparent idealism of Communism. All of which is understood as a possible motive rendering Armstrong's treachery plausible. But there are discreet challenges to the moral complacency of the free world. Even experience of American democracy isn't an unanswerable argument.

Gromek has lived in New York, and, with very little feeling one way or another, has rejected it to return to his police-state (Hitchcock is careful not to detail possible reasons why Gromek doesn't just *love* New York, so we can assume he was just a failure, a misfit, or power hungry as only tyranny could satisfy). A testy, authoritarian, élitist, old Professor has succeeded where the American government, with all its freedom of inquiry, has failed. Ironically, it's the Communists who are perfectly ready to let the Countess choose freedom, and it's the Americans who keep the iron curtain down. She can't find a sponsor (reminding us that private enterprise has its limitations where charity is concerned, and we may also remember the variety of jokes about the low social status and wretched existence of Polish ethnic groups in the U.S.A., so that even if she gets there she's unlikely to be much less forlorn than she is here). It's not America but Pi, with its East German patriots, who represent the golden mean between individualism and collectivism, forming a personal human group, which is closer, warmer than patriotic abstraction. The avarice of the stagehand represents the *other* face of the capitalist spirit: the miserly counting of coins, in return for which life and freedom are *sold*. The film's moral polarity nevertheless remains identical, whether or not the stagehand is a West or an East German. If the former, the criticism of capitalism is obvious, if the latter, the capitalist spirit is criticised, even though combined with an additional criticism of Communism, for permitting only the pettiest and meanest applications of that human greed, whose ineradicability is the unanswerable criticism of Communist ideals (not that we see much of those). Not for one second, therefore, are we tempted to suppose that Communism in any shape or form might, even amidst a tangle of errors, offer any moral or human positive whatsoever. Gromek and Lindt are affable enough, at some time or other, but one would hardly expect all Communists to glower unrelentingly under all circumstances whatsoever, particularly after Khrushchev had replaced Molotov as the image of Russian Communism in the West. And both Gromek and Lindt turn reassuringly sinister, or threatening, or irascibly authoritarian, just in time for all our sympathies to uncomplicatedly revert to Armstrong's purpose. The freedom bus is run by volunteers, which vindicates private idealism against any Socialist need for compulsion, and neatly balances any implied criticism via the Countess's lack of private sponsors. And it really isn't surprising that she can't find any, given her bizarre appearance and unrealistic ways, for which she is quite arguably at fault, in terms of human relationships, even though we feel sorry for her. And even if Armstrong leaves her in the lurch, it isn't at all clear that she wasn't ready to denounce him if he didn't help her, or, even if she wouldn't actually have gone quite as far, that she would have refused to help him so that if he leaves her in the lurch it's her fault rather than Armstrong's, especially as he's under duress, with the fate of world peace on his shoulders, and it would be unfair to expect him to feel more than mild qualms about her. A shot of cleaning ladies working away in a hotel which is at once old-fashioned, bleakly joyless, and palatial, is clearly meant as a condemnation of a system which has lost all capitalism's vitality while having got no nearer equality. One might easily take the film's moral as a plea to hold a greater concern for those groaning under the Communist yoke and for a more militant and daring adventurism in reaction to the Communist bloc; particularly if taken in conjunction with *North-by-North-West* and *Topaz*. And obviously no one but a diehard Stalinist can feel very complacent about the West's inaction in response to Nagy's plea for help against the Red Army.

The neutralist world, of scientists and Scandinavians, is a grey confusion. The cold fog is matched by the bookseller's, whose 'religious books are in a hell of a mess'. The allegiances of scientists are dubious, for their intellectual objectivity often goes with an emotional inadequacy. A nervous, middle-aged character runs after Sarah and Michael, to be very crisply treated by the latter. One wonders if he is pathetically in love with Sarah, and one of nature's losers.[1] But on the other side of the curtain the shambles are red, not grey. As Robin Wood observes, the plot's form is that of a hero's descent into the underworld, i.e., into Hell (where Eurydice follows to retrieve her scientific Orpheus!), and Hell, of course, is red. It is the stage flames of Hell which inspire Michael to shout 'Fire!' The red confusion matches the grey one, and if the ship is filled with shivering scientists because the heating has failed, the red signifies the hottest flames of all. The opening shows faces confusedly emerging from a red-tinged fog, which, in the context of another moral balance, might have implied that the grey and the red are identical. But here it means something more like 'Beware of confusing the grey and the red and not remem-

---

[1] As such, he recalls the detective in *The Lodger*. Both detectives and scientists are, in a sense, intellectuals, and searchers after objective knowledge. Mythically, the former tend to a combination of legalistic unemotionality, moral fundamentalism, and paternalistic assurance, which facilitates a bland amorality (as per *Blackmail*); the latter to scientific unemotionality, and moral impartiality, leading to an inept subjectivism in morals, which depend on group loyalties, and not, as scientists suppose, on objective logic.

bering the difference!' and even, if we assume that the director of *The Birds* is more hawk than dove, 'Beware of grey, cold, Scandinavian neutrality! Its real colour is red!' From this viewpoint the film, far from criticising the West, merely affirms it, all its individualistic corruptions included, against a Communism which is as total a negation of man and hope as a kind of plain-clothes Hell.

Torn Curtain struck French critics as politically somewhat archaic. And it annoyed not only the French left (less for its criticisms of Stalinist régimes than for its approbation of America), but one or two Gaullists (who weren't at all in agreement with its overtones about America's presence in Europe, or the identification of anti-Communism with American interests). The prominent focus of allegiance is not Germany, or Poland, but either America (Pi devotes itself largely to getting one American scientist out with his secrets), or to a vanished past (the Countess's). Ironically therefore the film supports Stalinist contentions that resistance to Communism in Eastern Europe is largely a matter of American intervention, and pursues American interests. About European allegiances and interests the film shows a purely nominal interest. It is up to the critic's intuition as to whether this is because Hitchcock is resigned to *realpolitik* (losers get forgotten), or because he feels that American audiences will only get confused or exasperated by anything so un-American as Eastern Europe for its own sake, or because he intends some sort of tragic irony, or because he feels that freedom versus Communism is the only genuinely political issue in Europe today, or because he combines several or all of these attitudes. One can, of course, imagine other variations on the same basic storyline. Just let's suppose that for young, dynamic, clean-cut Michael Armstrong we substitute a German-American whose father had been a colleague of Lindt's before the Nazis came to power. Lindt had been consigned to a concentration camp for his left-wing views, and, if he is somewhat tetchy now, it's understandable. But our Michael's father, however, worked for the Nazis, and prospered exceedingly there before doing even better and coming to America, just like Werner von Braun and his Mr. Hyde, Dr. Strangelove. The tensions between Lindt and Michael then acquire some moral complexity. Furthermore, Sarah would then have had some real reason to fear Michael's secret propensity to technological fanaticism, which might well induce him to change sides as blandly as his father. If, moreover, Sarah had been involved in Gromek's murder, not only would our dearly beloved Julie Andrews image have soiled its angelic hands with the messy blood of human *realpolitik*, but her *ecstasy* at Michael's loyalty would immediately have been transmuted to horror as the atrocious torture-killing dragged on. Again the Countess, a safely piti-able and sinfully mean nuisance, might have been replaced by, say, an ex-fighter-pilot crippled by a brave resistance to the Nazis and since studiously ignored by his relatives in America (George Seaton quoted an analogous case which he came across in the course of researching on a film). What if Gromek's stay in New York, coinciding with the Depression, had left him with impressions of poverty, violence and venality such that he can offer some recognisably realistic criticism of the American way of life? What if the film had accepted that, for some purposes at least, Eastern European Communism and patriotism might make common cause? There would certainly have been a risk of displeasing Middle American audiences more; but there would equally have been a chance of boring European audiences less.

As so often in Hitchcock, a multiplicity of briefly or lightly sounded possibilities, far from confronting conventional assumptions, merely act as concessive clauses which can offer no real opposition of our 'rooting interest'. Ingmar Bergman's *Shame* is no less resolutely anti-Communist, but its moral enquiry is in another class altogether—as, for that matter, is another study in Baltic climates, cold hearts, and American interventionism, Ken Russell's underestimated *Billion Dollar Brain*. Hitchcock's film can certainly claim its nauseous *tour-de-force* in the thoroughly *domestic* killing of Gromek. He retains that strong man's confidence throughout, until the finally weak fluttering of the hands; and it's as well that he does, for his continuing *threat*, his rela-tive absence of terror and pain, are *essential* lest our sympathies reverse or our sensibilities produce a nausea which has too little fun. As it is, this climax occurs early on in the film, as it must, for what comes after it exists partly to smother it, to incorporate it into a conventional attitude (even though, also Hitchcock's meticulous con-struction enables it to lend something of its strength to succeeding scenes). This double process explains why, so often in Hitchcock films, the strongest and uneasiest event occurs relatively early on, well before the end, as in *Sabotage* and *Psycho*.

Sharply beautiful as Hitchcock's clear and nuanced visuals are, as they go, the lack of dramatic substance results in most of the film's evaporating almost as rapidly from one's memory as *Dial M For Murder*. Perhaps, after all, Hitchcock was short of inspiration, and simply running for cover.

Ironically, this is just as much a tourists' film as the second version of *The Man Who Knew Too Much*. For by 1966 it was no longer rare to find people who had gone to Russia via Intourist, even though their political convictions were dyed a deep and permanent blue, and *Torn Curtain* takes one through just those first-class hotels. So the film homes in on the diminution of those tensions on which it also insists.

Topaz

Hitchcock's second full treatment of Cold War themes is set in 1962. Expertly he simplifies the structure of a long and sprawling novel, reputedly based on fact, by Leon Uris, into a tale of five cities.

In Copenhagen, U.S. intelligence agent Michael Nordstrom (John Forsythe) helps a high-ranking Soviet security official, Boris Kusenov, to defect with his family. The Americans are startled at Kusenov's air of superiority and ingratitude, although, as he observes, they are only rescuing him because of his usefulness to them.

In Washington, they acquire from him just enough information to confirm their anxieties on two topics which will soon be linked: first, Soviet activities in Cuba, and second, the existence in the highest security circles of France, and therefore NATO, of a Soviet spy-ring code-named Topaz. Nordstrom learns that copies of a secret Russo-Cuban trade pact are in the possession of Rico Parra, head of a Cuban trade delegation which is staying, pointedly, in Harlem. Parra's secretary, Uribe, is 'available', but not directly by Americans, and Nordstrom turns for help to his old friend from the French embassy, André Devereaux (Frederick Stafford).

Devereaux goes in turn to a Harlem florist, a coloured friend from Martinique, who is able to photograph the treaty.

Despite the pleas of his wife Nicole (Dany Robin) Devereaux falls in with Nordstrom's plea that he go to Cuba where, as an 'un-American' Frenchman, he can help confirm reports about Russian missile installations.

In Cuba, he is reunited with his lost love, Juanita de Cordoba (Karin Dor). She is the widow of a national hero, and her luxurious living is assured by her lover and landlord, Rico Parra. Secretly she heads a resistance network. At Devereaux's request she sends her servants out to photograph the installations. But they are arrested after a guard has noticed seabirds carrying scraps from their 'picnic'. Rico shoots Juanita, but the Cuban customs can't find the film and have to let Devereaux return to America.

Back in Washington, Devereaux finds his wife absent from their flat, and a Court of Inquiry awaiting him in Paris, for being too friendly with the Americans.

In Paris Devereaux invites his little circle of friends to a dinner. Its ostensible purpose is to help him plan his defence, but he also hopes to find evidence of Topaz, and pays particular attention to the Americans' suspect, a NATO economist called Jarré (Philippe Noiret). Jarré momentarily puts him off the scent, but Devereaux enlists the help of his journalist son-in-law, François Picard (Michel Subor). Picard pressures Jarré into agreeing to speak to Devereaux, but before he can do so, two hatchet men kill Jarré and wound Picard. They leave a telephone number which will be easy to trace; Nicole, horrified, confesses that the number is that of Jacques Granville (Michel Piccoli), a senior government official, with whom she has been having an affair during André's absence in Cuba.

In Hitchcock's original ending, Devereaux, presumably challenged to a duel by Granville, held a family conference and decided to accept the challenge, apparently under the impression that it was to be a formality for the sake of honour. In the early morning, it's pistols for two on a football field flanked with posters proclaiming that mineral waters are good for your health. Too late, Devereaux realises that Granville is shooting to kill. He is saved by a—presumably Communist —sniper, positioned in the stands to finish off an agent who has now become a liability. Apparently American preview audiences reacted unfavourably, and one can well imagine that they found this sudden incursion of an olde worlde aristocratic ceremony somewhat strained and alienating, particularly after the international topicalities with which Hitchcock doubtless intended a savoury contrast. Accordingly, the film unit was reconvened, and a second ending shot, in which Granville, who can't be arraigned for lack of evidence, flies East, as cool and amiable as ever. Conceivably the quiet shock of this last twist either disappointed or infuriated audiences, or both. At any rate, a third version appeared, in which the last we hear of Granville is a pistol shot overlaid over the front of his mews residence, implying his suicide. In Britain at least, both versions were shown, although the present writer has only seen the last. At any rate, all three versions go on to conclude with yet another anticlimax. On a Paris boulevard, an anonymous passer-by idly scans a newspaper whose headlines proclaim the safe resolution of the Cuban crisis. He drops it, and strolls off, revealing the Arc de Triomphe beyond. The bored indifference of the man in the street is contrasted with shots of all the Cold

War's unknown warriors, who, like Juanita and the servants, have suffered in the continuous war of freedom against tyranny.

The film's purpose is easily mistaken. Those who argued that Hitchcock deprived his film of all possible suspense by harking back to a crisis which we know was averted might as wlel have argued that all war films are dull because we know that the Allies won and the Axis lost. But the fates of individuals are still of interest in themselves. And even a known ending can have surprises along the way. In any case, we know that suspense can exist with a confidence in happy outcome, or even tragedy's inevitability effect, against which it is maintained by our sympathetic identification with the suspense experienced by the characters, who haven't got to the end of the story yet. It's quite clear that the historical event enhances Hitchcock's ironies. All sorts of personal intrigues, risks and sacrifices go on in the margins and shadows of history. They may have little or no effect upon the outcome, serving, here, merely to confirm what the U2 reconnaissance planes had spotted anyway. And if they unmask Jarré and Granville it is only for the reciprocal loss of Juanita and her friends. Other agents and traitors will take their place. Yet sacrifice, somehow, is never quite in vain.

Although those who see Hitchcock as a subtle and sophisticated moralist will remind us that *Topaz* is about personal codes of honour as well as political matters, the fact remains that it is also about political matters. One would hardly except a film-maker of Hitchcock's disposition to question the ideological assumptions of the widest possible American public, or to make even a deliberately weak case for the Communist countries. But the involvement of France and Cuba would have allowed him to touch on interesting and dramatically effective issues about less rigidly aligned nations and third world countries. Certainly some sort of case might well have been made for a kind of neutral opportunism which, however rascally, isn't at all unsympathetic. In the event Hitchcock emphatically reasserts the Cold War in terms of a monolithic polarity which, in 1969, was somewhat archaic. His film opens with shots of a military parade in Red Square, while an opening title informs us that Kusenov was troubled in his conscience by this menacing display and all that it represented, i.e. Communist imperialism. Not only the Russians, but Communists of every nationality, are continuously unleashing violence. Russians pull guns in the streets of neutral Copenhagen, Cubans pull guns and go rampaging through the streets of Harlem, Juanita's loyal aides are hideously tortured in Castro's jails, Granville has Jarré slain and *his*

chiefs have *him* slain. Thus the film maintains the usual polarity
between *our* side, whose resort to force is always minimal and reluctant, and the *other* side, whose violence is prompt, wanton, and
callous. Communism is not only gratuitously savage but also corrupt.
Juanita refers to Rico as her landlord, and he certainly maintains his
mistress in pre-revolutionary opulence. Uribe is even more meanly
corrupt ('He won't touch anything American.' 'Not even American
money?' 'Not from an American.') While the Americans stand by their
agents, the Communists slaughter their no longer useful friends.

That Cuba isn't quite on the level of other monolithically passionless
Communist regimes is conceded by the character of Rico, who, in
Harlem at least, appears to have a certain manly warmth. Even there,
his constant companion is a menacing, red-haired bodyguard, incarnating the suspicious violence of police states. While some misled
Harlem negroes applaud their Cuban culture-heroes, the Cuban
delegates smuggle prostitutes back to their rooms (so much for any
liberal scruples to the effect that Havana had become the brothel of
the U.S.A.; America is her own brothel and the Cubans are the
hypocrites!). Later, Rico's calm manliness reveals its obverse side.
When he interrogates Juanita's servants, whom he has had hideously
tortured, his voice is firm, almost kind and paternal, so unfeeling a
tyrant he is. His indifference gives an impression of slumbering
strength which bodes ill for the woman he loves when he learns of her
betrayal. Embracing her, he assures her, ragingly, gloatingly, that her
lovely body will be subjected to such hideous tortures . . . and then
shoots her, thus sparing her, although ensuring that she dies in terror.
And while one can't quite rule out the possibility of the sadistic
equivalent of premature ejaculation, it seems more likely that a certain humanity has twistedly reasserted itself, triumphing over his
country's security in, precisely, an individualistic, anti-totalitarian and
corrupt way. Similarly, the film counts on our being concerned for
Devereaux precisely because he identifies France's best interests with
America's, as opposed to his superiors, a sharp angry-eyed man and
a sort of Adolphe Menjou-type Pétain-cum-Blimp. It is these two who
cry 'A plague on both your houses' and try to follow an independent
French policy. But they succeed only in exposing not only America
but France and the whole of NATO to Russian infiltration.

Our heroes include not only the good Frenchman who works for
America against France, but a 'French' negro who works for America
against Cuba. Dubois hesitates as to whether he should pose as a
journalist for *Playboy* or for *Ebony*, and it takes a Frenchman to

advise him that the latter would be more acceptable to the Cubans. The choice of magazines suggests that the only choice good negroes need is between an inoffensive rakishness and suburban affluence. The only intimations of race prejudice comes from Parra, in so far as he will only be interviewed by *Ebony*, although of course this might be a primarily propagandistic calculation.

Hitchcock's quiet concern for surprises of race is entertainingly worked. The Cuban delegation, though surrounded by sympathetic negroes is headed by three conspicuously white ethnic types. Rico Parra is a Spanish type. His bodyguard's red hair suggests a Celtic (Basque) ancestry. Uribe is an extravagant and fascinating creation. Despite his Latin name, he first comes on looking like nothing so much as a caricature of James Stewart. Lean, stooping, with wryly twisted face, he seems part smalltown rustic, part inhibited accountant. Even his eccentrically polygonal spectacles evoke an expressionistic Harold Lloyd, before converting him into a mad scientist *à la Mabuse*. His face seems different every time one looks at it, even suggesting a touch of the slant-eyed, so that he is like a ragbag of miscegenation, like fanatic Herbert Lom in *North-West-Frontier* and the 'chigroes' in *Dr. No*. His 'availability' is a common enough American-capitalist characteristic (as a variety of American movies have reminded us), and one can read him either as something out of Al Capp or Damon Runyon (the mingling of whose rustic and urban types is commented on in *The Crazy Mirror*). Or one may take Rico Parra in Harlem as the equivalent of a gangster-type Mr. Big with a strong base in a ward ethnic vote, and Uribe as his WASPish front man and side kick. Corruption is universal, so idealistic revolutions can only be brutal tyrannies as well as corrupt.

Ethnic twists appear also in the choice of Nordic types elsewhere. The Russian security men are Nordic, essentially, but with lumpier faces, being less civilised (although the woman with them is squat, middle-aged and ugly). Our American hero is called Nordstrom, while Devereaux's long, narrow face would be much more at home in a Bergman film than in a Renoir. Presumably, Hitchcock is combining his love of absurdity with a denial of obvious racial types. This denial might appeal to the racial liberal as a denial of racism, while also appealing to the racial conservative, suggesting that, so far as international politics are concerned, racial prejudices exist only in the minds of muddle-headed Harlem negroes and Cubans who 'put on a show' (as Nordstrom says, and he isn't answered).

We can follow the line of thought further by decoding Hitchcock's intriguing, but characteristically cryptic, insistence on the personalities of Kusenov and his daughter. After the subtitle praising the purity of Kusenov's conscience, his first words express his contempt for the clumsy techniques of his American rescuers. His drastic, hard-edge calculation of their motivations, and his hardness in bargaining, compel our respect, without being at all likeable, given our assumption that a certain friendliness of style is an animal spontaneity even when it isn't very deep. And it's hardly balanced by the 'Please . . . please . . .' with which the Americans pressure him into posing for important photographs without allowing him any rest. Eventually Kusenov's continuous jeering seems to sum him up as a brilliant organisation man, a good family man, and an egoist. Like Lindt, in *Torn Curtain*, he suffers from megalomania, and he has done very well for himself and his by fleeing to the U.S.A. He's not only a Very Important Immigrant (and a successful counterpart to the unfortunate Countess in *Torn Curtain*) but his mixture of careerist individualism and reluctant co-operation with the state is an essentially 'American' attitude (vide *North-by-North-West*).

Consequently his go-it-alone, every-man-for-himself-ism, is disconcertingly unanswerable by his American hosts, for his absence of gratitude makes him almost an exemplar of the Ayn Rand philosophy. Not that Hitchcock directs these surprises towards anything like a the profound reflection on the paradosical dialectic, or yin and yang, or give and take, between individualism and patriotism. Our shock of surprise, here, is an inarticulate one, 'pure' emotion. And even if Hitchcock articulated it, he would have a variety of perfectly conventional answers in reserve: e.g., that freedom is never absolute, but always entails a compromise with responsibility; or, along more Hobbesian lines, that the state's functions include that of administering the spankings Grace Kelly should have had in *To Catch A Thief*, although Kusenov is a spoiled brat who's clever enough to get away with it. At any rate, he's ultra-American, and his unrelenting apoliticism is a corrupt, albeit invulnerable, contrast to the double patriotism (to France and America) of Devereaux. The polarity reads to America's credit: 'Only those states which allow themselves to be abused because they are so punctilious about the freedoms which they offer merit the voluntary sacrifice of all those who have high regard for the freedom of the individual.' America is the patient foster-father-figure who, just because he *allows himself* to be fooled, has all the more right to be defended.

Kusenov's cold, formal, megalomanic style effectively conceals from the spectator the extent to which the Russian expresses those contradictions within free societies which correspond to those expressed by Juanita's privileges within Communist ones. Just because he's stripped of the placatorily friendly mannerisms of his American hosts ('Please . . . please . . .'), the spectator feels confronted by him rather than identifying with him. Kusenov is proud of remembering just how many lumps of sugar each of his guests take, and, in a hilarious scene, their faces grow longer and longer as they suffer, childishly, under his needling oneupmanship. Yet he continues: 'A cigarette? Oh, you're smoking.' And this revelation of his childish and self-centred blindness is compounded by the fact that although he only offers a cigarette he's smoking a cigar whose length is exceeded only by that of Granville's, the other traitor and megalomaniac, who, in one of the film's three endings, defects in the reverse direction, from West to East.

Not that the film equates a lack of patriotism with megalomania. For these two are complemented by a third, Jarré. He is burdened with the limp leg, the flabby figure, and the sad brown eyes, of the boy who has always been bullied at school, and the scene in which the wry and experienced diplomat is bullied by the brash young journalist is one of Hitchcock's finest bullying scenes. Perhaps we feel a certain sympathy for him, or at least sense the pathetic satisfactions of his secret retaliation. The film's quintet of traitors is completed by Devereaux and Juanita, who perceive that patriotism is not enough and combine their narrower loyalties with a sense that America is the bastion of world freedom, so that her safety is humanity's. On her behalf they selflessly accept martyrdom rather than seek immunity. For Hitchcock, all true patriotisms are pro-American. No other nationalities exist.

As to Granville's motives, Hitchcock shows no curiosity whatsoever, leaving the critic with the opportunity of postulating any which he feels best fits Hitchcock's pattern. If we approach it from a purely practical viewpoint it rather looks as if Hitchcock has run out of simple reasons and doesn't feel like embarking on any complex ones. Status and wealth can't apply since Granville is a top person already. Conscience and egoism are pre-empted by Kusenov, and a psychological grudge by Jarré. Giving Granville reasons of conscience which balance Kusenov's would complicate the Cold War moral polarity, as would those reasons which are surely the most interesting in themselves and in the context of the film. For Granville might be trading secrets with Russia *partly* to *obtain* secrets which will help him build up his department (normal organisation man procedure), and *partly* because he is a narrowly dedicated patriot who believes that France's best interests lie in steering a devious course between the two cold war blocs. We can continue the paradox. It's thanks to the neutralist policy aspects so fiercely fought for by Granville and his friends that Devereaux can get to Cuba to procure secrets from Nordstrom. And so 'la ronde' of espionage spins on in its orbits of Machiavellian paradox, and it is, after all, in America's best interests that her allies should follow their independent policies. But as it is Granville, in terms of the Hitchcock motif, would seem, by the size of his cigar, to be a bigger, smoother megalomaniac than Kusenov. He corresponds, perhaps, to the ironically expressionless face of the British Museum God. He is the God of Ironic Absurdity—in plain clothes. . . .

In British Cold War movies between 1947 and 1960 the usual reason suggested for the defection of British scientists was a combination of wrong-headed idealism and insufferable megalomania. It wasn't until well after a thaw had set in that *Ring of Spies* conceded that anything as normal as greed, weariness, and an ordinary kind of chip on the shoulder might apply. One may well find that film, flawed as it is, more interesting, psychologically and morally, than Hitchcock's intriguing yet somewhat mechanical idea of having a stock character go from East to West. He engineers a similar, enlivening surprise for Devereaux on his trip to Cuba. One would expect that Parra, as a strong animal male with landlord status, would be the bully and Juanita his victim. But the pattern is less simple. First, Juanita isn't offered sympathy by Devereaux, an emotion we take for granted and don't waste too much time with. Instead, he playfully chides her for infidelity, whereupon she playfully slaps his face, leaving open three implications, which, in ascending order of strength, are, that like Kusenov, she likes luxury, or that it is somehow normative that a hero's widow should have a powerful man as lover, even if she's a traitor, or that she is exploiting Parra's fascination with her for patriotic reasons. The expected bullying of Juanita by Parra is preceded by a surprise (Parra loves her so much that she can turn him out of her house even though he rightly suspects that Devereaux is both her lover and a spy) and concludes in another (although he makes sure she dies in fear, his killing her is sparing her). In this lady-and-the-commissar variation on the lady-and-the-groom story, the lady is a perfidious heroine and a *femme fatale* (like Eve exploiting Van Damm). Even in a People's Democracy, class deference lingers on, and it's never quite clear where Parra's love of Juanita ends and his inverted snobbery begins, how far she is protected by his vulnerability in love, or, by the natural authority of her class, or by her public prestige as a national hero's widow.

Following a usual Hollywood formula, the tragic and interesting stories are relegated to secondary roles, where their challenges to consensus optimism are briefly upsetting but not too much so. In fact we have to be reminded of them by the final montage. Certainly the moral problems of espionage (including the dirty things agents have to do to, or ask of, their allies as well as inflict on their enemies) had been far more trenchantly aired in Anthony Asquith's *Orders To Kill* and Jack Lee's *Circle of Deception*, long before the later films based on Len Deighton and John Le Carré. But as well as seeing Hitchcock's film as lumbering ultra-cautiously in their rear, one should see it also as a deliberate defence of the American espionage network, presenting it as a structure which, without being perfect, comprises, essentially, dedication and nobility. It is easy for the man in the street, reading his newspaper, to pontificate about the immorality of diplomats and spies, but it is he, not the Nordstroms and the Devereaux of this world, who should examine his conscience and appreciate what is being done for him. The ending is an almost direct reference to the final shot of that bravely dissident film *The Ugly American*, where a typical American televiewer gazes blankly at his set, neither understanding nor caring about the efforts of an American diplomat (Marlon Brando) to prevent American intrigue from unleashing an unnecessary war in a little country in the corner of South East Asia. Hitchcock's film is an apologia for the C.I.A., among other, less political and more interesting things.

It is lifted out of the class of mere propaganda by its style's dedication to the continuity: espionage-diplomacy-negotiation-domesticity. These diplomatic spies emanate something of the quality of organisation men, more or less loyal, with their wives, to their corporations. Hitchcock brilliantly sets forth the *temps-mort* of office existence. Rico Parra, looking for a file, notices the absence of a briefcase from its expected place and looks vaguely round the office for it. His still diffuse focus of attention is distracted by a grease-stained document enfolding a forgotten hamburger. He interrupts his secretary to ask for two clean copies, and has a blank moment before recalling what it is he began looking for. The involvement of suspense with such a *temps-mort* is simple enough, once one has thought of it, but to think of it is a stroke of genius, for its absurdist intrication of everyday realism and tragic matters. As the NATO committee assembles for its climactic conference, a longshot allows us to observe their leisurely but definite separation into three groups, the hasty trafficking of dignified yet furtively confidential emissaries between them, and then a rapid, oddly imperceptible drift which leaves Granville isolated. We shift to close-up as he becomes aware of a spatial and spiritual change in his position, and then a colleague politely intimates, 'The Americans would rather you weren't at the conference, Charles . . .' The manner catches just the disingenuously tactful shift of blame to the Americans, and the covert affirmation implied by this acquiescence in their wish. If *North-By-North-West* takes grey flannel suit man out of his urban executive role and drags him through a geography of American loneliness, the key-signature of *Topaz* is that of the implosive solitude which comes near a Machiavellian view of existence, as of politics. *Topaz* might have been inspired by a line in *The Lady Vanishes*: 'You can't judge a nation by its politics'—inspired by it only to refute, or to balance, it.

Certainly, in *Topaz*, Freedom, American style, takes the place of the Florentine prosperity which meant so much to Machiavelli, and which makes of him a jingoist rather than a moral nihilist. Hitchcock extends Machiavellianism from its usual reference, to political matters, to show how relationships of every kind, including the most personal and intimate, are either dominated, or extensively infiltrated, by private schemes, by secret alliances, by devious bargains, by ambiguous clauses, by the balance of power. Every human relationship is a diplomatic affair. Occasionally a political matter is settled by the melodramatic gun, but more often by knowledge or the possession of some secret which is always likely to recoil upon the man who uses it: 'How do you know that?' Clearly, the diplomats are merely a special breed of organisation man; and the disruption of marriages is not a particular hazard of diplomacy, but derive from the unromantic fact that every wife is also married to her husband's social and professional position. The private sphere is constantly invaded by the professional, although it may also redeem the merely professional. Nordstrom and Devereaux are, almost idyllically, friends, but none the less make careful appeal to the favours they have done each other in the past. Those reminders are not merely for the benefit of the audience. Some at least of Devereaux's previous visits to Cuba were inspired by his continuing love for Juanita, about which he lies and bluffs to his wife much as he might to a foreign diplomat. She forces him to the patriarchal cry, 'I forbid you to mention that woman's name in this house!', an order which implies a lie ('Your suspicions are poisoning

our marriage! She is only "that woman".'). Finally she confesses her
affair with Granville, even though Hitchcock carefully tells us that her
confession has no prudential, personal or patriotic necessity (the telephone number can be traced anyway). But even the spider webs of
deceit which diplomatic ingenuity can spin must hang, in the end, from
certain commitments, which have to be *honoured*, and with all the
everyday virtues which they entail: truth, loyalty, standing by one's
word. There is honour among diplomats, as between unfaithful marriage partners. If the *rapprochement* between political and personal
loyalty is disturbing, it is far from nihilistic. And Hitchcock allows
the anticlimatic and admonitory end to distract us from a conclusion
which might with equal ease be drawn from *Topaz* and which not all
spectators would find reassuring. If the traditional virtues assert themselves along with the Machiavellian virtues, it is not for any reason in
metaphysics or in the nature of man. *Realpolitik* commits us to them.
Morality is an ineradicable constituent of expediency, and that it is
the *condition* of immorality is our reason for not betraying it.

It is natural therefore that alongside Hitchcock's moral concerns,
a *realpolitik* of human relationships should reassert its sway. However Nicole suffers when she learns of André's infidelity, and however he suffers when he learns of her *quid pro quo*, none the less his
extramarital sexual affair has a quality of physical and moral beauty
such that neither we nor, it seems, André, and certainly not Juanita,
with her last gift of a book of poems, would wish things otherwise.
There is no more question of Jansenism than in *To Catch A Thief*,
particularly since this love is at once romantic, cool, and Machiavellian. For André accepts Juanita's infidelities with Parra, and her
deceiving of Parra. His is a well-modulated love, without possessiveness, without jealousy. The Hitchcockian sense of subtle ascendancies
appears over and over again, as between the Americans and Kusenov
(an egoist who *doesn't* betray his family!) and between Dubois and
Uribe (the former corrupting the latter in a silent, beautifully choreo-
graphed mime which is also curiously reminiscent of the seduction of
an inhibited and puritanical homosexual). But to stress the sexual
aspect would be to commit the fashionable error of seeing a quality
of life force (the charm of the guiltless fixer) in its narrowly sexual
aspect only and omitting life force as force. If persuasion is seduction,
seduction is control. A joy in the guiles of force appears also as
Kusenov's security guards are ambushed by a group of tough blonde
American strong arm men who, turned sideways on to them, move
back and forth, to impede them but without looking at them, in a

beautiful visual equivocation as between accidental jostlings in crowds and relentless military drill. We are anxious about Dubois precisely because his confidence suggests *hubris*, and because his balding front and his delicacy suggests he might be one of nature's losers (cf. *Marnie*), as, later, the equally confident Mendozas prove to be. In a theoretical way, one might postulate their fate as a quiet punishment inflicted on us for the complacency which Dubois's success has encouraged for us. But if this connection is made then we ought also to make another which reverses it. For an equal pride of life and self-assurance is shown by young Picard, confronting Jarré. And even after he has been wounded, he looks at the blood and the holes with romantic delight, also enjoying being the centre of his family's concerned admiration and attention.

We have previously suggested how much Hitchcock's intricate structures of motif owe, not only to his intuitive flair, and his lifetime's elaboration of his craft, but also to the presence of certain preoccupations which are doubtless personal ones, even though, one suspects, he is careful to indulge only those personal preoccupations which he is sure loom suitably large among his public's consensus. The intricacy is nowhere more apparent than in the rendezvous which he contrives between the themes of freedom, homes and egalitarianism.

The Kusenovs escape as a family. Having landed in America, they are driven past the Capitol, whose dreamlike whiteness inspires his daughter to mistake it for the White House, a glimpse of which so moves her that her father looks at her, contemptuous of feminine sentimentality. The theme of *public* and *private* residences having been introduced, the Kusenovs' enter their 'safe house', to be greeted by their domestic staff, who smile and bow with that ready friendliness which is a common enough American style but which takes on a sharper meaning when the object of their shiny servility is a Communist secret policeman. Some spectators will feel uneasily indignant (despite an early reminder that only good treatment attracts defectors —itself a Machiavellian calculation). Others will find this reminder of servility and inequality in America a relatively gentle tit-for-tat for Rico's corruption. Women spectators may see mainly an enjoyably wish-fulfilment escape from their domestic service problems.

Later, Kusenov dismisses the servants, saying he will serve coffee himself. Briefly we wonder whether he hasn't, after all, mellowed a little towards his servants as towards his guests, and become informal, anti-hierarchical, like Nordstrom and André (the latter, as a European rather than American, briefly, in distress, regresses to a patriarchal form of speech). But if Kusenov serves coffee it is only to demonstrate his chilly perfection on the personal level also. He has adopted only the icily egoistical streak of American life. His daughter, as a younger person, and as a girl, and with something of her mother's simplicity, has less of a problem, and we see her, later, seated at her piano, before a sunlit window in one of Hitchcock's beautiful interiors. A reference to the bourgeois interiors of the Dutch school is no more incongruous than references to Stalin's daughter. This domestic scene is beautiful not only for its sunlit contentment, but for a contented apartness. She is the piano-playing daughter of an American home forty years ago. Perhaps she is, or will be, a little lonely, a little apart. Perhaps her contentment is a comment on the pace and dissatisfaction of contemporary America; quite probably Hitchcock intends to suggest, but not to underline, both senses.

The scene is a conclusion of a series of notations which imply, without actually telling, a story. They may have arisen, in the first instance, merely as a way of adding a dramatic dimension to melodramatic events. In the porcelain museum, Hitchcock cuts between (a) Kusenov's daugher, (b) the young Russian security man separated from her in space, apparently a stranger to her, and (c) the porcelain at which she gazes, its lovers kissing in a gently curving movement. As Hitchcock, faithful to Eisensteinian montage as pure cinema, must have known it would, the porcelain leads us to wonder if she, and he, were lovers, or linked by some sentimental bond—thus complicating the pursuit, and delicately sounding the theme of treacherous lovers which swells with Parra and Juanita, Nicole and Granville. Perhaps, the security man, in pursuing her, is stoically putting a cruel totalitarianism before love. Perhaps he had other hopes and aims in mind of giving her a chance to refuse to escape. At any rate, instead of assenting to his presence, she drops the porcelain, and chooses freedom. It is not the only 'accident' in which she is involved; a few moments later, she stumbles, while being chased, into a bicycle, as if some unconscious, masochistic accident-proneness expressed a longing to be caught. We can play with the implications as we will. Maybe her escape is the result of her subservience to her father (and his conscience). In dropping the porcelain, obediently, she is destroying a love affair which, she sensed, might have developed: and her longing for love makes her accident prone. Or: unaccustomed to freedom, the initiative frightens her. Or: as a young person, with a totalitarian and patriarchal formation, she is torn between (a) a natural love for freedom, (b) obedience to the system, and (c) obedience to her father, a conflict which, briefly, makes an accident-prone masochist of her. Finally she sits before the piano, in the free sunlight of America, but still within her home. Is she—convalescing towards an adaptation? or failing to make it, and so a victim of Kusenov's conscience? Is this a converse of *The Birds*: the home becomes a cage?

At any rate, the image shimmers, like a self-contained tableau, subtler even than the Kusenov's meeting with their new domestic staff, which we also sense as a climax, although maybe we don't quite know why, and are meant not to know. (It is true that any exegesis of a lyrical passage is likely to be misleading, since the lyric is not the exegesis, and may be a defence-mechanism against it as surely as the manifest content of a dream exists to conceal the real feelings which though it may briefly break through it, it does not, as a whole, express.)

The film includes another beautiful interior, by a window, curtained this time. André is stripped to the waist, Juanita clad in a negligée of which the cool white curtains, with their scalloped centre, are an echo. Their poses are at once intimate (it is surely after love), yet their position, facing each other across a table, suggest a separateness veiled by graciousness. The blues and whites are slightly cold, and André goes on to explain the electronic spying devices which will result in her death in an embrace. Human beings waste little time in intimacies. Purpose is Machiavellianism, for good as well as for evil. In another climactic domestic interior, Rico shoots Juanita, her purple dress spilling out around her, over the flagstones.

The Kusenov servants are balanced by Juanita's, all personally devoted, all friendly, all giving impeccable service. At this heroine's all is *luxe, ordre, calme et volupté*. In the free world, a merely social and functional inequality is perfectly compatible with spiritual equality. As romantically as Scottie in *Vertigo*, Hitchcock connects it with the heritage of the Spanish aristocracy—noble, and doomed. The implications about Cuban history are, to put it mildly, controversial. The film's original ending may have included another variation on the theme of family diplomacy. It seems that a Devereaux family con-ference (on, possibly, a new basis of honesty and therefore equality) preceded André's decision to duel with Granville. If Nicole advised against an unnecessary risk (as one might have expected her to, after her denunciation of André for helping America) then, in this case, her advice would prove only too realistic, since Granville cheats. One can also imagine a scene in which she would like to advise against it, but, given Europe's patriarchal residue and her own guilt she allowed herself to be overruled by André's feeling that he ought to live up to some sort of code. Nor can one dismiss yet another possibility, that Nicole persuades André to accept the challenge against better judgement, because she's still soft on Granville and doesn't realise that he's a fellow-traveller first and a Frenchman second. Each of these three possibilities makes sense in terms of a pattern, whereby olde-worlde honour, though noble in Cuba, is perilous in France, where its vital urge should be subsumed into America's mixture of *realpolitik* and reliability, which are proved by its honouring of its pledges to Kusenov and its saving of André's reputation in the nick of time. At least one can see how Hitchcock's sense of pattern, far from being a rigid and academic matter, helps to make scenes more rich and complex than they might appear if considered on a purely point-by-point basis, although, to repeat a comment on the intricacies of *To Catch A Thief*, the structure exists to enrich the scenes as they go, and to create an impalpable yet affecting atmosphere without complicating the much simpler moral. Many contradictory submorals may exist within a perfectly conventional polarity.

Suggested, no doubt, by both the theme of homes, and the involvement of France, food and wine, here, has its little subtheme. There is a hamburger inside a document, there is a camera in the loaves which the gulls betray to the guards, Juanita's pantry conceals the laboratory, meal to which André summons his colleagues, ostensibly for their help, actually to seek the traitor. No bait without its hook. The natural Machiavellianism of commensalism. Thus the positive aspects of diplomatic relationships, in every sphere, are counterbalanced by the negative reading. Paranoia is an appropriate response to a Machiavellian opponent, and it should have a non-clinical sense, whereby, confronted with any offer whatsoever, one seeks to ascertain the element of self-interest within it, and where that element will lead, rather than to take anything at face-value. Such a paranoiad reading may seem common sense, or depressing, or calling for stoic acceptance, or a confidence in one's own life-force. As in *Marnie*, Hitchcock's film accepts all four readings, but insists on the last as giving life meaning, so emphatically, indeed, as to result in a certain sentimentality about the morality of politics. 'Our side' is not only objectively justified, but consists of much nicer people. The other side is not only politically wrong, but personally nasty. Our cunning is exhilarating, its cunning is malicious and mean. This creates another problem of suspense. For our side displays a calm self-defence which is traditionally invulnerable, as audiences, by now, sense it to be. Furthermore, the theme requires of the characters a stoic self-control, and it's far from easy to suggest this yet to create the powerful feelings which would assert anxiety against this implied invulnerability. As a result, the film's upper lips are stiffer than in any English movie, while the characters respond as bleakly and minimally as in a standard television drama—to which the film's human interest is too often reduced. This, I think, is the root cause of its dryness.

Otherwise it possesses a panoply of Hitchcockian virtues, notably, that bold clarity which so curiously paraphrases the expressionist fog, and that substitution, for the blurred, looming entities of situations and entities in Kafka, of a kind of lamination effect, of mystery existing behind mystery, of danger existing behind danger, and a stoic acceptance of the absurd. *Topaz*, in particular, possesses this strange sense of suspension between acceptance and despair—alongside the sentimental aspects which are sufficiently conspicuous to inspire one's mixture of admiration for consummate craftsmanship, and lack of involvement, except of an intellectual-aesthetic sort.

Hitchcock doesn't bother to explain, because he knows we can work out why Juanita and her aides mislead Devereaux (and the audience) as to where they hid the film. If he knew where it was, his reactions might have betrayed it. (For between friends, there is also a benevolent Machiavellianism; perhaps between friends, above all.) But such a motive is not altogether convincing, since Juanita and André both show such coolness that there's no reason for her to suppose that he's so weak as to need mothering in this way. One certainly can't justify Hitchcock's not showing *us* where Juanita really hid the film on the grounds of our identification with André. For the latter's airport departure isn't shown to us, although a simultaneous event, which he could not have seen, Juanita's being shot by Parra, is. Hitchcock's deceit of us, like Juanita's deceit of André, is altogether gratuitous, a device forced on Hitchcock to intensify suspense against the non-responsiveness and assurance of his rightous characters. Possibly also he wished to spare us the obvious, dramatically uncomplicated search of André, realising that the *idea* of a search was all that was needed, and could be relegated to what, in visual terms, was the invisible background, to a far more passionate and unpredictable climax. The two simultaneous 'scenes' would strengthen one another in a fascinating 'double composition'. Another tactful use of misimplication occurs when Kusenov is led precipitately towards the photographers. We assume that this is for a press photograph, and that Nordstrom's protest against press publicity indicates America's equivalent (but minor) forms of persecution of the individual. Later the point is made that Kusenov's arrival is a secret of which the French can only have heard through Moscow. We don't bother to think back, but if we did we would deduce that the photographs were purely for identificatory or archival purposes. The apparent meaning has a second function, serving to maintain the theme of press information which has its culmination in Picard's interrogation of Jarré and its anticlimax in the final shot.

Whether or not the slow, restrained, strainedly casual stalking through the porcelain workshop-museum featured in the original, it sets the film's style. For a chase in which everyone loiters, pretending to concentrate on delicate objects, attunes us to diplomatic masks. Already so much is so intensely at stake behind little tics and composed voices as to establish a wavelength in which *only* little gestures and pauses betray the important issues which those involved hardly dare let themselves feel; for they must question, calculate, probe, pick up a telephone. The immobile, in a sense implosive, drama is rendered fully visual by Hitchcock's magisterial deployment and variation, not only of space, as in the scenes already mentioned, but of every index which might render thought visible. As often, overhead shots coincide with, or prefigure, climaxes: Juanita sinking to the floor, Jarré spread-eagled in what seems to be the road until, from street level, we see him lying on the roof of an automobile. Two visits to his home are preluded by a vertical shot down the stairwell, the camera abruptly jerking to one side to centre on the people mounting it.

Frenzy

As the new-broom young Minister for the Environment gives his proud little speech about a newly pollution-free stretch of Thames, one corpse, female, nude, comes floating along it. A necktie is tied too tightly round its neck. Although Hitch doesn't wait too long before letting us in on the identity of the 'necktie murderer', we're briefly uncertain whether to opt for Bob Rusk (Barry Foster), the cheery young Cockney Covent Garden coster, or for bad-tempered ex-Squadron-Leader Richard Blaney (Jon Finch). At any rate Blaney's estranged wife (Barbara Leigh-Hunt) and then girlfriend (Anna Massey) are shortly found raped and strangled. Eventually the culprit is cornered by Inspector Oxford (Alec McCowen), who's given some moral support by his scatter-brained wife (Vivien Merchant), while she prattles away intuitively over her gruesome attempts at *Cordon Bleu* cuisine.

Roughly, Robert is to Richard as, in *Strangers On A Train*, Bruno is to Guy. Here too the charming, queerish, mother's boy befriends the worried sporting man (here, an ex-Squadron-Leader) and murders his wife (and girlfriend too). But in this case he doesn't declare himself, and his social status is inverted (he's Cockney not playboy). The transference of guilt operates, to its usual limited extent. The irascible innocent finishes by attacking a sleeping man, battering him about the head, only to discover that it's a woman, strangled, nude, and that he's rekilling a corpse, in the spirit of *The Trouble With Harry*. In that film, the cadaver moulders amidst autumnal leaves; here it nestles in a sack of potatoes. And where Bruno's fingers strain and stretch for an incriminating monogram, Rusk breaks the corpse's clutching fingers to retrieve the incriminating initial. This body also only narrowly avoids a double death, being all but run over by a police-car (!). Hitch's early revelation of the murderer's identity is a common practice of his, indulged as early as *Blackmail* and *Sabotage*. And critical wonderment thereat arises from an elementary confusion between the mystery thriller and the suspense thriller. Here suspense obviously derives from our knowing who the killer is.

The film is set in 1972, i.e. post-Swinging London, or rather Sagging London. An early conversation between city gents establishes the benefits brought by Jack the Rippers to the tourist trade, and sets the key for a certain nostalgia for London in the era of *The Lodger*. *Frenzy* certainly catches the contemporary capital's penchant for falling awkwardly between all possible epochs. Oxford's assistant, Sgt. Spearman, could be described as a canny cross between Mr. Memory in *The Thirty-Nine Steps* and Marcel Levesque in Feuillade's *Judex*. Blaney might almost be an angry young man now dejectedly pushing middle-age, but as an ex-Squadron-Leader turned tippling barman he substitutes a seediness as per *Hangover Square*. Bob Rusk is post-Michael Caine Cockney all right, but all the old school tie ironies cluster about under the theme of an ex-serviceman's old boy net, the coupling of the Inspector's surname and his soft suave style, and his final, cool line: 'Mr. Rusk, you're not wearing your tie.' Anna Massey and the redhead theme (Rusk's hair dyed red just like his dear old Mum's) briefly evokes *Peeping Tom*'s, but here she gets hers too. Blaney spends one night in a Salvation Army men's hostel, the next in the London Hilton. The crowd mumbles something like 'Cor, another necktie murderer!', much as the crowd would have done in

The Lodger, had it had sound. Hitchcock allows Anthony Schaffer's script to perpetrate, not only every Cockney cliché in the Lord Willis book, yea, even unto 'Pull the other leg, it's got bells on!' (about which see *A Mirror for England*, p. 51), but also permits a story exposition whose clumsy creaking may well be as consciously archaic as Hitchcock's own get-up amongst the Thames-side crowd. His air of unctuous gloom and his black bowler are both as anachronistic as an Edwardian undertaker's man. The pictures on the hotel's walls would only be appropriate in an 1880 boarding-house. The killer's flat suddenly flares with greenery-yallery Tretchikoffs. The film plays with silence and sound in circa-1930 style, e.g. the Judge's sentence is concealed and revealed by the closing and opening of a glass door. Or again, the camera remains outside a room as we wait for the off-screen scream of a woman discovering a corpse. During the second murder the camera tracks back to stress that traffic would drown any screams (either way, London takes no notice). If Hitchcock is frank about orgasms, 1970-style, the violence remains considerately stylised, 1930 style. The hand-held camera is conspicuously post-Nouvelle Vague, with a certain loss, amidst the restlessness, of the old Hitchcock crispness. Anything more than one brief touch of impressionism and expressionism would have been out of place in this cool world. The sense of modern life as a *musée imaginaire* of subcultures and, almost, subepochs, is pointed when Blaney's friend promises to whisk him from his American-style hotel in London to his English-style pub in Paris.

If the film and the capital are both indeterminately adrift between epochs, the plot thematic is firmly structured around the linking corruption lurking within sex, food and money. Rusk rapes Mrs. Blaney, her legs forced conspicuously apart, and a few shots later Mrs. Oxford takes the lid off her latest dish, to reveal a soggy quail with its legs lifted up and apart. Rusk's grapplings with the barmaid's body in the potato sack, and its conspicuously protruding foot, are reiterated as the Inspector's utensils prod at a slithery little bundle of pig's trotter. The snapping of the dead girl's fingers is echoed in Mrs. Oxford's brisk breaking of a breadstick. Meat is corpses. We are all eaters of the dead, violently slain for us. Decency is a matter, not of kind, but of degree.

Covent Garden is a herbivorous rather than a carnivorous food-market, but the equation corruption = corpses = food is carried through to food = money. Blaney storms out of a pub and a job over his supposed theft of a drink. Later a customer complains over the stench of an outdated Scotch egg. Nailing advertising myths about friendly British pubs, Hitchcock's 'Mine Host' here (Bernard Cribbins) is a thoroughly sneaky character who palms rotten food off on to his customers if he can and whose real reason for firing his barman is sexual jealousy. Smells recur when Blaney is incriminated by his dead wife's powder on his banknotes. The cheery Cockney makes the odd few quid on the side as a copper's nark but complains that all these coppers make it tricky giving short weight. The polluted river probably smells and suggests corruption on a massive scale. Topically enough, Covent Garden is still a little oasis of old London, menaced by the pollution of 'improvement' schemes, i.e. bland, characterless, money-making office-blocks. The stench of contamination has its positive uses also. Rusk is betrayed by the smell of potatoes on the clothes brush with which he cleaned himself up at (returning to the gourmet theme) a transport caff.

Pollution infests human relationships. Blaney's rage has wrecked his marriage, and, perhaps, attracts the women whom Rusk dooms with the phrase: 'You're my type of woman,' i.e. the masochistic type, as his requirements of the marriage agency make quite clear. Inspector Oxford's meek forbearance in the face of his wife's gastronomic horrors suggests that a little taint of masochism may attend that decent kindness that makes the world go round. As if to substitute absurdity for easy amorality, the suspicious and the irascible are in no better nick. Blaney's been steadily sinking for years, the sneaky publican has never got further than furtively pawing the girl he covets, and Mrs. Blaney's suspicious, puritanical and kinky-faced secretary is a clear case of sexual repression complicated by sado-masochism. Her potential relationship with Rusk might give food for thought, if he weren't so insane as to be beyond placation. Mrs. Oxford applies a kind of torture by cosiness, and her cushiony imperceptiveness looks like plumping up again after her little comuppance.

If all the men weren't losers too one might speak of misanthropy. Mrs. Blaney's marriage bureau matches a mild man with a battle-axe widow who will undoubtedly cow him by comparisons with the mythified excellencies of her dear departed. Suddenly we are back in the world of music-hall songs, and the funny thing is, of course, that though entertainment fashions come and go, all this keeps right on happening, all over the place, as Renoir's *La Chienne* (for Paris 1930) and *Sailor Beware* (for England 1955) serve to confirm. But as Blaney and Oxford represent contrary (and equally gruelling) attitudes to the horrors of domesticity, so another moral polarity subsists as between the extreme of Blaney's rage—i.e. the apparently affable and level-headed Rusk—and the extreme of Oxford's devotion to duty, i.e. Sgt. Spearman. The latter accepts Mrs. Oxford's titbits with a politely eager face which is the mask of duty and insensitivity combined. Rusk, on the other hand, enjoys extremes of lust coolly, inconsiderately and undutifully, and gets, in the end, the worst of all possible worlds. Even so, those who can't stoically discipline, insensitise themselves to, their ambivalence, enjoy only derisive pleasures.

'Lovely . . . lovely . . .' he murmurs, rapt, as he stands between Mrs. Blaney's legs. But he hasn't removed his clothes and neither cares, nor notices, as she slips her bra-cups back over her breasts, in a gesture no more derisory than her murmuring of the 23rd Psalm, antiphonally with his eerie aestheticism. Although his post-coital backlash becomes a murderous rage, and his behaviour differs from Inspector Oxford's complacent assumption that the murderer's in the later stages of his 'disease', where he's impotent and only the murder provides the thrill. But if law-and-order is not quite right about Rusk, it's disastrously wrong about Blaney, goading him to a homicidal rage. The machinery of justice is no more wrong than a decent common sense, of which it is only a mobilised form. None the less it's further from the truth than Mrs. Oxford's intuitions. And their apparent sentimentality inspires in us the deepest mistrust of her clairvoyance as does its co-existence with an imperceptiveness about food which all but suggests an intense if unconscious negativity towards her man, like a touch of Mrs. Blaney's spinsterly secretary's towards men. These negative reactions within the everyday are echoed in the two little dolly girls who, hearing the secretary's scream as she discovers her employer's body, shrug and move on. That scream *might* have been Mrs. Blaney's call for help. As the barmaid endures her calvary, the camera tracks, in a lyrically elegiac movement, back down the empty staircase, using two more passers-by to distract us from the jolt of a step down, until it has crossed the street to end in a long shot of a bland façade. By now its quality of elegy is all but lost, and any scream would be drowned by the mighty roar of London's unstoppable traffic. Blaney's women are as sensible about his innocence as they are unaware of Rusk's intentions. The police reverse the pattern, thus being wrong on two counts instead of one. But any sexual pattern is broken by Hetty (Billie Whitelaw), the female hawk, perched on a sofa with hair and arms outspread, like fate, or Justice, or a fury, or a soul-sister of The Birds.

Not that these fifty-seven varieties of solipsism leads us to nihilism.

Blaney deserves our trust, because he is innocent. Those who sense he's all right include his fellow-patients in a prison hospital, rough tough brutes who pool their sleeping-pills to send a warder off to bye-byes. The very notion of so many hefty blackguards being given sleeping-pills is hilarious, with all the overtones of anxiety, insomnia and infantilisation by bedtime sweetie. Their gentle altruism, doubly touching in this gang of veteran hard cases, is all for a negative purpose (a revenge murder), and nearly gets Blaney's goose cooked for good. Fortunately, Oxford's conscientious scruples save him from himself. Oxford will doubtless help Blaney by arguing that Rusk smashed his victim across the head as well as strangling her, and the final outcome will presumably be another, albeit benign, miscarriage of justice, Blaney getting off scot-free with a forgivably brutal and sneaky murder attempt.

The 23rd Psalm may seem ironic in so far as Mrs. Blaney is promptly strangled. Its deeper spiritual assertions aren't undermined, but later Hitchcock disturbs anti-religious complacency too, with Oxford's (hardly definitive!) remark that sexual and religious mania often walk hand-in-hand. The film floats relaxedly, affably, in moral uncertainties akin to the sense of co-existing cultural periods. And doubtless the two issues aren't altogether unconnected.

The dramatic tone possesses a similar sense of flux. As intimately as Hitch observes the sexual aspects of the rape, so his camera stresses the violence of strangling which the victim's reactions soft-pedal. That discrepancy contributes to the film's at times almost inconsequential air, its bizarre good humour, mixed with the coolness of its none the less quite assured moral judgements. Critics have even spoken of our 'identification' with Rusk as he scrabbles with the corpse's fingerbones on the back of the truck, although our involvement is, surely, rather more complex than 'identification' alone suggests.

If, ingredientwise, this is Hitchcock in Hammerland (whose Grand Guignol sideline he inspired with *Psycho*), the overall tone is neither atrocious nor sensational nor tragic nor comic nor deeply dramatic. It's strangely mellow, and its co-existence with a variety of gruelling and cynical elements creates an odd, unique, almost indecisive mood. One might attribute it to the aforementioned loss of crispness, to an older exile's enforced passivity when faced with a company of actors steeped in 1960's behaviour-styles, and to only limited help from a screen play which is neither slick nor profound. But the 'indecisiveness' is also reminiscent of that in other septuagenarians' films: Fritz Lang's, Dreyer's, Renoir's. A mixture of identification and detachment, concern and tolerance, nostalgia and irony, generate the wisdom of age, which counterpoints a modern relativism and allows Hitchcock's sempiternal absurdism a little more play, in terms, not of poetic melodrama, but of easy-going everyday informalities.

Its almost mellow air hardly perfumes an insidious distaste—the fresh autumn fragrance of decay. Its stream of, not so much consciousness, as sensation (tastes, sudden silences), compounds the association: food → bodies → pollution (even *Cordon Bleu* becomes pollution). Of itself, decay might creep ever more extensively through minds, through society, save for the resistance opposed, stoically—one might almost say, 'God knows why'—by a firm sense of duty, in alliance with an unstable balance of 'hard' evidence and 'soft' intuition. Most conspicuous in the 'collaboration' of Inspector Oxford and his wife, it is extended also through a subsidiary contrast, between Oxford's gustatory masochism (the condition of his openness?) and his Sergeant's impassive politeness.

Following a general Hitchcock tendency, women tend to be trusting, yielding, and victims, although man-haters and battleaxes lurk in the margins, and the female hawk. Men, if not complacent, incline to bitterness or rage (like Blaney) and thus become victims too, although Oxford's meek tact doesn't spare him his nightly martyrdom. A critic saw Rusk as a male avenger against a regiment of women so monstrous that half our sympathies go with him. That's a matter of taste, and not mine, and Rusk's cheeriness hardly redeems him, since he's a mean little copper's nark as well. Any simple sexual polarity is denied by the variety of males and females, and even the loners become potential sexual partners, because of the film's context. Its central setting is a marriage-agency, and one might, of course, argue that Mrs. Blaney's marriage-agency makes her a quasi-madam, exploiting sexual loneliness for money. It's an interpretation one must reject, since it would also indict the food-market which is the movie's other network (and Hitchcock's movie-making too). But given the general shiftiness of marriage-like relationships, and the significance of separations, the film is almost a counter-pattern to *The Birds*. No home, here, can confirm and consolidate itself upon the shifting sands of contemporary London (dormitories, dosshouses, penthouses, hotels . . .) and this feeling gives a special sense to the sad track-back from a house across a street and to the ferocious defence of her home by Billie Whitelaw. She's thoroughly safe, thoroughly prudent, thoroughly suspicious, the 'hawk' whose savage defence of her home is really egoism and would also make social loyalties impossible. The English

Inspector affirms what Melanie in her phone-booth denies—and both shots involve momentous words obscured by glass. *Frenzy* is the antithesis to *The Birds*—for no principle, in Hitchcock's world, is sure and certain to be good and safe.

As diversely as the women, the men are ferocious, or deceptive, or weak. Oxford's mealtime masochism parodies the Jack Sprat recipe for perfect marriages: her gourmet delicacies torture her husband. And Rush strangles the women whose bodies wring from him an adoring cry. Nourishment is also punishment, but 'each man kills the thing he loves'. The strangler's and his victim's rival litanies of physical adoration and spiritual power are linked in a space-time continuum (the closest possible intimacy), yet establish minds so disparate that the sequence feels as if it's the result of cross-cutting (and not just from face to face). The double, contrary, irreconcilable streams-of-consciousness (we recall *Murder*) becomes a montage, in Eisenstein's sense, a collision of *shocks*, whose synthesis leaves us with some awkward options. We might rate sexual pleasure as more real than the religious afterlife, or make an uncertain bet on Christian reality, or opt for a double nihilism. Two psychological absolutes confront each other; each seems belied, for sexual pleasure is wretchedly brief and the prayer unanswered. And despite their absolutism, both protagonists seem almost conversational, concerned with detail, calm, one calculating the squeeze, the other reciting the psalm. Nurture and torture, embrace and combat, intimacy and incomprehension, don't just interlace each other, but are conditions of each other, interimpregnate each other; and in that sense the film is the antithesis (not the negation) of *Psycho*. For all its violence, the film has little sense of spiritual energy; London has lost its heart.

In a curious way, the mixture of consolation and destruction which goes on between human beings recalls the association food → bodies → pollution. Commensalism becomes cannibalism, and eating or drinking becomes a kind of pollution by ingestion, until the corpse pollutes the river. The equation verifies, though in a quite non-gnostic sense, Douchet's remark on meals as the transformation of matter into mind —or, here, food (stale pork pies, alcohol, birds) into sensation, which our mediocre moralities exist to indulge and to resist. Indulgence and resistance find their 'naked' confrontation as Rush rapes and murders Mrs. Blaney. But their instinctual spiritual absolutes remain in doubt, perhaps only a by-product of, an extrapolation from, the sequence man-food-home-society. Each man as an uneasily open system, sadly subject to fallible systems and to gusts of folly and of wisdom which are neither insane nor sane. Our everyday is a sequence of little madnesses.

Bibliography

AGATE, James, *Juno and the Paycock* in *Around Cinemas (1st series)*, Home and Van Thal, 1946; *Jamaica Inn, Suspicion* in *Around Cinemas (2nd series)*, Home and Van Thal, 1948.

AMENGUAL, Barthelemy and BORDE, Raymond, *Alfred Hitchcock, Premier Plan*, Serdoc, 1960.

ANDERSON, Lindsay, in LAVALLEY, op. cit.

AURIOL, Jean-George, *Festival Hitchcock* in *La Revue du Cinéma*, July 1948.

BAZIN, André, in LAVALLEY, op. cit.

BOND, Kirk, *The Other Alfred Hitchcock* in *Film Culture*, no. 41, Summer 1966.

BORDE, Raymond, and CHAUMETON, Etienne, *Panorama du Film Noir Américain*, Editions du Minuit, 1957.

BRAUDY, Leo, in LAVALLEY, op. cit.

BRUNIUS, Jacques, *Every Year In Marienbad, or The Discipline of Uncertainty*, in *Sight and Sound*, Summer 1962.

Cahiers du Cinéma, no. 39, October 1954; no. 62, August–September 1965, and *Cahiers du Cinéma in English*, no. 2, 1966.

CAMERON, Ian, *Hitchcock and the Mechanics of Suspense* in *Movie 3*, October 1962; *Hitchcock 2: Suspense and Meaning* in *Movie 6*, January 1963; and in *Movie Reader*, Studio-Vista, 1972.

CAMERON, Ian, and JEFFREY, Richards, *The Universal Hitchcock*, in *Movie Reader*, Studio-Vista, 1972.

CHANDLER, Raymond, in LAVALLEY, op. cit.

CORLISS, Richard, *Topaz* in *Film Quarterly*, Spring 1970.

DOUCHET, Jean, *Alfred Hitchcock* in *L'Herne Cinéma*, no. 1.

DURGNAT, Raymond, *Films and Feelings*, Faber & Faber, 1967.

DURGNAT, Raymond, *The Crazy Mirror*, Faber & Faber, 1969.

DURGNAT, Raymond, *Images of the Mind* in *Films and Filming*, March 1970–November 1970.

DURGNAT, Raymond, *A Mirror for England*, Faber & Faber, 1971.

Etudes Cinématographiques Special No. Nos. 84–87: *Alfred Hitchcock*.

FOX, Julian, *Reader's Letters: Rebecca*, in *Films and Filming* October 1970.

GRIERSON, John, in HARDY, Forsyth, ed. *Grierson on Documentary*, University of California Press, 1966; Faber and Faber, 1967.

HITCHCOCK, Alfred, and interviewers, in *Take One*, September 1966 and November 1968.

HITCHCOCK, Alfred, and BOGDANOVICH, Peter, *The Cinema of Alfred Hitchcock*, The Museum of Modern Art, 1962.

HITCHCOCK, Alfred and TRUFFAUT, François, *Hitchcock*, Secker and Warburg, 1967.

HOUSTON, Penelope, *The Figure in the Carpet* in *Sight and Sound*, Autumn 1963.

JOHNSON, William, *Marnie* in *Film Quarterly*, Fall 1964.

LAVALLEY, Albert J., ed. *Focus on Hitchcock*, Prentice-Hall, 1972.

LEHMAN, Ernest, *North-by-North-West* (Filmscript), Viking Press, 1972.

MILLAR, Gavin, *Hitchcock versus Truffaut*, in *Sight and Sound*, Spring 1969.

NAREMORE, James, *Filmguide to Psycho*, Indiana University Press, 1973.

PERKINS, V. F., *Rope* in *Movie*, no. 7, February 1963, and in *Movie Reader*, Studio-Vista, 1972.

PERRY, George, *The Films of Alfred Hitchcock*, Dutton Studio Vista, 1965.

ROHMER, Eric, and CHABROL, Claude, *Hitchcock*, Editions Universitaires, 1957.

SICLIER, Jacques, *Le Mythe de la Femme Dans le Cinema Américain*, Editions du Cerf, 1956.

SIMSOLO, Noel, *Alfred Hitchcock*, Seghers, 1969.

STANBROOK, Alan, *The Lady Vanishes* in *Films and Filming*, July 1963.

THOMSON, David, *Movie Man*, Secker & Warburg 1967.

WOOD, Robin, *Hitchcock's Films*, Zwemmer-Tantivy, Barnes, 2nd edition, 1969.

Filmography

Date usually signifies first release, sometimes year of production. D = Director, P = Producer, S = Screenplay (including ad-aptation, additional dialogue, or other writing credit), ex = based on an original work by, PC = Production company, R = First released by, W =With (leading actors only).

Always Tell Your Wife, 1922, D, Hitchcock, Seymour Hicks, P, Hitchcock, PC, Wardour, W: Clare Greet, Ernest Thesiger.

Aventure Malgache, 1944, PC, M.I.O., W: Moliere Players.

Birds, The, 1963, P, Hitchcock, S, Evan Hunter—ex Daphne Du Maurier, PC, Universal, R, Rank-Universal, W: Rod Taylor, Tippi Hedren, Jessica Tandy, Suzanne Pleshette.

Blackmail, 1929, P, John Maxwell, S, Hitchcock, Charles Bennett, Benn W. Levy —ex Charles Bennett, PC, British International Pictures, R, Wardour, W: Anny Ondra, John Longden, Sara Allgood, Charles Paton.

Bon Voyage, 1944, S, J. O. C. Orton, Angus McPhail—ex Arthur Calder-Marshall, PC, M.O.I., W: John Blythe, the Moliere Players.

Champagne, 1928, P, John Maxwell, S, Eliot Stannard—ex Walter C. Mycroft, PC, British International Pictures, R, Wardour, W: Betty Balfour, Gordon Harker.

Dial M For Murder, 1954, P, Hitchcock, S, Hitchcock—ex Frederick Knott, PC, R, Warner Brothers, W: Ray Milland, Grace Kelly, Robert Cummings, John Williams.

Downhill, 1927, P, Michael Balcon, S, Eliot Stannard—ex David Lestrange (= Constance Collier), PC, Gainsborough, R, Wardour, W: Ivor Novello, Ben Webster, Isabel Jeans.

Easy Virtue, 1927, P, Michael Balcon, S, Eliot Stannard—ex Noël Coward, PC, Gainsborough, R, Wardour, W: Isabel Jeans, Franklin Dyall.

Elstree Calling, 1930, D, Adrian Brunel, Hitchcock, S, Val Valentine, PC, British International Pictures, R, Wardour, W: Anna May Wong, Donald Calthrop, Gordon Harker.

Farmer's Wife, The, 1928, P, John Maxwell, S, Hitchcock, Eliot Stannard—ex Eden Phillpotts, PC, British International Pictures, R, Wardour, W: Lillian Hall-Davies, Jameson Thomas.

Foreign Correspondent, 1940, P, Walter Wanger, S, Charles Bennett, Joan Harrison, James Hilton, Robert Benchley, PC, R, United Artists, W: Joel McCrea, Laraine Day, Herbert Marshall.

Frenzy, 1972, P, Hitchcock, S, Anthony Shaffer—ex *Goodbye Piccadilly, Farewell Leicester Square* by Arthur La Bern, PC, Universal, R, Rank, W: Jon Finch, Alec McCowen, Barry Foster, Barbara Leigh-Hunt, Anna Massey, Vivien Merchant, Bernard Cribbins, Billie Whitelaw.

I Confess, 1952, P, Hitchcock, S, George Tabori, William Archibald—ex Paul Anthelme, PC, R, Warner Brothers, W: Montgomery Clift, Anne Baxter, Karl Malden.

Jamaica Inn, 1939, P, Erich Pommer, Charles Laughton, S, Alma Reville, Sidney Gilliat, Joan Harrison, J. Boynton Priestly—ex Daphne Du Maurier, PC, Mayflower Pictures, R, Associated British, W: Charles Laughton, Maureen O'Hara, Leslie Banks, Emlyn Williams.

Juno and the Paycock, 1930, P, John Maxwell, S, Hitchcock, Alma Reville—ex Sean O'Casey, PC, British International Pictures, R, Wardour, W: Sarah Allgood, Edward Chapman, Sidney Morgan, Marie O'Neill.

Lady Vanishes, The, 1938, P, Edward Black, S, Alma Reville, Sydney Gilliat, Frank Launder—ex *The Wheel Spins* by Ethel Lina White, PC, Gainsborough, R, Gaumont British, W: Margaret Lockwood, Michael Redgrave, Paul Lukas, Dame May Whitty.

Lifeboat, 1943, P, Kenneth MacGowan, S, Jo Swerling—ex John Steinbeck, PC, R, 20th Century Fox, W: Tallulah Bankhead, William Bendix, Walter Slezak, John Hodiak.

Lodger, The, 1926, P, Michael Balcon, S, Hitchcock, Eliot Stannard—ex Mrs. Belloc-Lowndes, PC, Gainsborough, R, Wardour, W: Ivor Novello, Marie Ault, Arthur Chesney, Malcolm Keen.

Lord Camber's Ladies, 1932, D, Benn W. Levy, P, Hitchcock, S, Benn W. Levy—ex Horace Annesley Vachell, PC, British International Pictures, R, Wardour, W: Gertrude Lawrence, Sir Gerald Du Maurier, Benita Hume, Nigel Bruce.

Man Who Knew Too Much, The, 1934, P, Michael Balcon, S, A. R. Rawlinson, Edwin Greenwood, Emlyn Williams—ex Charles Bennett, D. B. Wyndham-Lewis, PC, Gaumont British R, G.F.D., W: Leslie Banks, Edna Best, Peter Lorre.

Man Who Knew Too Much, The, 1955, P, Hitchcock, S, John Michael Hayes, Angus MacPhail—ex Charles Bennett, D. B. Wyndham-Lewis, PC, Filmwite Productions, R, Paramount, W, James Stewart, Doris Day, Daniel Gelin, Bernard Miles.

Manxman, The, 1929, P, John Maxwell, S, Eliot Stannard—ex Sir Thomas Hall Caine, PC, British International Pictures, R, Wardour, W: Carl Brisson, Anny Ondra, Malcolm Keen.

Marnie, 1964, P, Hitchcock, S, Jay Presson Allen—ex Winston Graham, PC, Universal, R, Rank-Universal, W: Tippi Hedren, Sean Connery, Diane Baker, Martin Gabel.

Mountain Eagle, The, 1926, P, Michael Balcon, S, Eliot Stannard, PC, Gainsborough, R, Wardour, W: Bernard Goetze, Nita Naldi.

Mr. and Mrs. Smith, 1941, P, Harry E. Edington, S, Normal Krasna, PC, R, RKO Radio, W: Carole Lombard, Robert Montgomery.

Murder, 1930, P, John Maxwell, S, Hitchcock, Walter Mycroft, Alma Reville—ex *Enter Sir John* by Clemence Dane (= Winifred Ashton) and Helen Simpson, PC, British International Pictures, R, Wardour, W: Herbert Marshall, Norah Baring. German version *Mary*, D, Hitchcock, W: Alfred Abel, Olga Tchekowa.

North-by-North-West, 1959, P, Hitchcock, S, Ernest Lehman, PC, R, M-G-M, W. Cary Grant, Eva Marie Saint, James Mason.

Notorious, 1946, P, Hitchcock, S, Ben Hecht—ex Hitchcock, PC, R, RKO Radio, W: Ingrid Bergman, Cary Grant, Claude Rains.

Number Seventeen, 1932, P, John Maxwell, S, Hitchcock—ex Jefferson Farjeon, PC, British International Pictures, R, Wardour, W: Leon M. Lion, Anne Grey.

Number Thirteen, 1922, P, Hitchcock, PC, Gaumont-British, R, Wardour, W: Clare Greet, Ernest Thesiger.

Paradine Case, The, 1947, P, David O. Selznick, S, David O. Selznick—ex Robert Hichens, PC, Selznick International, R, British Lion, W: Gregory Peck, Ann Todd, Charles Laughton, Ethel Barrymore.

Pleasure Garden, The, 1925, P, Michael Balcon, S, Eliot Stannard—ex Oliver Sandys, PC, Gainsborough, R, Wardour, W: Virginia Valli, Carmelita Geraghty, Miles Mander.

Psycho, 1960, P, Hitchcock, S. Joseph Stefano—ex Robert Bloch, PC, R, Paramount, W: Janet Leigh, Anthony Perkins, Vera Miles.

Rear Window, 1954, P, Hitchcock, S, John Michael Hayes—ex Cornell Woolrich, PC, R, Paramount, W: James Stewart, Grace Kelly, Wendell Corey, Thelma Ritter.

Rebecca, 1940, P, David O. Selznick, S, Philip MacDonald, Michael Hogan, Robert E. Sherwood, Joan Harrison—ex Daphne du Maurier, PC, David O. Selznick, R, United Artists, W: Laurence Olivier, Joan Fontaine, Judith Anderson.

Rich and Strange, (USA—*East of Shanghai*), 1932, P, John Maxwell, S, Alma Reville, Val Valentine—ex Dale Collins, PC, British International Pictures, R, Wardour, W: Henry Kendall, Joan Barry.

Ring, The, 1927, P, John Maxwell, S, Alma Reville, Hitchcock, PC, British International Pictures, R, Wardour, W: Carl Brisson, Lillian Hall-Davies, Ian Hunter.

Rope, 1948, P, Sidney Bernstein, Hitchcock, S, Hume Cronyn, Arthur Laurents—ex Patrick Hamilton, PC, Transatlantic Pictures, R, Warner Brothers, W: James Stewart, Farley Granger, John Dall.

Sabotage (USA—*A Woman Alone*), 1936, P, Michael Balcon, S, Charles Bennett, Alma Reville, Ian Hay, Helen Simpson, E. V. H. Emmett—ex *The Secret Agent* by Joseph Conrad, PC, Gaumont-British, R, G.F.D., W: Sylvia Sidney, Oscar Homolka, John Loder.

Saboteur, 1942, P, Frank Lloyd, Jack H. Skirball, S, Peter Viertel, Joan Harrison, Dorothy Parker—ex Hitchcock, PC, Universal, R, G.F.D., W: Robert Cummings, Priscilla Lane, Otto Kruger.

Secret Agent, The, 1936, P, Michael Balcon, S, Charles Bennett, Alma Reville, Ian Hay, Jesse Lasky Jr.—ex (play) Campbell Dixon—ex *Ashenden* by W. Somerset Maugham, PC, Gaumont-British, R, G.F.D., W: Madeleine Carroll, John Gielgud, Peter Lorre.

Shadow Of A Doubt, 1943, P, Jack H· Skirball, S, Thornton Wilder, Hitchcock, Sally Benson, Alma Reville—ex Gordon McDonell, PC, Universal, R, G.D.F., W: Joseph Cotten, Teresa Wright, Macdonald Carey.

Skin Game, The, 1931, P, John Maxwell, S, Hitchcock, Alma Reville—ex John Galsworthy, PC, British International Pictures, R, Wardour, W. Edmund Gwenn, Jill Esmond, John Longden.

Spellbound, 1945, P, David O. Selznick, S, Angus MacPhail, Ben Hecht—ex *The House of Dr. Edwardes* by Francis Beeding (= Hilary St. George Saunders and John Palmer), PC, Selznick International, R, United Artists, W: Ingrid Bergman, Gregory Peck, Leo G. Carroll.

Stage Fright, 1950, P, Hitchcock, S, Alma Reville, Whitfield Cook, James Bridie —ex *Man Running* and *Outrun the Constable* by Selwyn Jepson, PC, Associated British, R, Warner Brothers, W: Marlene Dietrich, Jane Wyman, Michael Wilding, Alastair Sim, Richard Todd, Dame Sybil Thorndike, Joyce Grenfell.

Strangers On A Train, 1951, P, Hitchcock, S, Whitfield Cook, Raymond Chandler, Czenzi Ormonde—ex Patricia Highsmith, PC, R, Warner Brothers, W: Farley Granger, Ruth Roman, Robert Walker.

Suspicion, 1941, S, Samson Raphaelson, Joan Harrison, Alma Reville—ex *Before the Fact* by Francis Iles (= Anthony Berkeley), PC, R, RKO Radio, W: Cary

Grant, Joan Fontaine, Nigel Bruce, Sir Cedric Hardwicke, Dame May Whitty Isabel Jeans.

Thirty-Nine Steps, The, 1935, P, Michael Balcon, S, Charles Bennett, Hitchcock, Alma Reville, Ian Hay (= John Hay Beith)—ex John Buchan, PC, Gaumont-British, R, G.F.D., W: Robert Donat, Madeleine Carroll, Lucie Mannheim, Godfrey Tearle, Peggy Ashcroft.

To Catch A Thief, 1955, P, Hitchcock, S, John Michael Hayes—ex David Dodge, PC, R, Paramount, W: Cary Grant, Grace Kelly.

Topaz, 1969, P, Hitchcock, S, Sam Taylor, Hitchcock—ex Leon Uris—ex news-story, PC, Universal, R, Rank-Universal, W: Frederick Stafford, Dany Robin, Michel Piccoli, John Forsythe.

Torn Curtain, 1966, P, Hitchcock, S, Brian Moore, PC, Universal, R, Rank-Universal, W: Paul Newman, Julie Andrews.

Trouble With Harry, The, 1956, P, Hitchcock, S, John Michael Hayes—ex John Trevor Story, PC, R, Paramount, W: Edmund Gwenn, John Forsythe, Shirley MacLaine.

Under Capricorn, 1949, P, Sidney Bernstein, Hitchcock, S, Hume Cronyn, James Bridie—ex Helen Simpson, PC, Transatlantic Pictures, R, Warner Brothers, W: Ingrid Bergman, Joseph Cotten, Michael Wilding, Margaret Leighton.

Vertigo, 1958, P, Hitchcock, S, Alec Coppel, Samuel Taylor—ex *D'Entre les Morts* by Pierre Boileau and Thomas Narcejac, PC, R, Paramount, W: James Stewart, Kim Novak, Barbara Bel Geddes, Tom Helmore.

Waltzes from Vienna, (USA—*Strauss' Great Waltz*), 1933, P, Tom Arnold, S, Guy Reginald Bolton, Alma Reville—ex Guy Reginald Bolton, PC, Tom Arnold, R, G.F.D., W: Jessie Matthews, Esmond Knight, Frank Vosper, Fay Compton.

Wrong Man, The, 1957, P, Hitchcock, S, Maxwell Anderson, Angus MacPhail—ex *The True Story of Christopher Emmanuel Balestrero* by Maxwell Anderson, PC, R, Warner Brothers, W: Henry Fonda, Vera Miles, Anthony Quayle.

Young and Innocent (USA—*A Girl Was Young*), 1937, P, Edward Black, S, Charles Bennett, Edwin Greenwood, Anthony Armstrong, Alma Reville, Gerald Savory—ex *A Shilling For Candles* by Josephine Tey (= Elizabeth MacKintosh), PC, Gaumont-British, R, G.F.D., W: Nora Pilbeam, Derrick de Marney, Percy Marmont.

Index